Henry Ward Beecher

Bible Studies

Readings In The Early Books Of The Old Testament With Familiar Comment

Henry Ward Beecher

Bible Studies

Readings In The Early Books Of The Old Testament With Familiar Comment

ISBN/EAN: 9783337099886

Printed in Europe, USA, Canada, Australia, Japan

Cover: Foto ©Lupo / pixelio.de

More available books at **www.hansebooks.com**

BY
HENRY WARD BEECHER

EDITED
FROM STENOGRAPHIC NOTES OF T. J. ELLINWOOD
BY
JOHN R. HOWARD

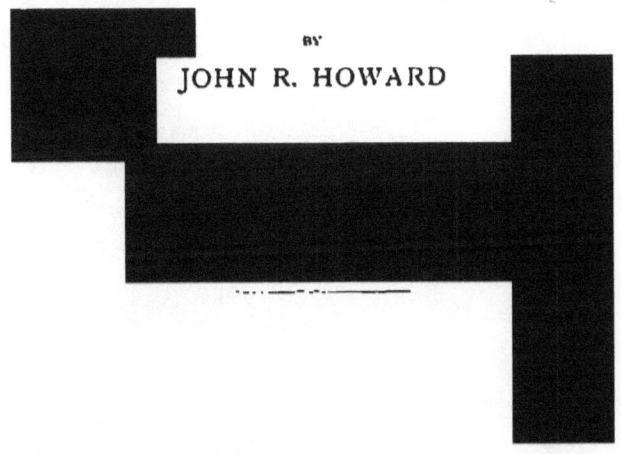

NEW YORK
FORDS, HOWARD, & HULBERT
1893

COPYRIGHT, IN 1892,
BY T. J. ELLINWOOD.

PREFACE.

THE lectures on the early Old Testament books contained in this volume were delivered in Plymouth Church, on Sunday evenings, during the autumn, winter, and spring of 1878-79, and were given, it may be presumed, in accordance with a comprehensive plan, cherished by Mr. Beecher, which included the desire, repeatedly expressed by him, that he might find opportunity to preach a course of sermons on the later historical books, the Prophets, and the Psalms. That this desire was not realized cannot but be deeply regretted by those who are aware of the power and skill of Mr. Beecher as an expositor of Scripture, and who therefore can form some conception of how he would have handled those topics, and especially the themes suggested by the matchless hymns of David.

These Lectures were not published immediately after their delivery, because at that time a series of Mr. Beecher's morning sermons was being issued in his paper, the *Christian Union;* but, following my usual custom as reporter of his utterances, I preserved full stenographic notes of them. It was evident that a more than transient purpose actuated their author in giving them forth, and from the first I felt that they ought not to be allowed to perish. After Mr. Beecher's death this feeling took on the form of a conviction of duty, which has resulted in their preparation for the press; and they are now, with the consent and approval of the family of Mr. Beecher, offered to the public.

It is probable that of the many hundreds of reported discourses of Henry Ward Beecher no series could be selected that would be perused with greater interest or profit than these "Bible Studies."

The present time, when there is such widespread and earnest attention paid to the study of the Scriptures, would seem most opportune for the appearance of this work; and it is sent out in the hope that through its instrumentality multitudes will be led to a better understanding of the Word of God, and a greater love and reverence for it.

T. J. ELLINWOOD.

INTRODUCTION.

BY THE EDITOR.

PROBABLY the thing which will most surprise those who for the first time have knowledge of these Bible Studies will be their modern spirit. The world of scholarship, criticism, and theological thought moves fast when once it starts; and since 1878, when these lectures were delivered, great advances have been made, especially in the larger freedom of utterance which men of reverent love for the Bible and of lives consecrated to the service of God deem it their duty to take. The necessity laid upon them by the new philosophies of the divine methods—

> "That to the height of this great argument
> [They] may assert eternal Providence,
> And justify the ways of God to men,"

—has driven them into bolder denial of the mechanical theories of inspiration; the amanuensis-theories of Bible-writing; and the infantile conceptions of the ancient Hebrews concerning their national deity, Jehovah, as binding upon the faith and conscience of men after two thousand years' study of the ampler revelations made by "Jesus, the Christ of God."

Popular hostile critics of Christianity have found their chief success in holding it responsible for a belief in every statement of these artless, childlike records as indubitable facts, and in exhibiting the savage cruelties committed by the early Israelites under "immediate divine commandment" as inconsistent with the professed teachings of Christ; thus claiming a demonstration that neither the Old Testament nor the New is of divine authority, since they stand as one, and both cannot be true. And foolish Christians, in captivity to the form of sound words as to "all Scripture" being "given by inspiration of God" have largely accepted this cunning dilemma, and contended earnestly for the faith once delivered to the saints. Of late years, however, philology, literary criticism, and the study of the past with an ever-widening sense of historical perspective, have changed the views of scholars; and—especially during the past five years—have resulted in diffusing an entirely new atmosphere, enabling those who are not scholars to comprehend something of the divine methods of creation by growth, in things spiritual and in the mental, moral, and social nature of man as well as in the physical world. So that, although the views of these Bible Studies will not be new to scholars or to those of the laity who keep abreast of the times, they will be almost novel to a multitude of devout Bible students, while full of fresh suggestion and invigorating thought even to those who have long held the same position.

Moreover, their especial value lies along the line not of destruction but of conservation. As a Presbyterian minister wrote to Mr. Beecher just after the issue of his volume of sermons on " Evolution and Religion ":—

"It seems to me you keep all the most choice and precious things, only placing them on the right foundation; and how they can stand much longer on the old foundation I do not see. . . . . Surely your book will bring light to many."

The whole force of these lectures goes to throw off the cramping theory of " inspiration " which makes God responsible for all the evil that was done by the inchoate Hebrew people in his name. Thus the student is left free to follow this master expositor in rediscovering and newly appreciating the wisdom, the goodness, the grand foundation-work of Moses under the Divine impulse, which both served to build up the Israelitish nation and has entered into many of the soundest elements of modern civilization. To quote another opinion as to the " Evolution and Religion ": " Many will owe to this illumination no less than the renewal of a lost belief."

Whoever will at this date read Mr. Beecher's sermons and addresses in the time of our Civil War will not only be moved by their eloquence, he will be interested and surprised at their solid conservatism. In the realm of civil polity as well as in that of religion and theology, the man wrought out his own noble, generous, honest, essentially just nature; and, when he found what he believed to be truth, flamed it out upon his fellow men with the effective contagion of human sympathy and an unwavering faith in God and the goodness of God's ways.

There must have been a mighty satisfaction dwelling in the soul of such a man-helper as Henry Ward Beecher. Despite the innumerable criticisms breaking upon him from every quarter,—

some, just, which he tried to heed; the most, unjust, which he regarded much as boys do snowballs in a winter fight,—throughout his entire life he was inspirited by a continuous acclaim of gratitude, many-voiced as the ocean, from men and women who gladly owned to him their debts of deliverance from darkness and spiritual captivity. Amid the buffets of blame, which no man of such abounding activity would expect to escape, he received also unstinted praise and outspoken admiration. This doubtless pleased him, for, though not a vain man, he was an amiable one.

But neither praise nor blame weighed much with him. His whole being was devoted to serving his kind. And the solid fact —based upon the ceaseless testimonies of thousands during twenty, thirty, forty, fifty years, as his public life went on— that he was successfully doing what God had inspired him with the desire to do, must have brought to him a supreme contentment; must have been a part of that astonishing reserve of spiritual power, that kept his head erect and his face serene while his pulpit work went on with increased richness and effectiveness, in the midst of troubles that should seemingly have crushed him.

The particular series of Sunday evening talks about the early books of the Old Testament which form the present volume, given in the winter and spring of 1878-9, were taken down stenographically as they fell from Mr. Beecher's lips, by Mr. T. J. Ellinwood —for nearly thirty years his special reporter. While going over them in preparation for the press, I have been impressed with the feeling that in Mr. Ellinwood's heart, too, there must be a large portion of satisfaction, in the fact that his keen sense, intelligent appreciation, and skillful hand have been the means of preserving to the world the chief part of Mr. Beecher's public ministrations, during their most eventful and influential period. It is due to Mr. Ellinwood to say that, while great numbers of Mr. Beecher's sermons, lectures, prayer-meeting talks, public addresses, etc., were reported by him as a matter of business engagement, either with Mr. Beecher or his publishers, there were a multitude of others that he took down for the mere pleasure of taking them, and in the hope that at some time they would be used. The present series were among this latter class; and surely, those who read them, and who find them a torch of new light in exploring the decried or forgotten treasures of the Old Testament Scriptures, will not overlook the debt they owe to the man who caught them in the air, and gave them to the "art preservative" fourteen years after their utterance.

Mr. Beecher, without dispraising any other reports of his sermons, grew unwilling to be held responsible for any except Mr. Ellinwood's, and so wrote at the time of the establishment of "Plymouth Pulpit," the weekly pamphlet edition of his sermons, in 1868. This was after ten years of experience with Mr. Ellinwood's reporting of his rapid and often irregular outpourings.

The discourses of the present volume are not sermons,—excepting the two in the front of the volume, one on "Inspiration of the Bible" and one on "How to read the Bible." They are in fact Bible readings, interspersed with comment in most free and familiar fashion. In the preparation of them for the press, many careless colloquialisms and repetitions have been elided; iterations of Mr. Beecher's view of inspiration, and recapitulations of its bearings on the history,—necessary in addressing congregations containing many different people from week to week, but surplusage in a connected printing of the whole series,—have been omitted; here and there, incomplete statements of his views, thrown out hastily and liable to misconstructions, have been reinforced from other and more careful statements made by the author elsewhere; and some of his interpretations, which to the old-style reader might seem almost irreverent, or at least "rationalistic," in their reduction of a passage to a common-sense meaning, have been confirmed by foot-note references to the text or margins of the Revised Version of the Old Testament, which was not published until six or seven years (A. D. 1885) after the delivery of these discourses.

In all this, however, scrupulous care has been taken not to mar or interfere with the spirit or essential form of the author's utterances, but to keep well within the line of revision pursued through many years under Mr. Beecher's own eye, and subject to his direction, in others of his lectures, sermons, and books.

The attentive reader of these Bible Studies will lose no living belief in the ancient Scriptures as containing the Word of God to men, while he will gain new and larger views of their worth for Christian life to-day—and that, not in spite of the new philosophy of growth, but in full harmony with its irresistible advance.

JOHN R. HOWARD.

New York, December, 1892.

CONTENTS.

		PAGE
PREFACE,		3
INTRODUCTION,		5
I.	THE INSPIRATION OF THE BIBLE,	11
II.	HOW TO READ THE BIBLE,	31
III.	THE BOOK OF BEGINNINGS,	47
IV.	ABRAHAM,	65
V.	ISAAC,	83
VI.	JACOB,	103
VII.	JACOB AND JOSEPH,	125
VIII.	JOSEPH,	145
IX.	MOSES,	163
X.	EMANCIPATION,	185
XI.	THE WILDERNESS AND SINAI,	205
XII.	THE SABBATH,	229
XIII.	MOSAIC INSTITUTES: HUMANITY,	248
XIV.	MOSAIC INSTITUTES: THE HOUSEHOLD,	267
XV.	MOSAIC INSTITUTES: SOCIAL OBSERVANCES,	281
XVI.	THE FEAST OF TABERNACLES,	297
XVII.	IN THE LAND OF MOAB,	315
XVIII.	CAMPAIGNS OF JOSHUA,	332
XIX.	A TIME OF DEGRADATION,	351
XX.	GIDEON,	367
XXI.	JEPHTHAH,	383
XXII.	SAMSON,	400
XXIII.	NAOMI AND RUTH,	420

I.

THE INSPIRATION OF THE BIBLE.

"But now we are delivered from the Law, that being dead wherein we were held; that we should serve in newness of spirit, and not in the oldness of the letter."—Rom. vii. 6.

For the general purpose of bringing home especially the more ancient of the Hebrew Scriptures to your consideration and your confidence, unembarrassed by the theories which have been given and which turn the Bible very largely into a book of disputes, I purpose, in this series of Sunday evening lectures, first, to discuss somewhat the meaning of "inspiration," as applied to this source of our faith, and then to go over with you the chief historical books of the Old Testament, trying to find what there is in them for us of the modern day.

Good and scholarly men have taken the declaration that "all Scripture is given by inspiration of God," and given to it what I think is an erroneous construction. I hold inspiration to be a fundamental fact; but they have proceeded to form a theory of inspiration, not out of the Word of God, but out of their own idea of the action of God upon the human soul. Then they have brought that theory forward as a criterion by which to interpret the Bible; and when facts have confronted it and seemed to contradict it, they have been tempted to go into a wrestling with and a wrenching of those facts, and to adopt a system which is inconsistent with all fairness, all straightforwardness, and all honesty. To a very large extent in our own time men have been deterred from reading the

---

Sunday evening, November 3, 1878.

Word of God; some by disgust at what seemed to them dishonest methods of interpretation; and some by despair because they could make nothing of it, as taught.

Look at the way in which this book is held, by thousands and thousands in the community, with abject indifference! It is as if it were not, so far as they are concerned. They have no curiosity, no appetite that leads them to desire the Word of God. And many of those that have a desire for it are thrown back from it when they see what are the methods of interpretation which are brought to bear upon it. Some men spiritualize every part of it, as if it were all a book of symbols, not carrying its true meaning in the letter and upon the face of it; as if it merely prefigured something outside of itself. Other men exactly reverse this, and give a literal interpretation to every part of the Bible; they unspiritualize it and degrade it by carrying men toward matter. Still others (and I am sorry to say that among them are men who have been much blessed by reason of their zeal and appetite for doing good) have been very pernicious in their influence upon the popular acceptation of the Word of God, their method being to give a spiritual interpretation to every material fact and a material interpretation to every spiritual fact, and so to work it both ways out of the range of ordinary reason, and put it beyond the operation of common sense, by which men are guided in the household, in the affairs of business, and in matters of State.

Now, if the Word of God is ever to be as powerful as it ought to be among men it must have an interpretation that will bring it home to the bosoms of men, so that they shall understand it as they understand any great and important truths in human life; and instead of imitating those who first form a theory of inspiration and then undertake to make the Bible conform to it, we must go humbly to the Word of God and see how it is made up, and ask what the facts are, and then out of the facts form a theory of inspiration—for I hold that the Bible was written by inspired writers. Everything that is in it, looked at exactly as it is, without perversion, must go to make up our theory of what inspiration admits or includes in itself.

I pass by briefly the definition of "revelation," which is making known to men things not known before.

As to the Word of God itself, it does not claim to be a book of revelations. It contains revelations; but at first it did not stand on that ground, nor did it base its authority thereon. Indeed, there are very few revelations, as such, in the Bible. There are records innumerable of things that men at large had not found out, but that they were capable of finding out. Men were told in the Word of God much valuable truth, as a child is told by its mother, for the sake of early instruction, many useful things that it has not yet learned, but that are within its reach. In a certain sense revelations may consist in disclosures of things which lie within the sphere of a man's reason. And at particular periods of the world, and for special purposes in the conduct of human affairs, it has pleased God to make extraordinary revelations, through extraordinary men, unfolding to men at large things which they did not know, and which they could not find out in the then stage of the world, but which afterwards, when they came to investigate, were plain and easy for them to comprehend.

Men laugh and say, "If we can ascertain such things by natural reason, what is the use of revelation?" Of course, if the race were to wait long enough, they could find out many things that were revealed in the Scriptures; but for purposes of education these things were wisely made known in the childhood of mankind. Beneficently, with a view to man's earlier development, some things were anticipated to which men would evidently have come if they had been let alone.

And yet, there are some things that human reason of itself could not compass; as, for instance, the nature of God, the character of the other life, the destiny of man, and the great moral principles on which God administers his government in this world. These are spiritual elements that men unaided cannot understand. I do not undertake to say that men may not, in later periods of large and multifarious knowledge and by scientific methods, arrive at right conclusions in regard to these elements also; but there are now many questions which no man can fathom except by the light which is thrown upon them by revelation. Because there are things revealed that are within the reach of men's investigations, it does not follow that there are not other things revealed which are beyond the pale of human research.

But revelation is the smallest part of the Word of God. There is far less of it than of narrative and of history. Divine inspiration educed the material, and men "spake as they were moved by the Spirit"—that is, under the inspiration of holy feelings they were competent to record with substantial accuracy the experiences that sprang from the influence of the divine mind upon the human mind. For inspiration is something much broader than revelation. It may be very generally defined as being a divine influence that quickens the faculties of men. Whether it acts directly upon individual human minds (I believe it does, at times); whether it acts indirectly upon the human mind through institutions (and I believe it does that also); or whether it inspires mankind at large with a knowledge of the truth or with the light of truth,—it is an action of the divine mind upon the human mind, either in the mass or as individuals, so as to secure— What? Such a presentation of the truth as shall work toward morality and spiritualized manhood.

The whole drift of the Bible is to be a practical book—a book to teach men the highest way of life; to teach them how to live so as not to be degraded by their senses; so that they shall be able to meet the inequalities of life; so that it shall be possible for them to use the world without abusing it; to teach them how to live in this world so that they shall come to a higher and better one. If there ever was a book the aim of whose teaching was that the man of God might be thoroughly furnished unto every good work, that book is the Bible—as we commonly call this collection of ancient sacred Scriptures.

Now, let us see what Inspiration, as it is derived from an examination of the Book itself, must include. There is an impression that in the larger understanding of inspiration there is a limitation of the interpretation of God's Word; on the contrary, I believe that the larger liberty gives the larger power.

First: Any adequate theory of inspiration must admit of the incorporation of all existing records into the Word. Genesis, in its earlier chapters, unquestionably was made effulgent with the combination of several then-existing records of things. They are very plainly marked in the original. The whole style and the whole use of language demarks them one from another. So, at the very first step into the Bible we find that inspiration, as it were, gathers up documents, statements of fact, that existed before, and makes them part and parcel of the inspired record; and that with which the Word of God begins it goes on with. Whole books were selections from existing literature. There is no question but that the book of Esther was taken bodily out of the records of an Oriental monarch. Without doubt the ten genealogies came from the public records, made just as any other genealogical records are— just as the public documents in Brooklyn are made, that are in the hands of the county clerk, and of which one might make a transcript. And so many existing documents were brought together in the making up of the Bible that, if it was produced under inspiration, we must see that inspiration admitted—nay, directed—the taking into the Word of God much of the literature that had sprung up in the ordinary course of human thought and procedure.

Then, *secondly:* Inspiration, to be applicable to the Bible as we have it, must admit the incorporation of statements, in regard to incidental facts, which originated in the usual faulty, errant operation of the human mind. If any theory of inspiration admitted such inaccuracy as vitiated moral principles, and misled men as to conduct, as to disposition, and as to great spiritual tendencies, it would be fatal to every scheme for the elevation of men to which it might be applied; but inspiration is consistent with such a presentation of solid truths as is adapted to the welfare of the human race, while yet this presentation is made through vehicles that carry with them the limitations and imperfections of human language and human thought, not only, but also the peculiar characteristics of the period, the nation, and the man inspired to declare it. We do not destroy the moral purpose of a document when we show that it is misspelled, or that there are literary or statistical mistakes in it, provided the mistakes are quite irrelevant to the main end. It is destructive of any theory of the inspiration of the Bible to claim that every word and letter which it contains is infallibly correct. That claim, carried out logically or consistently, would do one of two things: it would destroy the Bible itself, in the faith of just-minded men and honest-minded interpreters; or it would put men on a system of twisting and twirling metaphorical statements. It would lead to discriminations which would make men special theorists, and result in erroneous judgments on their part. Indeed, it has resulted in just that.

To say that there were "ten thousand" when there were only five thousand does not invalidate the practical intent of conveying the fact that there were *a great many*. The use of specific numbers to indicate a strong statement of a large number is thoroughly Oriental, and natural in an Oriental book. To say that there was a flood of forty days if it lasted only twenty days does not disprove the fact that there was a great cataclysm or phenomenon of nature, lasting an unusually long time. This does vitiate a theory of inspiration which makes every figure in the Bible accurate, which spells every word right, and which places every element in its correct place; but the record itself disputes any such theory of inspiration as that; for that would hold it morally responsible for inaccuracies, misstatements which are contained in the record, and would make the whole thing false in respect to the great moral ends for which any communication is made.

If it be said that one man, in writing a portion of the Scriptures, said one thing, while the opposite was said by another, that may be an utterly unimportant error. It is stated in one of the Gospels that Christ went to Nazareth before certain events happened, and by another it is declared that he went after the happening of those events; but what difference does it make whether he went before or after? He *went*. If the theory of inspiration insists that exactitude as to facts is indispensable to its divine origin, then it makes a great deal of difference; but if the theory of inspiration takes no note of incidental errors provided they do not vitiate the great purpose which divine truth was intended to bring forth, then it does not amount to any difference. At any rate, no man can critically examine the text of the Old Testament and the New and not find these internal and external vehicular inaccuracies; and I take the ground that the true theory of inspiration admits of those incidental errors of time, place, etc., which do not alter the general drift of the text, nor the impression it was designed to make on men, the object being to "thoroughly furnish them for every good work." A truth may be valid, and yet be clothed with imperfect views and erroneous statements, and even urged upon low grounds.

"Honor thy father and thy mother, that thy days may be long upon the land which the Lord thy God giveth thee."

What is the drift of this passage? Is it to teach men how to live a great while? No. People want to live a great while, anyhow. That does not indicate inspiration. That is inherent. The drift of the passage is *Honor thy father and thy mother;* and the motive applied was, comparatively speaking, a low one; but it was probably the only motive by which, in the early ages of the human race, children could be touched in a way to make them treat their parents with filial reverence. A great thing longevity was thought to be; and there was a distinction made between the length of days of those who honored their father and mother and those who disregarded them. It was not the highest motive; nor, for us, could it be the true one: but, for the slaves just escaped out of Egypt, it was wise.

So in every age human nature must be dealt with in the best way in which it can be reached; and if there be one thing that is shown all the way through the divinely inspired record it is the adaptation of methods, institutions, and revelations of truth to the weaknesses and necessities of men in each particular age. The garment was made to fit the figure. The manner of teaching was in accordance with the need of the time and nation in which it took place. Not perfection, but right direction, was the aim.

Thirdly: Inspiration as properly viewed may include a whole statement of material truths, good and bad, which make up a complete history, without either criticism, judgment, determination, or characterization. The sins, the evils, the mistakes of good men are not approved because they are stated without any application to them of moral discriminations and condemnations.

In the early periods of history, in the record, for instance, of the patriarchal age, we are confronted with conduct which would drive a man from society if it were committed to-day. We permit in a child things which, if he were to continue them until he became grown, would deprive him of good standing and throw him out of society. And in the infancy of the race things were permitted which, judged by our modern standards of honor and right, would condemn a man as utterly base. They were bad then, and they would have been worse in every age since, by reason of the growing light that has been brought to bear upon truth and duty ; and yet they are narrated in the Word of God without a single protest. Conduct was allowed in the past which was far less criminal than it would be in our age : but it was criminal then ; and nevertheless, there it stands, apparently unrebuked.

Look at Jacob, much of whose conduct would be condemned from beginning to end, according to any modern canon of moral criticism. He outwitted, with the connivance of a cunning mother, his elder brother. He was politic all the way through. While he was a politician, he always thought of himself, and looked out for "Number One." He was selfish and cruel. And yet, he is not criticised; there is no stamp of dishonor put upon him. He acted in these things by the light and the low morality of the age in which he lived, making mistakes and committing offenses that would be outrageous if they were committed in our day; and yet he stands up as one of the three great patriarchs—Abraham, Isaac, and Jacob.

Divine inspiration, in the record, then, admits the telling of the imperfections of men, of their sins, of their crimes, without stopping to lay upon them the law of criticism or of condemnation. The duty of placing censure upon these things is left to men who apply the moral and spiritual principles given in the inspired record. It is not to be held that a wrong thing is approved because it is not in words disapproved. It is simply to be held that the authors of the Scriptures stated things as they were,—good, bad, and indifferent.

Fourthly: A true view of inspiration admits of partial statements of truth—such as may come within the limit of misunderstanding, at any rate. To state to an audience a truth larger than the receptivity of that audience is, to all intents and purposes, not to state it to them. To explain to children in the nursery the operation of the Federal Courts as compared with the operation of the State Courts, would be to explain to them nothing at all, because they have not the elemental knowledge without which they cannot perceive the condition of things, nor cluster together facts and make comparisons. You tell them nothing if you tell them that which is larger than they can take in. And if the inspired record was to be used to any advantage it must be adapted to the level and capacity of that age of the human mind to which it was originally addressed. It is not possible for God, except by working a miracle, except by changing natural law, to make known to men the great universal truths of their being which ally them to the unseen world. Only so much of these truths can be put into any record as shall be comprehensible, either by the time in which the record is given or by the time which shall come after.

Now, the inspired record states truths in such partial forms that they will be comprehensible to men according to the measure of their understanding. Take, for instance, the doctrine of immortality. There is not a word in all the institutes of Moses—in the five books called "The Pentateuch"—which indicates that there is such a thing; and yet these are the foundation-books of the Jewish economy. In our time, through the teachings of Jesus, that transcendent fact is disclosed; but in the beginning, for reasons unquestionably wise, though not made known, the inspired records did not develop that side of truth. It made known much of God, much of the divine government, much of duty; but of that revelation which lies at the very foundation of the New Testament it made no mention. And what are you going to do about it, when you make a theory of inspiration, except to say that inspiration admits of partial, alphabetic, statements, capable of coming to more complex and fuller forms in later days?

Men are shocked when it is said that an inspired record may teach by stating things that are not. Well, it can, and it does. What are you going to do with the parables of Christ? There is not one of them that is not a little fiction. They were all artificial; they were invented; but they were apt, and among the best of means, especially among the Orientals, who teach so much by stories, of instructing men in higher truths. Here were falsities, so far as facts were concerned, employed for the purpose of making verities known.

The way to bring a child to a true knowledge is to tell him things that are not true. If you were to banish all the fairy stories, all the fables, all the made-up tales in Sunday-school libraries; if you should take away all of what some people call lies—accounts of things that never happened, what would become of childhood? Now, in all times of the development of the human race fiction has gone before fact, and has been used as a means of bringing men to fact. Although when men have grown to maturity it is not so necessary that there should be fiction to help them to fact, yet, in the adolescence of mankind, in their infantile condition, fiction was essential as an instrument by which to lift them from a lower to a higher plane. Imaginative elements, instead of tangible actualities, have been employed with continual benefit; and we find them employed nowhere more than in the Word of God, both the Old Testament and the New. No man need be afraid to look upon this thing, and say, "It is so."

The honored, and most deservedly honored, Dean Stanley, who is present in our great city adjoining, said a most wise thing in regard to this very subject, when he declared that it was not so important to have a theory of inspiration as it was to ascertain what are the actual facts about the Bible; "for," said he, "the theory that ultimately is to prevail must be that theory which includes in itself all the facts." Therefore, as these things are facts, we must take the ground that the inspired record admits of statements that are fictitious for the sake of helping the imagination and the reason to rise from a lower plane to a higher one. Any theory which includes all the facts must make room for that fact.

Fifthly: The fact of a document having been given under inspiration in no way limits or mars the freedom of the human mind in interpreting the truths taught. In other words, we are to interpret inspired language by precisely the same laws of interpretation which we apply to any other documents. Language which is used by inspiration is just the same as that which is used without it: and the laws of interpretation applied to inspired documents are precisely the same as those applied to documents of any other kind. Those laws are well ascertained and unvarying, and in the main are accepted by every school of thought and denomination of religion: and we are not to go to the Word of God, to the inspired record, with the idea that we must handle holy things in a different way from that in which we handle other things. There is no sanctity in the inspired record such that the attitude of a man's mind should be different in dealing with it from what it is in dealing with any other record or truth. We are to be guided by the same rules of judgment when we go to the Word of God as when we go to any other word. And this, not to destroy it, but to save it—to take it out of the realm of superstition and out of the twilight of ignorance, and bring it into the daylight of reason and common sense. What we want is to rescue the Bible from the mists and fogs that have surrounded it, and lay it open before the judgment of mankind, and say, "Fearlessly inspect it; read it; think about it!" It will stand that, and will be all the stronger for it. I am tired of a mystic interpretation of the Bible which takes it away from matter-of-fact people by wrenching it out of its true relations, and substitutes clouds that have no rain in them for substantial realities. I am in favor of seeing the Word of God handled in the way that any other documents would naturally be handled, by well ascertained laws of reason applied to interpretation.

It is not meant, then, that, in teaching the inspired Word, we should say to man's reason, "Stand aside, and hear what God says." The apostle commanded men to search the Scriptures, and see if things were not as he declared them to be. The whole Word itself is a challenge to the reason. Yea, God himself appears, in the light of a drama or representation, saying, "Let us reason together." Throughout the Old Testament and the New, men are invited to reason, *reason*, REASON!

Sixthly: On all subjects of mental experience or investigation we must accept an interpretation according to the best light, analogical, which we have in regard to the thing stated; and when we come to read the Word of God carefully the things that are beyond the reach of human investigation are very few. Those that are so are stated in such a manner that we cannot apply to them analogical experimental laws. They are given so vaguely, with so few facts, that men cannot fathom them.

As to immortality, for instance, Paul presents an example of the growth of the seed. The seed dies in order that a better thing may come out of it. The Scripture tells us that the state beyond is one of transcendent glory; but what that glory is, John says, does not appear.

So, when we speak of the revelation of truths that lie beyond the reach of human investigation, beyond ordinary experience, beyond scientific reasoning, we can give only a very faint interpretation of them, and we take them unquestioningly. I take the fact of continued existence without questioning. The fact of the resurrection—not of the material body but of the spiritual body—I also take without questioning. The statement that personal identity and recognition shall be given to us in the other life I cannot reason upon; I can only accept it as a simple fact: but the purpose of other forms of truth that are there, and which lie within the reach of human investigation, we must ascertain by studying the facts by which they are illustrated. You will admit this in respect to lower forms of truth, though you are not accustomed to admit it with regard to higher forms.

When the Bible speaks of things that you cannot learn anything about by turning from passage to passage of Scripture, seek information concerning it elsewhere. If it speaks of silver you may turn to Matthew, or Revelation, or Isaiah, or any other of the books of the Old and New Testaments, and you will not gain as much light in regard to it as you will by taking a piece of silver ore, or a bar of bullion, or a dollar piece, and looking at that. You go to *silver* when you want to know what the Bible means in speaking of "silver." When it speaks of snow, or trees, or clouds, or rivers, or lions, or anything within the reach of your knowledge, you go to that thing to find out what is meant. You interpret most of what is in the Bible by things that are outside of it. When the Word of God mentions material things, you do not consider it any violation of that word to go outside of it to ascertain what it means.

The same thing is true in respect to persons. We know what father and mother are, not because the Bible teaches us what they are, but because of our relations to them and our intercourse with them. It teaches us what their duties are; but what they themselves are we learn outside of the Bible. We carry our outside knowledge as a light with which to interpret that inside Scripture which refers to them. We do the same with regard to kings, to princes, to laboring men, to seamen, to men in all relations and situations.

We take the things of which the Bible speaks, and carry the knowledge we gain of them back and employ that as a means of interpreting the Bible. This is normal and legitimate,—nay, necessary.

The same is true of mental operations. When the attributes of the mind are spoken of in the Bible we ascertain what those attributes are, not by going to the Bible itself, but by observing their manifestations in human life. What justice, love, and goodness are, of which so much is said in the inspired record, we learn outside of that record —not inside of it. This Book is paper and ink; it is not love. It does not love when it says "Love." No love flames from the text when love is spoken of. But go home, after a long absence, to your mother, and see what love is. Meet your sweetheart after a prolonged separation, and see what love is. Go to life for life-facts. Take the things that are actual for the interpretation of real truths. · Life is a better interpreter of the Bible than old commentaries are, although old commentaries are not unuseful.

Seventhly: Inspired writings may contain statements which in an after-age would require no inspiration. That is also true of revelation. It may be needful that things be revealed to men by the direct telling of God in one age which at a later period would need no such direct telling. One says, "You pretend that these are revelations; when there is not a schoolboy in our day that could not find them out, without having them revealed to him." Very likely; but in an early and undeveloped age a thing may be required to be made known through special methods which at a later period would not be required to be thus made known. It does not follow, that, because at a later period men could help themselves, they could have done it at the beginning. We put a bottle to the mouths of babes; but it does not follow, because when the child is forty years old he does not suck the bottle, that he did not need to suck it when he was a babe. Things are adapted to the wants of infantile helplessness which would be absurd at a time of later disclosure.

Men attempt to show that things in the Bible which are claimed to have been miracles were not miraculous because they lie within the sphere of natural laws; but in the early ages natural laws not understood were miracles; for miracles in any age are facts that transcend the knowledge and skill of the men who live in that age.

Childhood is taught by certain methods. Ripe age supersedes those methods, but it does not despise nor reject them. I have left off the clothes which I wore when I was three years old; but I do not despise them. I put them on three-year-old children, or grandchildren. So it is in respect to the Word of God. It was given for different periods; and it stands to reason that this fact can be no objection to the divine record. On the contrary, it is eminently conducive to our faith in the efficiency of inspired things.

Hence, we find the New Testament boldly saying what some modern preachers would not dare to say. Hear Paul declare:

"Now we are delivered from the Law, that being dead wherein we were held."

If I were to come here and say, "The Old Testament law is dead and gone; I don't care for that any more," how would a paragraph flame out in the morning newspapers, and be heralded all over the country, "Beecher don't care for the Old Testament; he says it is dead!" Well, Paul says it; and people, without opening their eyes in astonishment, swallow it, as if it were all right enough. But Paul taught that, in the adaptation of means to ends, after a fact had served its purpose it ceased to be necessary. He took the ground that things which were essential in the childhood of the race could be dispensed with when it came to manhood. But only if replaced by something better; for, after declaring that the Law was dead, and that men were not held by it any more, he went on to say:

"That we should serve in newness of spirit, and not in the oldness of the letter."

He denied the authority of Mosaism as applied to men who live by the spirit of Christ, although indispensable to earlier periods. And he was right. An egg-shell is very necessary before the chicken is hatched; but would it not be very absurd to insist that the chicken should always wear the shell? The earlier statements, the earlier institutions, and the earlier methods of the Bible, when they had accomplished their appropriate work, were superseded by other provisions, and that without implying any contempt of these old instrumentalities. They were adapted to the object which they were meant to serve—namely, the development of human life as it originally existed.

We give medicine to men because they are sick; and if this medicine is rightly adapted it gives health, and thus renders itself unnecessary, so that it may thereafter properly be ignored. The Bible is full of medicine, as it were, that has served its purpose—the record of statements, institutions, and customs that related to the primitive conditions of mankind; and any correct theory of inspiration must make room for this fact.

And, finally: The unity of the Bible is not like the unity of a modern work. The Bible is simply a library-shelf filled with books. If the writings constituting the Bible, by different authors, were bound up separately, as modern books are, they would make forty or fifty volumes, written in different languages, under different institutions, and for different purposes, by men that had no sort of connection with each other; and yet, when brought together, though they may not be arranged with accuracy so far as order of time is concerned, as a series they have a certain spiritual unity, and that is all the unity there is about them. External unity in the books of the Bible is utterly wanting; but interiorly they are one. That is, they all bear on the general questions of man's sinfulness, his duty, his righteousness, his relations to God and eternity; they are uniform in that regard; while in their outward characteristics they are very different one from another.

I think one of the most interesting things in England is the Winchester Cathedral. It represents every order of Gothic architecture, from the old Saxon down to the latest developments in this direction, running through four or five distinct periods. In one part of the building you see represented the most ancient, in another more modern, in another still more modern, and in another, the most modern Gothic architecture. The whole constitutes a magnificent pile. It represents several different schools, with hundreds of years between them; but the peculiarities of these different schools are brought together so that, although the individual elements in them are unlike, they compose a unit which is admirable, and serves the purposes of the church, at the same time that it is beautiful to the eye.

In old Warwick Castle, before it was destroyed by fire outwardly, you saw the most irregular and strange grouping. One century built one side, with its tower, of a particular kind of wall. Another century built another side, with its palatial residence and magnificent halls. By accretion, with the growth of architecture, it came into its more recent condition. Now, outwardly, it represented very different epochs and very different architectural ideas, strangely grouped together; but inwardly it was a place fit for a noble to live in. All its parts were brought into domestic uses, and it answered the purposes of a refined and cultured household.

The Word of God is filled with books which, though written in different ages, have an interior unity. They are united in telling man how he shall be in harmony with God; how he shall live above his animal life, so as to be immortal; how he shall learn the secret of happiness in years to come; how he shall be forgiven for sin and avoid it. There is but one voice in these books in regard to the history of men; they are in perfect accord in this respect; whereas, in respect to the instrument, the literary implement, by which the great truths of the gospel are conveyed to men, the exterior elements of the Bible are exceedingly diverse.

From this general statement it will appear that the setting aside of any book that is bound up in the Bible will not invalidate the others. We know very well that Luther did not believe the Epistle of James was a canonical book, and that he set it aside. We know very well that there are modern critics who suppose parts of "Isaiah" were not written by the author of that book, and should not be ascribed to him. We know very well that some of the earlier historical books are supposed by critics to be invalidated because they seem to show traces of being compilations of still earlier documents, and as they say could not have been written by Moses or any single writer.

As for myself, I say that if even it should be proved that some of the books of the Bible are not authentic, and must be rejected—as I do not believe it will, and that others though in the main correct contain more or less errors which must be eliminated, it would not destroy the Bible, any more than to take a rotten joist from an imperfect place in a house would destroy the house. In taking out from the Bible whatever is false, you simply take out something that does not belong there. Therefore, to criticise a single book does not alter the whole canon. *The Bible* remains.

If men go to the Old Testament, then, and undertake to give to all that is there an interpretation under the impression that every word and sentence has been forged in the soul of God, and put into his Word by his own direct influence, instead of its being a demonstrative system adapting the amount and the method of truth employed to the nature of the minds to be operated upon through the instrumentality of other minds inspired and aroused to wisdom by the Holy Spirit, making use of natural objects, society, all available means, for teaching and developing the human race,—then one of two things must happen : either the Bible must give way or they must give way.

This Book is elastic; and if you put a cast-iron frame about it, if you cramp it by theories and philosophies, it cannot stand—it will die of suffocation. If you are going to save the Bible, you must proceed on the Bible ground: take facts as they are, and act according to those facts. If men will go to the Word of God simply for the purpose of knowledge, to profit withal, and not to find material for controversy, not in a spirit of criticism, not even for literary enjoyment; if men will go to the Scriptures with the wish that they may be thoroughly furnished for every good work; if they will go to the inspired record as they would go to any other document in which they were profoundly interested, to seek for what is right and pure and good, and to be built up in holiness—if men will go in that way to the Bible, they will find there treasures that are not to be found in any other quarter. It is the history of the evolution of the highest forms of human nature. Along with this history are accounts of wars, revolutions, catastrophes. There are records of lives and achievements of men of God. The Book is filled with facts and lessons that men would not willingly let die. I could not afford to let go what it has taught me of the experiences of mankind in the patriarchal age. I could not afford to lose those grand old figures of the Israelites, more majestic than any sphinxes. I could not afford to have destroyed the records of their captivity, and of their wanderings in the desert. I could not afford to give up the knowledge that I have gained of the commonwealths that sprang from the polity of the great lawgiver of the ages. Greater than he has never been upon the earth, as a mere human being. I could not afford to lose the magnificent wisdom and poetry and spiritual experience of those grand old statesmen of the Israelitish nation. I cannot afford to dispense with one of the records of those wonderful triumphs of human nature under God's guidance. The world has been marching through a wilderness amidst conflicts and victories, and the records of these victories and conflicts are infixed as jewels in the Word of God. They stand there to brighten our lives on our pilgrimage, to encourage our faith and hope, to cheer us in our childhood, to help us in our manhood, and to comfort us in old age.

I love the Word of God; and the more I free it in my mind and use from superstition, from narrow ecclesiasticism, and bring it into the atmosphere into which it was born and in which it has lived,—the more I make it the man of my counsel, the guide to my path and the lamp to my feet, —the sweeter it is to me. The more I give to its interpretation the largeness, the variety, and the liberty which in every other direction we have learned to employ, the more profoundly am I affected by the inspiration of God's Word.

II.

HOW TO READ THE BIBLE.

"Thy word is a lamp unto my feet, and a light unto my path."—Psa. cxix 105.

THIS Psalm is, in the original, a literary curiosity, after a manner that was apparently delightful to the Oriental mind — the formation being something like acrostics in our times, every letter of the alphabet having its section. But while the outward form is somewhat peculiar, the inward form is still more striking. It clusters together, from every point of view, the expressions of the sweet psalmist, whoever he was, as to the Word of God, both in the written Scriptures and in unwritten nature.

The language is unmistakable, not once nor twice, but many times, in which, while speaking of the precepts of God's Word as written in his time, he also speaks of the law of the Lord as it is made manifest in nature. It conforms, therefore, to our idea of the two Revelations—the Word and the World.

You will observe that the point of emphasis in the passage I have read is the *guiding power* of the Bible; and if at the time this was uttered, when comparatively a small portion of the Scriptures had been written, that portion of it which we are now almost inclined to reject, certainly largely to neglect, was so much esteemed by this ancient writer, how much more would he have rejoiced if he had seen the fullness of the revelation of God as he is made known in Christ Jesus, and in the New Testament writings of the disciples of Christ!

Sunday morning, October 20, 1878. LESSON : Psa. cxix. 97–144.

More especially for the advantage of the young, I wish to speak to-night on the subject of *Reading the Bible*. There are many difficulties connected with this in our time. There have been so many questions raised concerning it from the outside, the authenticity of the books of the Bible has been so much disputed, there have been suggested so many scientific objections to it, the reality of the things in it has been so much contradicted, that there has come to be a kind of haze or mist in the view of many cautious, critical minds around about the Word of God. They are not prepared to say that there is not something in it, that it has no authority, that it is without influence ; but they say that the claims which have been made for it cannot be sustained, and that we cannot believe as our fathers did. It seems as though there had been a kind of drifting away from the Bible on the part of people who fifty or even twenty-five years ago would never have thought of recession.

Then, if one undertakes to read the Bible he is like a country lad going into a strange city where a foreign language is spoken. He has not been brought up to the habit of reading it intelligently. It is in fact a library rather than a book. It comprises the sacred Scriptures of the Israelitish people. It represents their then whole literature, and substantially their entire philosophy and legislation and law ; and parts of that which is now collected into one volume are separated in their origins by hundreds and thousands of years.

If we were to gather together the events of Cicero's life, and of the life of Sallust, and then, coming down through the medieval ages, should stop once in a hundred years and pick up the facts of that period, and so on to our own day, and if we were to combine these all in a single volume, it would have as much claim to logical unity as the writings of the Hebrew Scriptures have, that were brought together simply by mechanical means.

The Bible was not all given at once. It gradually unfolded through many centuries, representing different ages, different civilizations, different languages; and now we have the results brought together and bound up in one book. When a man reads this collection without any knowledge of it historically or structurally, and without any foregoing familiarity with its contents, I do not wonder that he stumbles.

It befell me, once, to go to a neighboring manufacturing town, and to reach it at about nine o'clock in the evening; and for the first and only time in my life I undertook to find a friend's house in a strange city at night. I could not tell whether the street upon which I entered was going out of town or into town; I could not tell whether if I turned to the right or to the left I was going toward the center or away from the center of the place; I was helpless; and it was only by rousing the people in a house that I was able, at last, to find my way and reach my destination.

Now, going into the Word of God is very much like one's going into a town of whose streets and lanes he knows nothing. A man is taught that he should read the Scriptures. Let him, for instance, sit down and read in Solomon's Song, in order to ascertain whether he was a good man or not. What sort of a time would he find there? Suppose he went into the book of Chronicles, and fell upon one of those long genealogical lists, or upon the account of David's woes? He has heard that this book is a guide to his feet and a lamp to his path, but, stumbling upon such passages, it would not be strange if he found no meat in them. A man who did not know where to go, in search of curiosities, objects of fine art, or what not, in this great city, might wander up and down its streets aimlessly and uselessly. There is a great advantage in knowing where to apply for what one wishes to find. And in reading the Bible, it is important to know how to read and what to read—for this book is not, as I have already said, an essay or philosophical treatise, whose various parts, being united, make a perfect whole, but is a cluster of books brought together through long periods of time, having different immediate objects, and subserving different local ends. The only unity is one of general spirit, making for righteousness of life.

Then there is another difficulty (and it is not a small one)—namely, the enormous amount of rubbish that has been gathered around about the Scriptures. You know how it is with the cities of the East that are now being exhumed. In Egypt they are digging down to old cities under centuries of accumulations of sand. In Assyria they are doing the same. Jerusalem itself lies forty feet below the level of the present city; if you would walk the streets where the prophets walked you must go down through rubbish to get where they were. But no statue, or pyramid, or sphinx, or treasure sought was ever covered down with learning and other accumulations as the Word of God is. If you doubt it, read the commentators. Take a little of Adam Clarke, and Matthew Henry, and other writers on the Bible. There is a great number of these commentaries (less than a thousand volumes); and it is almost incredible how about every element—as it were, on every letter—of the Book, in regard to whatever is connected with it, in one way or another, there is a special plea.

To a very large extent, moreover, these commentaries have proceeded on a radically false principle. You will perceive how hard it is for a man to get the right point of view in reading the Bible. I hold that the theory of the literal inspiration of Scripture is a theory of the devil, and that it will lead a man who is logical and consistent as straight into infidelity as possible. The theory that every word and every letter of the Bible is inspired of God—in other words, that by an irresistible impulse God put certain thoughts in men's minds and hearts, without any volition on their part, so that they were impelled to say exactly what they did say—is the absolute destruction of any belief in inspiration. Under this theory a single error, certainly a series of errors—of a material, exterior, or physical kind—the showing that dates are false and statements incorrect, the discovery that inconsistencies exist, that one part is not in exact agreement with another part—these things utterly ruin the faith of the believer in literal and verbal inspiration, and so, his faith in any inspiration.

It is true that the Bible is an inspired book—but in a much higher sense than that which is thus claimed for it, and which is pragmatical, pharisaic, and minifying. I have already dealt with this, but for the young there may be a further consideration of some points. The grander and truer theory of inspiration is that under God's providence all the moral sentiments and noble tendencies of mankind have been growing in the direction of divine truth; that there has been a guidance, a general enlightenment, of the human race, in every age, especially among certain peoples; that men have developed great moral principles, and some to a large degree have grown into heavenly knowledge; that the counsel and secret thoughts of God were thus indicated by human growth in grace; that exceptional persons were raised up in every period who could see what was thus made known, and who made a faithful record of what had transpired under this inspiration of God; and that statements were made by them of the experiences of the inspired race, so far as they were unfolding out of nothing into something, from lower to higher forms of knowledge. This theory of the inspiration of Scripture is quite reconcilable with the fact that there are mistakes of letters and words and even of historic statements in it here and there, without lessening its spiritual value.

Now, if it was necessary, for the development of the truth, that holy men should be inspired of God, they were nevertheless *men*, and you must take their utterances as infallible only for the purpose of moral and spiritual instruction, making allowance for the imperfect operation of their minds by reason of the limitations to which they were subject as men. In other words, if God employs instruments he must employ them with all their defects and liabilities; and as he did use men, he used them with all their defects and liabilities. Therefore, that in the Bible there are literal mistakes, verbal mistakes, literary mistakes, and statistical mistakes, is not strange at all.

These do not detract from its authenticity as a genuine document, or its authority as a spiritual guide.

For example, in showing on the chart where the Gedney's Channel runs through to New York, suppose the channel should be put down exactly right, but that in giving the depth of some outside place or in representing some other minor detail—the name of the maker of the chart, or what not—there should be a mistake; so long as experience proved that there was no error in the location and width and dept. of the channel, and no error that rendered vessels in passing through it liable to danger or inconvenience, would you denounce that chart as unauthentic? The fact that there was in it a minor mistake here and there which did not interfere with its practical use would make no difference with its real value, and you would not think of finding serious fault with it.

If we insist, as many people do, that the writings of the Old and New Testaments came directly from the mind of God, then the slightest variation from accuracy in any statement of fact would be fatal, because we should say, "God cannot lie"; and yet there are many errors of this sort in the Scriptures. If it be claimed that the penmen of the Gospels were absolutely infallible, we have a test case. All the four Evangelists state that there was written in three languages over the cross of Christ the declaration, "This is Jesus, King of the Jews." Here was an instance in which there was the actual writing of a legend or inscription; and, according to the theory of verbal inspiration, four witnesses that saw it, and wrote it down, were kept absolutely from making a mistake, so that the four writings would be just the same; and yet, every single one of them differs from all the others in recording it. Matthew has it one way, Luke another, Mark another, and John another. There is not, however, any such variation as invalidates the fact that is stated. The general statement is the same, but the way of copying or remembering the inscription differs in the several cases. They do not all have it the same, letter for letter and word for word, but they have the substance alike, and their minor variations of memory evidence their common honesty and trustworthiness.

So of matters concerning dates and numbers. A person says, "I ate strawberries at your house last June." In fact, it was in July; but what is the difference, so far as the validity of the occurrence is concerned?

And there may be in the Bible errors of time, certain dates may be wrong, numbers may be incorrect, and they may seem all the more erroneous because the use of numerical terms differed in antiquity from their use at the present time. The frequent employment of familiar incidents was often accompanied by exaggerations. For instance, *forty* was used as we now use *a hundred*. We say, "I have been there a hundred times," simply meaning a great many times. You recollect that the flood prevailed *forty* days, that the prophet fasted *forty* days, that Christ fasted *forty* days, that Moses was *forty* years old before he went into the wilderness, that he was *forty* years in the wilderness, and *forty* years more in the desert. *Forty* means, here, *a great many*, instead of a definite number; and the same is true of many other figures in the Bible.

I am instancing the theory of verbal inspiration to show that those writers and commentators on the Word of God who follow this theory have undertaken to reconcile contradictory passages by spiritualizing them, by wrenching them out of their literal meaning, and giving them a metaphorical signification, or *vice versa;* so that when a man comes to read the Bible according to their notions he feels that he has come to Babel, and that there is confusion worse confounded. If he is a clear thinker, and a straightforward philosophical man, the result will be that if he really believes the commentators he will lose all confidence in the authenticity of the Scriptures. I do not wonder that multitudes of men turn away from the Bible with disgust under such circumstances.

Right between extreme metaphoricalism and extreme materialism stands the Word of God itself, claiming to be simply a book from which a man can thoroughly furnish himself for right living. It gives enough of God to enable you to understand the moral character of the universe. It gives enough of human nature to enable a man to perceive what ails him. It gives directions enough in regard to every one of the faculties of the human soul and every one of the paths of life to enable a man who wants to walk in the way of righteousness to find that way. It gives as much information as one needs to make him thoroughly honest and upright. Nay, more, there is in it all that is necessary to enlighten a man's understanding and fill him with faith and hope and love. No man can go amiss in regard to any of these things who reads the Bible wisely and diligently.

Notions have been formed from the Old Testament that good men (as, for instance, David) committed great offenses; that treachery was allowed; that cruelty was permitted here and there ; that God winked at these things. I do not undertake to discuss that subject now, although I shall do it later ; but whatever may be said about the divine moral government in the primitive ages of the world, the question is for every man's own self, whether there is not, if he really desires to learn how to live right, material in the Word of God to enable him to do it. There certainly is. For a man who undertakes in earnest to ascertain what to do with his thoughts and feelings and conduct as regards his fellow men or himself individually, in the household, in civic affairs, and in business or economic matters, there is no book in the wide world which contains so much and such varied information as the Bible. You can spin and weave it into anything you like; from it have been formed medleys of every description; but when one says, "How shall I be a better man?" he finds that question answered better in the Word of God than anywhere else : when you come to the ground of its ethics there is no dispute. It may be difficult for you to know what Ezekiel meant—I do not suppose he himself knew ; it may be difficult for you to understand what John saw in the Revelation; you may have a very imperfect notion of Daniel's beasts, and of a great many other mystical and prophetic things; there may be applications and parallelisms of history which you cannot reconcile; in regard to all these things there is ground for difference of opinion: but on the subject of *essential manhood* there is *no* difference of opinion. Men are at substantial agreement respecting it. The Roman Catholic Church and the Protestant Church see eye to eye so far as such matters are concerned. The sects may differ about philosophies and theologies, but not about honesty, purity, truth, hope, love and joy in the Holy Ghost. Men may differ in regard to doctrines and forms and ceremonies, but not in regard to hardness of heart, obstinacy, and all other elements that come into play in our daily life. About these, men are at agreement in all churches. So much of the Bible as it was meant that we should *live by*—is perfectly plain.

If you want to know whether or not pride is beneficial, there are no two voices in the Bible about that. If you take the testimonies of Scripture for centuries and thousands of years you will find that they have always been the same concerning the affections. In the patriarchal age, in the time of Christ, and all the way down to the present, you will find the same teaching on the subject of selfishness. In the earliest day, and from that time down, you will find the same witness borne as to what prayer is. In regard to meekness, the Psalms are just as explicit as the Sermon on the Mount. Indeed, the Sermon on the Mount was largely drawn from the Psalms. Respecting the experiences of men in sin, and under fear and remorse, the statements are precisely the same in the Old Testament as in the writings of the Apostles. Here is a book whose instructions, though written at widely different periods, agree in every essential particular. Here is a book, portions of which were written hundreds of years after other portions, the later authors having sometimes no knowledge of the writings of those who preceded them, and yet there is identity of faith and experience. They are all precisely the same in regard to the great issues of life and character, and the ways in which man can attain reconciliation with God and hope of immortality. With an evident development from lower to higher completeness, the similarity of kinship and spirit from beginning to end is uniform and constant.

Therefore, under that system of moral inspiration which God has been carrying on in all nations and in every age of the world,—under that process of unfolding in which men rise through social refinements and affections to a larger development of human life,—under that divine scheme, the race have everywhere and in all ages come to the same results. They have found the law of human life. Just as a man finds the law of electricity or light, so men, through thousands of years, have found what are the qualities of character which fit them for time and eternity; and the united testimony of mankind on that subject is both comprehensive and simple, and is absolutely without any objection whatsoever from critics or infidels.

If men come, then, to the reading of the Word of God through commentators, there is a use in that of which I will speak by and by; but if an ordinary man, like any one of you, should say to me, "Mr. Beecher, I want to live a better life," my advice to him would be, "Steer clear of commentators; read the *Bible*—not what folks have written about the Bible." "Well, how shall I read?" "There are a hundred ways; but the way above every other way is to read for the purpose of learning how to be a right-minded man and how to live right."

As regards the structural errors, the literary mistakes, the arithmetical inconsistencies, that are found in the Bible, they neither invalidate the general drift of the history recorded in it, nor change the evident tenor of its instructions. If one is really studying the text of Scripture, its formation and its nature, if one is going into a philosophical analysis of the structure of the Word of God, as a teacher in a Sabbath school or a preacher of the gospel, commentaries, judiciously selected, may be of great use to him now and then; but as a general thing they are not essential. And though there may be some advantages in being able to read the text in the original Hebrew or Greek, this is not so important as may be supposed. The number of instances in which the meaning is not sufficiently brought out in our translation are comparatively speaking but few. Here and there minor errors may exist,—the sense may be obscured, rectifications of statement may be desirable, passages may be transposed and taken out of their proper connection,—errors of printers, of translators, of copyists, of editors, and, for what we know, of authors; but the marrow of this book is not touched by any of these discrepancies. Commentaries may be useful for teachers, and by and by may have a sparing use for ordinary readers of the Word of God; but as a general rule the book itself is its best commentator.

If you ask me, "How shall I read the Bible?" I say, in the first place, you may read it for philosophical knowledge, for knowledge of antiquity, for local historical knowledge; you may read it for the sake of the literary pleasure to be derived from its study; you may read it on account of its poetry and its magnificent prophecies; but you must not understand, by this, that you are to read the Bible for those things alone. You must not suppose, for instance, that all the prophets were "prophesying" in the sense of *foretelling*, and valuable on that account. Jeremiah, Isaiah, and Ezekiel were reforming statesmen; and, although here and there foretellings were mixed up with their discourses, the greater part of their prophesying was *preaching;* their exhortations applied to human affairs, and were replete with the most sublime symbolism. Nothing in other literature can approach in grandeur the utterances of the prophets. They are equal to the Psalms of David in this respect. There is no high feeling, there is no low feeling, there is no feeling of joy or sorrow, of exhilaration or despondency, that has not its voice in the Psalms. Every passion that inflames the soul has its lyrical expression there. Nowhere else are portrayed doubts, fears, thanksgivings, confidences, as they are set forth in the Psalms of David. A man is fortunate who knows how to describe his own emotions in the language of David—only, our emotions are so small that we are like David in Saul's armor when we undertake to walk in the language of the Psalms.

The dramas of the Old Testament prophets are extremely beautiful. The book of Job is a magnificent drama, as truly as Shakespeare's plays; but it is not a historical document. The story of Ruth is unsurpassed for beauty. The history of Joseph and portions of other Bible histories have no superiors in literature. To those who know how to wisely cull from the contents of the Old Testament it is a magnificent reading-book. There is nothing that children listen to with more interest than portions of the Scriptures; and there is nothing to which persons in old age cling with more tenacity than some of its passages. It was not, like many of our modern books, artificially gotten up for purposes of making money. It is a book of simplicity, in which are recorded the experiences of men who did the best they knew how to do. It is, to a great extent, a statement of what were living facts. It therefore possesses the elements, not only of simplicity but of universality, power, truth, and beauty.

You can read the Bible also for controversy; but that is venomous reading. It may be necessary to gather together, for the illustration of a common truth, different passages written in times of warfare, or during periods of revolutions of thought such as those which occurred in the lives of Luther, and Wesley, and other reformers, when great changes were wrought; it may become essential to collect various representations of truth, draw them up in battle array, and with them bear down on opposing views and teachings; but such a use of this book seems to me to be infelicitous. It certainly is uncongenial to me.

I have spent nearly forty years in the ministry, and during the early part of that period my work was more or less controversial. I was born not far from the time of the split between the Old and the New School Presbyterians. I was brought up in the gladiation of a theological seminary. You may think I do not know much about theology. You do not know how much I know about it, for I have tried to forget all that, and to recover from the scars and wounds inflicted by a controversial reading of the Bible.

If I had preserved the love-letters of my mother written before she was married to my father, as I have fragments of a few of them, and I should make them parts of a controversy on the subject of the affections of mankind, and I should fight those affections up hill and down, one with this passage and another with that, until there was not a line in the letters that was not associated with some intellectual battle, how utterly would they be emptied of their beauty and sweetness! How, after I had made wads of them to fire at views different from those which I chanced to hold on the subject under discussion, should I divest them of those features which gave them greatest value and attractiveness!

Now, the Bible is filled with the tracks of warriors. The prophets have been drawn up, like athletes, and led here and there by one set of controversialists to oppose another set. The whole New Testament has been marshaled, with regimentals on, to put down the Unitarians, the Universalists, the Arminians, and the Arians. The tocsin has been sounded in this great book, and all parts of it have been summoned to battle array. Every man in the conflict has been armed with a text as a sword, and the Word of God has been made to do service as a magazine of artillery. The good news called "the gospel"—the glad tidings that God so loved the world that he gave his Son to die for it; the invitation of Christ, "Come unto me, all ye that labor and are heavy laden, and I will give you rest,"—these things theologians have hardly listened to, although the whole creation has groaned and travailed in pain until now. Notwithstanding the New Testament teems with expressions of the deepest feelings of sympathy and compassion for human infirmity, these, its profoundest elements, have been for a large part unheeded by so-called religious teachers. Instead of using the Bible as a means of help to men in the great exigencies of life, they have made a wanton, wasteful use of it, for purposes of controversy. They go into the Word of God in a spirit utterly at variance with the spirit in which it was written.

But suppose a man, in the right spirit, desires to read the Bible for purposes of guidance and direction, then how should he read it? Well, that simplifies the matter. In the first place, you want to read the Bible with reference to your own state. You want to know how to carry yourself in the world. A good book to read with that object in view is the Proverbs of Solomon. I wish every man who does business in New York would read those proverbs. Some parts of that book can be read with great profit by every one. In it are laid down precepts for secular conduct. On the subjects of virtue and vice, of giving way to unwarrantable appetites, of right and wrong methods of administering property, of hard-heartedness toward one's neighbor, of extortion or usury, of hospitality, of truth-speaking, of being puffed up with pride,—on these and a thousand other important subjects which relate to right living, you will find wise criticisms, witty epigrams, wholesome counsels, in this book of Proverbs.

Then, when you have read that book for the right ordering of your life, take a pencil and mark the passages in it whose injunctions you are willing to follow. Make a little cross on the margin opposite those passages that you have made up your mind to adopt as your rule of practice ; and put an interrogation point over those passages that you think are so hard that you cannot promise to live up to them just yet.

This is business. If I were to deal with you in a commercial way, I should say, "Be so kind as to mark the things which you have to sell with the prices at which you are willing to sell them, that I may not be laboring under any misapprehension." So in counseling you in regard to reading the Bible—and particularly in advising you as to your use of the Proverbs—I am impelled to make a similar request.

Take this book, and mark the things you have no hesitation in following, and those you fear you cannot follow. Study especially those passages that you think have a personal bearing upon you—upon your nature or disposition, upon your duties to your neighbors, upon your relation to business. You may find, when you come to honestly square your life with the rules laid down in the Proverbs, that you will be obliged to break this or that partnership, that it will necessitate your changing your companions, or that it will otherwise completely revolutionize your life. This I call *rubbing the Bible in.* So employed, it is a lamp to your feet and a light to your path. I instance the book of Proverbs alone; but you know as well as I do how this same method may be followed throughout this great Library of Life—and especially in the books of the New Testament.

Now, then, let those who will, ridicule Moses and make fun of the prophets as much as they have a mind to. You will have business enough to carry your life by those parts of the Bible that commend themselves to your judgment as being true and wise. It is a book that exposes, in their glaring deformity, your meanness, your pride, your vanity, your lust, your inordinate appetites; and if you are going to follow its directions you will need God to help you. Nothing is truer than that if we wish to escape from the lower instincts of animalism and organize our life on inspirations of higher spiritual wisdom nothing but God can enable us to succeed.

Therefore, let me close the lessons of to-night by urging that while you are reading this book you let go up to the throne of grace a silent prayer that the Spirit that originally sent it forth may give you the inspiration which was given to those through whom it came, and make you honest in obeying its injunctions. If you lied to other people as much as you lie to yourselves, there would not be a man on earth that would believe you. If you deceived other people as you deceive yourselves, you would be given over to utter unbelief in the eyes of your fellow men. Therefore ask God to deliver you from lying and self-deception. Ask him to give you light not only to read the Bible aright but to discern what it reveals. Ask him to take away all those hindrances that prevent your being just as true, pure, and honest, as this text requires you to be.

I am not asking you, to-night, young men outside of the pale of religion, to come into the church; I am not asking you to accept the doctrines of Christianity: I am asking you with honesty and sincerity to read the Word of God; to take it with an earnest desire to ascertain whether or not it is what it claims to be—a light to show you how to walk; a book that is able to thoroughly furnish you for every good work in this life. I simply invite you to make this experiment. Is it an unreasonable request? Is it not wise for you to read with the purpose of knowing what you are, what you were designed to be, and how you may work out your true destiny? You are brought into circumstances that make you feel that you are not living aright, and are not ready to die; and is not this a simple, rational way in which to endeavor to arrive at correct conclusions on so important a subject?

I beseech of you, receive, in the spirit in which I have spoken these things, my advice in this matter. Read, as I have asked you to, this book, which has guided so many thousands out of darkness into light; this book on which your father leaned for support; this book from which your mother drew consolation. Do not throw it disdainfully aside. Do not despise the foundation on which holy men in every age have stood and worked.

III.

THE BOOK OF BEGINNINGS.

"And beginning at Moses and all the prophets, he expounded unto them in all the Scriptures the things concerning himself."—Luke xxiv. 27.

THIS was spoken of our Master after his resurrection. You see here, with a little modification of the language, how the Old Testament books, or the religious books of the Israelites, were named at the time of our Saviour. They were called "The Law of Moses," "The Prophets," and "The Scriptures," or "The Writings." This was the threefold definition, in which were included all the books of the canon now called "The Old Testament." Where it is translated, "Beginning at Moses and all the prophets, he expounded unto them in all the Scriptures the things concerning himself," it is really the equivalent of saying that he interpreted Moses, the Prophets, and the other Scriptures in respect to himself—these three.

The Old Testament, for a variety of reasons, has passed out of use for many men and women who call themselves Christians. They think that it is an imperfect guide as respects modern times, though relatively perfect as respected ancient times ; that it was superseded by the more full disclosure of spiritual truths by the Saviour, and by the Apostles under inspiration, and that we do not need to go back to it as at school children go back to their hornbook; that men learn certain necessary lessons, so that, having learned them, and their schoolbooks, as it were, being superseded by other and better ones, they have no longer use for them. This is all the more so be-

---

Sunday evening, November 10, 1878. LESSON : Psa. xxvii.

cause there are so many parts of the Old Testament that have inherent difficulties in them; because there are so many things recorded which men are supposed to be obliged to believe, but which strain belief to the uttermost; because there are such wondrous miracles, such remarkable phenomena, such associated historical statements, so many things that, according to modern and ordinary interpretation, seem exaggerated if not absolutely erroneous. Rather than take such statements and difficulties implicitly they find it easier to put aside the whole book; and because it is hard to get gold out of the rock they throw the rock and the gold all away in a heap, and let them alone.

Now, it is true that the Old Testament stands on a different ground in relation to us from the New; but it does not follow from this fact that there is not in it present and future medicine for Christian men; and it is my desire, in the discourses which I give on this subject, not so much to criticise for the purpose of tearing to pieces, as to present the Old Testament even in its more questionable parts in such a way that they can be received and used with personal profit by men of our time. Luther said of it, "It is the most useful and beautiful of books." There is eminent beauty in it to those that know how to find it; and it is far from being without usefulness, although it be a record of the first things that are known to us.

Having discussed the question of inspiration and rejected the theory of a limited and verbal inspiration of these writings,—accepting, rather, the theory of the inspiration of the human race by its holy men that are competent to receive divine impressions,—and holding the Word of God to be a record of the best thoughts and feelings which have existed in every age over which the record passes, I propose to apply that theory in some detail to the successive books of the Old Testament; and if it shall seem to any of you that, in the course of this, I set aside unnecessarily a good deal, or depart too widely from old-fashioned notions, I call your attention to the fact that everybody, without exception, in the whole Christian

world, has set aside whole books of the Old Testament—
and not individuals alone, but the churches themselves.
For where, in the world, is there any man who ever teaches
that *Leviticus* is binding on us? The whole instituted
religion of the Israelites has been set aside; the altar is
gone, the tabernacle is gone, the temple is gone, the priest
is gone, and the forms of worship are gone. We leave
them utterly. If, therefore, to any it should seem auda-
cious to teach a change in reference to the books either
before or after the ritualistic books of the Jews, comfort
yourselves, quiet your disturbances. If I do it at all, I do
that which the whole church has done.

In the Old Testament the five books of Moses are called
" The Law," " The Law of Moses," and " The Book of the
Law of the Lord." The Rabbis called it " The Five-fifths
of the Law." In more modern times it is called " The Pentateuch "—*pentateuch* being a Greek word which signifies *five
books*. It is made up of Genesis, Leviticus, Exodus, Numbers, and Deuteronomy. In Hebrew the Israelitish books are
named mainly from some word or sentence in the first verse.
Our names differ from those employed in the Hebrew
scrolls. *Genesis* signifies *beginning* or *beginnings;* it is a
book that contains a history of the beginnings of things in
the world. *Exodus* signifies *going forth*, or *emergence;* it is
the history of the deliverance of the Israelites from bondage, and their traversing the desert. *Leviticus* is so named
because it is the book that treats of all the forms and ceremonies of the priesthood, and of their worship, that worship
being conducted by the Levites—the sons of Levi. *Numbers*
is a general history, and it is called *Numbers* simply because
it records, takes the census of, Israel. *Deuteronomy* is, literally speaking, the *Second Law*,—a recapitulation, a second
law-giving or enunciation of the Law.

If Washington's farewell letter had included the whole
history of the colonies in brief, and the theory of the Constitution, with the general features and the policy of the
free commonwealth, that would have been exactly a parallel
of Deuteronomy, which is in the form of a farewell letter of

Moses to the people, and contains a recital of their history, and the laws and ordinances imposed upon them by God through Moses.

To-night I propose to consider only a portion of the book of Genesis. It is not my object to go into it in minutiæ and detail, but to give a general view of it.

This book may be said to be divided into two parts. The first twelve chapters contain the history of that vast space anteceding the appearance of Abram; and the rest is an account of the patriarchs, Abram, Isaac, and Jacob, of their wanderings, and of their posterity down to the period of their inclusion in the Egyptian kingdom.

My purpose, then, this evening, is to take simply the first division of Genesis, including the first twelve chapters, leaving out connecting and minor elements.

This history may be said to be an account, first, of Creation; second, of the Garden of Eden; third, of the Flood; and fourth, of the Tower of Babel; or an account of the creation of the Terraqueous Globe, of Man in his primitive Condition, of the Corruption of Men, of their Destruction by the Flood, of the Dispersion of Men, and of the Origin of Languages.

Before entering upon that, let me say a word on the subject of authorship. These books have universally been attributed to Moses. In modern times very severe debates have occurred on this subject. I do not consider it a subject of very great importance so far as practical utility is concerned whether he wrote them or not. The mere name of the author of a book is not half so important as the nature of its contents. The result in my mind is about this, that these books were very largely produced by Moses or under his direction: either compiled—as the first twelve chapters; or, as the subsequent chapters, formed from legends, traditional histories, or other material, giving the same sequences, accounts of the patriarchs down to his own time, and then adding his own personal history, and the history of the different tribes and of their wanderings until they came to the Promised Land.

I have no doubt that the substantial basis of the books was from the hand of Moses, or that they were written by some clerk or Levite under his direction. But that there were not corrections and re-editings of them by other hands is not so plain. These may have been made at a comparatively late period, during the reign of the kings, and not far from the Babylonian intrusion.

If this seems to be tampering with the inspired authority, we are to consider that the rights of a book and an author were different in a primitive age from what they are in a later age, when, by development, authorship has become a business, and passed out of a crude and rude state into a regulated state, with methods and rules. When, in an early period, books were made on sheets of lead or on prepared skins; when but one book existed in a nation; when it was a thing unknown to the common people, except as they occasionally heard it read; when it was a phenomenon standing unique and apart from every other mode of intercourse—then there were no established rules or laws. In the medieval age, certain men, thinking they would honor and glorify God if they added to sacred Scripture some theories of their own, not doubting that they were true, committed what are called "pious frauds," that in our day would be not only exceptionable but manifestly improper. For a man in this age of the world to tamper with history, for instance, to inject into the writings of Froude or Gibbon statements and comments as if from the pens of Froude or Gibbon, would be a high offense at the court of public sentiment; it would be an outrage: but in the early time, when there was no trade of book-making, when there was no author's profession, a man jotted down what he knew of his people, and subsequently some man who came after him added what he deemed to be the further ascertained facts concerning that people, and nobody thought it to be criminal. In the simplicity of an infantile age men set down what was before them; and it was an operation without guile, for there was then no way of putting together for preservation additional facts, except by incorporating them in the single record with facts already set down. And in later days critical acumen may be able to point out, in ancient and modern documents, where the line runs between the genuine and the spurious, or the earlier and the later.

The question of the authorship of Moses is very much to historical and literary criticism, but is very little to common readers. It makes comparatively little difference to me whether Moses, or a Levite or some scribe in the reign of the kings, wrote what are called "The Books of Moses." Here are these historical books handed down to us, and our reception of them is to depend upon their interior contents, rather than upon their authorship.

Let us consider, now, the accounts in Genesis—the Creation, Adam and Eve, the Tower of Babel, the Dispersion of Men, and the Change of Language. In regard to all these, they are to be neither accepted nor rejected as scientific or historical statements made in our day would be. You are to bring to bear upon them the same rules of criticism that you apply to any ancient document.

Here comes in the principle enunciated last Sunday night, that the inspired records are relative to the want of the age in which they were made, and that a record which was suitable to the condition of the understanding of an early period would not be suitable to the condition of the understanding of a later period. If any man holds the theory that God, in the beginning, sat down and wrote things which he wanted to be true of the children that he created on the earth, and that those things were to be equally true at the beginning, the middle, and the end of existence; in other words, if any man has the idea that the inspired records are a continuous narrative, an uninterrupted overflow of divine thought given to men, and that they in some way proceeded from God, as Mill's philosophy proceeded from Mill, as Cowper's poetry proceeded from Cowper, or as Milton's works proceeded from Milton—then he must take everything as its stands in the Word of God without modification. But there can be no fact more indisputable than that the Bible is not a continuous narrative, nor an uninterrupted overflow of divine thought to men.

The Old Testament is made up of a score or more of books, between which whole centuries roll. They are composed of histories of different nations in different stages of development, adapted to the conditions of men in given times and circumstances, and their uses were related to those times and circumstances. Therefore, a truth that may be brought out in a large measure in a later day in an earlier and far distant age might have been brought out simply as a twilight truth. There is noonday revelation in the New Testament; in the Old Testament is early morning revelation. Those early statements of the beginnings of things in the world were designed, primarily, for the times in which they were written and to which they came. They were adapted to unripe and childlike conditions of the human race. They presented the thoughts that were in them in forms that were useful at that time, even if they should cease to be useful in later days. We are to interpret them by the light of the later inspiration of the human race, and not to undertake to interpret the later inspirations of the human race by being tied up to these earlier ones. A scientifically ascertained fact in a later day is not to be set aside for the sake of "saving the Scripture," as men foolishly say. The testimony of God in the whole history of the human race is more important than to maintain a special form of teaching or truth that existed in the early primitive times.

Take, then, the history of Creation. It is declared, apparently, on the face of Scripture, that God in six days created the earth, and all the things that it contained. The very first debate originated in the now unquestionable fact that creation was not a peremptory and instantaneous thing. Over against the old interpretation of Genesis, there rises the divine record of the rocks. Geology in our times says that between one period and another of this earth ages rolled—that one thing was not created on

Monday, the next on Tuesday, the next on Wednesday, the next on Thursday, the next on Friday, and the next on Saturday. Evidence to the contrary has accumulated in so vivid and compulsory a manner that at last a theory has been settled upon that the "days" meant in Genesis were *periods*, and much illustrative matter is brought to bear upon it.

I am not especially interested in that debate. I am satisfied that by "days" ages were meant. All is pictorial, and adapted to that idea. But I have no doubt that those who first received the books supposed that ordinary days were referred to. I question whether they could have understood periods of time such as we now begin to understand in this connection. So it is held, by the intelligent teachers now in orthodox churches, that the creation of the world was a work, not of literal days of twenty-four hours each, but of periods which may have been thousands of years long.

As a part of this, was the idea that Creation, as delineated in the book of Genesis, was, when it took place, instantaneous, and by the voice of command; that God spoke, and it was done. It is recorded, "God said, Let there be light, and there was light." It is also recorded, "God said, Let the earth bring forth;" but is it to be supposed that instantly he saw things creeping and growing and forming? The disclosures of the globe are disproving this conception of instantaneity in creation, and showing that the method by which things were created was, as it still is, one of gradual unfolding. In every department new links are being added to the chain until the evidence is becoming irrefragable that the mode of making the world has been by succession, one thing growing out of another.

Now, science, rightly so called — not in its tentative suggestions, not in its first shrewd guesses, but in its ascertained facts and modes—is the voice of God, just as much as the divine decrees on Mount Sinai were the voice of God. A fact is a voice of God. It shows what his thought has been, it illustrates what he has executed, and there is no going behind it. To deny it is perilous. If it be different from what the record has been supposed to be, if the ascertained facts of creation are not such as they have hitherto been understood to be, we must accept the later record, the growing revelation : for there is an inspiration that begins things, presents them partially ; there is a later inspiration that gives them a larger development, so that they are seen in a more clarified state; and there are final inspirations that bring them out in full completeness.

The process by which, in the progressive painting of a fine oil portrait, are brought out, first the rude outline, then the crude filling in, and then the perfecting of every part, is the same process as that by which, under God's inspiration, the primitive races were developed from their primitive condition, step by step, to higher states, until in these later days we have larger understanding, more comprehensive knowledge, and may hope to be nearing the final or full form of things. The inspiration of the race is not by fits and starts; it is by gradual development. It began with the beginning of man, and holds on with him, and will continue clear down to the remotest period. We have not come to the end of inspiration yet.

Study it as you may, in the light of God's riper revelation, the Old Testament history of creation gave to antiquity characteristics of the sublimest nature. There is nothing low or mean about it. Even as measured by transcendent modern refinement, it is grand in the extreme, and is worthy of a place—the very highest place—in any literature. It is a revelation that life and the world sprang from the forces of the divine will, and not from chance ; that the world has not come from mere ether, finding its way anonymously, but that it is the result of power, gradual, prolonged, differentiated, under the divine method— that it is a creation of God. That fact stands effulgent, in the record.

Moreover it is monotheistic. In the cosmogony of other

nations, the creation and government of the earth were ascribed to multitudes of little gods; in Genesis they are represented as the result of unitary divine thought, so that there is harmony throughout the whole universe.

Now, if you take the narrative in this larger way it is very extraordinary. How came it? It was prepared at the time of Moses. It is acknowledged to be a primitive document, or a compilation of primitive documents, wrought into the form of a book, by the hand of whoever was the early scribe or author of that part of Genesis. How happened it that away back in the beginnings of the world such a grand conception of the highest result of the creative power of God was given to primitive men?

Look at the details as they have been since disclosed to mankind. The order of creation is substantially ascertained. Much is now supposed to be understood by men of science as to how it took place. Not that there is exact knowledge on the subject; but there is such marked identity between the recorded order of procedure and the result of actual scientific research as to make it impossible that this should have been accidental. Here is the oldest document concerning the proceedings of things far back of any recorded history; and when the inspired Word is compared with the record of God in the rock, in the soil, in the whole structure of the globe, it is found to be in the main correct.

Such an account as could be developed in its details at this age of the world would have been absolutely useless to an early period, just as a treatise on optics would be of no use to children in the nursery; so if all that is included in geology, geography, botany, ethnology, and biology had been put into the account of Genesis in the early period, there would have been no one on earth competent to understand it. It would have been like eloquence to a babe in the cradle, or philosophical knowledge to a child.

The next notable passage in the book of Genesis is the account of the Garden of Eden, in which it is said our first parents, Adam and Eve, were placed. This has been held to be a literal statement of fact. I do not so take it. I side with that large number of devout Christian men and scholars who think this to be an allegory, containing a profound spiritual meaning; who think that the *man* is the fact—not the story in which the meaning of the fact is conveyed. Our Lord and Saviour, when he undertook to impart the highest truths, followed the universal custom of his race and time, and invented parables, inclosing these truths in them. The New Testament is full of parables; and the Old Testament is all alive and glowing with Oriental poetic imagery.

But the church has given this statement of the Garden of Eden a literal rendering. It is supposed that Adam and Eve were created perfect. I shall not stop to refute this belief. It is supposed that the fate of their whole posterity was made to depend upon their conduct; that when they fell, all that should come after them fell with them; that on account of their guilt the whole human family have been laid under a curse, and that you and I and everybody are to be condemned because Adam ate an apple the eating of which was forbidden. That may do in a theological seminary, but not in the minds of sensible men. We are responsible for what we do ourselves, but not for what our ancestors did. Am I responsible for all the iron that my grandfather forged out on the anvil, though I had nothing to do with it? Am I responsible for all that my Welsh ancestors did centuries ago I am responsible for my own conduct, for what I myself do; but I am not responsible for that which took place before I was born. And to say that the whole human race are morally responsible for Adam's act in eating an apple contrary to the divine command, and are therefore guilty of "original sin," is absurd. I will admit actual transgression on the part of Adam, but I will not admit "original sin" on our part. Theologians hold that every man has had sin "imputed" to him on account of the sin of his great ancestor — Adam. To such devices men are obliged to resort in maintaining erroneous doctrines!

But whatever may be set aside, this remains: That man was not created an immutable and untemptable being, fixed as a crystal. A dove holds fast to the creative idea: it is a perfect dove from the beginning to the end. An eagle begins an eagle and is always an eagle. Everything runs after its nature unerringly, without mistake, except man. He is a fallible being. He has it in his power to make his condition, and to avoid evil; but he is temptable and mutable. He is placed in circumstances such that he has larger sovereignty, with plenary power to determine his own lines of action. He is organized on a higher range than the mere animal. This statement is the fact in the allegory; and it is a fact transcendent. Adam, who is represented as being temptable, liable to sin, and yet as having power to choose between good and evil, stands for the human race, as the prototype, the allegorical man, the first parent. He has a numerous posterity; for there is not a man in life that is not, as Adam was represented,— mutable, liable to go astray, ready for deterioration. Adam, as an allegory, stands to represent what is the nature of man as distinguished from the brute in creation. Spiritually, he stands related to posterity in all the ages and everywhere. The statements of primitive history, of the beginnings of things, point undoubtedly to the condition and destiny of mankind.

I have no doubt, then, that this record of Eden is a record of facts; but I do not at all believe that it is a record of facts in such a sense as many men suppose it to be.

Now as to the story of Noah and the great Flood. It is known that the earth is round, that the world is divided into continents, that there are Africa, Asia, Europe, and North and South America, and that there are the Atlantic and Pacific oceans, the frigid oceans and the vast Indian ocean; but there was a time when men supposed that the world was flat, and that they saw the whole of it in a two-days' journey, in the provinces east of the Mediterranean, the Black, and the Caspian seas, and that it was there submerged.

Doubtless there was anciently a great deluge; I have no doubt that there was a time when, as far as men could see, the earth was covered with water; unquestionably there was something which answered to the preservation of animals in an ark; but to suppose that the whole terraqueous globe was deluged, that all living things except those which were preserved in the ark were drowned, and that every insect, every bug, every worm, every mosquito, every butterfly, and every animal, were gathered together in pairs, and placed in the ark, and kept there during the flood—to suppose that all these creatures, of which there are thousands and thousands of species, were so gathered together, is too much for me. I can swallow a good deal, but I cannot swallow the sum total of all the organized animals on the globe! How many animals did Noah gather together in pairs and put in his ark? All the more common ones he might have carried through the Flood, but not the animal kingdom as we understand it. That would have been impossible. As a testimony to the corruptions of men, as a witness to the great natural law by which God cuts off the wicked, this account is important, and has great force. We are to interpret the story of the Flood as they interpreted it to whom it was given,— as a lesson of the judgment of God; but not by taking the whole of modern knowledge, and carrying it back to antiquity, and undertaking to make that ancient statement include all that has subsequently been evolved by instruction and research into the multitudinous myriads of the animal kingdom. This is the record of a fact; but not of the fact theologically ascribed to it in modern days.

Next in order comes the history of the Tower of Babel, as an explanation of the different languages of the globe. I have no doubt that, at the time, this was the very best account of that history which could be made. I have no doubt that it is a faithful representation of the understanding in that age of the fact of the differing languages of the races of men. I have no doubt that there was some answering fact in the history of the people—namely, that there was a scattering of the builders of that tower, and that to this was attached the impression that they went forth speaking, from that hour and moment, different languages, as a lesson against heaven-defying ambition. Yet even such a fact would in our day find a more natural rendering,—namely, that when men were divided and scattered abroad, out of that circumstance sprang a variety of new conditions, associations, and wants which led—as they always do lead—to the necessity of differences of language.

Looking back over the ground we have trodden, I remark, first, by way of application, How little is the knowledge that is given in the record of the Old Testament! Of the immense periods of time from the history of the first man on earth down to the account of Abram, it would seem as though the thing spoken of occurred within the space of a few scores or, at most, hundreds of years; but between the beginning of the human race on earth and the time of Abram must have elapsed thousands and thousands and thousands of years.

Yet I have given you the substance of the whole history of that period which is recorded. Thousands of years past,—the most momentous years that have been gone through by the human race,—and not a line nor a word! Thousands and thousands of men, in thousands and thousands of years, unfolded without a record! How infantile was the race as represented by the record when we first begin to get some thought and knowledge of them! And their condition at that point in their history when the record first speaks of them, as they were beginning to emerge toward manhood—how low, how uncivilized, how crude, how nearly animal it was! What knowledge had the human race then of the world on which they dwelt? None. Did they understand the law of the sun or of the planetary bodies? Not at all. Did they have any conception of the laws generally which govern physical things? Far from it. There was no revelation, no inspiration, which taught them these things. Was there anybody or anything which said to them, "This is the globe on which God has appointed your destiny; these are the laws by which, observing them, you are to maintain life?" No. Not a syllable was there disclosed to the primitive human race on these subjects. What did man know of men? What is there in the record which speaks of man's own personal self and the knowledge of it? There is no evidence that man ever knew that he was a thinking being or that there was a beginning of thought in him. No man knew that there was a heart with such force that it carried life through his whole body. No man was aware that he had a liver in which the devil resided. No man understood the structure of his being, outward or inward. In respect to his creation, his development, and his destiny there was no instruction given. What knowledge of ethics, of right and wrong, was given to him? None. There is no trace in the Old Testament record of the setting up of any ethical system that met the wants of men in society Indeed, there was no society. Men were wanderers in the desert. They were a pastoral people. They were savages. Life was slowly evolved. Those ideas which lead to the performance of duties had not yet been impressed upon the mind. The whole system by which men are to regulate their conduct toward each other was not proclaimed even in its beginnings until you come far down in the Old Testament record.

What provision was made for true worship in all the period before Abram's time, yes, and throughout all the patriarchal period? Polytheistic systems had grown up among the Phœnicians, Assyrians, Babylonians, and Egyptians; but, as I shall show next Sunday night, there was among all the early Hebrews not a church nor a tabernacle known, and there was no order of priests. There was now and then an altar; on special occasions, intermitting at rare epochs, there were prayers; but the whole series of Hebrew religious services were of comparatively modern date. The attempts to carry back the church to that early period and to prove its existence by records in the primitive

Scriptures, involves such violent stretchings of fact and application as ought to make an honest man blush with shame. I do not think there is any conscious deceit; but to undertake to harmonize the ancient inspired records with modern religious developments leads to an amount of unconscious dishonest quibbling that would cause a man who indulged in them to be turned out of a law-court. Even where the judges themselves were partial in his favor, I do not think, according to the procedure of human affairs, that such improbabilities as have been brought forward by interpreters of the Word of God in regard to views and doctrines would be tolerated.

How restricted, when we look at it, do we find the knowledge and the nature of God's moral government to have been! There was no divine teaching on these subjects, so far as the inspired record is concerned, until long after the time of Abram. There are hints of crude worship by Abel and Cain, and recognition of God by Enoch and Noah. But there was no literature of Jehovah. There was vague knowledge of God and creation, but almost nothing else was taught to men until a vastly later period. Putting his hand through the great dark antecedent period, and gathering out of it all the elements that were known of God and religion and morality, Moses brought together the early teachings; but what were they? The Stories of Creation, the Garden of Eden, the Flood, and the Tower of Babel. These were all there was, and they covered no man knows how many thousands of years of the existence of the human race. Yet there are men who attempt to take the advanced knowledge of these later days and carry it back to primitive facts, and give to them the same interpretation that they give to facts that are transpiring among us to-day. It is a monstrous misuse of the Old Testament. It is the very way to kill the Scriptures dead—if they could be killed. When this history of the primitive condition of the world was first dawning into twilight, men saw men as trees walking. The wind they were accustomed to think of as the breath of God. When the lightning flashed they thought it was his eye flashing over the earth. When they heard the thunder they thought it was his voice, and they said, "God is speaking." In their infancy men looked at all the facts about them with uninstructed eye and undeveloped philosophy, and the best that they got out of them is put down in the sacred writings, and is precious and valuable. Here is the history of the beginnings of the human race. You have a chance to measure the difference between man at the beginning of time and man in our day.

Is it not a striking fact that not only at that ancient period but away down to the time of Christ, immortality was not known to the Jews? There is not a trace of it, not a word concerning it, in the five books of Moses. It is not wrought into precept or statement; it is not made a sanction or an authority; it is not mentioned in any way; it is utterly unknown in the early Scriptures; and even in the later prophets the allusions to it are dubious.

Take this history, then, as a twilight inspiration of the nascent race, as a record of their progress, as a disclosure of their development, of the simplicity and beauty of their lives, and it has a moral power as well as great beauty and transcendent excellence. Let it stand to show what men's ideas were at the beginning of their history. Let the historical documents of the Bible, the simple statements of the Old Testament, not be damaged by being interpreted according to the laws of modern science. Let them remain as instructive allegories, or as the best account that could be given in those early days, of phenomena which men could not understand.

I read the accounts in this old Book with ever-growing pleasure. I read them with more profit than I did in childhood, when I held, in common with the uninstructed church, that they were exact inspirations and revelations. I now walk in those dim aisles of antiquity, and hear the lisping syllables of primitive man, and behold the way of God toward him, and draw lessons as to how we are to deal with the savage and the wants of men from seeing how God dealt with nascent man,—for the bottom of society represents the beginnings of the world. There is degradation in the communities in which we dwell; nay, the primitive animal instincts of man are in our very selves; and we have need of the wisdom that comes from the inspection of the divine method as God infuses himself into institutions and policies and manhood itself, by adapting his truth to the conditions and wants of mankind.

Remember Him who spake as never man spake, saying to his disciples, "I have many things to tell you, but ye are not able to bear them now." Christ adapted his instruction to his disciples, even so late as that period when he was on the earth, according to the measure of their understandings, and not according to the largeness and fullness of the truth as he understood it ; and how much more may we presume that the same thing would have been done by God's providence when the human race was but as a babe in its cradle, unknowing and incapable of knowledge!

And if, according to the measure of their knowledge, the race in times gone by were responsible not only for conduct but for character ; if the law of cause and effect was just as powerful in the moral kingdom from the beginning as the law of cause and effect is in the physical kingdom ; if they, in accordance with the small light they had, were under condemnation for disobedience,—as all these ancient histories show that they were,—how much more responsible are we, how much more shall we be amenable to the law of cause and effect, and how much more shall we be under condemnation—we, upon whom has come the knowledge that has been gathered through successive ages, that has accumulated, and that has rolled down upon us, if we do not therewith lay the foundations of purified life, and furnish the motives of a nobler manhood !

IV.

ABRAHAM.

"Looking unto the promise of God, he wavered not through unbelief, but waxed strong through faith, giving glory to God, and being fully assured that, what he had promised, he was able also to perform. Wherefore also it was reckoned unto him for righteousness.—Rom. iv. 20-22.

It is indispensable, if we take the full comfort of sacred Scripture, that we should wholly get rid of that natural but very incorrect idea that it is something, in all its nature and parts, which is perfect,—unless we reckon imperfection as an element of perfection, as we must. For if it be true that the scheme of creation in the mind of God is to evolve from the lowest conditions a race from ignorance, little by little, to more knowledge, and from a low estate of virtue, step by step, to a higher; if, in other words, it is a part of the divine plan that the beginnings of things shall be infantine, then it is indispensable that the economy of these beginnings shall have the nature of imperfectness.

It is therefore entirely in accordance with this whole divine plan, and it takes nothing from the sanctity of Scripture, to find that in the early periods there is the record of much that bears unmistakably the stamp of imperfection. Otherwise it would not be a truthful or a fitting record. If you represent men as having observed, before the era of observation was developed; if you speak of men as having discriminated between the physical and the spiritual, before the time came when human nature was able to do this; if you describe the early simplicity of the

---

Sunday evening, November 17, 1878. Lesson: Heb. xi. 1-16.

pastoral lives of a people according to the conditions of men in civilized society,—you carry doubt and unbelief back upon these early periods to every man that is philosophical, that loves truth and is sensitive to it: but if ancient records come down to us bringing memorials of earlier days having all the mistakes of imperfection in them, they carry their own evidence of being a transcript of those rude, unknowing, superstitious times.

So we may, in some sense, say that imperfectness is one of the signs of genuineness. As the history of a child, if written, will be a history of prattle, of misunderstanding, of obliquity in various ways; as in order to be a true history it must contain an account of these imperfections, so the earlier records of a remote people may well be expected to bear in themselves these evidences of veracity.

The Arabian, the Persian, the Jew, the Christian, the Mohammedan, all hold in sacred reverence the name of Abram. This name is more celebrated than any other in universal history. We marvel at this, for Abram was not a military hero. He was not a founder of cities. He was not the king of an empire. Nor was he, for aught that we know, a great thinker, nor a teacher, in any particular sense of the term. No line fell from his pen. No golden sentence has been preserved from his lips. Unlike Confucius, or Zoroaster, or Buddha, or Moses, he founded no system either of philosophy, of religious belief, or of worship. He was a wandering shepherd, and nothing more than that. If you would see his living image, as it exists to-day in real life, go to the original, the Bedouin sheik with his turbaned head, his cloak, and his long spear. This wild chief of the wandering tribes of the East may not be your conception of Abram which is founded upon the pictures of modern artists, but without doubt it is the very life-form of the patriarch.

The history of this great chief is very simple; it would seem, at first, as though there were but little in it for comment; and yet, upon consideration, there is in it more than can be encompassed in any discourse—more than the plan of these Bible lectures will permit me to enter upon. I must skeletonize it.

He was called by name, first, *Abram*—"Father of Elevation" or "Great Father"; but in later life *Abraham*—"The Father of Multitudes," owing to the promise which was made to him, that his posterity should be as numerous as the stars in the heavens, or as the sands upon the seashore. He was "the father" pre-eminent. He was the founder of a nation, without being, at the same time, a pretender to anything that he was not. He did not profess to be a god, or a demigod. In regard to heroes, the founders, the lawgivers of all lands of antiquity, you shall find in their history the beginnings enshrouded in the pretense that they were in intimate communion with God, in the same sense in which holy men are in communion with him. Not so Abram. He never moved out of the simple sphere of the shepherd life. But he is known universally as "the father," and is termed familiarly in the literature of many nations yet, not "Abram," nor "Father of the Faithful," nor "Father of Multitudes," only, but "The Father." And it is a little remarkable that, reaching down through the space of thousands and thousands of years, we find, when the new system came in, and the last great Teacher appeared, that he taught us to begin the very approach to God with the phrase, "Our Father, which art in heaven." This is antiquity connected with the later periods of life.

Abram was the ninth descendant of Shem, son of Noah. After the increase of Noah's posterity in Armenia they came down from the mountainous country into what is called Mesopotamia, the southern part of it—Chaldea. Abram is said to have dwelt in Ur with his father and brethren. An Ur used to be located at a point where the Tigris and Euphrates empty into the gulf; but there were three or four or five places by that name, and the best knowledge we have of it is that it was probably the Ur lying far to the north of the mouths of the Tigris and the Euphrates—that it was in the upper part, near the Armenian mountains.

Abram's family were idolaters. Legend says that Terah, his father, was a maker of idols. Abram was seventy years old when he heard that inward Voice, the call of God, commanding him to leave all his associates and associations, and go forth, the great emigrant of antiquity. His first move was only a march of a day or two, from Ur to Haran, which lies to the west of Ur. For five years he dwelt there, where his father died. Then the impulse returned, which was to him as a voice of God calling him a second time; and he set his face westward. Is it not remarkable that since the great incursions from the North to the South in Asia and Europe, emigration has been from the East toward the West—never from the West toward the East, as if men followed the sun—as if they sought to see what fields he saw in his constant circuits?

Abram passed the Euphrates. The ford probably remains where this patriarch describes it as being. It is probable that his journey took him not far from Damascus, and thence southward until he reached the river Jabbok, along which his grandson, Jacob, found his path on his return from the same region in Padan-Aram.

What this "call" was that Abram heard, no man can now define. The impulse, we cannot doubt, was a high and sacred one; but it was the impulse of an emigrant—not that of a conqueror who, with a sense of ambition and conscious power, went forth to subdue new territories. He went out, with his small band, as an emigrant, with the promise that he should have a great posterity. It lay in the future. Compare the feelings of this great original patriarch in going forth from Mesopotamia with the feelings with which thousands and tens of thousands have left their homes in days since—the Pilgrims that left England, and came, over the stormy sea, and landed on the shores of New England; those emigrants that, dropping further down, early made their home in Virginia; those other emigrants that streamed out from the Eastern states and found the great basin of the Ohio, the plains of the Rocky and Sierra Nevada mountains, and California itself; and the stream that has never ceased to flow, simply with the latent hope of bettering their condition, without half the conviction that belonged to Abram—of a call from God, and the divine assurance that he should be the founder of a great nation in which all the earth should be blessed. Nevertheless, these emigrants go on laying foundations, suffering hardship, accumulating treasure, and establishing institutions, whose full benefit will be known only to their children or to their children's children.

Whether in the dreams of sleep, whether in some appearance to the senses, or whether under the influence of vivid imagination so strong that his subjective state became objective—whether in one or other of these ways this call of God was made to Abram, we are not now to determine. All we know is that we are to suppose not that God spoke in an audible voice out of the heavens to him, but only that Abram received spiritual impulse, knowledge, and strength, which set him upon his journey. He was the father of emigrants.

It is not difficult to trace the route which he pursued, because it was the route of the great caravans. There were but few routes of travel at that time. The East is not even now diversified with highways. Roads are almost unknown there; and those that exist are for the most part not for wheels but for the camel and the ass. Roads for wagons and chariots in the Orient are still unknown in any such sense as that in which we have them in this country.

Entering the country of Canaan not far below the issuing of the Jordan into the Sea of Galilee, Abram's first point of rest was taken under a tree. He spread his tent—he who, except in Egypt, never, to the end of his life, dwelt under a roof. There, as shepherd, he lived for a brief period. Then, that his flocks might have the benefit of larger pasturage, he moved south to Bethel. After that, still going south, he went to Mamre. While there famine overtook him, and he descended into Egypt, the great granary of the East. How long he dwelt there we cannot ascertain accurately. That he remained there until he had greatly increased his household, and enlarged his possessions of silver and gold and flocks, we are definitely informed. Here occurred one of those episodes which are a blemish upon his memory—undoubtedly a blemish, but not such a blemish as criticism in modern times has made it to be. His wife was his sister by his father, but not by the mother. It is probable that she was more nearly in the relation of what we call a niece than in that which we esteem as a sister. At any rate, she seems to have been beautiful; and in going down to Egypt, fearing that the king would imprison her in his harem, and that in order to possess the wife he would slay the husband, Abram besought her to represent that she was his sister and not his wife, thus deceiving the king. He was rebuked afterwards when on the king's learning the truth she was restored unharmed to him; and they dwelt peacefully in Egypt.

Years afterwards, Abram returned from thence to Gerar in the southern part of Palestine, where Abimelech was still king. Strangely enough, to those who read with criticism, precisely the same story is told of Abram and his wife in relation to Abimelech,—as though he twice represented that she was his sister and not his wife, and as though the second time she was restored to him with a rebuke. Is it probable that this thing took place twice? No. It is far more likely that two different documents, each giving this account, have been embraced in the Mosaic history.

We find substantially the same literary error occurring in the New Testament. In one of the gospels an account is given of a visit of Christ to Nazareth, as though it occurred at one period of his life, and in another it is declared that he visited it at another and later period of his life. The two records are precisely the same. Those who advocate the verbal and literal inspiration declare that there was no mistake in the reckoning—that he did go twice thus to Nazareth. It is said that on Sunday, twice, he went into the Synagogue: that a book was given him both times ; that he opened it at the same place both times, and read the same Scripture, and gave the same interpretation ; that both times he was set upon and dragged out ; that both times there was an attempt to throw him down a precipice ; and that both times he escaped out of their hands. Thus men resort to inconsistencies and absurdities instead of simply saying that both visits were one, that one Evangelist who gave the account was correct, but that the other was mistaken as to the date.

In regard to another occurrence in Christ's ministry there is a discrepancy—his driving out from the Temple the money changers and those that sold doves and beasts. One of the Evangelists puts it at the beginning of his ministry, and another at the close. Verbalists, in order to save themselves from saying that there was a mistake of date in either narrative, say that it occurred twice. They tell us that Christ went into the Temple on two occasions and said the same thing both times, and drove out the same men that sold doves and animals, and the same money changers. There is no reason why men should sacrifice their common sense, and insist upon putting the Scripture to a rack that would ruin it if they could succeed in pressing against it this doctrine of verbal, absolute, literal inspiration.

The patriarch returned from Gerar to Bethel. It was here that the memorable discussion took place between the herdsmen of Abram and the herdsmen of Lot. Lot was Abram's nephew. They appear for a time to have dwelt together with common possessions ; but in consequence of the increase of the amount of property and in the number of herdsmen and servants there began to break out jealousies and contentions. The nobility of the patriarch is made manifest in the settlement of this question. It might very well be employed as a type of the proper settlement of controversies in later days of the church. He says to Lot, "The country is before you. Make your choice. If you will go to the south I will go to the north ; or if you will go to the north I will go to the south. Let there be no contention between us. Take your way and I will let you alone, and I will take my way and be let alone." So Lot went down to the interior of the luxuriant plains where Sodom and Gomorrah lay; and he derived the natural consequences—relaxation and corruption; while Abram kept to the hills, rude, rugged, harsh, in many respects, but giving vigor, manhood, simplicity, and virtue. Abram was evidently a broad-minded, able manager, for in whatever place he sojourned it is recorded that his possessions and his household increased.

Not far from the time of this division, not many years after it, one of those events took place which developed the greatness of the patriarch. It seems that there had been, from the east and the northeast, an invasion of the great king, Chedorlaomer, who had taken possession of all the cities of the plain and the country far around, and taxed them. He had no right in these places any more than England has in India, but he did what England has done; he took with a strong hand and held under tribute nations that he had no business with. It is recorded that the king gathered his forces and swept the people and their possessions away with him, traveling by the line of the Jordan clear up toward Damascus.

Then it was that Abram gathered together the three hundred servants born in his own household, with such confederates as he could, and, marching day and night, surprised the king and his forces, routed them, followed them, and scattered them utterly, bringing back the herds and the captives, and restoring them to their homes.

It is memorable that on the return he met Melchizedek, King of Salem; and it is very remarkable that this priestly king, so far as can be gathered from the original, was a worshiper, not of Abram's Elohim or Jehovah, but of another God. He was not in agreement with Abram; but he was truly religious, probably a worshiper of one God, and therefore, under whatever name, of Abram's God.

When this king offered, if Abram would restore the captives, to give him the goods, the old chief towered too high to accept anything as payment. Said he, "I will not take anything that is thine, lest thou shouldst say, I have made Abram rich." So he took nothing, and sent all back to their original possessors.

The remaining events in Abram's history are few, but of transcendent importance. It had been promised to him that he should be the father of many generations. Yet he was now ninety years old, and no child had been born to him. Then comes, not so much the history of Abram, as the record of one of the customs of the country and the race. By his wife's wish he married, in a secondary way, the bondwoman Hagar; and by her was born a son, Ishmael. The history of Hagar and Ishmael, if it has not given rise to a great deal of doctrine, has given rise to a great deal of art, of romance—for it is a romance; and the pictorial story in the old Scripture compares favorably with the efforts of modern art.

But Sarai, the wife, after she had arrived at an extreme old age, gave to her lord and master a direct and legitimate heir, in Isaac. Then broke out in Abram's peaceful family jealousies and difficulties, such as polygamy always entails, and always will entail. The result was, as might be expected, that the wife was mightier than the husband, and she drove forth Hagar and her child, and Abram's reputation as master in his own household was at a discount. In reality, Hagar was a great deal better off in the wilderness with her son than she would have been in Abram's tent with that woman to despotize over her. To go forth into the wilderness in that day was not so hard a thing. She went forth from no house, from no luxuries, simply from a tent. She went forth from nothing to nothing; and although history records a temporary suffering at first, it also records relief and prosperity almost immediately; for Ishmael became the father of a great nation.

After this occurred one of the most striking events in the history of Abraham (for from the birth of his son he took the name "Father of Multitudes"). He was moved by the voice of God (whatever that voice may have been: whether it came to him in a dream, whether it was a vision, an impression received by him, or what it was, I do not undertake to say) to follow the example of all the nations around about him that on great occasions were offering their children to the gods.

We have a half-instance of this in the later history of Jephtha and his daughter. That military chieftain dedicated to sacrifice the thing that first should meet him coming out from his house on his return from battle, if he should have victory. Under memorable circumstances parents were accustomed to dedicate their firstborn to the gods, and the dedications consisted in sacrifice.

Such was the impulse that was brought to bear upon Abraham. He had received the promise that he should be the father of many generations; but the fullfillment of direct posterity was delayed until he was a very old man; when Isaac was born he was impelled to dedicate him to his God, and when he was well grown—under the absolute paternal right of life and death in the household, common to the time—to consummate the dedication by final sacrifice. The simple narrative of how Abraham took his son and laid him upon the altar is too exquisite to be touched with the finger of commentary. I think there is nothing in any literature comparable to the father and son on their way to the sacrifice. Abraham bound Isaac on the altar, and stretched forth his hand to slay him, when he heard a Voice calling upon him to forbear. A ram caught in the thicket was offered up by Abraham in place of his son. The faith which, it is said in the New Testament, led Abraham to believe that God was able to give him Isaac back from the dead, reveals the feelings that were in the father's mind. He was under the impression that in spite of the promise of a multitudinous posterity, God had called him to give up his son; and his faith in God was such that he implicitly proceeded to obey.

We are not to measure this by the light of our moral sense. A man who in our day should thus offer a son for sacrifice would be denounced by multitudes of men and legions of angels; but that which would be outrageous if done in the manhood of the race is not to be so judged when done in the infancy of the race; and it was certainly a masterpiece of sincerity in Abraham to give up for his religion (that was the amount of it), for his faith in God, every hope that had cheered him in his long pilgrimage, and on which he had fed, that in him should the nations of the earth be blessed. Since the blessing was to come through Isaac, as his only lineal heir, to offer Isaac up in sacrifice was to blot out the whole prospect, so far as the power of Abraham could determine cause and effect; but he did not draw back from what he deemed his duty, and it was a remarkable exhibition of faith and conscience.

I call to your attention the account of the death of Sarah, and of the tomb at Machpelah. I will read it. I do not know where you will find anything more beautiful than this account:—

"Sarah was one hundred and seven and twenty years old: these were the years of the life of Sarah. And Sarah died in Kirjath-arba; the same is Hebron in the land of Canaan: and Abraham came to mourn for Sarah, and to weep for her.

"And Abraham stood up from before his dead, and spake unto the sons of Heth, saying, I am a stranger and a sojourner with you: give me a possession of a burying-place with you, that I may bury my dead out of my sight. And the children of Heth answered Abraham, saying unto him, Hear us, my lord: thou art a mighty prince among us: in the choice of our sepulchers bury thy dead; none of us shall withhold from thee his sepulcher, but that thou mayest bury thy dead. And Abraham stood up, and bowed himself to the people of the land, even to the children of Heth. And he communed with them, saying, If it be your mind that I should bury my dead out of my sight; hear me, and entreat for me to Ephron the son of Zohar, that he may give me the cave of Machpelah [the double cave], which he hath, which is in the end of his field; for as much money as it is worth he shall give it me for a possession of a burying place amongst you.

"And Ephron dwelt among the children of Heth: and Ephron the Hittite answered Abraham in the audience of the children of Heth, even of all that went in at the gate of his city, saying, Nay, my lord, hear me: the field give I thee, and the cave that is therein, I give it thee; in the presence of the sons of my people give I it thee: bury thy dead.

"And Abraham bowed down himself before the people of the land. And he spake unto Ephron in the audience of the people of the land, saying,

But if thou wilt, I pray thee, hear me: I will give thee money for the field; take it of me, and I will bury my dead there."

He could not bury his dead in another man's ground, even though it were generously given him; he insisted on paying for it. And, with a delicacy equal to his generosity, Ephron fixed a price and received it from the lordly chieftain. So Abraham came into possession of this cave; and I presume that his dust and the dust of Sarah, of Isaac, and of Jacob lie in that very same place to this day. Over it has been built a temple of reverence, and the Gentile is not allowed to enter there. Beneath is the original cave; and there is no reason to suppose otherwise than that the bones of the three patriarchs and their families yet lie in it.

The disposition of Abraham not to mingle himself with the inhabitants of the lands, not to take on their customs, not to dwell in their cities, not to adopt their languages, not even to bury his dead in the sepulchers where their dead were buried, but to maintain separateness of organization and life—this disposition falls in with the whole thought and aspiration of his life, to be the founder of a new and multitudinous family.

There is one more history that I shall allude to, and that I will not defile with criticism nor with commentary. It is a history such that I do not see how any man who has read it can wish to tear it to pieces. It is the pleading of Abraham with the angel of the Lord when the destruction of Sodom and Gomorrah was determined upon.

I will not occupy the time by reading the account, but will beg you to read it as the representation of a great soul pleading for others, in that remote period when disinterested benevolence was not known, as a term, nor as a fact except to pre-eminent natures.

If by any this mode of looking at early history in the light of modern ideas be accounted unnatural and not useful, I reply that it is useful in the sense in which the Ten Commandments are useful; in the sense in which the Beatitudes of Christ are useful; in the sense in which the example of the sinless One is useful; in the sense in which the precepts of the New Testament are useful. The histories in the Old Testament of the earlier periods of the world may not be thought to be authoritative; but if any man is disposed to reject them as not useful on the ground of their particular nature, of their special method, or of the literary elements in them, I beg him to pause and reconsider the matter. There is not in the history of any nation anything more charming in its simplicity than the history of the early periods of the human race as given in the Old Testament. If there is anything in the history of Abraham that seems to butt against your views of science and philosophy as to what a divinely inspired record should be, I wish you would read the absurd Arabian legends, the fantastic stories told by the Mohammedans in the Koran and in their literature, and see the wide difference. If you would see what the human element really was in the history of antiquity, go back to the Hebrew Scriptures and you will find it. Of course, when you go back to these Scriptures you will find a vast difference between simplicity, truthfulness, and righteousness as measured by modern rules and judgments, and those same qualities as measured by the standards of Old Testament periods. These stories are marvelous to us; it is difficult for us to comprehend how such things as occurred in those times were tolerated by good men; but if we could see the circumstances in which they originated, if we could go back to the literal facts, we should look upon them more leniently than now we are disposed to do; while the very honesty of the stories is proof of their truth and trustworthiness.

Take into consideration the career of the great founder of the Israelitish people, and for that matter of the Christian church—for the Christian church is but the outcome, the fruit of that people: they both had the same life. Does it seem to you that this man of God could not fitly be the leader of that people? Do you say that he was a slaveholder, that he was a polygamist, and that he was at times given over to deceit? These things were not the same in that age that they are now.

Slavery then was not a curse but a blessing. It was not a degradation to be gathered into a household, as slaves were at the beginning, to be treated with kindness, to be instructed, and to receive whatever advantages were accorded to the children of the family themselves. There was a great difference between Hebrew slavery and Roman slavery. Hebrew slavery invariably accounted a slave to be a man, not only, but as being in near connection with his master, and as inheriting or having a right to all the amenities of the family. Roman slavery began by dispossessing a man of manhood, and making him a chattel, classing him with furniture and horses and mules, and allowing him no rights. Under the Roman law the slave had no rights; but under the Hebrew law he had all rights—that is to say, his servitude was very little more than that of a hired servant. At a later period the privilege of emancipation was given to him.

In the early periods of the race, when there was no distinction made between a person and property; when a man bought his wife as much as he did his cow; when his children were salable; when the doctrine of personal rights had not been unfolded, or had been defined but to a limited degree; when the differentiation of society had not taken place, the old patriarch held slaves without guiltiness. But this is not justification of the modern slaveholder, slavery in the early ages and slavery now not being by any means the same thing.

Do you object to this founder of the Jewish nation, who was a polygamist, being held up as a pattern and exemplar of virtue? A polygamist in these days is certainly not to be commended; we cannot condemn such a man too severely: but polygamy was a custom that belonged to the nascent race. In the early time, when men were not enough advanced socially and morally to discriminate between right and wrong courses, it was tolerated as faults are tolerated in children until they are old enough to correct them themselves.

As to the deception of Abraham, I do not wish you to

make it any less than it was, but I do not wish you to judge him as you would a man that would tell a falsehood in our day. You will bear in mind that the animal kingdom below us has craft, cunning, as an instrument of self-protection with which to meet brute force. Savage nations, a little above the animal, retain these traits (indeed, we civilized Christian nations have not altogether outgrown them); and Abraham, though he stood on a vastly higher plane in most respects, believing that his life was in peril, to save himself (not from any mercenary motive or motive of pleasure) resorted to deceit and falsehood. Of course the great patriarch should not be revered for that; but ought we to sit in judgment upon him with the same severity that we should upon a man who did the same thing in this age of the world?

How is it to-day with war? Is it not full of organized deceit which everybody justifies? Is it not thought to be right to lie to the enemy because he is an enemy? Is not war an organized lie? How is it with diplomacy? Does it not abound with falsifications, with promises made to be broken, with falsehoods organized into custom and method? How is it with commerce? Look at the rivalries, the secrecies, the misdirections, that exist between those who are antagonists or competitors in business. How is it in statesmanship and politics? Is falsehood unknown there? How is it even with newspapers? Is straightforwardness highly developed among them? Do they altogether account it to be a fatal wrong for them to stand up for their party by exaggeration and misrepresentation? Is it not true that in many departments of human society, nowadays, men for the sake of self-interest justify themselves in the practice of deceit? And is it right for these same men in the sanctuary and elsewhere to condemn Abraham, because to save his life he said that his wife was his sister? He did wrong; such falsifying would be condemnable at this period of time; but at that remote age, when the race was at so low a level in the matter of education and development, his offense was but as a speck on his garments, compared with evils that are indulged in and tolerated in modern Christian society.

What, then, is the reason why Abraham has been so great? One conspicuous reason is that he was the founder of the household, and not of a kingdom. He was a father and not a king—the father of the faithful—the father of a multitude. You must not think of him as in his life the ruler of a great nation. He was great in that the household was his sphere. It was transmitted from son to son. It went down to the nation that grew up after them, and from that day to this, one of the distinguishing and magnificent peculiarities of the Israelitish people is that they have maintained the household. I take it upon me to say that all over the world the education of the children of the household is nowhere more remarkable and admirable than among the descendants of Abraham. This is one of the strongest points of their history. Their family love, their fidelity in the culture of their children, their putting these things above everything else, is worthy of all imitation. They have brought down from Abraham, through all the periods of history, to our time, the example of the family. To them we are indebted for much of the dignity and the blessedness of the monogamous household. And you will find that development and power in their noblest and best forms have never gone aside from the nations in which the household has been fostered and honored. Civilization in its highest types will never succeed in any community where the ideal of the household is lost or has never been possessed. It lies at the root of every rightly conceived commonwealth, and is its foundation. The influence of the father and mother on the children and the influence of the children on the father and mother are the beginning of prosperity in national life. Thus, as Abraham was the father of the household he stands high in dignity and power.

Not only has Abraham this claim, but he shows essential dignity and magnanimity of character in his transactions. The course he pursued with Abimelech was such as to call forth from that king the testimony, "I perceive that God is with thee;" and any man whose nature is so large that others, looking upon him, see the force and goodness of his being, any man who, in the eyes of those around about him, is walking in the spirit and in the communion of God, any man whose portrait is universally painted as that of a great nature—any such man, even if we had no great instances of his courage, enterprise, daring, and fair dealing throughout his whole history, might safely be presumed to be one worthy of honor and of reverence.

Abraham's personal purity, his self-control, and his eminent sense of justice fitted him to be the prototype of a great nation. His faults were faults even in the age in which he lived; but as he had not been trained to higher things, as there were no institutions to aid him in overcoming them, his finding his own way out of them in a trackless wilderness, his ability to conceive and choose for his own the idea of an invisible, supreme God, and his establishing himself in a larger and truer life than others lived in his time, mark him as a very superior nature.

Lastly, his faith in God's promise that he should possess the land, that his posterity should be multitudinous—that *faith in the future* which was the source of his inward life, and which, though he dwelt in a tent, and was a stranger and a pilgrim, led him to look forward continually to a city that had foundations, whose builder and maker was God—that faith ought to be an encouragement to every soul that is striving to rise from a lower plane to a higher. It is this which gives him his great name, "Father of the Faithful," and which has made him known even to this day in all the Orient as the "Friend of God."

In that far away period, then, stood the great chief, who had all the while thought of life, who founded a noble household, and who established in the family an economy of consecrated happiness. He lived, according to the day in which his lot was cast, not only a notably efficient and successful life, but a higher and nobler life than is to be found in any of his contemporaries; for in the midst of idolatry, of gross superstitions, of lust, of all that was low and debasing, Abraham cleansed his ways from whatever was vile, he showed himself to be a father of justice, he was faithful to his children, he believed in one God, to the end of his life he was witness to monotheism as distinguished from idol worship in every direction, and he transmitted this doctrine to his sons, and through them to their posterity, as they have given it to the whole world—for monotheism is, even by Moses, its teacher and the organizer of it as a religion, referred back to the great patriarch.

There is, then, abundant evidence in the inspired record of facts which justify the greatness of soul that has been attributed to this grand man, and that makes him a most conspicuous figure on the horizon of antiquity. We may look back and venerate him without hesitation, as much as they do who sprang from his loins.

V.

ISAAC.

"And the Lord appeared unto him the same night, and said, I am the God of Abraham thy father: fear not, for I am with thee, and will bless thee, and multiply thy seed for my servant Abraham's sake."—Gen. xxvi: 24.

I AM endeavoring, in the Sunday-night readings which I am giving from the Old Testament, not alone to interest you in local histories, nor alone to benefit you by drawing lessons from special passages, but so to present the subject matter of the Old Testament as to give you a more enlightened conception of the sacred writings, and a clearer and better view of the doctrine of inspiration, that you may enjoy in a larger degree than many people now do the study of the Scriptures—particularly of the primitive Scriptures; for we are to bear in mind that between the beginning and the end of the sacred writings there stretches a period of probably some four thousand years.

In the purview of the early book, the book of beginnings, Genesis, there are three great periods of time: first, the vague, remote, and indefinite period before there was a history or a record—the prehistoric period; second, the patriarchal period, which comes within the nebulous border of the historic; and, third, the period of organized society, which begins with the life, the legislation, and the institutions of Moses. Here you have three distinct eras.

The first deals with the world at that period which stretches away back to the beginnings of things and comes down to the Flood, and a little after. Of that great period

---

Sunday evening, November 24, 1878.

there is very little known; and the Word of God does not undertake to carry the torch into it and state exactly how things were. It has, however, clustered together the best thoughts, the best histories, the best views, that prevailed at that time, and transmitted them to us, that we may have light thrown upon the state of the human mind preceding organization and modern instruction. Of that great nascent period of the human family before there were governments, when chiefs and their tribes represented all there was of order, when men were creeping up from the lowest forms of savagery and barbarism, it is of profound importance to know something of what was the economy of providence during that era, and what were the ideas of men of that time about that economy. We are told by scientists of our day that there has been a great development and evolution from germinant forms of the great vegetable kingdom and of the lower animals; and also an unfolding of growth in social, moral, and spiritual elements among men: yet we are surprised to find described in the Old Testament a long period in regard to which precisely this state of facts is to be recognized.

This book of beginnings tells what were some of the nebulous, shadowy, imaginary, fantastic notions which prevailed at that time. These we do not want to change by putting a modern interpretation on them; we want them to remain just as they are. They are the infantine thoughts, feelings, and ideas of men—not ripe ones of later days. Men are attempting, by straining their catechisms, to save the Book, ignoring the fact that there was a long space of time when men were but little better than savages, and that the Book records many of their unintelligent notions.

We have in that Book the beginnings of those evolutions which originate in a low state of mind; and we ought to take it as it is; and any theory that does not take it so is false and mischievous.

When you come down to the period of the patriarchs, you will find there ignorance, superstition, immorality, and wickedness, but you will find these mingled with heroic traits and great virtues, though without symmetry and proportion. In judging of this period you must, of course, apply the higher ethics of the Gospel to every fact and phase ; that is to say, though lying may not have been as really culpable in Abraham as it would have been in Paul, although it may have been more excusable at the beginning than at the end of the history of the world, as in a little child it is less condemnable than in a man fifty years old, nevertheless it is lying ; and while the Sacred Record never attempts to varnish anything that the utmost simplicity records of infirmity, fanaticism, blundering, or cruelty, while it never sets over against these things any plea of abatement or any word of commiseration, while it gives them as they are, it is our wisdom to take them as they are. We want to know how men lived at that time.

Under the false notion of inspiration it has been undertaken to represent the patriarchs as free from superstition, whereas they were not free from it. It is supposed that men were so directly under the guidance of God that they knew clearly what was right and duty; but the facts show that they did not—that there was no such guidance. There is no question that there were men who took dreams for revelation; there is no doubt that men thought God spoke to them when it was nothing but their imagination that spoke to them—noble and inspiring as that might be; and the attempt to bolster up improbable statements by special pleading will not save Sacred Writ—nay, will damn it in the end. You must take these statements just as they are, and simply say, "Here, in the unfolding series of human experience, men came to a point where they did not know ; and they were mistaken in such and such things."

The very evidence, to me, of the inspiration of the Old Testament Scriptures, is, that I find in the records of the early days what we ought to expect in those days— infantine knowledge and infantine moral strength in infantine men, and a simple history which reflects the condition of primitive morality as consisting of imperfect notions grouped under religious belief. If, in writing the biography of a child, I should put into that child's early life mature thoughts that would have been impossible to him, I should make him monstrous in the eyes of men—I should destroy the simplicity that is expected in childhood, and make a little monster instead of a little man; and the attempt to substantiate the imperfect and erratic notions of antiquity by bringing the morality of our day to bear upon them, to subject them to the light which we have gained, to strain the text of the narrative and make it conform to facts as they exist five thousand years later than the time in which the actors lived—that process, through which many a man has put the Scripture, cannot but have the effect of undermining men's confidence in it. Daniel Webster once said that one of the evidences of Christianity was that religion had survived in spite of the pulpit; and I say, One of the evidences of inspiration is that the Bible has lived in spite of the treatment it has received at the hands of its friends.

From the beginning of the world to the time of Abraham, religion, in the modern sense,—in the sense in which we hold it,—had not sprung up. A definite and regulated system of moral precepts governing the disposition and outward life was absolutely unknown, except such as were organized by various Pagan priesthoods. When men say that Adam and Eve were "created perfect human beings," it is supposed that they were like human beings who should be perfect in the light of the experience of these later days. It has been the notion of thousands of men, that they were like a trunk packed with goods already made up, and that when they started they had what no other human beings ever possessed except by gradual unfolding through ages—that it was innate—that in infancy they had perfectness as an element instantaneously conferred upon them. Any such notion as that is a simple myth. From the beginning to the time of Abraham, I repeat, religion in any modern sense had not sprung up. Religion during that period consisted of occasional, vagrant moral impulses. There was the original thing in men, but this had only fitful developments here and there, and these developments were sometimes right and sometimes wrong.

Next came the patriarchal period, beginning with the high-minded Abraham, and descending to his children's days. Religion then had developed so that it had a much broader current and a far deeper channel; and yet, even as late as that, religion was very humanly errant. Among the Chaldees of Abram's kin it had grown into a system of idolatry and priestcraft, from which he had the God-given impulse to break away. Even morality was not formulated except in a few directions. How could it be, when society itself was not born? Can you formulate morality before commerce, manufactures, and agriculture come in to define the relations of citizens one to another? It was before there were any conditions such as we understand by morality. There was no regular government except in chiefs. What are called *kings*, in connection with the tribes of Canaan, and certainly in connection with the patriarchal families, were no more than chief shepherds. There was, among the people who were to be the moral teachers of the world, no government with regular officers, gradations, implements, and instruments. There were no institutions of any kind. What sort of institutions can you have where the whole of a tribe live in tents, feeding their flocks from pasture to pasture, and have no abiding place, no unfolding sequences, no laws as to commerce, no officers of justice, no churches or places of worship?

Now and then there was an altar, as a special thing. Abraham built two or three, and Isaac two or three; but they were not permanent. They were rude appliances on which to offer particular sacrifices. In those times men were bare of everything that belongs to society life as we understand it. Even the household had not been unfolded. Property in persons was yet believed in, as it was long afterwards. The wife was bought and the children were owned. And what insanity is it to attempt to find in those infantine conditions the type and pattern of modern religious usages and beliefs! They are the beginnings. Genesis is rightly named. Esteem it for just what it is—a book which records the beginnings—not the endings nor the intermediate stages, but the *beginnings*—with their rudenesses, their errors, their lies, their superstitions, their crimes, their evils of every kind. Then you will have something of great value. You will know exactly what mankind were, at successive steps. Otherwise you will have a medley, a fantastic mixture, neither old nor new, which, whether true or false, right or wrong, will be of no earthly use.

The patriarchs are not to be set up as our models. Not everything that they did was right. They were not exemplars for us, nor were they fit to be. They were not our teachers. They did not teach anything. Abraham never spoke a word that anybody remembered for instruction or religious knowledge. He was as dumb as Adam, and Adam was as dumb as silence or death itself. Genesis is a book in which we see sprouts, buds, and leaves, and here and there fruit, but small and immature.

Isaac was the son born to Abraham after he had attained a very great age. It is recorded of those that lived before the Flood, that they were not married, usually, until they were three or four hundred years old. There be some who escape the difficulty, by saying that numbers meant differently then from what they do now; there be others who escape it by saying that this was mere surplusage, arithmetic run mad, the magnification of the Oriental mind; and there be still others, who, on physiological grounds, say (and there is as much probability in that direction as in any other) that the nascent human race were a flabby product that did not live as much in a hundred years as, in the developed and riper state, men live in five years, and that they were not as far advanced in three hundred years as, in the more compact and vitalized, nerve-grown races of modern times, men are at twenty. You will find, if you inform yourselves on this subject, that by many it has been supposed that the livers of the far remote periods were giants either in imagination or reality, but that they did not come to their majority and maturity until they had lived two or three hundred years.

Now, in some line of these reckonings of longevity, Abraham begat Isaac after he had attained to an extreme old age; and when it was announced to him that Sarah, his wife, should bear him a son, it seemed simply ridiculous, and she, hearing it, laughed behind the door; and when the son was born she laughed again; and everybody has laughed ever since, so to speak, at the fact. So Isaac, being born, was called *Laughter;* he grew up and that was his name—*Laughter;* for that is the meaning of the word *Isaac.*

Isaac stands, as respects the other two patriarchs, Abraham and Jacob, as a sweet and beautiful valley between two hills. He was not the equal of Abraham in dignity,—in that kind of wild grandeur that the old patriarch had,—nor was he the statesman and politician that Jacob was. He had neither the enterprise nor the amount of being that Abraham had; for, although there is very little that Abraham has transmitted to us, and although his history is vague, we see that wherever he went everybody stood in awe of him, and we inherit his one great idea. He was recognized on every side, by his dependents, his equals, and his superiors, as a great man. He had an immense quantity of being. There are men of such structure of mind that, although they add very little to literature, are felt wherever they go, and Abraham was such a man. He towered up by reason of this native greatness. But Isaac was of a milder and far inferior type. Colorless, he was. He was peaceful, pleasant, harmless, useful, but in no sense romantic. There was not one thing in his life that in and of itself stirs the imagination. There was not a phase of his character the contemplation of which would lead one to an involuntary exclamation of admiration. There was a good deal about him that would tend to make a person feel like swearing—I mean "swearing" in a mere interjectional form, not profane swearing. His mildness and timidity and peace-loving ways ran to the very edge of cowardice, and quite over the border of honesty.

We hear very little of Isaac until he is twenty or twenty-five years of age. The chronology of the Old Testament is very uncertain and variable. There is no absolutely accurate date as to the birth of Isaac, but it is supposed, from the tenor of the narrative, that he was about twenty or twenty-five years old when he was led by his father to the summit of the mountain to be offered up a sacrifice, as Abraham thought, in obedience to the will of God. The offering up of children was a common practice, growing out of superstition, in all the neighboring nations, and in one way or another Abraham was made to believe that he was called of God to offer up his son Isaac.

Now, a young man twenty-five years old, living in our time, would not be apt to make a long journey to the top of a mountain, and carry wood in order to be himself sacrificed: but Isaac, who was a very obedient son, did; and he was bound by his father, and laid upon the pile, and was about to be slaughtered when he was rescued by a voice that Abraham thought was the voice of a superior Being, and saved from destruction.

That is the first considerable fact that appears in the life of this patriarch; and although it represents filial obedience on the part of Isaac, and his great confidence in his father when he found out what was about to be done, it does not represent what we should call Anglo-Saxon pluck. I do not think my father ever could have got me on to a woodpile to kill me. I cannot say that I should have great admiration for anybody that would submit to a thing like that.

Passivity, resignation—these were the traits that pervaded the life of this man. His brother Ishmael could not have been dealt with so. That child, born to Isaac's father through a handmaid, and adopted by Sarah until Isaac was born, had a different spirit. Abraham could not have laid him on an altar to sacrifice him, and did not try.

Not until he was forty years old was Isaac married—not until his mother's death. That same gentle, meek, yielding, complying nature that he had, which bound him to his father's wishes, seems also to have clasped him around about his mother; and her death, although it is alluded to by only a single word, throws a flood of light upon it.

"Isaac brought her [the one to whom he was about to be married] into his mother Sarah's tent, and took Rebekah, and she became his wife; and he loved her: and Isaac was comforted after his mother's death."

So, on becoming forty years old, Isaac was married. Most men, under such circumstances, would have selected whom they would marry; but in this case Isaac was true to his reputation, and his father picked out his wife for him. I will read the history. It is a perfect poem of the transaction, and it gives an insight into the internal economy of society and the notions of men at that time.

"Abraham was old, and well stricken in age: and the Lord had blessed Abraham in all things. And Abraham said unto his eldest servant of his house [it was supposed to be Eliezer], that ruled over all that he had, Put, I pray thee, thy hand under my thigh [that was the mode of taking an oath, and is yet in many Oriental countries]: and I will make thee swear by the Lord, the God of heaven, and the God of the earth, that thou shalt not take a wife unto my son of the daughters of the Canaanites, among whom I dwell."

There was wisdom in that. They were not only idolaters but they were vile and corrupt. They were the torment and the contempt of the Israelites in all the after period; and most of the defections into idolatry came through the solicitation of the women of the land around about. Abraham discerned that through such stock as that he could not bring to his posterity the blessings which had been promised through him, and in which he firmly believed.

"But thou shalt go unto my country, and to my kindred, and take a wife unto my son Isaac."

He was to go back to Mesopotamia, to Haran, to the old stock out of which Abraham himself came.

"And the servant said unto him, Peradventure the woman will not be willing to follow me unto this land : must I needs bring thy son again unto the land from whence thou camest?"

Isaac had nothing to say all this time.

"And Abraham said unto him, Beware thou that thou bring not my son thither again. The Lord God of heaven, which took me from my father's house, and from the land of my kindred, and which spake unto me, and that sware unto me, saying, Unto thy seed will I give this land ; he shall send his angel before thee, and thou shalt take a wife unto my son from thence. And if the woman will not be willing to follow thee, then thou shalt be clear from this my oath : only bring not my son thither again. And the servant put his hand under the thigh of Abraham his master, and sware to him concerning that matter."

Abraham's God was the God of heaven and earth. Eliezer's God was the God of his master ; afterwards the God that the Israelites worshiped was the God of Abraham and Isaac and Jacob ; and everybody's God ought to be "*the God of my father and my mother.*" Eliezer said :—

"O Lord God of my master Abraham, I pray thee, send me good speed this day, and show kindness unto my master Abraham."

When a man of great sagacity lays out a wise plan and then prays God to fulfill it, it is pretty apt to come to pass. And when Eliezer was appointed to select a wife for Isaac, he was first sagacious and then devout. He desired to select one that was generous, that was serviceable, that was willing to work, that was hospitable and pleasant ; and so he thought that a test might determine, among the women that should go out at eventide to draw water, who was the one that Isaac ought to have. He would have said, of course, that it was the way "pointed out." It was pointed out—through the common sense and sagacity of Eliezer. He prayed :—

"Let it come to pass, that the damsel to whom I shall say, Let down thy pitcher, I pray thee, that I may drink ; and she shall say, Drink, and I will give thy camels drink also : let the same be she that thou hast appointed for thy servant Isaac ; and thereby shall I know that thou hast showed kindness unto my master. And it came to pass, before he had done speaking, that, behold, Rebekah came out, who was born to Bethuel, son of Milcah, the wife of Nahor, Abraham's brother, with her pitcher upon her shoulder. . . . . And she went down to the well and filled her pitcher, and came up. And the servant ran to meet her, and said,

Let me, I pray thee, drink a little water of thy pitcher. And she said [looking upon him and his caravan], Drink, my lord: and she hasted, and let down her pitcher upon her hand, and gave him drink."

Was there, probably, ever water that tasted sweeter?

"And when she had done giving him drink, she said, I will draw water for thy camels also, until they have done drinking."

Surely, to draw all the water that ten camels who had traveled for days across a desert wanted to drink was no small token of this woman's energy and efficiency ; and to do it under the circumstances described in this narrative bespoke of not a little kind-heartedness.

"And she hasted, and emptied her pitcher into the trough, and ran again unto the well to draw water, and drew for all his camels. And the man wondering at her held his peace, to wit whether the Lord had made his journey prosperous or not."

The damsel was beautiful, and, according to the habit of that country, accomplished. She could not play the guitar, nor the piano, nor do we know that she could embroider. We do not know whether or not she could dance ; but she could *work*. This was an accomplishment very much in vogue at that time.

"And it came to pass, as the camels had done drinking, that the man took a golden earring of half a shekel weight [he understood woman nature], and two bracelets for her hands of ten shekels weight of gold ; and said, Whose daughter art thou? tell me, I pray thee: is there room in thy father's house for us to lodge in? And she said unto him, I am the daughter of Bethuel the son of Milcah, which she bare unto Nahor. She said moreover unto him, We have both straw and provender enough, and room to lodge in. And the man bowed down his head, and worshiped the Lord."

Courting by proxy had thriven very well thus far.

"And he said, Blessed be the Lord God of my master Abraham, who hath not left destitute my master of his mercy and his truth: I being in the way, the Lord led me to the house of my master's brethren. And the damsel ran, and told them of her mother's house these things. And Rebekah had a brother, and his name was Laban: and Laban ran out unto the man, unto the well. And it came to pass, when he saw the earring, and bracelets upon his sister's hands, and when he heard the words of Rebekah his sister, saying, Thus spake the man unto me, that he came unto the man ; and, behold, he stood by the camels at the well. And he said, Come in, thou blessed of the Lord."

A man who brings gold bracelets and earrings is not to be left out in the cold.

"Wherefore standest thou without? For I have prepared the house, and room for the camels."

Laban had an eye to business all through life.

"And the man came into the house: and he ungirded his camels, and gave straw and provender for the camels, and water to wash his feet, and the men's feet that were with him. And there was set meat before him to eat: but he said, I will not eat, until I have told mine errand. And he said, Speak on.

"And he said, I am Abraham's servant. And the Lord hath blessed my master greatly; and he is become great: and he hath given him flocks, and herds, and silver, and gold, and menservants, and maidservants, and camels, and asses. And Sarah my master's wife bare a son to my master when she was old: and unto him hath he given all that he hath. And my master made me swear, saying, Thou shalt not take a wife to my son of the daughters of the Canaanites, in whose land I dwell: But thou shalt go unto my father's house, and to my kindred, and take a wife unto my son. And I said unto my master, Peradventure the woman will not follow me. And he said unto me, The Lord, before whom I walk, will send his angel with thee, and prosper thy way; and thou shalt take a wife for my son of my kindred, and of my father's house. Then shalt thou be clear from this my oath, when thou comest to my kindred; and if they give not thee one, thou shalt be clear from my oath. And I came this day unto the well, and said, O Lord God of my master Abraham, if now thou do prosper my way which I go: Behold, I stand by the well of water; and it shall come to pass, that when the virgin cometh forth to draw water, and I say to her, Give me, I pray thee, a little water of thy pitcher to drink; and she say to me, Both drink thou, and I will also draw for thy camels: let the same be the woman whom the Lord hath appointed out for my master's son. And before I had done speaking in mine heart, behold, Rebekah came forth with her pitcher on her shoulder; and she went down unto the well, and drew water: and I said unto her, Let me drink, I pray thee. And she made haste, and let down her pitcher from her shoulder, and said, Drink, and I will give thy camels drink also: so I drank, and she made the camels drink also. And I asked her, and said, Whose daughter art thou? And she said, The daughter of Bethuel, Nahor's son, whom Milcah bare unto him: and I put the earring upon her face, and the bracelets upon her hands. And I bowed down my head, and worshiped the Lord, and blessed the Lord God of my master Abraham, which had led me in the right way to take my master's brother's daughter unto his son. And now, if ye will deal kindly and truly with my master, tell me: and if not, tell me; that I may turn to the right hand, or to the left.

"Then Laban and Bethuel answered and said, The thing proceedeth from the Lord: we cannot speak unto thee bad or good. Behold Rebekah is before thee; take her, and go, and let her be thy master's son's wife, as the Lord hath spoken.

"And it came to pass, that, when Abraham's servant heard their words, he worshiped the Lord, bowing himself to the earth."

Now, if this had been the man himself, Isaac, I should not have wondered; for a true man, who finds a woman he sincerely loves, and sees in her a return of admiration and of love, ought to be lifted into the highest realm of solemnity; and a deep, pure, and true love is always humble; and the man under such circumstances must say, Why should I be loved? Why should such a one as she love such a one as I? But Eliezer felt it for his master. Poor Isaac!

"And the servant brought forth jewels of silver, and jewels of gold, and raiment, and gave them to Rebekah: he gave also to her brother and to her mother precious things."

Courting their daughter, and courting her mother

"And they did eat and drink, he and the men that were with him, and tarried all night; and they rose up in the morning, and he said, Send me away unto my master. And her brother and her mother said, Let the damsel abide with us a few days, at the least ten; after that she shall go. And he said unto them, Hinder me not, seeing the Lord hath prospered my way; send me away that I may go to my master. And they said, We will call the damsel and inquire at her mouth."

However dear the life of home may be, when once a woman has given her trust and her love, her home thereafter is where her heart is. And, according to the fashion of her day, this young woman's heart already went out to her appointed mate.

"And they called Rebekah, and said unto her, Wilt thou go with this man? And she said, I will go. And they sent away Rebekah their sister, and her nurse, and Abraham's servant, and his men. And they blessed Rebekah, and said unto her, Thou art our sister, be thou the mother of thousands of millions, and let thy seed possess the gate of those which hate them."

Two great blessings that belonged to the idea and imagination of that age! Let her have a great family of children, and may they have power over their enemies.

"And Rebekah arose, and her damsels, and they rode upon the camels, and followed the man: and the servant took Rebekah, and went his way.

"And Isaac [who all this time had been at home waiting] came from the way of the well Lahai-roi; for he dwelt in the south country. And Isaac went out to meditate in the field at the eventide: and he lifted up his eyes, and saw, and, behold, the camels were coming. And Rebekah lifted up her eyes, and when she saw Isaac she lighted off the camel. For she had said unto the servant, What man is this that walketh in the field to meet us? And the servant had said, It is my master: therefore she took a veil, and covered herself. And the servant told Isaac all things that he had done.

"And Isaac brought her into his mother Sarah's tent, and took Rebekah, and she became his wife; and he loved her: and Isaac was comforted after his mother's death."

The void was filled.

If you can find anything better than that, I should like to be permitted to divide the secret with you. Was there ever anything more exquisitely simple? Did you ever come across anything more in accordance with the instincts of unperverted human nature? It is a pastoral poem, while it has the structure, the firm foundation, at least in part, of a history.

Isaac lived, as his father Abraham had, for a long period. At last twins were born to him—Esau and Jacob. Esau was the firstborn, and Jacob the second. Esau was therefore entitled to all the advantages conferred by the laws of primogeniture in vogue in that desert land; and next Sunday night I shall discuss the character of Jacob, and shall have occasion to show some of the facts in respect to these two brothers.

I can only add a few words in closing, with regard to the history of Isaac. The greatest memorial of his life was the many wells that he digged. Some men build hospitals by way of handing their names down to posterity; some erect churches; some establish institutions of civic economy; but in ancient days, and especially in pastoral countries where yet there were long, cloudless, dry seasons, he that dug a well was considered to have done a great public service. Down through the limestone rocks some wells were made with a spiral path around the sides, by which one could descend to the bottom and procure water; and there were other wells, from which water was drawn up by a rope. It was no small achievement and at no small expense of time and labor; so that to have dug a well was almost to have the title of a prince.

Isaac dug one well, and the servants of Abimelech drove his people from it. Abraham would have stood his ground and kept it, but Isaac gave it up. He dug another, and his herdsmen strove with the herdsmen of the king of Gerar; but Isaac loved peace, and gave up that well. He dug a third, and I think that third—either the third or the fourth—he was permitted to hold. As it was dug so far away from the herdsmen of the king that it was beyond their interference, he called it Rehoboth (*Broad-place*), saying, "For now the Lord hath made room for us."

Then took place his nefarious, or what is alleged to have been his nefarious, intercourse with King Abimelech. It is the Abrahamic legend over again: famine, refuge in a richer country, telling the king that his wife was his sister (lest he should be killed for her possession), and reproof of the lie by the nobler-minded king.

When Isaac became very old, and was about to die, there occurred that scene of perfidy and craft which throws the light of interpretation somewhat upon Rebekah. I need not say that the woman who was courted at the well, who took the rings and bracelets, who went home, and, facing her parents, told them just what had happened, who accepted a suitor that was five hundred miles off, and who, when appealed to as to whether she would stay a few days or go immediately, said, "I will go"— I need not say that she was not a woman that would be very severely governed by the mild, sweet-tempered Isaac. I have no doubt that there was government in that family, but I do not think Isaac maintained it!

Well, when he was old, and could no longer see, and felt that his death was approaching, Isaac, according to the custom and manner of the country, wished to bestow his blessing, and all the authority that went with it, upon his firstborn. Desert chiefs, like later monarchs, had absolute power, and could nominate their successors; David, for instance, nominated Solomon; the king transmits his government and authority to his first son, or to his favorite descendant; thus the ascendency of a tribe is prolonged: and Isaac was to give over his chieftainship.

"And it came to pass, that when Isaac was old, and his eyes were dim, so that he could not see, he called Esau his eldest son, and said unto him, My son: and he said unto him, Behold, here am I. And he said, Behold, now I am old, I know not the day of my death: Now therefore take, I pray thee, thy weapons, thy quiver and thy bow, and go out to the field, and take me some venison; and make me savory meat, such as I love, and bring it to me, that I may eat; that my soul may bless thee before I die. And Rebekah heard when Isaac spake to Esau his son. And Esau went to the field to hunt for venison, and to bring it."

The law of counterparts was in force then, as it is now. We love that which we do not have but which others do have, and which makes up and completes us. A strong, vigorous man likes a sweet, delicate, twining woman for his wife. A vigorous, strong, manly woman likes a quiet, peaceful, unobtrusive man for her husband. And Esau, who was a bold and dashing fellow, won the gentle heart of his father Isaac. Jacob was politic, shrewd, keen; and his mother, who was of an imperious nature, liked these traits in him. So the father loved Esau, and the mother loved Jacob. They indulged in favoritism, which is enough to destroy any family—to breed hatred even between twin brothers as these were.

"And Rebekah spake unto Jacob her son, saying, Behold, I heard thy father speak unto Esau thy brother, saying, Bring me venison, and make me savory meat, that I may eat, and bless thee before the Lord before my death. Now therefore, my son, obey my voice according to that which I command thee. Go now to the flock, and fetch me from thence two good kids of the goats; and I will make them savory meat for thy father, such as he loveth: And thou shalt bring it to thy father, that he may eat, and that he may bless thee before his death.'

Now a stanch, honest man would have said, That is a trick: I won't! But Jacob did not revolt from it a bit. He was a politic man.

" And Jacob said to Rebekah his mother, Behold, Esau my brother is a hairy man, and I am a smooth man: My father peradventure will feel me, and I shall seem to him as a deceiver; and I shall bring a curse upon me, and not a blessing."

From the beginning, you see, he had just those traits which go to make a politician.

"And his mother said unto him, Upon me be thy curse, my son: only obey my voice, and go fetch me them. And he went, and fetched, and brought them to his mother: and his mother made savory meat, such as his father loved. And Rebekah took goodly raiment of her eldest son Esau, which were with her in the house, and put them upon Jacob her younger son: and she put the skins of the kids of the goats upon his hands, and upon the smooth of his neck: and she gave the savory meat and the bread, which she had prepared, into the hand of her son Jacob.

"And he came unto his father, and said, My father: and he said, Here am I; who art thou, my son? And Jacob said unto his father, I am Esau, thy firstborn; I have done according as thou badest me: arise, I pray thee, sit and eat of my venison, that thy soul may bless me. And Isaac said unto his son, How is it that thou hast found it so quickly, my son? And he said, Because the Lord thy God brought it to me. And Isaac said unto Jacob, Come near, I pray thee, that I may feel thee, my son, whether thou be my very son Esau or not."

I think Isaac had an inkling of the boy.

"And Jacob went near unto Isaac his father."

It was a very critical time.

"And he felt him, and said, The voice is Jacob's voice, but the hands are the hands of Esau. And he discerned him not, because his hands were hairy, as his brother Esau's hands: so he blessed him. And he said, Art thou my very son Esau? And he said, I am. And he said, Bring it near to me, and I will eat of my son's venison, that my soul may bless thee. And he brought it near to him, and he did eat: and he brought him wine, and he drank. And his father Isaac said unto him, Come near now, and kiss me, my son. And he came near, and kissed him: and he smelled the smell of his raiment."

The old man was not as foolish as he seemed. There was a subtle fear running through his mind, and yet he did not say so. He tested it in these various ways. Having smelled of his garments, he blessed Jacob, and said:—

"See, the smell of my son is as the smell of a field which the Lord hath blessed: Therefore God give thee of the dew of heaven, and the fatness of the earth, and plenty of corn and wine: Let people serve thee, and nations bow down to thee: be lord over thy brethren, and let thy mother's sons bow down to thee: cursed be every one that curseth thee, and blessed be he that blesseth thee."

There is the old patriarch's benediction on his son. Not a word of what we call religion, or aspiration, or personal nobility, but much of harvests, vineyards, fields, and sovereignty. That was all that lay in the great patriarch's blessing. He gave it in full faith that the blessing Abraham had received and bequeathed to him was also his to bestow upon his successors; yet the element of superstition is clear, in his belief that a blessing, although secured by fraud, must be a blessing still.

"And it came to pass, as soon as Isaac had made an end of blessing Jacob, and Jacob was yet scarce gone out from the presence of Isaac his father, that Esau his brother came in from his hunting. And he also had made savory meat, and brought it unto his father, and said unto his father, Let my father arise, and eat of his son's venison, that thy soul may bless me. And Isaac his father said unto him, Who art thou? And he said, I am thy son, thy firstborn Esau. And Isaac trembled very exceedingly, and said, Who? where is he that hath taken venison, and brought it me, and I have eaten of all before thou camest, and have blessed him? yea, and he shall be blessed. And when Esau heard the words of his father, he cried with a great and exceeding bitter cry, and said unto his father, Bless me, even me also, O my father. And he said, Thy brother came with subtilty, and hath taken away thy blessing. And he said, Is not he rightly named Jacob [*Supplanter*]? for he hath supplanted me these two times: he took away my birthright, and, behold, now he hath taken away my blessing. And he said, Hast thou not reserved a blessing for me? And Isaac answered and said unto Esau, Behold, I have made him thy lord, and all his brethren have I given to him for servants; and with corn and wine have I sustained him: and what shall I do now unto thee, my son? And Esau said unto his father, Hast thou but one blessing, my father? bless me, even me also, O my father. And Esau lifted up his voice, and wept."

Which was the nobler boy of the two?

"And Isaac his father answered and said unto him, Behold, thy dwelling shall be the fatness of the earth, and of the dew of heaven from above; and by thy sword shalt thou live, and shalt serve thy brother: and it shall come to pass when thou shalt have the dominion, that thou shalt break his yoke from off thy neck.

"And Esau hated Jacob because of the blessing wherewith his father blessed him: and Esau said in his heart, The days of mourning for my father are at hand; then will I slay my brother Jacob. And these words of Esau her elder son were told to Rebekah: and she sent and called Jacob her younger son, and said unto him, Behold, thy brother Esau, as touching thee, doth comfort himself, purposing to kill thee. Now therefore, my son, obey my voice; and arise, flee thou to Laban my brother, to Haran; and tarry with him a few days, until thy brother's fury turn away: [This was probably the last time she ever saw her son.] until thy brother's anger turn away from thee, and he forget that which thou hast done to him: then I will send, and fetch thee from thence: why should I be deprived also of you both in one day?"

She did lose both of them; and it served her right. Her act was an infamous piece of treason. There was not a redeeming feature in it. It was an outrage.

Isaac was a connecting link between Abraham and Jacob. The three were the great figures in antiquity. They certainly are not to be the exemplars of instructors of modern times, but they represent the highest reach to which morality, the household, and religion had risen at that early period; and they were men so much beyond their times and above their people that they were the best material that could be selected with which to lay the foundations of that structure which has outworn the ages. Abraham, with his lofty faith in the invisible God and his lordly power over men; Isaac, with his affection and humility, and his placid sagacity of managing and increasing his great inheritance of wealth; and Jacob, crafty, courtly, diplomatic, persevering, gifted even with inspiring visions of spiritual things—out of these what a wondrous stock has grown!

That I may not do Isaac injustice, I will say that there are many qualities that are essential to a rounded-out character, which are not needed in laying the foundations of a state, and that many a man, as I shall show next Sabbath evening, may be eminently fitted to establish a commonwealth who is not personally a man that we should greatly admire.

If there is to be a nation founded, there must be a foundation laid in riches. No nation was ever built up on sand. Nations are of necessity established on property.

Property is not a mere thing of vulgar value. It represents the forethought, the purpose, the wisdom, the self-denial, the ingenuity of the human mind. It represents the conflicts which men go through against nature. It represents the subjection of natural law to the uses of men. It represents the highest endeavors of mankind in certain directions; and on these states are built. Poverty may have excellence, but poverty in a whole commonwealth is absolutely incompatible with civilization; and it was necessary that the foundations of nationalities in those early times should be laid in the substantial elements that result in the power of acquiring property. The instinct of home was great in Isaac. The power of accumulation, the policy and wisdom of maintaining what he had, and the capacity to transmit his possessions to another generation—all these were in him. In so far as the heroic element was concerned he was absolutely devoid of it; but in so far as the great elements that went to build up a commonwealth were concerned he had them in no inconsiderable degree, notwithstanding his quietness, meekness, and gentleness—perhaps even largely because of them.

Not intellectual, not largely inspired in the direction of morality, but being guided by faith that the promise of his father Abraham should be fulfilled to him, and that he should be, in succession, the father of many generations of posterity, according to the measure of his wisdom and strength, he sent forward the blessing; and then he died, and was buried in Machpelah: and his body has turned to dust, and his bones have crumbled.

But his posterity still flourish upon the earth.

VI.

JACOB.

"Verily I say unto you, Among them that are born of women there hath not risen a greater than John the Baptist: notwithstanding, he that is least in the kingdom of heaven is greater than he."—Matt. xi. 11.

JOHN was the latest of the prophets, and, in respect to spiritual understanding, respecting ethics or morality, in regard to that internal spiritual purity which the Gospel contemplates, and according to the declaration of our Master, he was incomparably higher than any that ever preceded him. Higher, then, was he, than the old prophets, Jeremiah and Isaiah; higher than David or Samuel; higher than Moses, or Abraham, or Isaac, or Jacob. And yet, Christ says that the least in the new kingdom will be greater than John; how much higher, then, will he be than all the antecedents of John!—for this is a rule of measurement, and it goes straight back to the very beginning. Commencing at zero it gradually and steadily rises through the ages until it comes to the highest point in the old dispensation, in the person of John the Baptist; and then it passes into a new state—namely, the development of a spiritual condition which is the result of a direct personal converse or intercourse of God with the human soul.

This sentence, then, goes clear back to the beginning. Ancient saints have been overdrawn. We have seen them through the golden dust of superstition. In poems, in moral treatises, and endlessly in sermons, we have had an indiscriminate exaltation of these men; not so much as

---

Sunday evening, December 1, 1878. LESSON: Psa. xxiii.

great factors, and as marking important eras in a vast circle of divine providence, but as great saints. They were great factors, and they did mark important eras in the vast circle of divine providence; but in regard to their personal power and excellence we have been brought up on false, exaggerated, and unreasonable views. The popular conception of these men has been strained in a way that was unnatural. That which they were thought to be was impossible under the circumstances.

So, when you bring out the simple facts in the actual Scripture history, plainly, as they lie there, you are met with surprise, and I do not know but with indignation. Men feel that you are taking away their God. They say, "You are stripping the Bible." No: not of anything that is worth keeping. I am correcting your erroneous convictions and misconceptions. I am saving the Bible from falsehoods that have been fastened upon it. Otherwise it could not stand the shock of such men as Ingersoll, whose whole force lies in the fact that he is fighting the misconceptions of a spurious interpretation; whereas the Word of God, under a true rendering, would pass unscathed and unharmed. The critical examination that is going on inside and outside of the church is such that we are bound to go back to first principles, and establish ourselves on the simple truth.

These remarks are required, before the unfolding of the character of Jacob, in many respects the most faulty, and yet in many respects the greatest, character in Hebrew antiquity. As a picture he is less grand than Abraham, but as a founder of nations he is greater than Abraham. He not only was not perfect, but he was imperfect to the degree that if he had lived in our day he would have been ranked among miscreants and criminals; and yet in his own day he was a man of transcendent moral power. If you think those two things are inconsistent or irreconcilable, I hope to show you, before I am done, that they are not.

We must, in the first place, get some little conception of

how far back these men lived—at what point the history of Scripture discovers them to us. It is admitted, on all hands, that in regard to the Greek people there was no true history—nothing but fabulous history—until you come down to the Trojan war of which Homer sang. Then there begins to be some historical basis or foundation. But Abraham lived seven or eight hundred years before that period. He lived a thousand years before there was any considerable authentic history of Greece. He lived 1167 years before the reputed founding of Rome. At the time that he and Isaac and Jacob lived there was no historical knowledge, no national history of China, of India, of Persia, or of Assyria. At that remote period only Abraham's own nation, Chaldea, represented organized government in Asia, and only the ancient Egypt towered up in all the wide stretch of antiquity as a civilized nation. And it was in those early days that Abraham pushed westward to begin with tents and caravans his search for the Promised Land, and that the history of the patriarchs took place.

We must, then, go back in our imagination, and ask ourselves: What was life at that time? What were men? What was known? What was yet unknown? And let us be sure that we take things just as they are—not as our fancy would like to have them.

With these statements I begin the history of Jacob. I had hoped to finish this history to-night, but it may be more than can be properly disposed of in a single discourse.

Jacob was a twin brother; Esau being the other and the firstborn. The first picture we have of them is given to us in the twenty-fifth chapter of Genesis: Esau was a daring hunter, a man of the field, Jacob being a "plain" —or quiet—man, dwelling in tents. War and hunting were the two elements of heroism known in that period. Esau, then, was a stirring, energetic, outside-living man, while Jacob was a peaceful man who loved home. Isaac loved Esau because he did eat of his venison; but Rebekah loved Jacob.

You never would, from this record, so condensed is it,

get any definite conception of the age of these brothers at the time of which we speak. You will bear in mind that the transaction which is first related could not have taken place much before they were fifty years old; for Jacob was seventy-eight years of age when he conspired with his mother to defraud Esau of his blessing, as related in the last lecture,—old enough to have known better! Although we have not a definite record of the period that elapsed between this event and the previous transaction, which we are now to review, we may presume that it was not more than twenty-five years. Probably it was not near so much.

"And Jacob sod pottage: and Esau came from the field, and he was faint: and Esau said to Jacob, Feed me, I pray thee, with that same red pottage; for I am faint: therefore was his name called Edom [Red]. And Jacob said, Sell me this day thy birthright. And Esau said, Behold, I am at the point to die: and what profit shall this birthright do to me? And Jacob said, Swear to me this day; and he sware unto him: and he sold his birthright unto Jacob. Then Jacob gave Esau bread and pottage of lentils; and he did eat and drink, and rose up, and went his way. Thus Esau despised his birthright.

What was the birthright? It was to inherit the place of his father, and whatever was included in that. As in the case of Abraham and Isaac, so Jacob, if he succeeded, would become head of the tribe and head of the property; and as there had been no differentiation between the chief and the priest he would be head of the tribe in religious matters. He would be king as well as priest and chief. He would stand at the highest point at which it was conceivable for a person to stand among his people.

Measured by any standard of moral feeling to-day, this whole transaction was mean and despicable to the last degree. If you mince matters you do violence to your own judgment, and do no good to history. It was an unmitigated piece of scoundrelism—for whoever, in any age, violates the great natural instincts is a scoundrel. There is no use of putting other than right epithets on such a proceeding as this. It was driving a hard bargain with a brother, by simply exercising superior commercial foresight. It was taking him when he was weakened by travel, and when he was so faint that he had no fair use of himself—when he said of his condition, "I am at the last gasp; I am dying; and if I die what is the use of the birthright to me?" Taking him in that strait, Jacob made Esau swear that he should become the inheritor of all that pertained to the proprietorship of his father's possessions. Can you conceive of any such thing taking place without feeling the waters of indignation roiled in your whole soul? It is abominable. And the most remarkable thing in regard to this transaction is, that from the beginning to the end of the Bible there is not a single word of criticism upon it. It is related elsewhere with the most astounding comment; for, if you turn to the twelfth chapter of Hebrews, and the fifteenth verse, you will find this statement:—

> "Looking diligently lest any man fail of the grace of God; lest any root of bitterness springing up trouble you, and thereby many be defiled; lest there be any fornicator, or profane person, as Esau, who for one morsel of meat sold his birthright. For ye know how that afterward, when he would have inherited the blessing, he was rejected: for he found no place of repentance, though he sought it carefully with tears."

After he had been cheated of his birthright, his weakness being taken advantage of, his extremity being the point at which the screw was brought to bear, after he had purchased his life by yielding up his honor and dignity, Esau is reprobated because he suffered himself to give up his birthright; and yet there is no condemnation of Jacob. Such is the treatment in the Scripture of this transaction, which no sane man can look upon except with loathing and indignation. Esau, the one that is wronged, is made to bear the blame. Why is this? In a purely spiritual point of view, looking at these men as representing the progress of nations and of the human race, the man who had a conception of the grandeur of chieftainship, of the priesthood, of the household, and of the relations of the promises of God to the future welfare of mankind—the man who had these things in his mind, evermore awakening a dream of greatness and excellence throughout all the time to come, was superior to the man who had no such conception—no ambition of that kind.

Esau had an ambition as a conqueror of wild beasts, as a man of enterprise in matters physical, but he was without the instincts of statesmanship; without the instincts of a founder of nations; without the instincts of a man of honor. He was low-toned. He is blamed because he was blameworthy. On the other hand, while these facts do not alter the criminality of his brother's conduct, the spiritual outreaching of Jacob was a noble thing, though it incited him to so mean, so ignoble, so criminal an act. That is the inward meaning of the New Testament reference to the matter. The act was intrinsically wicked, and there is no use of defending it; it was shameful, judged by any code in any age; but such an act would not be so wicked and shameful committed by some men in some ages, as it would committed by other men in other ages. It was not so blameworthy in that early period as it would have been in our day, or in a civilized time. It was done before there was any national life or public sentiment to direct or correct human conduct. It was done before there were moral or reformatory institutions. It was done by a Bedouin Arab in the wilderness—by a shepherd living in tents. It was done thousands and thousands and thousands of years ago, in the very twilight of existence. Craft, as a resource of weakness against strength, is always developed in early ages; and before the light of a better moral sense is thrown upon it craft is not regarded as a crime. In the early ages of every nation craft is looked upon as a virtue. You do not need to go back to antiquity to find this out. It has been so in every past age. It is indeed as really so in our day as ever it was at any previous time, though not so widely. In certain lines it is tolerated now as much as it was at any earlier period of the world. It has always been regarded as a trait of genius for a man to be able to outwit his fellow men; and in an age when every man's life hung on a thread, as it were, and self-defense was a thing of almost universal necessity, it was less culpable than it is now.

We dwell in a land where we do not think anything about personal self-defense. We have armies and navies, we have institutions, we have forts and soldiers, we have even policemen, and our defense gives us no concern; but let a man live on the border of civilization, so that every night he carries his scalp not knowing where he will find it in the morning, let a man be so situated that his safety depends on perpetual vigilance, let a man be obliged to hide from danger on the right hand and on the left, let a man find himself in a society where he must take care of himself or be set upon and beaten down by strong and designing men, and he will think a great deal about self-defense.

The first development of the natural man in those early ages was to resist violence with violence, where there was strength for resistance; but where there was not strength, to duck under—that is, to disguise, to deceive, to resort to craft, to outwit the adversary.

A man knows that his enemy is tracking him: he digs a deep pit; he covers it with brush; it looks like good, firm ground; he shows himself on the other side of it; the skulking enemy springs after him, and down he goes into the hole, and is trapped by the man that he sought to kill. The man who has escaped death feels pretty triumphant under the circumstances; and he owes his life to craft.

That old spirit is not so far gone but that, nowadays, if a man had an adversary hard after him, he would resort to some dexterous trick, or some form of deceit, in order to save his life. It is just this that prevails in the early development of the human race, before they have the advantage of the instruction that comes from the accumulated experience of men, and from the increasing light of revelation or inspiration.

You will find in Greek history that one of Homer's heroes, Ulysses, is crafty. Homer chuckles in showing how sharp he was, and how he outwitted everybody. Many of the scenes in early history are best described by fairy stories. I think they are better delineations of the condition of men before they were educated or developed than anything else, unless it be the Old Testament Scriptures. You will find that in such stories lying and stealing are not thought to be wrong. The little hero, being pitted against a giant, tells him all sorts of lies, and betrays him into cutting his own throat, or doing something else that amounts to his destruction. With your knowledge of cause and effect there is to you an element of inconsistency and untruthfulness in fairy stories, but in olden times men did not know anything about cause and effect. Natural law was not understood then. The theories on this subject are a later development. They have come in since the Roman era.

One of Macaulay's essays, which is worthy of your reading on many accounts, is that on Machiavelli (a name that has passed into universal use as a type of craft or deceit). In order to present a fair exposition of Machiavelli, Macaulay gives an account of public feeling in Italy, where corporations and dynasties had crushed out the people, where they resorted to all manner of deceit and craft and cunning, and where the state of public feeling was thoroughly in favor of lying. It was regarded not only as smart, but as sagacious, philosophical, and justifiable. If Shakespeare's play of "Othello" were performed in any Northern nation *Othello* would be the hero, and *Iago* would be despised with loathing, as a base, intriguing scoundrel; but in Italy of Machiavelli's day it would be the other way, and it would be said, "That old beef-eating Othello is despicable, but that splendid manager Iago is an admirable fellow." Deceit and craft were, according to the prevalent conception, public sentiment and law.

However, we need not go back so far as antiquity or even the Middle Ages for an example of one man's cheating another out of his birthright, because he has the power. That is not a thing simply of the past. I should like to know what right England has in India, except the right which comes from her power to cheat that nation out of its hereditary possessions? I should like to know why England is in Afghanistan, except because she has the ability to force her way there by reason of the weakness of the Afghanistani, and compel them to submit to her government? I should like to know what right there was in the confederated nations of Europe to divide and distribute Poland, except the right of superior force? It is a gigantic game of Jacob over again. I should like to know what right this government of the United States has to dispose of the Indians and of their territory, making treaty after treaty, violating one almost before another is formed, starving them and cheating them by unscrupulous agents, and pursuing them with an army whose officers blush, and say at every step, "The Indians are right and we are wrong"? I think our age is not so far advanced that we can afford to be severe on Jacob. If, with all the light of the Gospel, with eighteen hundred years of Christian instruction, with the experience of empires and nations, with the modified morality that makes our households what they are, with the manhood and all the refinements of life—if, with these advantages, we can stand calmly by and see such things done without horror and protest, is it becoming in us to be very much shocked at what was done six thousand years ago? Disconnected from and unsurrounded by any mitigating circumstances, it was an abominable deed; but it was done at a time when men did not know how abominable such deeds were.

But do you say, "Jacob, notwithstanding, was accepted for a great, providential work"? Yes, he was, in spite of this—not in consequence of it; just as England and America are to-day. Providence must work with the materials it has. If it worked only with perfect men it would never work at all. All the way down, God works with everything that can be made to conspire with his purposes, restraining the wrath of man, and causing the remainder thereof to praise him.

But one modicum of relief in the contrast lies in the vulgarity of Esau's nature, and in the ambition or craving for eminence that is manifested in Jacob. It is a very slight alleviation, however.

The next point in Jacob's history is his conspiracy with his mother to deceive his father, her husband, and to complete the bad bargain of fraud already entered upon against his brother Esau, by securing for Jacob the patriarch's dying blessing, which was the last will and testament of the old chief. I read last Sabbath evening in Isaac's history, and shall not repeat to-night, the painful details of this very disgusting conspiracy between a mother and one son, as against the husband and father and the other son. It was a calculated fraud; it was a deliberate purpose formed to defraud; and judged by our modern standards as applied to the household it has in it almost every element that could make it despicable. You cannot speak of it too severely, on its merits.

And that is not the whole of it. I think the most extraordinary part of the matter is that both Jacob and his mother believed themselves to be eminently religious, and neither of them showed at that time, or at any subsequent time, the slightest sign of remorse. They gave no evidence that they thought they were doing wrong. So far as the recorded history of the transaction is concerned, there is nothing to show that in after years Jacob was convicted of this as a sin, or looked back upon it with regret; and yet he was seventy-eight years old when he committed it. And nowhere has any writer in the Bible borne any witness against the disgraceful proceeding. It must stand, therefore, as a prodigious testimony of the low moral development of men in that early age, when such an unparalleled outrage could occur without condemnation, or even criticism.

From how low a state, then, has the family of man arisen! Do not attempt to palliate this act, except to show that it was the act of men in an undeveloped age, and that we are not to apply to them the severity of condemnation which we apply, in this later age, to ourselves, who have better instruction.

They violated no moral sense that was in them; and the measure of the wrong, in so far as the wrongdoer is concerned, lies not in the mischief that the act works outwardly, but in his responsibility to his best understanding inwardly. Since they were so rude and low that they had no moral sense which was violated, the act did not work upon them such demoralization as the same act would upon us.

The attempt of some persons to explain this by saying that Jacob acted under divine inspiration, that he obeyed the decrees of God, and that it was right because God inspired it, is futile. I do not think that style of reasoning exonerates the culprit, and the effect is to debauch the moral ideas of mankind. It is to charge God with inspiring deceit and cunning and with violating the great law of love. It does not justify the actor, but tends to destroy the faith of mankind in God. We are to abhor the doctrine that *a thing is right because God says it*. Things are not right because God says them; but he says them because they are right. There is no inspiration on the part of God of any such doctrine as that things are right or true because God says them. There is no need of falling back on any such debasing theory. "Let God be true," says the sacred Writ, "and every man a liar." Maintain the integrity of moral government in the universe, and let saints, patriarchs, and inspired men go as they may. Whatever criticism you put upon men, do not destroy the confidence of the world in the integrity, justice, truth, and purity of God.

Men are led to this by having a vicious theory of inspiration—a theory of inspiration that is not contained in the Bible, and that is utterly inconsistent with the Bible. I believe in the inspiration of the Bible from beginning to end, but not in its inspiration in every part alike; and the inspiration I believe in is very different from plenary and verbal inspiration.

Now, as to the consequences of this transaction. They are related without comment. First, we have a revelation of the effect of these proceedings upon the man Esau.

'And Esau hated Jacob because of the blessing wherewith his father blessed him: and Esau said in his heart, The days of mourning for my father are at hand; then will I slay my brother Jacob."

It is as if he had said, "The old man will die before long, and then I will kill Jacob." A lovely condition of affairs it was—a son waiting for a father to die before he should kill his brother!

"And the words of Esau her elder son were told to Rebekah: and she sent and called Jacob her younger son, and said unto him—"

What? Not a word of regret; not, "We have made a mistake, and let us rectify it"? Nothing of the sort; but,

"Behold, thy brother Esau, as touching thee, doth comfort himself, purposing to kill thee. Now therefore, my son, obey my voice; and arise, flee thou to Laban my brother, to Haran; and tarry with him a few days, until thy brother's fury turn away; until thy brother's anger turn away from thee, and he forget that which thou hast done to him: then I will send, and fetch thee from thence: why should I be deprived also of you both in one day?"

That was the counsel of the mother—the beautiful Rebekah, whose courtship had been so charming!

There is another scene connected with this affair. Rebekah goes to her venerable husband, and says to him,—

"I am weary of my life because of the daughters of Heth: if Jacob take a wife of the daughters of Heth, such as these which are of the daughters of the land, what good shall my life do me?

"And Isaac called Jacob, and blessed him, and charged him, and said unto him, Thou shalt not take a wife of the daughters of Canaan."

The good woman judged very correctly as to the right line of appeal.

"Arise, go to Padan-aram, to the house of Bethuel thy mother's father; and take thee a wife from thence of the daughters of Laban thy mother's brother. And God Almighty bless thee, and make thee fruitful, and multiply thee, that thou mayest be a multitude of people; and give thee the blessing of Abraham, to thee, and to thy seed with thee; that thou mayest inherit the land wherein thou art a stranger, which God gave unto Abraham. And Isaac sent away Jacob: and he went to Padan-aram unto Laban, son of Bethuel the Syrian, the brother of Rebekah, Jacob's and Esau's mother."

So, then, he had got out of the scrape! The stolen blessing was to stand in full force, and he was to be snugly married. Well, that must surprise every person of a fresh and unvitiated conscience; unless he is relieved by the evidence which we have of the utterly undeveloped moral sense of men in that early age.

When Esau saw that Isaac had blessed Jacob, and sent him to take a wife from Padan-aram, he went and married elsewhere to vex his mother, and did other things that we do not need to dwell upon. We will go on with the history of Jacob.

He went—in the western part of Palestine, across the hills, probably in sight of Hebron and Jerusalem—through what was afterward Samaria; he traversed the valley of the Jordan, crossing it somewhere; he most likely followed the then track of caravans south of the sea of Galilee, stretching up toward Damascus, and eastward to Mesopotamia and Haran, where Abraham had sojourned.

"Jacob went out from Beer-sheba, and went toward Haran. And he lighted upon a certain place, and tarried there all night, because the sun was set; and he took of the stones of that place, and put them for his pillows, and lay down in that place to sleep. And he dreamed, and behold a ladder set up on the earth, and the top of it reached to heaven: and behold the angels of God ascending and descending on it. And, behold, the Lord stood above it, and said, I am the Lord [or, Jehovah] the God of Abraham thy father, and the God of Isaac: the land whereon thou liest, to thee will I give it, and to thy seed; and thy seed shall be as the dust of the earth; and thou shalt spread abroad to the west, and to the east, and to the north, and to the south: and in thee and in thy seed shall all the families of the earth be blessed. And, behold, I am with thee, and will keep thee in all places whither thou goest, and will bring thee again into this land; for I will not leave thee, until I have done that which I have spoken to thee of."

There is all the rebuke he got for his sin of unparalleled treachery and deceit, for this abominable outrage of the most sacred of relationships. It is very fortunate that it was a dream. He thought it was a revelation directly from God. Like the people of his day, like barbarous nations nowadays, and like the under-classes in our own country, he thought dreams to be realities, and took his dream to be a fact; but in all this history there is not a trace of any consciousness on his part of having done wrong. He committed a series of acts which would have driven any man out of our society, which would not be tolerated in any civilized community; and yet, in that early age, before moral virtue had been developed, it was so little thought of as a fault that it not only did not trouble his memory, but his sleeping thoughts made visions of God sanctioning and confirming the blessing.

When Jacob dreamed, lying, weary from his journey, in the open field, and restless, as men are when they dream, all he saw was God declaring that by his providence he would take care of him, and fulfill in him the promise made, that he should be the father of many generations, and inherit vast possessions. There was no revelation to him of moral government, no disclosure of virtue, no development of the idea of higher manhood or rectitude, but simply the assurance of imperial dominion.

" Jacob rose up early in the morning, and took the stone that he had put for his pillows, and set it up for a pillar, and poured oil upon the top of it. And he called the name of that place Beth-el [the House of God] : but the name of that city was called Luz at the first. And Jacob vowed a vow, saying, If God will be with me, and will keep me in this way that I go, and will give me bread to eat, and raiment to put on, so that I come again to my father's house in peace ; then shall Jehovah be my God."

Well, suppose Jehovah would not have done these things, who would have been his god then ? This is a clear act, by a crude, undeveloped man, bargaining with his God, and saying, to all intents and purposes, " I will be your servant if you will be my protector." That is the plain English of it.

"And this stone, which I have set for a pillar, shall be God's house : and of all that thou shalt give me I will surely give the tenth unto thee."

Such a transaction in our time would be regarded as worse than simony ; but at that time it was perhaps as well as could be expected.

We now come to another of those beautiful idyls of the Old Testament. Just as men, traveling over California mountains, go through rude and hirsute places, toiling laboriously, severely taxing their strength, until they come to some intervale, some charming little valley, where everything is pastoral and delightful, where the clear crystal stream gives them refreshment, and they sit and talk of their hardships, so we go through these rugged parts of history, and all at once strike upon the most exquisite pictures.

"Jacob went on his journey, and came into the land of the people of the east. And he looked, and behold a well in the field, and, lo, there were three flocks of sheep lying by it; for out of that well they watered the flocks: and a great stone was upon the well's mouth. And thither were all the flocks gathered: and they rolled the stone from the well's mouth, and watered the sheep, and put the stone again upon the well's mouth in his place."

That is to say, this was their custom.

"And Jacob said unto them, My brethren, whence be ye?"

We are to think of him as we would think of a magnificent old Bedouin chief of to-day, as being a pattern of etiquette and courtesy, and as addressing the shepherds in stately, admirable language. A modern traveler, going to seek his fortune, would very likely have said, " Halloo, boys ! what are you doing here?" You might expect from him some such curt and rude form of address ; but not so with wanderers in the wilderness of the East. Even though they took your life they took it with extraordinary grace and dignity ! So Jacob salutes these men with,—

"My brethren, whence be ye? And they said, Of Haran are we. And he said unto them, Know ye Laban the son of Nahor? And they said, We know him. And he said unto them, Is he well? And they said, He is well: and, behold, Rachel his daughter cometh with the sheep. And he said, Lo, it is yet high day, neither is it time that the cattle should be gathered together: water ye the sheep, and go and feed them. And they said, We cannot, until all the flocks be gathered together, and till they roll the stone from the well's mouth; then we water the sheep.

"And while he yet spake with them, Rachel came with her father's sheep: for she kept them. And it came to pass, when Jacob saw Rachel the daughter of Laban his mother's brother, and the sheep of Laban his mother's brother, that Jacob went near, and rolled the stone from the well's mouth, and watered the flock of Laban his mother's brother."

It was not the only time that love has uncovered deep wells. You recollect that, in his father's courtship, it was Rebekah that watered the camels of Eliezer, the steward ; but in this case it is changed, and Jacob waters the flock of Rachel.

"And Jacob kissed Rachel, and lifted up his voice and wept."

That is not usually the effect of such a salutation! Nevertheless, that simple statement is most penetrating and revelatory. It is a master-stroke. All the way through Jacob's weary journey of probably two or three weeks—following upon the exhaustive excitement of the conspiracy for the blessing and the subsequent fear for his life at the hand of Esau—there was uncertainty, except so far as his hope was confirmed by the conviction of his dream, as to whether or not he should find his mother's brother; but when he beheld at the well Rachel, of his own kindred and household, the whole uncertainty was dispelled; and when she recognized the relationship, and suffered herself to be kissed by him, his heart gave way to the tide of gladness which swept through him. His feelings were akin to those of men who, wrecked, have drifted along upon a dark sea on a raft, and are almost spent, when at last, as the morning breaks, they see a ship bearing down upon them for their relief, and, in spite of famine, cold, and wretchedness, lift up voices, feeble though they be, of joy, and shed tears of thanksgiving, and shout, "We are saved! we are saved!" And for depth or impressiveness, there are no tears like those which love and joy shed.

"It came to pass, when Laban heard the tidings of Jacob his sister's son, that he ran to meet him, and embraced him, and kissed him, and brought him to his house. And he [Jacob] told Laban all these things. And Laban said to him, Surely thou art my bone and my flesh. And he abode with him the space of a month."

Thus far he was a guest.

"And Laban said unto Jacob, Because thou art my brother, shouldest thou therefore serve me for naught? Tell me, what shall thy wages be? And Laban had two daughters: the name of the elder was Leah, and the name of the younger was Rachel. Leah was tender-eyed [sore-eyed, it may be—a matter of small importance to you; but it would have been a matter of great importance to you if you had been in her place. Ophthalmia is a well-nigh universal complaint in Oriental countries, where the glare of the sun, the shining sands, and the want of proper cleanliness affect the population to a degree almost unknown in Occidental lands. Leah, it may be presumed, was weak-eyed]; but Rachel was beautiful and well-favored. And Jacob loved Rachel; and said, I will serve thee seven years for Rachel thy younger daughter."

Jacob was pleased, and Laban had made a very good bargain. He had sold his daughter at an excellent market price—for it was a sale. It was in a day when men sold their children. The practice is not quite abandoned yet.

"Jacob served seven years for Rachel [where, in the English language, is there anything more beautiful than the remainder of this sentence!], and they seemed unto him but a few days, for the love he had to her."

How love lightens burdens, shortens the road, and takes away care! Love is the universal solacer of pain, and the universal reconciler of evil. It is the one great element whose concentration and permanence make eternal life.

"And Jacob said unto Laban, Give me my wife, for my days are fulfilled."

I will not go through the details of this history. Jacob found that Leah had been apportioned to him; and he then renewed the bargain for Rachel, and served seven years more for her.

I will not read the pitiful thirtieth chapter of Genesis. It is full of revelations of the effects of polygamy, and of the condition of the family in an early age, with its ignorance, with its coarseness, with its jealousies, and with its occasional beauties. In the main it is enveloped in a low, chilly, foggy atmosphere. It is a very sad chapter in many respects.

"And it came to pass, when Rachel had borne Joseph, that Jacob said unto Laban, Send me away, that I may go unto mine own place, and to my country. Give me my wives and my children, for whom I have served thee, and let me go: for thou knowest my service which I have done thee."

Laban was a good bargain-maker. He said:—

"I have learned by experience that the Lord hath blessed me for thy sake. And he said, Appoint me thy wages, and I will give it."

Then a new bargain was made; and Jacob, having been overreached a great many times, contrived to overreach his father-in-law in this case. He agreed to continue to serve Laban for all the cattle that were ringstreaked, speckled, and spotted; then he devised methods that brought a due measure of the products of the flock to his side; and he did not seem to suffer in his conscience from any such reasons. But the great increase of his possessions

—of the children of his household and of his flocks—excited the jealousy and hatred of the family of Laban.

"And he heard the words of Laban's sons, saying, Jacob hath taken away all that was our father's; and of that which was our father's hath he gotten all this glory. And Jacob beheld the countenance of Laban, and, behold, it was not toward him as before. And the Lord said unto Jacob, Return unto the land of thy fathers, and to thy kindred; and I will be with thee."

It is not stated that this was uttered by a voice from out of heaven. It might not have been even a dream. It might have been simply a strong impression that was made upon his mind, as if it were from above, that he had better depart, and seek again the region of the land of his fathers.

"And Jacob sent and called Rachel and Leah to the field unto his flock, and said unto them, I see your father's countenance, that it is not toward me as before; but the God of my father hath been with me. And ye know that with all my power I have served your father. And your father hath deceived me, and changed my wages ten times; but God suffered him not to hurt me. If he said thus, The speckled shall be thy wages; then all the cattle bare speckled: and if he said thus, The ringstreaked shall be thy hire; then bare all the cattle ringstreaked. Thus God hath taken away the cattle of your father, and given them to me."

There is an unspeakable simplicity of coolness in that statement, attributing directly to God the results of his own shrewd planning. Have good men altogether got beyond that, even yet?

"And the angel of God spake unto me in a dream, saying, Jacob: and I said, Here am I."

So he gave to his wives an account of the command of God, as he interprets it, that he should emigrate and go westward.

"Then Jacob rose up, and set his sons and his wives upon camels; and he carried away all his cattle, and all his goods which he had gotten, the cattle of his getting, which he had gotten in Padan-aram, for to go to Isaac his father in the land of Canaan. And Laban went to shear his sheep: and Rachel had stolen the images that were her father's."

It seems that Jacob's wives were idolaters. The patriarch's own household were in the habit of worshiping idols.

"And Jacob stole away unawares to Laban the Syrian, in that he told him not that he fled. So he fled with all that he had; and he rose up, and passed over the river [the Euphrates], and set his face toward the mount Gilead.

"And it was told Laban on the third day that Jacob was fled. And he took his brethren with him, and pursued after him seven days' journey; and they overtook him in the mount Gilead. And God came to Laban the Syrian in a dream by night, and said unto him, Take heed that thou speak not to Jacob either good or bad. Then Laban overtook Jacob. Now Jacob had pitched his tent in the mount: and Laban with his brethren pitched in the mount of Gilead.

"And Laban said to Jacob, What hast thou done, that thou hast stolen away unawares to me, and carried away my daughters, as captives taken with the sword? Wherefore didst thou flee away secretly, and steal away from me; and didst not tell me, that I might have sent thee away with mirth, and with songs, with tabret, and with harp; and hast not suffered me to kiss my sons and my daughters? Thou hast now done foolishly in so doing. It is in the power of my hand to do you hurt: but the God of your father spake unto me yesternight, saying, Take thou heed that thou speak not to Jacob either good or bad. And now, though thou wouldest needs be gone, because thou sore longedst after thy father's house, yet wherefore hast thou stolen my gods?"

Then comes a revelatory scene. Jacob, in a towering passion, knowing not that Rachel had taken the idols, denies that he has done any such thing, and offers to have his goods ransacked. Rachel hid them, sitting on them, and alleging a false reason why she should not get up, and the father could not find his gods.

"And Jacob was wroth, and chode with Laban: and Jacob answered and said to Laban, What is my trespass? what is my sin, that thou hast so hotly pursued after me? Whereas thou hast searched all my stuff, what hast thou found of all thy household stuff? Set it here before my brethren and thy brethren, that they may judge betwixt us both. This twenty years have I been with thee."

Then Jacob recounts his fidelity in service, and what he has suffered, and ends by saying:—

"Thus have I been twenty years in thy house; I served thee fourteen years for thy two daughters, and six years for thy cattle: and thou hast changed my wages ten times. Except the God of my father, the God of Abraham, and the Fear of Isaac, had been with me, surely thou hadst sent me away now empty. God hath seen mine affliction and the labor of my hands, and rebuked thee yesternight."

There followed a reconciliation and a covenant, and they part. Jacob moves forward, and comes near to Jordan again by way of the river Jabbok, with varied experiences. There he hears that Esau, with his men, is coming, and he is greatly afraid. The generalship which he manifests under the circumstances is worthy of exposition ; I cannot give it to-night, but will resume the subject next Sunday evening. After making his politic arrangements, while he was waiting at night on the river bank to learn the result, there occurred a mysterious scene, memorable for a dramatic reason, as well as for other reasons, and to me interesting because it has given rise to one of the most magnificent specimens of spiritualization to be found in any language.

"And Jacob was left alone; and there wrestled a man with him until the breaking of the day. And when he saw that he prevailed not against him, he touched the hollow of his thigh; and the hollow of Jacob's thigh was out of joint, as he wrestled with him. And he said, Let me go, for the day breaketh. And he said, I will not let thee go, except thou bless me. And he said unto him, What is thy name? And he said, Jacob. And he said, Thy name shall be called no more Jacob, but Israel [Striver with God]: for as a prince hast thou power with God and with men, and hast prevailed. And Jacob asked him, and said, Tell me, I pray thee, thy name. And he said, Wherefore is it that thou dost ask after my name? And he blessed him there. And Jacob called the name of the place Peniel [The Face of God]: for I have seen God face to face, and my life is preserved. And as he passed over Penuel the sun rose upon him, and he halted upon his thigh."

Amid the frivolous and mischievous spiritualizations that are taking place in the Bible-reading of our day, I present to you a specimen by Charles Wesley of what we may regard as a sublime spiritualization of this passage, and of that most mysterious event in the history of Jacob:—

> Come, O thou Traveler unknown,
>   Whom still I hold, but cannot see,
> My company before is gone,
>   And I am left alone with Thee;
> With Thee all night I mean to stay,
> And wrestle till the break of day.
>
> I need not tell Thee who I am,
>   My misery or sin declare,
> Thyself hast called me by my name,
>   Look on Thy hands and read it there;
> But who, I ask Thee, who art Thou?
> Tell me Thy name, and tell me now.

JACOB.

In vain Thou strugglest to get free,
  I never will unloose my hold;
Art Thou the man that died for me?
  The secret of Thy love unfold;
Wrestling, I will not let Thee go
Till I Thy name, Thy nature know.

Wilt Thou not yet to me reveal
  Thy new unutterable name?
Tell me, I still beseech Thee, tell;
  To know it now resolved I am;
Wrestling, I will not let thee go
Till I Thy name, Thy nature know.

'Tis all in vain to hold Thy tongue,
  Or touch the hollow of my thigh;
Though every sinew be unstrung,
  Out of my arms Thou shalt not fly;
Wrestling, I will not let Thee go
Till I Thy name, Thy nature know.

What though my shrinking flesh complain,
  And murmur to contend so long,
I rise superior to my pain,
  When I am weak then I am strong;
And when my all of strength shall fail,
I shall with the God-man prevail.

My strength is gone, my nature dies,
  I sink beneath Thy weighty hand,
Faint to revive, and fall to rise;
  I fall, and yet by faith I stand—
I stand, and will not let Thee go
Till I thy name, Thy nature know.

Yield to me now, for I am weak,
  But confident in self-despair;
Speak to my heart, in blessings speak,
  Be conquer'd by my instant prayer;
Speak, or Thou never hence shalt move,
And tell me if Thy name is Love?

'Tis Love! 'Tis Love! Thou diedst for me;
  I hear Thy whisper in my heart;

The morning breaks, the shadows flee,
   Pure Universal Love Thou art;
To me, to all, Thy bowels move—
Thy nature and Thy name is Love.

My prayer hath power with God; the grace
   Unspeakable I now receive;
Through faith I see Thee face to face—
   I see Thee face to face, and live;
In vain I have not wept and strove;
Thy nature and Thy name is Love.

I know Thee, Saviour, who Thou art—
   Jesus, the feeble sinner's Friend;
Nor wilt Thou with the night depart,
   But stay and love me to the end;
Thy mercies never shall remove—
Thy nature and Thy name is Love.

The Sun of Righteousness to me
   Hath rose with healing in His wings;
Wither'd my nature's strength, from Thee
   My soul its life and succor brings;
My help is all laid up above—
Thy nature and Thy name is Love.

Contented now upon my thigh
   I halt, till life's short journey end;
All helplessness, all weakness, I
   On Thee alone for strength depend;
Nor have I power from Thee to move—
Thy nature and Thy name is Love.

Lame as I am, I take the prey,
   Hell, earth, and sin with ease o'ercome;
I leap for joy, pursue my way,
   And as a bounding hart fly home,
Through all eternity to prove
Thy nature and Thy name is Love.

VII.

JACOB AND JOSEPH.

I MUST recur occasionally to the fundamental theory upon which I treat the early history in the Old Testament—a theory totally different from that which regards the inspiration of the Scriptures as "plenary" and "verbal." You are to bear in mind that the Bible itself does not anywhere declare what inspiration is. It merely says that Scripture has been inspired to one purpose—namely, "for instruction in righteousness, that the man of God may be perfect, thoroughly furnished unto all good works." It goes no further.

But if you go to the facts I think you will find that the inspiration spoken of is primarily the inspiration by the divine Mind of the reason and moral consciousness of nations and races. It is the inspiration of the evolution of moral truth among mankind, of which the Scripture is a partial record; and it is a partial record which takes account only of that part of the dealing of God with the human race which lies within the channel or along the line of the Semitic race—the Israelites.

In treating of the patriarchal age, therefore, I have represented men just as they are there depicted, in the old record. It is impossible to read many of the scenes that belong to the early conditions of the human race, and to those venerated names that we have been trained to look upon through the luminous medium of the modern church and through all the poetic inspirations and incidental colorings that have been given to them—it is impossible to go

---

Sunday evening, December 8, 1878. LESSON: Psa. lxxvii.

back and take them just as they were in their low estate, and not to a great extent lessen the veneration of many for them; but I cannot help that. It must be.

I closed last Sunday evening's discourse with an account of the vision that came to Jacob in the night. In that vision his name was changed, and whereas he had been called "Jacob," after that he was called "Israel." "Jacob" signifies *a Supplanter;* and "Israel," "*a Striver, or Prevailer, or Prince, of God.*" Such became his name; and from this time many of the faults of Jacob disappeared, and we come, not to a high plane, but certainly to a better account of him than in anything that has preceded. It was time for a man nearly a hundred years old to behave!

We had proceeded in Jacob's history to the approach of his brother Esau to meet him, with his men. For, tidings having been borne to Esau that Jacob was coming back with great possessions, Esau started out to meet him with a band of four hundred men.

The generalship which Jacob manifested here was admirable. It was not heroic, but it was in accordance with his settled character. He was essentially a man of policy. He had not a single element of the heroic in his nature. He was a man of peace, quietness, and good management. He was sagacious, far-sighted. And when he heard that Esau was coming out to meet him, being greatly afraid and distressed, lest Esau should slaughter him and his, in revenge for the past, Jacob sent droves of sheep, goats, camels, kine, and asses before him as so many presents to "my lord Esau," from "thy servant Jacob."

Then he divided his great family. Mark the order!

"He divided the children unto Leah, and unto Rachel, and unto the two handmaids. And he put the handmaids and their children foremost, and Leah and her children after, and Rachel and Joseph hindermost."

If any fury was to burst upon anybody, the ones he esteemed least should get the first blow. Therefore the two handmaids and their children were placed foremost; Leah, the wife that he had been cheated into having, and her children came next; and Rachel, who was the one on whom his heart always rested, his dearly beloved Rachel, and her then only son, Joseph, came last of all. And then "he passed over before them."

The brothers meet. Jacob had the birthright and was the superior according to the customs of that age. But he "bowed himself to the ground seven times, until he came near to his brother."

Whatever Esau might have thought of what he would do when he met Jacob after so many years of separation, his now venerable brother, not taking on any airs of superiority, nor defying him, but doing the most reverent and humiliating obeisance to him—bowing himself once, then coming a little nearer and bowing again a great deal lower, then advancing a step or two further and bowing still again, and so on until he had bowed seven times, and had come almost to his feet—disarmed Esau's bitterness toward him, if he had any.

I cannot help, and you cannot help, feeling a great deal more sympathy with Esau than with Jacob; but Jacob for the purposes of building a commonwealth was better timber than Esau; for Esau was a man not of forethought, adapting means to ends, holding to them, and overruling his feelings by his judgment: he was a man of impulse; and his primary impulses were generally strong. When he was mad, he was *very* mad; when he was gay, he was *very* gay. He was subject to circumstances, and according to his impulses he was blown hither and thither. He was well-fitted to be the head of nomadic plundering tribes, but was not the right sort of a man to found a nation that was to be built up. Yet, for dramatic effect, Esau was the finer fellow. He was bold, dashing, and in some respects admirable.

"Esau ran to meet him [Jacob], and embraced him, and fell on his neck, and kissed him: and they wept."

Kissing, in the old times, seems to have been connected with tears!

"And he lifted up his eyes, and saw the women and the children; and said, Who are those with thee? And he said, The children which God hath graciously given thy servant. Then the handmaidens came near, they and their children, and they bowed themselves. And Leah also with her children came near, and bowed themselves; and after came Joseph near and Rachel, and they bowed themselves."

It appears that Rachel was even put behind Joseph; she was the dearest of all.

"And Esau said, What meanest thou by all this drove which I met?"

Now, that was nature; and Jacob had a quick sense of what was nature. That must be a very bad man who, being approached by reverential women and by little children, can resist the appeal that is made to his sympathy; and when it is made in connection with large presents of various kinds it is very likely to come near to the heart; and Jacob did not mistake human nature in this case at all. He sent, first, the cattle, and they stood around, too; and then he sent the women in climacteric succession, and the little children; and it touched the heart of Esau, and his first impulse was very generous.

"What meanest thou by all this drove which I met? And Jacob said, These are to find grace in the sight of my lord. And Esau said, I have enough, my brother; keep that thou hast unto thyself."

Still he was not insensible to entreaty.

"And Jacob said, Nay, I pray thee, if now I have found grace in thy sight, then receive my present at my hand: for as much as I have seen thy face, as though I had seen the face of God, and thou wast pleased with me."

It was very well that he had no pride that choked him. You and I could not have said that, and been sincere. For him to make up with his brother with the compliment that he was as a god to him was carrying humility to the extreme.

"Take, I pray thee, my blessing that is brought to thee; because God hath dealt graciously with me, and because I have enough. And he urged him, and Esau took it."

Jacob did not misjudge in that point, either.

Now Esau, when he was at his best, when his best affections were uppermost, was a very pleasant brother; but Jacob knew him too well to think it worth while to spend many days with him. The weather might change. So when, in the first gush of brotherly recognition and affiliation, Esau said, "Let us take our journey, and let us go, and I will go before thee," Jacob said to him :—

"My lord knoweth that the children are tender, and the flocks and herds with young are with me: and if men should overdrive them one day, all the flock will die."

That was good shepherd-sense.

"Let my lord, I pray thee, pass over before his servant: and I will lead on softly, according as the cattle that goeth before me and the children be able to endure, until I come unto my lord unto Seir."

There, too, was a dexterous and rare stroke of policy. It was a timely thing for Jacob to say then.

"And Esau said, Let me now leave with thee some of the folk that are with me. And he said, What needeth it? let me find grace in the sight of my lord."

Here was Esau, that had submitted to a very disgraceful series of cheatings and conspiracies on the part of Jacob to obtain supremacy and secure rights of primogeniture. After an absence of twenty years Jacob returns, and, fearing his brother's anger, he humbles himself to that mode of address. But this is to be said: In Oriental countries a great deal of such ceremoniousness does not mean any more than you mean when you say "Good-bye." Interpreted, it is, *God be with you;* but you never think of that. "Good-bye," "How do you do?" and Good morning," are modes of address which, if filled out with their primitive meaning, would have a very weighty significance; but as they are ordinarily employed they signify very little; and much of Oriental address is to be set down simply as belonging to the manners of the race. Even down to the present day Oriental salutations by the way are burdensomely, and indeed absurdly, ceremonious. Nevertheless, the attitude of Jacob before Esau, as I have said, was extremely politic, and not at all heroic.

"So Esau returned that day on his way unto Seir; and Jacob journeyed to Succoth, and built him an house, and made booths [corrals, I suppose; fences that they might be saved from wild beasts, or plundering Arabs] for his cattle."

How long Jacob lived there is uncertain—probably not

less than five or six years. It may have been ten years. We have no definite knowledge on this point.

"And Jacob came to Shalem, a city of Shechem, which is in the land of Canaan, when he came from Padan aram; and pitched his tent before the city. And he bought a parcel of a field, where he had spread his tent, at the hand of the children of Hamor, Shechem's father, for an hundred pieces of money. And he erected there an altar, and called it El-elohe-Israel [God, the God of Israel]."

At this point there comes in a view of the social condition that surrounded Jacob. The thirty-fourth chapter contains, what I shall not read, an account of the conduct of his sons toward the Shechemites or the Hivite community. The Hivites were decendants of Noah. They are called Midlanders, but I think they might more properly be called villagers, as they lived in a town. It seems that Jacob had but a single daughter, Dinah ; and, according to the loose manners that prevailed in that age, the oldest son of the king, seeing her, wooed her with unwilling consent, and, loving her, desired that she should be affianced to him, and sought at the hands of Jacob permission to pay a large dowry and make her his accredited wife ; but as he had put shame upon her, the brothers felt it to be an outrage against their family. Their only sister had been humbled ; and although it was proposed to give her honorable wedlock,—to make her, as it were, a ruler in the land,—they utterly refused it. They however pretended that if the whole city would submit to the Abrahamic rite of circumcision, so as to become members of the house of Israel, they would consent. Strangely enough, according to the narrative, these conditions were complied with by the entire community; but then, selecting the most favorable time, the brothers, with their servants, fell upon them and completely destroyed the inhabitants of the city, except the women and children.

Jacob himself was thoroughly indignant ; the outrage he never could forget; but he was politic, and he did not interfere; he raised no difficulty; and when he came to speak of it you will observe that he said to Simeon and Levi ;—

"Ye have troubled me to make me to stink among the inhabitants of the land, among the Canaanites and the Perizzites: and I being few in number, they shall gather themselves together against me, and slay me; and I shall be destroyed, I and my house."

They defended themselves, saying, "Should he deal with our sister as with an harlot?"

They stood for the moment on higher ground than he did. The outrage to Dinah had been an indignity to the whole household, and they justified their revenge for this natural reason; but all Jacob thought of was its inexpediency. He feared that it would array all the inhabitants of the land against him and his people.

He now journeyed from that neighborhood, thinking it convenient to get away from there, and went to see his father Isaac, who was still alive.

"And God said unto Jacob, Arise, go up to Beth-el."

To this, and more in the same connection, I shall recur. Isaac, we do not know how many years afterwards, dies, and Esau comes from the south,—from Mount Seir, or that region,—and he and Jacob go and bury their father with Abraham, in the cave of Machpelah, in the southern part of Judea, where still later Jacob himself was buried.

Before closing the history of Jacob, we will interpose an intermediate history. In order to that, it is necessary that you should have a larger view of the precise state of things.

From Abraham to Jacob not one solitary step, apparently, had been taken toward civilization. What Abraham was, that Isaac was, only weaker; and what Isaac was that Jacob was, a little more spread out. They were dwellers in tents—shepherds. They built no cities. The constructive talent was not with them. They did not develop husbandry. They were not tillers of the soil. They carried on no commerce. They did not buy and sell except at home and in the most limited sphere. Their business was in the fields, tending flocks. They had no literature, no books, no papers, no memorials or monuments with the exception of rude stones cast up upon occasion. There is no evidence that one of the patriarchs ever put his foot across a threshold. They lived out of doors, or in tents. What we call the fine arts were unknown to them. There was no formulated religion, there was no religious service of any kind, there was no domestic policy, there was no instruction in the household or outside of the household, by priest or prophet, down to the time of Jacob's death. If you would know what was the interior condition of the household after Jacob had reached the age of over a hundred years, read the account contained in the thirty-fifth chapter of Genesis.

"God said unto Jacob, Arise, go up to Beth-el, and dwell there: and make there an altar unto God, that appeared unto thee when thou fleddest from the face of Esau thy brother. Then Jacob said unto his household, and to all that were with him, Put away the strange gods that are among you, and be clean, and change your garments."

It seems that while this patriarch believed in the true God his multiform household were going to take with them their own idols, and continue their superstitious idolatry.

"Let us arise and go up to Beth-el; and I will make there an altar unto God, who answered me in the day of my distress, and was with me in the way which I went. And they gave unto Jacob all the strange gods which were in their hand, and all their earrings which were in their ears; and Jacob hid them under the oak, which was by Shechem. And they journeyed."

Up to this time, in the life of Abraham, Isaac, and Jacob, the condition of the household, and their patriarchal condition, might have been described by the simple term, *nothing*. And yet, here was the egg that was to be the eagle.

Now some other influences must come in; for, if there was to be no other influence except that of father and son in the shepherd life—unless there had been some interruption, some inoculation, some dislocation—they would have been Arab Bedouins to this hour: there could never have been any growth through pastoral life. The life of hunting is the lowest, and as long as that prevailed there could be no improvement among the people. Our Indians can never be improved as long as they remain hunters. The first step from hunting is pastoral life. When men depend upon gaining their food by hunting, pastoral life is impossible to them. They cannot thus lay foundations of permanence. There must always be one step beyond that before there can be great improvement—namely, that of agriculture, or husbandry. And it is not until that is supplemented by manufacturing that civilization begins to develop. When upon manufacturing there come constructive improvements, then the necessity of commerce enters in. Agriculture, manufacturing, and commerce are the three elements through which God has conducted the human family, and developed their social and moral nature. Such an education did not come in the patriarchal period; but it came through the mediation of Joseph. The history of Joseph, which is one of the most exquisite of dramas or stories ever read, was the first step of civilization; and without speaking of the later years of Jacob to-night, I shall run briefly through this story or history.

Egypt, at this time, was the only civilized nation of the world. Not only was there not another, but there never had been. It was before the era of semi-civilization in China. It was earlier than the civilization that existed under Babylonian and Assyrian emperors. There was on the globe but one nation that had institutions and civilization; and it was necessary to send the shepherds to school to that nation. The question was, How were they to be sent? On this subject there seems to have been no divine communication, no command of God, no conviction, in the mind of the patriarch; but, as shown by the history, the firstborn of Rachel's children, next to the last of the sons of Jacob, Benjamin coming after, was to be the instrument by which it was to be accomplished. We cannot trace the whole as it actually occurred. We can only glance at it through the incomplete but vivid sketches that remain to us.

Rachel had died. In the thirty-fifth chapter of Genesis, at the sixteen subsequent verses, is an account of her death. It is matchless for its natural simplicity and depth.

"And they journeyed from Beth-el; and there was but a little way to come to Ephrath: and Rachel travailed, and she had hard labor. And it came to pass, when she was in hard labor, that the midwife said unto her, Fear not; thou shalt have this son also. And it came to pass, as her soul was in departing [for she died], that she called his name Ben-oni [Son of my Sorrow]: but his father called him Benjamin [Son of the Right Hand]. And Rachel died, and was buried in the way to Ephrath, which is Beth-lehem. And Jacob set a pillar upon her grave: that is the pillar of Rachel's grave unto this day."

You will recollect, if you enter into the full poetic power of this scene, that when Herod destroyed the children, after hearing from the wise men, it was said that there was "a voice heard and lamentation and weeping, and great mourning, Rachel weeping for her children, and would not be comforted, because they were not." Rachel is regarded as the mother of Israel, and the figure was that when those children were slaughtered in Bethlehem, the very mother-form of Rachel rose out of her grave, which was in that neighborhood, and that her voice was heard in lamentation. Benjamin was the youngest son, born at the expense of her life. Joseph was about seventeen years old at this time. He was apparently the only pure and sweet nature in the whole twelve sons. What the other sons were is detailed in the recorded history. The terrible curse that Jacob pronounced against them on his death-bed, his judgment upon them, was a revelation of their nature, which was hard, coarse, cruel, and avaricious. Such were the twelve heads of the twelve tribes.

Joseph, being yet too young to become a servitor of his father's property, was sent with some other sons to assist. It appears that Jacob regarded him with special tenderness because he was the son of his old age. It is said that "he made him a coat of many colors"—which is a bad rendering. He made him a mantle which indicated rank, and made it long so that it reached down to the ankles, with sleeves that extended to the wrists. It was a mantle which represented a certain condition. "When his brethren saw that their father loved him more than all his brethren they hated him, and could not speak peaceably unto him."

Things were not bettered when Joseph, seeing their abomination, went back and told tales of them; and to make things worse, he had two unlucky dreams.

"And he said unto them, Hear, I pray you, this dream which I have dreamed: for, behold, we were binding sheaves in the field, and, lo, my sheaf arose, and also stood upright; and, behold, your sheaves stood round about, and made obeisance to my sheaf. And his brethren said to him, Shalt thou indeed reign over us? or shalt thou indeed have dominion over us? And they hated him yet the more for his dreams, and for his words."

He got himself into trouble with his father, too.

"And he dreamed yet another dream, and told it his brethren, and said, Behold, I have dreamed a dream more; and, behold, the sun and the moon and the eleven stars made obeisance to me."

That was a high-flying dream. It made such an impression on him that he went home and told it to his father, and his father rebuked him, and said unto him:—

"What is this dream that thou hast dreamed? Shall I and thy mother and thy brethren indeed come to bow down ourselves to thee to the earth? And his brethren envied him; but his father observed the saying."

Although the old father had thought it fit to rebuke Joseph, he rather liked the saying. There was something in the flavor of it which pleased his parental love.

Now, upon this state of facts, Joseph was sent by his father to look out for his brethren. He went to report their progress. When they saw him coming their ill-will broke out, and they said, one to another,—

"Behold, this dreamer cometh. Come now, therefore, and let us slay him."

They had probably had a conference on the subject before, and the time seemed to be at hand when they could avenge themselves. Reuben, the oldest, interposed. Being the firstborn, he had the general responsibility of the brood of brothers — and a precious brood they were! He said, "Shed no blood, but cast him into this pit that is in the wilderness."

There were many pits, caves, fissures, cracks, in that limestone country, and Reuben advised putting Joseph in one of them—for he meant to rescue him, and deliver him to his father. So Joseph was put in a pit by his brethren, and they sat down to their meal, and Judah, the next, interposed and said :—

"What profit is it if we slay our brother, and conceal his blood? Come, and let us sell him to the Ishmaelites, and let not our hand be upon him; for he is our brother and our flesh."

He was too precious to leave to perish in the pit, and seeing a band of merchants, Ishmaelitish traders, coming, they sold him to them. In those days merchants or traders took caravans down through the southern towns and villages, and bought anything or sold anything if thereby they could make money; and these Ishmaelites bought Joseph from his brethren for twenty pieces of silver.

"And Reuben returned unto the pit; and, behold, Joseph was not in the pit; and he rent his clothes. And he returned unto his brethren, and said, The child is not; and I, whither shall I go?"

What account should he give to his father? A touch of nature and of gentleness!

"And they took Joseph's coat, and killed a kid of the goats, and dipped the coat in the blood; and they sent the coat of many colors, and they brought it to their father; and said, This have we found: know now whether it be thy son's coat or no. And he knew it, and said, It is my son's coat; an evil beast hath devoured him; Joseph is without doubt rent in pieces. And Jacob rent his clothes, and put sackcloth upon his loins, and mourned for his son many days. And all his sons and all his daughters rose up to comfort him; but he refused to be comforted; and he said, For I will go down into the grave unto my son mourning. Thus his father wept for him. And the Midianites sold him into Egypt unto Potiphar, an officer of Pharaoh's, and captain of the guard."

So, strangely enough, circuitously, and by an unexpected course of events, the first steps were taken by which the Israelitish people were to build up a national life.

The history goes on to show that Joseph's wisdom and sagacity were appreciated. Passing by some sad scenes in the life of Judah, which are scarcely proper to read in public but which are invaluable as a part of the recorded history of this people in their uncivilized and early condition, we come to the selling of Joseph by the Ishmaelites to Potiphar, the captain of Pharaoh's guard.

"And his master saw that the Lord was with him, and that the Lord made all that he did to prosper in his hand. And Joseph found grace in his sight, and he served him: and he made him overseer over his house, and all that he had he put into his hand."

Potiphar's wife, a sensuous and corrupt woman, looked upon Joseph with eyes of solicitation, and sought to win him to her pleasure, which he resisted, because it would be both an evil recompense for the confidence his master reposed in him and a sin against God; and in that age and under those circumstances it was a trait of heroism which I think marked Joseph as one of the first in this long and remarkable line, that had reached the ground of high moral principle. The woman turned upon him in her anger, and slandered him to her husband, who, believing his wife, threw Joseph into prison. There for a time he remained in disgrace; but as it was known that he had interpreted certain dreams, and that the interpretations came out right, Pharaoh, who had dreams also (where men have not a great deal of knowledge they always have a good many dreams), called Joseph to interpret his dreams; and the interpretation came out right; and he was rewarded by being made a grand leader, next to Pharaoh himself.

Foreseeing years of famine, Joseph advised his monarch, Pharaoh, to build houses, and collect the surplus of the food in the land, and store it up. Then came the seven years of famine, and the people, soon exhausting their slender savings, began to be in want, and applied to their parental head, Pharaoh, for relief; and he turned them over to Joseph. And what did Joseph do? Had he any sense of right and justice toward the men, women, and children who appealed to him? Not at all. Upright and just, as we have seen him to be, he was of his age, and looked upon the people as slaves or cattle. He sold them corn. They bought, as long as their money held out; then they sold cattle to him for corn; and then their lands; and at last offered themselves as slaves, and he took possession of all these hungry, starving creatures. So, under his advice, the whole property and population of the land were brought into bondage to the royal family.

I need not say how this looks to us now. It did not look so to him then. At that time the ideas were not born which in our day we are proud of, and on which our prosperity rests. This history is of a man, and of a man standing high on moral principle, but living in a period before the true inspiration of the race had developed those lofty conceptions of the value of the individual man and of the rights of the people which prevail in the present age of civilization.

It came to pass while Joseph was thus engaged, that the famine—before it had driven the whole body of the people of Egypt into the snare and toils of the royal family, but while yet the Egyptian granaries were full—reached northward, or northeastward, and was felt in Palestine; and it was determined to send down to Egypt for corn. So Joseph's brethren went down. I do not know as I can read all of this. I never did succeed in reading the whole of Joseph's life without having my voice stagger a good deal.

"And Joseph's ten brethren went down to buy corn in Egypt. But Benjamin, Joseph's brother, Jacob sent not with his brethren; for he said, Lest peradventure mischief befall him. And the sons of Israel came to buy corn among those that came: for the famine was in the land of Canaan.

"And Joseph was the governor over the land, and he it was that sold to all the people of the land: and Joseph's brethren came, and bowed down themselves before him with their faces to the earth. And Joseph saw his brethren, he knew them, but made himself strange unto them, and spake roughly unto them; and he said unto them, Whence come ye? And they said, From the land of Canaan to buy food. And Joseph knew his brethren, but they knew not him. And Joseph remembered the dreams which he dreamed of them, and said unto them, Ye are spies; to see the nakedness of the land ye are come. And they said unto him, Nay, my lord, but to buy food are thy servants come. We are all one man's sons; we are true men, thy servants are no spies. And he said unto them, Nay, but to see the nakedness of the land ye are come. And they said, Thy servants are twelve brethren, the sons of one man in the land of Canaan; and, behold, the youngest is this day with our father, and one is not. And Joseph said unto them, That is it that I spake unto you, saying, Ye are spies: hereby ye shall be proved: by the life of Pharaoh ye shall not go forth hence, except your youngest brother come hither. Send one of you, and let him fetch your brother, and ye shall be kept in prison, that your words may be proved, whether there be any truth in you: or else by the life of Pharaoh surely ye are spies. And he put them all together into ward three days.

"And Joseph said unto them the third day, This do and live; for I fear God: If ye be true men, let one of your brethren be bound in the house of your prison: go ye, carry corn for the famine of your houses: but bring your youngest brother unto me; so shall your words be verified, and ye shall not die. And they did so."

Now comes the after part of the brutality of these men.

"And they said one to another, We are verily guilty concerning our brother, in that we saw the anguish of his soul, when he besought us, and we would not hear; therefore is this distress come upon us."

Thousands of men, in the midst of their wickedness, have no conscience at all, but when they are caught, and the legitimate results of wrongdoing begin to distill fear on them, that rouses conscience in them; and they see the nature of cause and effect.

"And Reuben answered them, saying, Spake I not unto you, saying, Do not sin against the child; and ye would not hear? therefore, behold, also his blood is required. And they knew not that Joseph understood them; for he spake unto them by an interpreter. And he turned himself about from them, and wept; and returned to them again, and communed with them, and took from them Simeon, and bound him before their eyes. Then Joseph commanded to fill their sacks with corn, and to restore every man's money into his sack, and to give them provision for the way: and thus did he unto them. And they laded their asses with the corn, and departed thence. And as one of them opened his sack to give his ass provender in the inn, he espied his money; for, behold, it was in his sack's mouth. And he said unto his brethren, My money is restored; and, lo, it is even in my sack; and their heart failed them, and they were afraid, saying one to another, What is this that God hath done unto us?"

They went back to their father, Jacob, and gave him an account of their treatment, telling him that they had been severely handled.

"The man, who is the lord of the land, spake roughly to us, and took us for spies of the country. And we said unto him, We are true men; we are no spies: we be twelve brethren, sons of our father; one is not, and the youngest is this day with our father in the land of Canaan. And the man, the lord of the country, said unto us, Hereby shall I know that ye are true men; leave one of your brethren here with me, and take food for the famine of your households, and be gone: and bring your youngest brother unto me: then shall I know that ye are no spies, but that ye are true men: so will I deliver you your brother, and ye shall traffic in the land."

They give their father an account, also, of their finding in their sacks the money that they had paid.

"And Jacob their father said unto them, Me have ye bereaved of my children: Joseph is not, and Simeon is not, and ye will take Benjamin away: all these things are against me. And Reuben spake unto his father, saying, Slay my two sons, if I bring him not to thee: deliver him into my hand, and I will bring him to thee again. And he said, My son shall not go down with you; for his brother is dead, and he is left alone: if mischief befall him by the way in the which ye go, then shall ye bring down my gray hairs with sorrow to the grave."

Whatever else Jacob was, or was not, he was a *father*. So they abode at home. But the famine continued, and pressed them, so that the father told them to go down again to Egypt for food. They replied that they could not go without Benjamin.

"And Israel said, Wherefore dealt ye so ill with me, as to tell the man whether ye had yet a brother? And they said, The man asked us straitly of our state, and of our kindred, saying, Is your father yet alive? have ye another brother? and we told him according to the tenor of his words: could we certainly know that he would say, Bring your brother down?

"And Judah said unto Israel his father, Send the lad with me, and we will arise and go; that we may live, and not die, both we, and thou, and also our little ones. I will be surety for him; of my hand shalt thou require him: if I bring him not unto thee, and set him before thee, then let me bear the blame forever: for except we had lingered, surely now we had returned this second time.

"And their father Israel said unto them, If it must be so now, do this; take of the best fruits in the land in your vessels, and carry down the man a present, a little balm, and a little honey, spices, and myrrh, nuts, and almonds: and take double money in your hand; and the money that was brought again in the mouth of your sacks, carry it again in your hand; peradventure it was an oversight: take also your brother, and arise, go again unto the man: and God Almighty give you mercy before the man, that he may send away your other brother, and Benjamin. If I be bereaved of my children, I am bereaved.

"And the men took that present, and they took double money in their hand, and Benjamin; and rose up, and went down to Egypt, and stood before Joseph. And when Joseph saw Benjamin with them, he said to the ruler of his house, Bring these men home, and slay, and make ready; for these men shall dine with me at noon. And the man did as Joseph bade; and the man brought the men into Joseph's house.

"And the men were afraid, because they were brought into Joseph's house; and they said, Because of the money that was returned in our sacks at the first time are we brought in; that he may seek occasion against us, and fall upon us, and take us for bondmen, and our asses. And they came near to the steward of Joseph's house, and they communed with him at the door of the house, and said, O sir, we came indeed down at the first time to buy food: and it came to pass, when we came to the inn, that we opened our sacks, and, behold, every man's money was in the mouth of his sack, our money in full weight: and we have brought it again in our hand. And other money have we brought down in our hands to buy food: we cannot tell who put our money in our sacks. And he said, Peace be to you, fear not: your God, and the God of your father, hath given you treasure in your sacks: I had your money. And he brought Simeon out unto them.

"And the man brought the men into Joseph's house, and gave them water, and they washed their feet; and he gave their asses provender. And they made ready the present against Joseph came at noon: for they heard that they should eat bread there.

"And when Joseph came home, they brought him the present which was in their hand into the house, and bowed themselves to him to the earth. And he asked them of their welfare, and said, Is your father well, the old man of whom ye spake? Is he yet alive? And they answered, Thy servant our father is in good health, he is yet alive. And they bowed down their heads, and made obeisance. And he lifted up his eyes, and saw his brother Benjamin, his mother's son, and said, Is this your younger brother, of whom ye spake unto me? And he said, God be gracious unto thee, my son.

"And Joseph made haste; for his bowels did yearn upon his brother: and he sought where to weep; and he entered into his chamber, and wept there. And he washed his face, and went out, and refrained himself, and said, Set on bread."

Then he feasted with them, taking pains to pay special attention to Benjamin, to see if there lurked toward him the same animosity he had experienced, on the part of the brethren. Then he sent them away.

"And he commanded the steward of his house, saying, Fill the men's sacks with food, as much as they can carry, and put every man's money in his sack's mouth. And put my cup, the silver cup, in the sack's mouth of the youngest, and his corn money. And he did according to the word that Joseph had spoken.

"As soon as the morning was light, the men were sent away, they and their asses. And when they were gone out of the city, and not yet far off, Joseph said unto his steward, Up, follow after the men; and when thou dost overtake them, say unto them, Wherefore have ye rewarded evil for good? Is not this it in which my lord drinketh, and whereby indeed he divineth? ye have done evil in so doing.

"And he overtook them, and he spake unto them these same words. And they said unto him, Wherefore saith my lord these words? God forbid that thy servants should do according to this thing. Behold, the money which we found in our sacks' mouth we brought again unto thee out of the land of Canaan: how then should we steal out of thy lord's house silver or gold? With whomsoever of thy servants it be found, both let him die, and we also will be my lord's bondmen. And he said, Now also let it be according unto your words: he with whom it is found shall be my servant; and ye shall be blameless. Then they speedily took down every man his sack to the ground, and opened every man his sack. And he searched, and began at the eldest, and left at the youngest: and the cup was found in Benjamin's sack.

"Then they rent their clothes, and laded every man his ass, and returned to the city. And Judah and his brethren came to Joseph's house; for he was yet there: and they fell before him on the ground.

"And Joseph said unto them, What deed is this that ye have done? wot ye not that such a man as I can certainly divine? And Judah said, What shall we say unto my lord? what shall we speak? or how shall we clear ourselves? God hath found out the iniquity of thy servants: behold, we are my lord's servants, both we, and he also with whom the cup is found. And he said, God forbid that I should do so: but the man in whose hand the cup is found, he shall be my servant; and as for you, get you up in peace unto your father.

"Then Judah came near unto him, and said, Oh my lord, let thy servant, I pray thee, speak a word in my lord's ears, and let not thine anger burn against thy servant: for thou art even as Pharaoh. My lord asked his servants, saying, Have ye a father, or a brother? And we said unto my lord, We have a father, an old man, and a child of his old age, a little one; and his brother is dead, and he alone is left of his mother, and his father loveth him. And thou saidst unto thy servants, Bring him down unto me, that I may set mine eyes upon him. And we said unto my lord, The lad cannot leave his father: for if he should leave his father, his father would die. And thou saidst unto thy servants, Except your youngest brother come down with you, ye shall see my face no more. And it came to pass when we came up unto thy servant my father, we told him the words of my lord. And our father said, Go again, and buy us a little food. And we said, We cannot go down: if our youngest brother be with us, then will we go down: for we may not see the man's face, except our youngest brother be with us. And thy servant my father said unto us, Ye know that my wife bare me two sons: and the one went out from me, and I said, Surely he is torn in pieces; and I saw him not since: and if ye take this also from me, and mischief befall him, ye shall bring down my gray hairs with sorrow to the grave. Now therefore when I come to thy servant my father, and the lad be not with us; seeing that his life is bound up in the lad's life; it shall come to pass, when he seeth that the lad is not with us, that he will die: and thy servants shall bring down the gray hairs of thy servant our father with sorrow to the grave. For thy servant became surety for the lad unto my father, saying, If I bring him not unto thee, then I shall bear the blame to my father for ever. Now therefore, I pray thee, let thy servant abide instead of the lad a bondman to my lord; and let the lad go up with his brethren. For how shall I go up to my father, and the lad be not with me? lest peradventure I see the evil that shall come on my father."

Joseph had proved his brethren pretty well, and found that they were better men than might have been supposed, and that they had a loving reverence and natural affection for their father.

"Then Joseph could not refrain himself before all them that stood by him; and he cried, Cause every man to go out from me. And there stood no man with him, while Joseph made himself known unto his brethren. And he wept aloud: and the Egyptians and the house of Pharaoh heard. And Joseph said unto his brethren, I am Joseph; doth my father yet live? And his brethren could not answer him: for they were troubled at his presence. And Joseph said unto his brethren, Come near to me, I pray you. And they came near. And he said, I am Joseph your brother, whom ye sold into Egypt. Now therefore be not grieved, nor angry with yourselves, that ye sold me hither: for God did send me before you to preserve life."

With many other gracious words he comforted them, he clothed them, he made a royal feast for them, and he sent them back to the father, to tell him all that was done, and bring the old man himself down to Egypt.

And so these wandering clans, these tribes that were the nomads of the desert, who after three hundred years had not taken a step in advance, were by this strange route, this romantic history, brought down into Egypt to receive, through the next four hundred years, the rudiments of that knowledge by which they were to become a nation to which the whole civilized world is indebted for its best laws, its noblest morality, its sweetest domestic affections, and its profoundest aspirations! From so lowly a beginning did there ever spring so grand a result in posterity?

As a seed no bigger than a grain of mustard seed, the smallest of all seeds, cast into the earth, grows and becomes a tree so large that the fowls of the air sit in its branches, so this rude nucleus, this warfare of wild passions, this wandering tribe of raw, rash men, developed at last a civilization founded, not upon art nor upon the intellect as in Greece, not upon organization and iron power as in Rome, but upon the deepest moral convictions of which human nature is capable.

Next Sabbath evening I propose to give some account of the closing scenes of the life of Joseph, and also of the history of the Israelites in Egypt.

This has brought us to the beginnings of what may be called the sound historical ground—the formation of institutions and the Mosaic economy ; and through these I shall go with such haste as is compatible with a fair conception of the benefits conferred by that economy upon the whole human family.

VIII.

JOSEPH.

I shall endeavor, to-night, to conclude what remarks I have to make on the first book of the Old Testament Scriptures—the book of Genesis—the book of the origins or beginnings of things.

Last Sunday night we closed with the account of the disclosure of Joseph to his brethren when famine drove them down to Egypt. In all literature there is not a more exquisite little interlude of history than that. To-night I begin with the tidings which went up with them on their return to the old man, their father, now over a hundred years of age, sitting in his tent, surrounded by his flocks and his serving men in Palestine. It was the saddest message, and the most joyful, that men ever carried to men.

The patriarchs, as they are called,—the twelve heads of the twelve tribes,—were obliged to go back to their father and narrate to him the history of their wickedness, their unnatural crime against their brother Joseph, and the still more heinous and cruel act against their father Jacob, whose sufferings they had with sealed lips caused through the years, when they let him know that the beloved of his heart, the firstborn of the dearest one, Rachel, was still alive. The time had come.

"And they went up out of Egypt, and came into the land of Canaan unto Jacob their father, and told him, saying, Joseph is yet alive, and he is governor over all the land of Egypt. And Jacob's heart fainted [stopped, it is in the original], for he believed them not."

No words can paint a natural phenomenon more exquisitely.

Sunday evening, December 15, 1878. Lesson: Psa. cxlvii.

The child has been away from home since he was six years old, upon the sea or land ; for fifteen or twenty years he has not been heard from, and is given up for dead. No tidings have come from him until some day in winter, when, as twilight is falling, he enters his father's house, where his mother, old and trembling, sees him, and sees him not. The father, gasping, says, "You are not my son!" When he says, "Mother, mother, I am your son," she neither believes him nor disbelieves him. Joy is sometimes so great that we cannot believe that it is joy to us, and we thrust it away as if it were a dream and an imposition.

"And Jacob's heart fainted, for he believed them not. And they told him all the words of Joseph, which he had said unto them : and when he saw the wagons which Joseph had sent to carry him, the spirit of Jacob their father revived."

How characteristic still! The sense of property in the old patriarch was always a very keen sense. He would not believe his boys, and he had good reason to doubt them ; but when he saw the property, that convinced him.

"And Israel said, It is enough ; Joseph my son is yet alive : I will go and see him before I die."

They went down to Egypt.

"And they took their cattle, and their goods, which they had gotten in the land of Canaan, and came into Egypt, Jacob, and all his seed with him : his sons, and his sons' sons with him, his daughters, and his sons' daughters, and all his seed brought he with him into Egypt."

Then follows the enumeration of them all. I am personally interested in one fact only. After mentioning the rest he comes down to Joseph's children—Manasseh and Ephraim ; then he names the sons of Benjamin — Belah, *Becher*, etc. It is always a matter of profound interest for one to be able to trace his genealogy !

"And he [Jacob] sent Judah before him unto Joseph, to direct his face unto Goshen."

There has been some dispute (of course there has ; there never did anything happen in the world that there was not some dispute about) as to where Goshen was. The best and most recent authorities, and I think the strong probabilities, place it upon the east side of the delta of the Nile in lower Egypt. It was not included in Egypt proper. Although it belonged to Egypt, it was a strip of territory extending about thirty miles, indefinitely, north or south, or east or west, between the delta of the Nile and the great wilderness beyond. It was a pastoral country, and was on that account in the possession of the horsemen of Pharaoh, with his cattle. There the king had directed Joseph to bring his father.

"And Joseph made ready his chariot, and went up to meet Israel his father, to Goshen, and presented himself unto him; and he fell on his neck, and wept on his neck a good while."

A silent scene—a scene to be thought of; but not in any way to be disturbed by exposition.

"And [at last] Israel said unto Joseph, Now let me die, since I have seen thy face, because thou art yet alive."

He felt as though after this there could be no other blessing half so great. He had reached the climax of earthly joy. Why should he not die in the blessedness of that moment? It was that same feeling that inspired Simeon, in later days, when he said, "Lord, now lettest thou thy servant depart in peace, according to thy word: for mine eyes have seen thy salvation."

"And Joseph said unto his brethren, and unto his father's house, I will go up, and shew Pharaoh, and say unto him, My brethren, and my father's house, which were in the land of Canaan, are come unto me; and the men are shepherds, for their trade hath been to feed cattle; and they have brought their flocks, and their herds, and all that they have. And it shall come to pass, when Pharaoh shall call you, and shall say, What is your occupation? that ye shall say, Thy servants' trade hath been about cattle from our youth even until now, both we, and also our fathers: that ye may dwell in the land of Goshen."

Then the compiler adds:—

" For every shepherd is an abomination unto the Egyptians."

That is to say, the pastoral life was next to the lowest. The hunter's life only was one step below it. The Egyptians were highly refined and cultivated—the only cultivated people on the globe; and they looked down on any man whose business was lowly. We have terms that convey the contempt they felt. When we speak of a cowherd or swineherd we use language which implies that Norman contempt of Saxon in which the artificers and agriculturists of Egypt indulged towards the wandering herdsmen of the plains, and which I have no doubt they expressed in good round Egyptian words.

It has been supposed, however, that Joseph's Pharaoh was of that Semitic race of Shepherd Kings who overran Egypt, and ruled tyrannically there for several hundred years; and that he welcomed these shepherds from Canaan as likely to be friends of his dynasty. However that may be, Joseph's brethren appeared before the king, and repeated their catechism very well.

"And Pharaoh spake unto Joseph, saying, Thy father and thy brethren are come unto thee; the land of Egypt is before thee; in the best of the land make thy father and brethren to dwell; in the land of Goshen let them dwell; and if thou knowest any men of activity among them, then make them rulers over my cattle."

Now comes one of the most unique and charming scenes, I think, in this pastoral history—the meeting between the king of Egypt and the wandering old sheik of the desert—Pharoah and Jacob.

"And Joseph brought in Jacob his father, and set him before Pharaoh and Jacob blessed Pharaoh."

He did not wait for the king's benediction. Ripe old man—for he *was* ripe. When he beheld this monarch in his regal splendor, which must have dazzled the eyes, one would think, of a man who had lived in tents and dwelt in a wilderness all his life, when Jacob was brought before the proudest monarch on the globe, he blessed him. There was dignity and pride for you! Without pretense, there was the rising of a man into his true position of superiority, by his benediction. So he set Pharaoh down in his proper place.

"And Pharaoh said unto Jacob, How old art thou? And Jacob said unto Pharaoh, The days of the years of my pilgrimage are an hundred and thirty years; few and evil have the days of the years of my life been, and have not attained unto the days of the years of the life of my fathers in the days of their pilgrimage. And Jacob blessed Pharaoh, and went out from before Pharaoh."

That needs nothing more.

The next scene is that in which Jacob blesses the children of Joseph, and adopts them into the tribal relation. There was no tribe of Joseph. There were two half-tribes, of Ephraim and Manasseh. These were the two sons born to Joseph while he dwelt in Egypt.

"And it came to pass after these things [you are to bear in mind that Joseph was a grand official of Egypt], that one told Joseph, Behold, thy father is sick: and he took with him his two sons, Manasseh and Ephraim. And one told Jacob, and said, Behold, thy son Joseph cometh unto thee: and Israel strengthened himself [summoned up the whole of his energy in his weak state], and sat upon the bed [probably upon the edge of the bed]. And Jacob said unto Joseph [this was a retrospect of his life], God Almighty appeared unto me at Luz in the land of Canaan, and blessed me; and said unto me, Behold, I will make thee fruitful, and multiply thee, and I will make of thee a multitude of people; and will give this land to thy seed after thee for an everlasting possession. And now thy two sons, Ephraim and Manasseh, which were born unto thee in the land of Egypt before I came unto thee into Egypt, are mine; as Reuben and Simeon, they shall be mine. And thy issue, which thou begettest after them, shall be thine, and shall be called after the name of their brethren in their inheritance. And as for me, when I came from Padan, Rachel died by me in the land of Canaan in the way, when yet there was but a little way to come unto Ephrath: and I buried her there in the way of Ephrath; the same is Beth-lehem."

There is something indescribably touching in the retrospect this old patriarch gives of his whole life. There were but two things that stood up in it, apparently. He had had a great experience both at home and at Padan-aram, and he had been for a long time an honored chief among the neighboring nations; but only two things seemed to remain to him worth remembering. One was, that God had appeared to him and filled his soul with a sense of divine presence, and promised him great blessings in his posterity; and the other was Rachel. These were the two great controlling facts of his life—*God* and *Love*. He was talking to Joseph, who was Rachel's first-born, long-delayed child, and he was overwhelmed with emotion.

"And Israel beheld Joseph's sons, and said, Who are these? And Joseph said unto his father, They are my sons, whom God hath given me in this place. And he said, Bring them, I pray thee, unto me, and I will bless them. Now the eyes of Israel were dim for age, so that he could not see. And he brought them near unto him; and he kissed them, and embraced them. And Israel said unto Joseph, I had not thought to see thy face: and, lo, God hath showed me also thy seed. And Joseph brought them out from between his knees, and he bowed himself with his face to the earth. And Joseph took them both, Ephraim in his right hand toward Israel's left hand, and Manasseh in his left hand toward Israel's right hand, and brought them near unto him."

That was the order of their birth; and the blessings of primogeniture were bestowed on the eldest.

Now, you recollect that Esau was first born and Jacob was second, and you remember the disgraceful trick by which Jacob superseded his brother, and became heir apparent, and inherited the blessings of his father Isaac. So when his son Joseph brought his boys, and they were in an attitude such that, in blessing, the right hand, that always carries the idea of power and prominence, should fall upon the first born, Jacob said nothing, but crossed his hands, and put his right hand on the second born, and his left hand on the first born. Through the old man's mind what a curious thread of thought and feeling must have run, that he should have done that!

"And he blessed Joseph, and said, God, before whom my fathers Abraham and Isaac did walk, the God which fed me all my life long unto this day, the Angel which redeemed me from all evil, bless the lads; and let my name be named on them, and the name of my fathers Abraham and Isaac; and let them grow into a multitude in the midst of the earth. And when Joseph saw that his father laid his right hand upon the head of Ephraim, it displeased him: and he held up his father's hand, to remove it from Ephraim's head unto Manasseh's head. And Joseph said unto his father, Not so, my father: for this is the firstborn; put thy right hand upon his head. And his father refused, and said, I know it, my son, I know it: he also shall become a people, and he also shall be great: but truly his younger brother shall be greater than he, and his seed shall become a multitude of nations.

"And he blessed them that day, saying, In thee shall Israel bless, saying, God make thee as Ephraim and as Manasseh: and he set Ephraim before Manasseh.

"And Israel said unto Joseph, Behold, I die: but God shall be with you, and bring you again unto the land of your fathers. Moreover I have given to thee one portion above thy brethren, which I took out of the hand of the Amorite with my sword and with my bow."

This inextinguishable love of the old patriarch was the crowning feature of his character.

Then comes the scene of the prophecy and blessing which Jacob bestows upon his twelve sons. I shall not go through this in detail; or, rather, I shall rapidly run through it, without giving all the explanations that are recorded, because I propose by and by to take the parallel scene of the blessings which Moses uttered in like conditions. It will be a matter of interest to see what was the blessing of Jacob upon the twelve sons, and what the blessing of Moses upon the twelve tribes; and under those conditions we shall recur to it. I will, however, give a few passages from the record on this point. It is a poem. On that account it has been objected to. It is said that folks do not make poems when they are dying. My reply to that is, that they never make them so well at any other time as then. It is said that this was a prophecy made after the event. It may have been, but there is no evidence that there was a necessity for any such strange procedure. I never admit a miracle if I can help it; and I never refuse to admit one if I cannot help it. I believe in miracles and in prophecies; and yet I do not believe that everything wonderful is a miracle; nor do I believe that everything said to be a prophecy is a foretelling.

"And Jacob called unto his sons, and said, Gather yourselves together, that I may tell you that which shall befall you in the last days. Gather yourselves together, and hear, ye sons of Jacob; and hearken unto Israel your father."

It is almost the voice of a bard, and not that of a feeble old man. Are you not familiar with the fact that often, when persons are dying, the whole force of their being goes to the head, so that they manifest transcendent powers in that hour? I know not why at such times men may not be prophets and seers of visions. When in the dying hour men think they behold father and mother and children waiting for them across the border, I know no reason why we should not believe that they see them. There is something sublime in the rising of this old man out of infirmity and almost imbecility in the last moment of his earthly life to pronounce these final utterances.

"Reuben, thou art my firstborn, my might, and the beginning [or first fruits] of my strength, the excellency of dignity, and the excellency of power: unstable as water, thou shalt not excel."

Effervescent as boiling or bubbling water would be a better rendering. It is as if he said, *Thy passions boil up, like water over a fire.* "Thou shalt not excel," would be better rendered, *Thou shalt not have priority or preference.* By reason of Reuben's transgression Jacob would not make him first, although he was his oldest son.

"Simeon and Levi are brethren."

Of course they were; but he meant in a disgraceful sense.

"Instruments of cruelty are in their habitations. O my soul, come not thou into their secret; unto their assembly, mine honor, be not thou united: for in their anger they slew a man [men], and in their selfwill they digged down a wall."

You recollect the history of the Shechemites. You remember how these brothers, by stratagem, acted by way of revenge for the wrong done their sister, destroying the whole male population of this people, driving off their cattle, and committing other depredations.

"Cursed be their anger, for it was fierce; and their wrath, for it was cruel: I will divide them in Jacob, and scatter them in Israel."

It came to pass that for the tribes of Simeon and Levi no territorial limits were appointed, but that they had assigned to them certain cities within the territory of other sons. The tribe of Levi was regarded as the tribe from which the priesthood came; and if I were disposed to spiritualize, as almost all ministers do, finding types and prototypes in the Sacred Scriptures, I should say the fighting qualities of theology in after times came from the tribe of Levi, who was a cruel and belligerent ancestor from the beginning.

"Judah, thou art he whom thy brethren shall praise: thy hand shall be in the neck of thine enemies; thy father's children shall bow down before thee. Judah is a lion's whelp: from the prey, my son, thou art gone up: he stooped down, he couched as a lion, and as an old lion; who shall rouse him up? The scepter shall not depart from Judah, nor a lawgiver from between his feet, until Shiloh come; and unto him shall the gathering of the people be."

You will recall that when the tribes went off to Babylon and were dispersed and lost, it was Judah that maintained his individual tribal existence; that temples were multiplied, and the continuity of religious feeling was with his tribe.

So Jacob goes on until he comes to Joseph, and then the old man's heart breaks out again with a freshet.

"Joseph is a fruitful bough, even a fruitful bough by a well; whose branches run over the wall: the archers have sorely grieved him, and shot at him, and hated him: but his bow abode in strength, and the arms of his hands were made strong by the hands of the mighty God of Jacob; (from thence is the shepherd, the stone of Israel:) even by the God of thy father, who shall help thee; and by the Almighty, who shall bless thee with blessings of heaven above, blessings of the deep that lieth under, blessings of the breasts, and of the womb: the blessings of thy father have prevailed above the blessings of my progenitors unto the utmost bound of the everlasting hills: they shall be on the head of Joseph [for Joseph was Rachel's son], and on the crown of the head of him that was separate from his brethren."

And it is said :—

"When Jacob had made an end of commanding his sons, he gathered up his feet into the bed, and yielded up the ghost, and was gathered unto his people. And Joseph fell upon his father's face, and wept upon him, and kissed him. And Joseph commanded his servants the physicians to embalm his father: and the physicians embalmed Israel."

He was embalmed after the manner of the Egyptians.

Then Joseph goes in to Pharaoh, and asks leave of absence to go up and bury his father, with Abraham and Isaac, in the cave of Machpelah. Permission is granted, and all the servants of Pharaoh, the principal officers of his household, the elders of the land of Egypt, and all the house of Joseph and his brethren, and his father's house except their little ones, their flocks, and their herds, which they left in the land of Goshen, went to make up the funeral procession.

"And there went up with him both chariots and horsemen : and it was a very great company. And they came to the threshingfloor of Atad, which is beyond Jordan. And there they mourned with a great and very sore lamentation : and he made a mourning for his father seven days."

That is to say, they gathered together, and went through ceremonies expressive of grief. There were appointed mourners who chanted funeral songs and uttered exclamations of sorrow. It was thought to be necessary to have a band of hired mourners at funerals in those times, as it is thought in our day that bereaved persons should robe themselves in garments that have been woven in the loom of midnight.

"And when the inhabitants of the land, the Canaanites, saw the mourning in the floor of Atad, they said, This is a grievous mourning to the Egyptians: wherefore the name of it was called Abel-mizraim."

Mizraim is the name of Egypt ; and it is called the *mourning of the Egyptians.*

When Joseph had returned from burying his father, and before his own death, his brethren, with the same sordidness which they had manifested all their life, counseled, " Now that Joseph's father is dead nothing will restrain him, and he will turn upon us ; " and they humbled themselves, and sent a deputation to him, with a lie, undoubtedly, saying ;—

" So shall ye say unto Joseph, Forgive, I pray thee now, the trespass of thy brethren, and their sin ; for they did unto thee evil : and now, we pray thee, forgive the trespass of the servants of the God of thy father.

"And Joseph [who was a great and generous soul] wept when they spake unto him. 'And his brethren also went and fell down before his face ; and they said, Behold, we be thy servants. And Joseph said unto them, Fear not: for am I in the place of God ? But as for you, ye thought evil against me ; but God meant it unto good, to bring to pass, as it is this day, to save much people alive. Now therefore fear ye not: I will nourish you, and your little ones."

That is, all his regal power was for their benefit.

Then came the time of his own dying. He said to his brethren :—

" I die: and God will surely visit you, and bring you out of this land unto the land which he sware to Abraham, to Isaac, and to Jacob. And Joseph took an oath of the children of Israel, saying, God will surely visit you, and ye shall carry up my bones from hence. So Joseph died, being an hundred and ten years old: and they embalmed him, and he was put in a coffin in Egypt."

What matters it to a man where he is when he is dead? What if one's body has been devoted to the surgeon's knife; or plunged in the depths of the sea; or has perished by the flame? No knife, no flame, touches the real man. The body is but the casket in which the jewel lies. And yet, to one that has a thought of the beautiful, how romantic— shall I say poetic?—how intensely natural, it was that Joseph should have longed to be buried by the side of his fathers—that, on account of the glory of the kingdom yet to be raised, which he saw, vaguely perhaps, he should have yearned to be with his ancestors!

I had always supposed that when my father had become old and feeble, he would desire to be buried in old Litchfield; but no; after he became so infirm that he was no longer able to remember words with which to convey what his wishes were, by signs and tokens he said to me, "Bury me by the side of that dear man" (he could not utter the name),—Dr. Nathaniel Taylor, of New Haven, as noble a man as God ever made, and whose heart was knitted to my father's heart, and his to his, with cords that death could not sunder. My father wanted to be buried by his side, if, peradventure, in the morning of the resurrection, when they rose together, they might, with equal wing-beat, fly, at the first dawn, and greet the smile of the Father's face.

Few are they that have this feeling. Unhappy am I, that have not a bit of it.

I have now gone through the book of Genesis: not by any means considering all the details that are of profound interest in it, but only giving a cursory view with reference to the general contents. It is a book of literature. If you accept it as literature it is a book full of benefit and of comfort; but if you undertake to make the book of Genesis authoritative and mandatory on belief and conduct you come wide of that benefit and that comfort. No man can unite it harmoniously with the later revelations of the truth in Christ Jesus; and no man can attempt to make every part of it harmonize with later known facts without demoralizing and injuring himself theologically. It is impertinence to take the utterances and experiences of a child five years old and apply them to a man fifty years old; and it is no less an impertinence to make the needs of nascent tribes a criterion by which to judge of the necessities of men who have arrived at full-grown manhood in the Lord Jesus Christ. As literature, the history of the early developments of the race is invaluable, but as dogma it is useless.

As I have said, the record of Beginnings may be divided into several periods. One is the nebulous stage, which treats of creation. After that comes the destruction, by the flood, of the human race. Then follows a very brief history of the descendants of Noah—especially that particular line which includes the primitive patriarchs, Abraham, Isaac, and Jacob. The last half, or perhaps two-thirds, is occupied in tracing the experiences of these patriarchs. They have produced upon the imagination of the Israelites, and upon the imagination of modern Christians, an impression that is illusory; and I propose, in the remainder of the evening, to give a glance at the actual condition and relations of these men.

In the first place, as I said in an earlier discourse of this series, the patriarchs were not the founders of the organized Jewish nation. They founded nothing. They had no theology. They had no formulated worship. They had no recognized laws. They had no government. The head of the family was the chief and the priest, and did that which according to his fathers' customs was supposed to be right. There were no religious institutions—no places of worship. They founded none, except here and there, for specific reasons, an altar,—as few in the time of Isaac as in the time of Abraham; and as few in the time of Jacob as in the time of Isaac or Abraham. And there was no progress made between the time of Jacob and the time of Joseph, when Jacob died in Egypt.

There is a sense in which these patriarchs stand at the head. A little rill in the mountains flows down and becomes the Amazon; but the Amazon is formed, not by that rill, but by the hundred side-streams that pour in. And yet, the Amazon is said to have had its origin in that little rill, no bigger than my finger.

In that sense the tribes had their origin in the old patriarchs; but when we follow them out, after they had lived two or three hundred years, there were only about seventy that went down into Egypt and took up their residence in the land of Goshen.

We must be very cautious, too, in attributing to them such intercourse with the divine Being as it is claimed in general religious literature that they had. It is not necessary to deny that they had conscious intercourse with God —I believe everyone has that who experiences any disclosure of moral sense; but there is no evidence that they had it in any such sense as it is ordinarily held that they had. In the magnified and exaggerated impressions of both modern and ancient times, I see no evidence of such intercourse. Because a man dreams that he talks with God, and that God directs him to do so and so, it does not follow that that is the teaching of God. The real and discernible personal relations between these men and God were occasional. They were not manifested by a steady stream of influence. They were often only in the form of dreams or impressions on the imagination. In a sense that raised them out of the sphere of natural causes, and indicated that they had direct personal intercourse with God, or that they experienced the operation of the divine mind on theirs, there were but two or three instances. Nothing that they ever did was above the ordinary moderate use of the common faculties. Their whole history unfolded itself naturally. Human nature in them had not risen to any great height. Their knowledge was very limited. Their idea of God— how extensive was it? They believed in one God; but how much was that one God, as they thought of him? What did they think of him? To Abraham he was "the Highest" of all the gods he knew of—the Supreme One—the only real one; to the later patriarchs, he was the God of Abraham, Isaac, and Jacob.

And what did God teach these men on the subject of veracity, and the indispensable necessity of it? There is no record on this point. There is no command which makes truth obligatory, nor is there any rebuke of its violation. There was a principle of honesty and integrity—a kind of varying, unstable principle on which men acted. This exists in every nation on the globe; society could not cohere without it: but that they had anything more in this direction than every tribe on earth has there is no trace. What teaching was given them in regard to polygamy—that vile cancer on the household? What were they taught of that great love which is the exaltation of human nature—the sacred love that exists between one and another? Is it conceivable that in the course of three lives, for nearly three hundred years, while men were supposed to be in intercourse with God, God should have had nothing to impart to his people on the subject of polygamy? However that may be, this evil was suffered to exist and to bear its evil results without rebuke, so far as the Old Testament Scriptures tell us. There was no preconception of the proper status of the household. What steps were taken toward civilization in this and other particulars were taken after their time. They remained shepherds till the very last. They had no laws, institutions, customs, or organized methods, that we should not criticise very severely.

This will appear more plain when we compare the condition of Israel on coming into Egypt with Egypt itself. Egypt was the one civilized nation on the globe when the patriarchs were thrown within her borders. It was a regularly organized government. It was not the best government that, in the light of experiments which men have since made, it was possible to have; but it was a better government than any contemporaneous nation had, and certainly better than these wandering tribes had. It was a stable government. It had a settled order of procedure. It embraced a set of wholesome laws. The Egyptians were an agricultural people. They led, as it were, the nations of the earth. They had also an active commerce; and agriculture and commerce go hand in hand. The agriculture and the commerce were not of the highest type, but they were very important, and it took centuries to compass their development. They had made some advance in art; their sculpture was above that of other nations and their architecture most impressive. In constructive engineering they were pre-eminent. Modern engineers even contemplate with admiration the wonderful feats they accomplished with but few and inferior tools. Gunpowder and nitro-glycerine were unknown; and yet the achievements of quarrying that were performed with poor instruments, we, with all our machinery and steam power, regard with astonishment. Think of carving the Sphinx out of a single rock! Look at the stones selected, from many quarries, for the pyramids, with a wisdom which would do credit to engineers of modern scientific experience. And consider the moving of these stones—for it is said that the methods of doing this were almost as marvelous as the pyramids themselves. And there was also a vast complicated institutional organization of religion, with some notable elements that may well excite our admiration. Here was a nation that had come up and developed to a remarkable degree, compared with which the other nations were as shavings alongside of magnificent trees of the forest.

And yet Abraham, Isaac, and Jacob made a profound impression on the imagination of the later Jewish nation. The Jews half created these Fathers of the primitive period. They clothed them with the luminous robes which they have worn. When they pronounced the names "Abraham," "Isaac," and "Jacob," they did not see those men as they were: they saw them as the heroes they had made them to be—what to the Greeks Hercules was. The patriarchs meant to them what the primitive heroes of almost every nation naturally mean; they were glorified by their originators.

And this estimation of the three great patriarchs has run through Christian literature perhaps even more than through the literature of the Jews. Jacob, the least Christlike, the least spiritual, of them, the man that had the shrewdest sense of property and good management, the politician and statesman, is sometimes extolled to a degree that borders on blasphemy. I have heard prayers commenced by references to him which made me shiver. To the Jews it was a common thing to say, "The God of Abraham, Isaac, and Jacob," or "The God of our fathers," thus exalting these men above all other human beings. To us, what are Abraham, Isaac, and Jacob but dim lights on the remotest horizon of antiquity? And when you come to closely examine them as to their manhood, religion, and spirituality, they will not bear the searching inquisition of the rules of our modern religious knowledge and feeling.

But it will be said, "How is it that the New Testament speaks of them as it does?" You will find that in the twelfth chapter of Hebrews it is shown that Abraham was regarded as having poetic thoughts, that he acted with reference to things which he could not see, things which he expected in the future, things in the air. So did Isaac and Jacob have thoughts of things which had not taken place, but which were to take place in the future, illustrating the power of men through faith in the invisible to act outside of the sensuous. That was a vast gain upon the low, material condition of men of their day. The New Testament speaks of them as they were estimated.

It is said that Christ spoke of them reverentially. That is true. He spoke of them as ancestors, as their descendants were accustomed to speak of them. But one recorded fact is striking: that when the very summit of his own life was reached, before his crucifixion, at the Transfiguration upon the side of the mountain, it was not Abraham nor

Isaac nor Jacob that came over, and in the air were spectators. It was Moses and Elijah that appeared and talked with him. It was Moses who was the founder of the Israelites, in any proper sense of that term; their institutions were derived from the hand of Moses; while their moral instructions came from the prophets, from the time of Samuel down to the end of the long line.

There were, however, three great elements which operated upon these ancient men, and which were transmitted from them to their posterity. First, and most important, there was firm and unwavering faith in the unity of God as distinguished from the polytheism of idolatry. While in other nations almost every natural phenomenon was supposed to be a god, it was borne in upon the mind of Abraham, and transmitted by him to his children, that there was but one God, and that besides him all objects or creatures that were claimed to be gods were idols and lies. The patriarchs held that there was one supreme Creator, Governor, Judge, God; and that truth has been transmitted by their whole posterity.

What if they did not meditate largely upon the attributes of God? What if they did not apprehend the elements of moral government? What if, in that early, twilight age, no religious institutions had yet been evolved? Here was the very center of all true religion—one God; and in that dark, desolate period, these men stood unwavering witnesses to that truth.

Then, next, was the purity of the household. When I hear men say that the life of the world has been wrapped up in its system of religious doctrine, my reply is that in connection with that, as one of the saving influences of mankind, has been the foundation of the family upon purity of life. The household is one ark that has gone far toward carrying nascent peoples and individuals over the perils of dark periods to safety; and the patriarchs, Abraham, Isaac, and Jacob, held their tribes together by the pure household, making the family an ark of purity and safety.

There was one more element in their lives that should be mentioned in this enumeration—namely, their hope in a future, although this hope never amounted to a firm faith. They did not go through the world with their heads down like browsing cattle; their thoughts were directed upward, to a land beyond, where they and their posterity were to dwell after leaving this mortal sphere.

These: *One God*, the *Household* intact and pure, and the *Hope of a Future*, were the three great elements that were developing in the patriarchal period. Though they had not then attained the degree of perfection which they have reached in modern times, they were rooted and grounded. And when we consider that they were, so to speak, the mere letters of the alphabet; when we consider that from these primal elements have been unfolded all the glory of later Christian civilization, we cannot but acknowledge their vast importance to the race, and derive from them a large conception of the methods of God in guiding his people from a low state to a higher.

I accept, then, this Book of Beginnings as the recorded history of the first faint dawnings of that life which has now become so wondrous in its development. I am grateful for the preservation of these records. I value them for the treasures I find in them. They are rich in sweet pictures, admirable touches of nature, which no man would willingly miss. Here were a people that were said to have been led of God; and I believe they were. I think he led them by natural laws—by evolution of their social and moral natures. The book of Genesis shows us the selection of the crude elements; their development and refinement must be seen in later records.

IX.

MOSES.

In pursuing our course of readings from the Old Testament Scriptures, we have completed the first book—the book of the beginnings or origins of things. We leave it with regret. It is a book of delight. It is a book in which the stories take on all romantic forms. It is the book of the infancy of the human race. The pastoral life and histories are poems, and we have taken great pleasure in them.

Now we pass on to the second book, with which definite history begins. We come down to times more nearly within our reach, more nearly within the domain of those instruments of thought by which men have learned to compass and record the truth.

This book is called *Exodus*, from its Greek name in the Septuagint. The Septuagint is the oldest Greek version of the Old Testament in existence. It was made, probably in the third century before Christ, for those who were dispersed abroad, and who spoke, principally, the Greek language, and it was the version commonly used by the Jews in the time of Christ, even in Palestine. In English, the book of Exodus may be called *The Book of the Going Forth, or the Departure.* It is divided, naturally, into two parts: the first nineteen chapters giving, mainly, the history of the departure of the Israelites from Egypt; and from the nineteenth chapter to the end, offering delineations of those institutions, civil and religious, which Moses gave to his people.

Sunday evening, December 22, 1878. LESSON: Psa. cvi.

Of course it is for me, to-night, only to make a beginning upon this great history; and in doing this I must call your attention to the relation which men of ancient thought sustained to the element of time. It might almost be said that in the records of the Old Testament, certainly in its primary, primitive books, the element of time was not thought of. I should almost say that the idea of *chronology* in a literary record had not, in that early day, been invented in such a sense as that in which we use the term.

For example, simply from the book of Genesis who could tell what the time-element was in that era? Who, merely from the Old Testament history, standing between the first Creation and the next natural period, the Flood, could determine the number of years that elapsed? There is no determination of the time-element at all, nor any attempt at it, in the Old Testament; the literary efforts made to determine this element have been made upon hints and incidental facts; and they have never been very successful. From the Flood to the time of Abraham—certainly hundreds of years—there is perfect silence on the subject in the record. From the call of Abraham to the death of Jacob in Egypt, during the patriarchal period, which is supposed to have extended through about two hundred and fifteen years, there is nothing in the narrative upon which a conclusion could be based. Things are not stated definitely, except as regards the ages of men. For the most part they are given; and even they are uncertain as to whether referring to men or tribes; and, for the most part, from those data we are obliged to make our own calculations as to the lapse of time.

Then from the descent into Egypt to the period of Moses, which we are told in the New Testament was about four hundred and seventy years, there is nothing in the older record that gives any idea of the length of the period. It was a timeless history. There appears in this, as in many other things, the impress of an infant race, an infant unfolding, an infant literature. Everything was nascent, undeveloped. And this carries with it a strong impression as to the reality and authenticity of these ancient scriptures. They are as old as men have thought them to be. They are not modern inventions. They bear upon their very face, in their very deficiencies and in their aberrations, the marks of antiquity. They existed before civilization and literature and learning were born into the world. If they had come down to us dressed as perfectly as our own histories are, we should at once have said, "These cannot be the histories of primitive races." The very antiquity of these scriptures is borne out by their incidental deficiencies.

This time-element is very striking when you consider it in its relations to the exactitude of the divine administration in the natural world. Look at the great sphere of astronomy, where everything moves according to accurate mathematical exactness and definiteness; there are no variations or exceptions: everything is positive. Look at the strict accuracy of proportions in chemistry, where all is definite, constant, always and everywhere. In physics the relations are invariably clear, and true to the ascertainable laws of cause and effect, structure and function. In contrast with the accuracy which exists in outward nature, striking is the lack, in this primitive record, of exactitude and definiteness in the processes of human action. It is as if the thoughts of men rose as clouds rise that take on vague forms—indeterminate shapes; and we see in the primitive history traces of this vagueness of thought strangely pervading the records themselves.

In connection with this lack of definiteness and exactitude as regards the time-element, we are to-night brought to the very edge of a gulf. More than four hundred years lie before us, between Joseph and Moses. Out of that period comes not a single voice. There is no evidence, in the Scriptures or elsewhere, so far as the Israelites were concerned, that there was an altar or tabernacle built. The indications are that those four hundred years were years of darkness, silence, mystery. We can penetrate it by using known laws, and by inference; but the record is dead. The sixth and seventh verses of the first chapter of Exodus are separated by four hundred years, without hint or sign.

"And Joseph died, and all his brethren, and all that generation.

"And the children of Israel were fruitful, and increased abundantly, and multiplied, and waxed exceeding mighty; and the land was filled with them."

This covered a period of four hundred years; and there is no record of the great space of time between. If we wish any memorial of it we must take the reflection, as it were, of backward beams of light. We have the history of the Israelites when they came out of Egypt; and as every effect must have a cause, taking the effects which were wrought out in four hundred years, we can come to some knowledge of the causes which must have been in existence during the time.

The question may arise as to whether these people were not under divine care during that period. We have seen that the Old Testament claims that Abraham was especially called of God, and was under his personal supervision and tutelage, that Isaac followed in the same line of divine convoy, and that Jacob was conducted from period to period under the constant inspection and guidance of God: but here spring up twelve heads of Tribes that cover four hundred years in which there is apparently no convoy, no declarative providence over them.

God employs nature. Nature is greater than institutions. It is the parent of institutions. All righteous institutions are but nature applied. God's communications to men by the living voice are not so solemn nor so sublime as the communications of God to men through the voices of nature round about us. Israel was not forgotten or abandoned because in the wisdom of divine providence she was left to vegetate, to become a people, and so to prepare for us a great after-history. This long period was required to develop a nation in numbers. At any rate, it may be said that one thing which did happen during those four hundred years was a mighty increase in the numbers of the nation. Could not that have been done in Palestine? It is very doubtful. It is more than likely, when you consider the preoccupation of the territory by warlike tribes on every side, that the posterity of Abraham and his descendants would have drifted north or east or south, and remained in a nomadic or pastoral life. Now a pastoral life scatters: an agricultural life condenses. The Israelites were carried to a condition in which they would be held together, and be able to keep all that they gathered, and to maintain a cohesive existence. Seventy souls went down into Egypt. It is the general opinion (though the estimates vary from a million to a million and a half, and even two millions), that a million souls came out of Egypt. Here, then, was the nest; and this was the brood!

The region inhabited by them was fitted, by its position, and by other circumstances, to the transition from pastoral to agricultural life. It was east of the easternmost branch of the Nile. It was within agricultural bounds. It included pastoral lands. So, about the patriarchs in Goshen, where they settled down and grew up, there was a land that had both agricultural and pastoral adaptations, with a constant tendency to pass from the pastoral to the agricultural, which is the next higher step in development; this had a civilizing effect. While it had its repugnances, it also had certain elevating influences which it exerted upon this nascent people. That they became to a very great extent agricultural, we know; and that the nomadic element was in them, we know. They never eradicated that. This is shown by the fact that Moses took a million of them and carried them into the wilderness, and for forty years convoyed them there. It would be impossible to take a settled nation and carry them into such a nomadic life. The possibility of their being induced to lead a wandering life was based upon the old instinct in them of the shepherd life. So, then, they had an addiction toward the agricultural without losing the pastoral.

Thus the Israelites were placed in this Goshen land, first because it fitted their pastoral life, and second because it afforded facilities for agricultural pursuits. It so happened that this was an important frontier of Egypt; that it was the weak side of that country, as toward the great Asiatic nations, which had overrun and were overrunning the Egyptian territory. Egypt did not need to guard itself on the west or on the south; for, although it had once been assailed and overrun from the interior of Africa, the likelihood of attack was not in that direction. The warlike people of Asia rose and multiplied, and threatened to roll over to the great valley of the Nile, that was the attraction of the universal world, on account of its wealth, of the glory of its art, and of the reputation of its monarchs.

Now, as I have said, the frontier was Goshen; and the Israelites were a plucky people. They never ceased to be such. Abraham did not fight in vain. He showed that he was a warrior. Not so with Isaac. He was quiescent. He was an everlasting member of the Peace Society. Jacob was politic. He was not, at the last resort, I suppose, unwilling to contend, but he lived by a diligent exercise of his brains in all matters that came to him. But the posterity of these three men showed that they had vigor, bone, muscle, irascibility, courage, cruelty, and capacity for vengeance. They were primitive warriors. It was nothing for them to destroy a city in order to satisfy their turbulence, their passion, their ungovernableness, the bad qualities in them. And when their posterity or their country was threatened, they were plucky and could be depended upon for defense. So, these Israelites, being put in Goshen to defend the frontier, were trained to a kind of semi-military feeling. It was shown when they first went into the wilderness. If brought to emergencies they were capable of meeting and overwhelming their adversaries. They were warlike; and the inner source of their power was the fact that they were being instructed in the art of war. In the history of the world, military training is for civilization next to moral training. That is to say, physical vigor, strength, and courage are indispensable to virtue and to power. Weakness in a nation is an unforgivable heresy.

Strength is the element of permanence. Weakness foretokens decay. In civilizing a nation the elements of courage and enterprise are blessed evidences of a condition which will take on polish. You cannot polish a pumpkin, nor lead. The things that are hard, and will hold polish, are the things that we burnish and brighten. There must be a great deal of human nature if you are going to make much grace out of it;—and there was a great deal of human nature among the Israelites.

Then, their position and family clannishness led them to keep aloof from the great body of the Egyptians. They did not mingle with them. I have no doubt that the Egyptians despised the Israelites, and I have no doubt that the Israelites paid them back in the same coin. While repugnances and prejudices that separate men in our day generally are not to be praised, but are to be disallowed, there are circumstances in which they are to the last degree desirable. It was so with the Israelites; and being placed in this valley of bounty, which produced everything that flourished in the tropics, they gradually separated themselves to a greater or less extent from the Egyptians. There is no other wall like hatred. At any rate, they did not deliquesce readily and mingle with the common people of that nation.

It is true that they were infected, to a certain degree, with Egyptian idolatry; and yet, in other things they were not affected at all by their contact with the Egyptians. They are spoken of in the historical record as having served the gods in Egypt. The great object of worship in Egypt was the sun. In all Oriental nations the sun and stars produced a most powerful impression upon the imagination—a sense of veneration. In Egypt the worship of the sun stood as in Palestine did the worship of Jehovah, the Everlasting, the Everliving. And they worshiped not only the sun but all the other powers of nature, with their hundreds of symbols in the celestial bodies and in vegetable and animal forms.

Thus the Israelitish people dwelt; and, though we have

no record or actual knowledge of their condition when they went out of Egypt, yet those four hundred years must have been years of vegetation, and of gradual unfolding, gradual strengthening, gradual preparation for the great drama in which this peculiar people were to act so sublime a part.

During this whole time, as I have said, there was no hero, no great priest, no towering patriarch. Four hundred years were waiting for the coming man; and when he came he was a man who, in proportions and in grandeur, was worthy of that long waiting. For until you come to the Advent there is no name in all human history that, for various excellence, can be compared for one single moment with the name of Moses, the man who, as a leader, so excelled as to gain a reputation unexampled—the man who delivered his people, not only, but whose leadership itself paled in the superior light of his power of organization and of administration. The foundations on which commonwealths are built to-day were laid in the Arabian desert; and the laws and customs and institutions which we cherish in our time with most tenacity, and for good reason, came originally from the hand of Moses, than whom nature has never produce greater man.

I shall not, to-night, attempt to discuss at all the disputed question of the real historical existence of one called *Moses*, and the genuineness of his labor. I do not sympathize with the extreme school that undertake to destroy all history, and to resolve everything into the nebulæ of remote antiquity. It seems to me to require a greater stretch of faith and more breadth of conception to suppose a character like Moses to have been invented than to suppose that he lived and performed the tasks that are ascribed to him. At another time I shall consider, in brief, the subject of the reality of Moses, and the substantial historic foundation of the history that is given of him.

With these preliminary remarks I turn to the first two chapters of the book of Exodus.

"And Joseph died, and all his brethren, and all that generation.

"And the children of Israel were fruitful, and increased abundantly, and multiplied, and waxed exceeding mighty."

You are to bear in mind that the promises made to Abraham, Isaac, and Jacob, iterated and reiterated, were promises of abundant posterity. The Oriental people regarded a large household as the greatest of earthly blessings. I need not refer you to the Psalms, in which, in various ways, this fact is proclaimed. To be without children was regarded as the greatest of misfortunes, and to be the mother of many children was considered the most significant token of divine favor.

So far as the physical is concerned, a wholesome out-of-door life, well tempered with labor and abundant food, increases population with remarkable rapidity. We know how it is in the insect world, the bird world, and the animal world. Let there be ample food and protection, and there will be increase at an extraordinary rate. And that which is true of the lower creation is true of the human family.

Now, there was a cradle for the Israelites. It was this land of Goshen, where they had sufficient food, where there was all needed protection, and where they had moderate labor. Therefore it was that they "were fruitful, and increased abundantly, and multiplied and waxed exceeding mighty," so that "the land was filled with them."

"Now there arose up a new king in Egypt, which knew not Joseph."

The dynasties of Egypt are infinitely perplexing. That there was a succession of dynasties in Egypt we know; but exactly the line of them and the number of them are matters of very much dispute and difference of opinion. It is, however, on the whole, generally held that what is called the Shepherd dynasty had at the time we are discussing come and gone—that the Egyptians had revolted and cast them out and the native rulers had again come to power. And, after four hundred years had passed from one dynasty to another, after one Pharaoh had succeeded another (for *Pharaoh* among the Egyptians, like *Cæsar* among the Romans, was the official name of the head of the state), is it strange that when they talked about Joseph this later Pharaoh did not know much about him? We look at it from the side of Israel, and we shall be in danger of taking sides exclusively with Israel and damning Pharaoh, as though there was no excuse, no palliation, nothing to be said for him. There is nothing to be said in extenuation of his conduct. Cruelty is cruelty in any age of the world, and wrong policy is wrong policy wherever you find it : nevertheless, considering what human nature is, it was perfectly natural that Pharaoh should not know the history of this people, but should concern himself more about Egypt at large.

Did Pharaoh reason about this matter? Their increase had been such that it had been brought to the royal ears. It had been represented to Pharaoh that they were a warlike people, that they were filling the land of Goshen, that they did not mix with the Egyptians, and that they did not worship as the Egyptians did. He looked upon them as a dangerous element because he thought they would be split up into parties and factions, and especially because they might take sides with the enemies of his country. In the event of invasion from without they might swarm on the side of the adversaries of the government. Such was the view which Pharaoh took ; and monarchs of that day were not very apt to go aside from selfish considerations any more than they are nowadays.

"And he said unto his people, Behold the people of the children of Israel are more and mightier than we: come on, let us deal wisely with them; lest they multiply, and it come to pass, that, when there falleth out any war, they join also unto our enemies, and fight against us, and so get them up out of the land."

He did not want to lose them, any more than the planters of the South once wanted to lose the negroes ; but he wanted to hold them in certain conditions.

" Therefore they did set over them taskmasters to afflict them with their burdens. And they built for Pharaoh treasure cities, Pithom and Raamses."

That is to say, "Let us subject this warlike tribe by the discipline of regular industrial organization. Let us give them so much to do that they will not have time for mischief-making. Let us employ them in building cities, military depots, and canals. Let us see to it that they are so fully occupied that they will have no opportunity for plotting treason. Let us break their spirit by exhausting their strength in useful labor." That was the plan.

"But the more they afflicted them, the more they multiplied and grew. And they were grieved because of the children of Israel. And the Egyptians made the children of Israel to serve with rigor."

It was a kind of brutal experiment; and when it did not succeed,—

"They made their lives bitter with hard bondage, in mortar, and in brick, and in all manner of service in the field: all their service, wherein they made them serve, was with rigor."

It was hard goodness; for if there was anything that the Israelites needed it was to have their wild discursive spirit tamed, and to be taught industry—how to do many things that they did thus learn. And when Pharaoh wanted handicraft men he had them. They were apprenticed out to Pharaoh. But, as we have seen, they still multiplied: it must have taken many years to reveal this briefly stated fact. So soon as that plan failed Pharaoh fell upon a new one: he summoned the Hebrew midwives, and gave them orders to destroy in birth the male children. Female servants were not to be dreaded in war, and they were useful as beasts of burden.

That order led to a series of deceptions, such as you will find among animals and in connection with the lower conditions of human society. The midwives deceived the king: and when he called them to account, they said the reason was that the Hebrew women did not employ their services; that they did not need them as the Egyptians did, and that therefore the children were born without their knowledge. They lied. The record goes further, and says,—

"Therefore God dealt well with the midwives: and the people multiplied, and waxed very mighty. And it came to pass, because the midwives feared God, that he made them houses."

That is, built up their households, or families.

There is no doubt that, to the Israelites, this lie that the women told in behalf of humanity was a virtue. Cunning and craft as against oppression has always been considered a virtue; and it is considered as much a virtue in our time as ever it was in the olden time. We organize it into method, and we practice in our diplomacy and military operations the same craft and deceit which were practiced by early nations.

Is it put down against any great soldier that he sent out couriers with letters containing false information, that he deceived the enemy, and caught them in traps that he set for them? I never heard any very vehement declarations against military cunning, which, to give the plain English of it, is lying. It is not fair, however, to suppose that God rewarded their falsehood. They "feared God" and protected what they believed to be his chosen people. They were instruments of great humanity. They were rewarded for their patriotism, their national spirit.

Failing in this attempt to destroy all the male children that were born, Pharaoh gave command to his people to issue a proclamation, saying,—

"Every son that is born ye shall cast into the river, and every daughter ye shall save alive."

It is to be presumed that such an edict as this was promulged chiefly along the banks of the river where a large part of the Israelites dwelt, and did not extend far to the north or southeast. If there had been a rigorous enforcement of it there could not have been such an augmentation of the nation as took place, and prepared them to go forth with such a great multitude. It must have had a limited application; and even in the small sphere where it was applied it is not to be supposed, while great cruelty was committed, and there was an extensive slaughter of children, but that the mother-love often outwitted the zeal of tyranny. At any rate, it was the beginning of the drama in which Moses was the hero. And here, again, we fall upon one of those beautiful pictures in which the natural heart breaks out in the most beautiful forms.

"And there went a man of the house of Levi, and took to wife a daughter of Levi. And the woman conceived, and bare a son: and when she saw him that he was a goodly child [I should like to know what mother ever did look upon her son without thinking that he was a goodly child], she hid him three months."

He could not have cried much, or they would have found him out. Moses was slow of tongue in after life; and it seems that he began early!

"And when she could not longer hide him, she took for him an ark of bulrushes, and daubed it with slime and with pitch, and put the child therein; and she laid it in the flags by the river's brink."

Even animals have the shrewdest instinct. Have you never seen a cat preserve her kittens? I have watched the operation at my country home. I have seen sagacity in the mother that was truly surprising, as she moved her young from place to place whenever she thought danger threatened them.

If that sagacity in a feline creature is so admirable, how much more admirable is it when, going up through many gradations, it develops itself in the human heart. And how shrewd this mother was! Did she not know that that part of the river was where the daughter of Pharaoh was accustomed to walk with her maidens, and at times to bathe her feet, and perhaps her person? And was not that the place to be chosen? After she had put the child in this little basket, that was made water-tight, his sister and she "stood afar off, to wit what would be done to him." They watched him. I do not believe he was out for a night. They would have him in over night and out again early in the morning; and then they would wait and watch. In that torrid region there was no walking at midday; and Pharaoh's daughter must have walked either at evening or in the morning—probably in the morning.

"And the daughter of Pharaoh came down to wash herself at the river; and her maidens walked along by the river's side; and when she saw the ark among the flags, she sent her maid to fetch it. And when she had opened it, she saw the child: and, behold, the babe wept."

Its cry was the sweetest oration and the most convincing that ever was uttered, doubtless. The daughter of the proud Pharaoh looked upon this alien child,—for she knew at once that it was of the Israelites ; and the babe wept ; and she was conquered.

"She had compassion on him, and said, This is one of the Hebrews' children."

Then the shrewd little sister ran up and said to her,—

"Shall I go and call to thee a nurse of the Hebrew women, that she may nurse the child for thee?"

It was a lucky thought. Pharaoh's daughter saw that it would be rather awkward for a daughter of the king to go back with a babe in her arms. She might not have many questions to answer, but there would be surmises about it ; and when the maid asked if she should go and get a nurse it was exactly what Pharaoh's daughter wanted to have her do.

"And Pharaoh's daughter said to her, Go. And the maid went and called the child's mother."

She was all ready for it. She had been longing for such a call. Do you suppose a child was ever hungry that the mother did not know it? Nature is often stronger than the tongue.

"And Pharaoh's daughter said unto her, Take this child away, and nurse it for me, and I will give thee thy wages.

"And the woman took the child, and nursed it. And the child grew, and she brought him unto Pharaoh's daughter, and he became her son. And she called his name Moses: and she said, Because I drew him out of the water."

Moses means *drawn out*. At that time they gave names, not as we do, repeating the same name over and over : they named their children from some circumstance ; as, for instance, when Rachel was dying she called her babe Ben-oni, "Child of my Sorrow"; but the father said, "No, Benjamin, Son of my Right-hand." And Moses was called by that name because he was *drawn out*.

"And it came to pass in those days when Moses was grown "—

That is all there is said in this history about his education. Later on we find the statement that he was *brought up in all the wisdom of the Egyptians*.

Egypt then was really glorious. Rome had not been thought of. Greece was a den of robbers. There was not a refined people in all Media, in Persia nor in Asia. There were conditions that prefigured civilization; but at that time there was but one radiant spot on the globe, and that was Egypt; and if there was to be a movement by the human race which should culminate in moral effulgence, it must be made there. Abraham's posterity were to go into Egypt. And then, Moses, being born, and being threatened with destruction, was rescued and put into the house of Pharaoh, where was to be found the very acme of the world in all philosophy, in all art, and in all religion as it had developed in the imperfect forms of idolatry—for, under all idolatry, there is a true element.

Under the religion of every nation on the globe that ever worshiped or that worships to-day there is an element of morality which that religion faintly and imperfectly tries to express. There are rude nations whose conceptions of God are made manifest by idols; and, although those idols are so distorted as to amount to a slander upon the Omnipotent, they shadow forth an element of truth.

And whatever was known of history in the time of Moses was nurtured in Egypt, and in the lap of Pharaoh. Whatever there was of mathematics (and there was a great deal), whatever there was of constructive engineering and architecture (and it was magnificent) centered there. And astronomy, geometry, medicine, and many manufacturing arts were there well advanced; while the science of war was both taught and practiced. And Moses was thoroughly educated in these things. As prince, he was also priest, and was broadly and thoroughly trained. He was encyclopedic. All this concatenation of events and elements was a preparation for the work he was to do afterwards. And what did this man think during all that time?

The Jewish writer Josephus details legends of the military exploits of Moses, who conquered Ethiopia for the Egyptians and took to wife the daughter of the defeated king. He seems to have completed a full round both of mental training and practical experience to equip him for his real life-work, which was not to be amid the splendor of Egypt, but among the degraded slaves who were his countrymen.

One trait that we honor is fidelity to one's own country. Moses was brought up with the knowledge that he was of Hebrew blood. He stood in a place of power. He was surrounded by magnificence. He had everything that the heart of man could desire. He had the energy that was necessary for ambition. But his heart constantly ran back to his own people. He thought of them sympathetically. That sympathy which led Jesus Christ to couple himself with mankind, and made him the Saviour of the world, was, though not in such grandeur and radiance, nor in such noble and heroic form, also in Moses. It would not have been strange if, amid the blandishments of a court, he had been dazzled into forgetfulness and contempt of his people. What if they were slaves, and in distress? All the more did they need somebody at Court to intercede for them. And yet, the methods pursued by Moses showed the inexperience of the age as well as of the man. The first effort he made for avenging his people was a miserable blunder in every way. It had in it no foresight, no plan. It was a mere blind impulse. Blind impulses are sometimes heroic; but oftentimes they are just the opposite. The narrative is brief.

"And it came to pass in those days when Moses was grown [There's chronology for you! *In those days*. It might have been when he was twenty or twenty-five years of age; but it was when he was about forty, as understood from other sources] that he went out unto his brethren, and looked on their burdens : and he spied an Egyptian smiting an Hebrew, one of his brethren."

If Moses had been nothing but a common man, and had knocked the Egyptian down, I should have said "Amen"; but Moses had in him the movement toward a larger sphere than that in which common men move, and should have acted accordingly, with a larger wisdom. Therefore in the act which he committed, and which is here narrated, he was rash ; noble in impulse, but not wise in method.

"And he looked this way and that way, and when he saw that there was no man, he slew the Egyptian, and hid him in the sand.

"And when he went out the second day, behold, two men of the Hebrews strove together : and he said to him that did the wrong, Wherefore smitest thou thy fellow ? And he said, Who made thee a prince and a judge over us ? Intendest thou to kill me, as thou killedst the Egyptian?"

Here you see what slavery brings men to. Moses interfered as a vindicator of one of his people who was smitten, and slew the smiter. Then he undertook to stop a quarrel, to act as a mediator between two men that were striving together, and one of them, an enslaved man out of whom hard bondage had driven his manhood, turned upon him, like a dog separated from another dog with whom he was fighting, and said, "Intendest thou to kill me, as thou killedst the Egyptian ?"

"And Moses feared, and said, Surely this thing is known.

"Now when Pharaoh heard this thing, he sought to slay Moses. But Moses fled from the face of Pharaoh, and dwelt in the land of Midian."

So, then, here was the first scene—a rash, impulsive endeavor to emphasize his detestation of the oppression of his people. He had expressed his sympathy for them ; but all he had accomplished was to excite their animosity, to bring himself into disgrace at Court, to make himself a vagabond ; and he ran away to save his own life. As to his people, they were oppressed more than ever before. The first effect of an attempt to break up slavery is to make the slave-master hold his victim tighter. When a lion has seized a lamb, woe be to the lamb if anybody tries to draw it out of his mouth ! Then the teeth grind it to powder. When power has long prevailed, and is confronted with resistance, or with attempts at emancipation or amelioration, the immediate result is not a help but a hindrance. Moreover, the first effect of attempting to lift men from a lower sphere to a higher is to make them your enemies. He that came to give salvation to the whole human race was rejected by those among whom he first sought to perform his mission. It is dangerous to touch the animal in men, if you would lift them up toward the angels; as Moses found, and as Christ found.

Next comes in one of those poetic pictures which so abound in the Bible. You will recollect how Abraham, then Jacob, and now Moses, carried on their courtship by the side of wells. These wells in antiquity seem to have been favorably placed.

"Now the priest of Midian had seven daughters: and they came and drew water, and filled the troughs to water their father's flock."

Women had rights in those days!

"And the shepherds came and drove them away: but Moses stood up and helped them."

Here was a courtly-bred man; and whatever the facts may have been in regard to the methods he employed in attempting to deliver his people, he was not going to see seven women wronged and not have a word to say in the matter. Thus he vindicated his gentlemanly nature—for he was a gentleman, every inch of him.

"Moses stood up and helped them, and watered their flock. And when they came to Reuel their father, he said, How is it that ye are come so soon to-day? And they said, An Egyptian delivered us out of the hand of the shepherds, and also drew water enough for us, and watered the flock.
"And he said unto his daughters, And where is he? why is it that ye have left the man? Call him, that he may eat bread."

So said the old hospitable priest of the wilderness.

"And Moses was content to dwell with the man."

There is a whole year represented in a sentence here, very likely. We are not told how long it was before he was contented to dwell with the man; nor are we told how long it was before Reuel gave him his daughter for his wife, which he did.

"And he gave Moses Zipporah his daughter. And she bare him a son, and he called his name Gershom [Stranger]: for he said, I have been a stranger in a strange land.
"And it came to pass in process of time [or, in the course of many days] that the king of Egypt died."

There's chronology again! *In process of time!* It is understood that Moses abode many years in the wilderness. He was forty years old when he went there, it is said. He abode there, we are told, about forty years. This was a time for discipline, for meditation, for education into patient submission ; and dwelling with this simple priest doubtless he ripened inwardly much of the knowledge he had derived from his intercourse with the Court of Pharaoh.

"And the children of Israel sighed by reason of the bondage, and they cried, and their cry came up unto God by reason of the bondage. And God heard their groaning, and God remembered his covenant with Abraham, with Isaac, and with Jacob."

You would suppose, from this statement, that God never thought of them for four hundred years, and that they waked him up, and that he said, "Oh yes, I recollect Abraham, Isaac, and Jacob"; but no, this is the infantine way of representing it. It is the way in which it was then perfectly natural for men to represent it. God's providence was watching this people all the time, and while the process of development was going on under the great stimulating influences of nature, it was God working upon them through natural laws, just as much as when he spoke from Mount Sinai, by his voice of thunder, or when he wrote the law upon the tables of stone. He was not then more actively engaged in working out the destiny of his people than when, in his providence, he was preparing them to increase and multiply in Egypt.

"And God looked upon the children of Israel, and God had respect unto them."

At this point we must leave the narrative to-night, to be resumed, God willing, next Sunday evening.

I shall now ask your attention for a single moment to the analogy which exists between our own experience and that which has been so perfectly sketched here. We have oppressed a great people in our midst. They made our wealth, they ministered to our luxury, and we despised them : not probably more than Pharaoh despised the shepherds ; but in our case there was a difference of complexion and feature; and this great nation walked in the footsteps of Pharaoh and despised the Negroes. Then came the efforts to bring to pass their emancipation, which, in their early stages, may well be considered as having been rash, as were the first attempts of Moses to vindicate his people. While I honor the testimony of Mr. Garrison, Mr. Phillips, and men associated with them, I do not regard them as being emancipators. As in the case of Moses, their first efforts for the amelioration of the condition of the slaves led to violent opposition, instead of accomplishing the end they had in view. I did not utter one word of criticism concerning them at that time; everybody was throwing stones at them, and, as you know, I stood with and for them in the matter of their free speech. But, as a matter of fact to-day, I do declare that the invective and abuse indulged in by those men did not promote emancipation, but had just the contrary effect. Although they did have an influence in the right direction, that influence was derived, not from the severe and rash statements they made, but from their appeal to that love of liberty, that sense of justice, which resides in every man who has not a personal interest in oppression.*

The first effect of agitation created by abolitionists such as these was not favorable to the cause for which they labored. In the Eastern cities, where commerce reigned, the church was well-nigh dumb on the subject of slavery. There was almost no testimony there in regard to it; and the indignant utterances of Garrison and Phillips were true,

---

*In a discourse preached February 10, 1884, in memory of Wendell Phillips, Mr. Beecher said: "He was an aristocrat by descent and by nature—a noble one, but a thorough aristocrat. . . . He was aristocratic in his pride, and lived higher than most men lived. He was called of God as truly as ever Moses and the prophets were: not exactly for the same great ends, but in consonance with them. . . . The power to discern right amid all the wrappings of interest and all the seductions of ambition was singularly his. To choose the lowly for their sake; to abandon all favor, all power, all comfort, all ambition, all greatness—that was his genius and glory. . . . He has become to us a lesson, an example, his whole history an encouragement to manhood—to heroic manhood."

if not wise. But in the great Western community, where I lived, the earliest emancipators and strongest abolitionists were in the church. The first vote I ever cast in a church in my life was in the Presbytery of Indianapolis, where I voted, in connection with every other man there, minister or elder, that we would neither license nor retain any man who held slaves, unless he could satisfy us that he held them against his own will, and for their benefit; and I bear witness that the leading men in the West gave their testimony against slavery along with Christian ministers. There are those whose memory goes back with mine to men who labored in poverty for this cause whose great ends were unknown, and are not known to-day, but who stand so high, I believe, that if I rise to the heavenly estate I shall hardly be worthy to unloose their shoe's latchet, shod with light as they are before the Throne.

To all the early anti-slavery men—especially the Eastern abolitionists — it was constantly said, "You only make slavery worse." Their early counsels, of repudiating the Constitution in the interest of liberty, were overruled by the providence of God, and, as in the case of the Israelites, events, in the hand of the Divine Leader, made way for wiser and more effective methods. And yet the impulse was right, and bold ; the beginning had to be made.

When Moses interfered for his people they themselves did not understand what he meant. They cried out against him. They resented his early attempts to emancipate them, which made their yoke heavier and their sufferings greater. It is the nature of slavery to make people ignorant and servile inside as well as outside.

I will not go farther with this analogy—because I have not developed the history of Moses and the emancipation which he wrought—except to say briefly that the lion would not give up his prey until he was smitten with the sword, and his own blood flowed. Our people, whatever they may have talked, refused to let the oppressed go free until He who smote Pharaoh with many plagues, and devastated his kingdom, came down in robust judgment, and blood flowed to the horses' bridles. The God that emancipated the Israelites emancipated the Africans, and let them go free. We are not, therefore, to read this history without some allusions and applications to current history among our own selves.

X.

EMANCIPATION.

In the very general survey which we have been making, for several Sunday nights, of the books of the Old Testament, we have finished the book of Genesis, and now enter upon the second book—namely, Exodus. The contents of this book are divided into two parts : that which gives an account of the going-forth of the Israelites from the land of Egypt,—the first twelve or thirteen chapters,—and that which gives a history, in part, of their wanderings, but especially of the institutions and customs which were framed by Moses, and which afterwards became the constitution, religious and civil, of the kingdom of Israel.

To-night we have come to the great drama of Emancipation. To me this history, which is usually called the "History of the Ten Plagues," comes bringing remembrances of my childhood. I was brought up when there were almost no books for children. An aunt, revered and beloved, who for a portion of the time acted toward me the part of a mother, was accustomed to promise readings from Scripture as a reward for good conduct ; and as I was (of course) a good boy, I almost always had the promised reward. Among the favorite themes chosen—although I was not quite old enough to enter fully into an understanding of that startling, memorable, and wonderful history — was the "ten plagues." On the whole, I think I took more satisfaction in the ten plagues than the Egyptians did. They were very dear to me. They gratified both the upper and the under nature in me—the sense of power,

---

Sunday evening, December 27, 1878. Lesson : Psa. cxxxviii.

and the sense of retributive justice, which is very strong in children and in uncultivated people. I would that I could look with the same eyes and the same unquestioning feelings upon them now that I did then. However, other things have come in, and on the whole the treasure of knowledge and the great comfort of Scripture are a thousand times more than they were in my childhood; the Book has grown as I have grown, and has twined itself into the habits of my thought and feeling and life.

I shall not undertake to interrupt the general course of the statement of the narrative to-night by pausing to discuss difficulties. There are enough of them. Whatever theory you may take,—whether you consider this as a poetical drama based upon history, or whether you regard it as a historical statement of facts and developments,—there are difficulties. For instance, we have, by the Gospel of Christ, been brought upon a moral ground which leads us to shrink from direct falsehoods; and yet, at the same time, they were practiced by Moses upon Pharaoh, and so related as if direct deceptions were commanded of God. It is said:—

"And thou shalt come, thou and the elders of Israel, unto the king of Egypt, and ye shall say unto him, The Lord God of the Hebrews hath met with us: and now let us go, we beseech thee, three days' journey into the wilderness, that we may sacrifice to the Lord our God."

The mention of the number of days was merely a mild pretense; what was meant, was, "Let us go." But we are told that Moses was commanded to say this. It is said that God commanded him to do it. Did God tell him to say so? If he did not, where is the narrative? If he did, where is God? There is a difficulty here, to which I shall on some other occasion address myself.

Then, again, if it had been: "When the Israelites go forth out of Egypt they shall requite themselves for what, as slaves, they have suffered, by taking possession of whatever they can; when they go out to the wilderness, to set up housekeeping, they shall remunerate themselves for laboring hundreds of years to increase the wealth of their masters, by helping themselves to an equivalent of that out of which they have been defrauded,"—that would have been according to the laws of war, and not unjust or immoral. But we are told that they were commanded to "borrow." They were commanded to make a pretense of only wanting a little while the articles they should ask the Egyptians to let them have, when they knew that they were going to keep them. This gives rise, not only to a question of truth, of veracity, but to a question of honesty. Our modern educated conscience takes exception (on Sundays!) to such pretenses.

Then comes that which has been the difficulty of ages—namely, God's "hardening" of Pharaoh's heart;—commanding him to do things, and then "hardening his heart" so that he could not or would not do them. All questions which cluster around this difficulty have existed through generations, and will exist. On whatever ground you put such questions, there are difficulties connected with them. These difficulties, as I have already said, I shall reserve for a separate discourse, in which I shall give them the best treatment I can.

There are two classes of men who read the accounts contained in the early chapters of Exodus. There are those that look at them from the standpoint of a belief in a personal God, who not only is able to work miracles, but does work, and in all ages has worked, miracles. There is to me no philosophical difficulty on the subject of miracles. If there be a personal God,—and, surely, I trust we all believe there is,—if the whole physical globe is, in some sense, a school in which he develops and educates the human race, his power to control material elements so that they shall further his supreme designs among men upon earth cannot seem strange; so, it is reduced to the simple question of fact, Does God work miracles? Did he work miracles?

The allegation that the order of nature cannot be interfered with, and that there is no evidence to show that it has ever been interfered with, amounts to very little with me. I can believe that new forces may be interposed parallel with stated and regular forces, if there be a ruling God, and if he chooses, for moral ends, to interpose them; and I can see that if done at all it would naturally be done in the infancy of the human race, as a substitute for higher methods until they were able to employ those methods. I can understand, in other words, that many miracles—all of which, except those of Jesus, were wrought through men—were merely the enabling of exceptional men to take hold of natural laws higher up than ordinary men could take hold of them, and use them with an efficiency, a scope, a skill, such as men at large cannot give them. I believe in miracles—not in everything that is called a miracle, but at large in a system of miracles; and, once admitting that, there is no difficulty in so far as miracles are concerned. It is just as easy to turn water into wine as it is to make a grape from which wine can be made. It is as easy for God to perform special acts, if he please to do it, as it is for him to do many other things that he does. If there is an end worthy of such interposition as may be necessary for the creation of a new law or method in the physical globe, I see no reason why he should not exercise his omnipotent power for the accomplishment of that end. And in a history that, however strange it may be to ordinary experience, unfolds itself miraculously, there can be no difficulty to those who believe in a God that can work by laws in a sphere higher than men can, or that can work for special ends by interposing parallel forces alongside of those working according to the usual natural laws.

There are those, however, who believe in religion and in the Bible to a great extent, but who believe in these things as families in reduced circumstances in England used to believe in old mansions and castles. There were the structures, with magnificent rooms in them; but then, it was cold and bleak, and the impoverished family were not able to furnish them and live in them. There were vast halls, once filled with kings, knights, and courtiers, but they were beyond the present family necessities. So, they were unused, except that they were given up to rats, owls, and what not. There are a great many persons who are so reduced in faith that they say, "The chambers of the Old Testament had better be shut up, for we are not able to furnish them and live in them." They make use of certain rooms in the New Testament, and say, "We are believers not in the whole Bible, but in a considerable part of it."

But, in one way or another, according to what seems to me their aims, I believe in the entire Scriptures. There are portions of the Old Testament that relate to the early unfolding of the race, which are not to be interpreted literally; but they remain as history and as literature, and are valuable for inspiration, for doctrine, for correction, for right-living, that the man of God may be thoroughly furnished to every good work.

There are men, however, who cannot thus accept the Bible. They are in our churches. They are under our ministerial care. They cannot manage the difficulties they find in the Word of God. They huddle themselves in portions of the New Testament, and say, "We believe in so much, and are inhabiting such and such chambers in the Bible, but there are rooms which we are unable to make use of."

Now, it seems to me that a great deal more than is being done might be done for those that are out of the way by reason of their lack of faith. For example, can these two classes of men—those who believe in the miraculous power and interposition of God, and those who believe that God never did nor does work miracles, and that everything comes to pass by the regular accredited forces of nature—can they both go together through the history of the emancipation of the Israelites and make profitable use of that whole statement of Scripture? I believe they can. For their sakes I suggest a supposition—and it is not at variance with what we know to have been the habits of men in early days. The suggestion is that the first historians were poets. They had the poetic instinct, so that primitive history, the history of the earliest nations, was more poetry than prose. It was more or less allegorical and dramatic. Suppose, then, that this history was presented as a drama; and not as an invented drama—not like one of Milton's great epic poems, as, for instance, "Paradise Lost," which was wrought out by the imagination, and is not a literal statement of fact, but originated in his own brain from a mere hint in the Bible. It is a magnificent poem, but it is imaginary from beginning to end, not being based on known, recorded historical facts. A great deal of the matter in this poem by Milton is from the Bible; there is in it a certain tone which reminds one of the patriarchs and prophets; but from the tentative brain of John Milton there came splendid recitations of scenes which never took place, and the like of which never occurred.

These, however, are very different from the allegory, "Pilgrim's Progress," which, later, John Bunyan wrote in his prison. In this allegory the outside history has no existence at all, and yet there is a most admirable inside history. The evolution of the universe by which a man rises from a lower life to a Christian life, and progresses in that Christian life, was never put into a sermon so successfully as it is set forth in this allegory. You have here an allegory founded on fact—an allegory all the circumstances of which are imaginary, yet which is full of truth.

Now, is it not possible that there may be an irregular, and in some sense an anomalous, internal drama which shall represent substantially the progress of historical events, and yet be so constructed that there shall be a filling up by the imagination of the intervening spaces concerning which there is no record,—a drapery, as it were, given to facts and sequences,—thus securing to nascent histories a larger form and a sublimer presentation?

I do not say that this is so here, but I say that it is possible, to such an extent that men who shrink from a recognition of positive miracles may look upon this whole history as a magnificent drama, adorned with imaginative elements, yet representing interiorly, with truth, the emancipation and founding of a nation.

Therefore, you can follow me to-night from either point of view—whether you regard the record as an allegory or a drama, or whether you regard it simply as a plain narrative of the wonder-working power of God, historical, and to be judged on historical grounds. I invite you thus to go with me, and take in this portion of Scripture.

We begin at the point where we left off last Sabbath evening. The birth of Moses and his preservation; the wonderful providence by which he received an education in the very heart of the most civilized nation of antiquity, being of the royal family by reason of his adoptive mother; the fact that he acquired all the wisdom of the Egyptians, and became a great logician, reputed soldier, and administrator,—these things were recited; but the record is void of much information which one would naturally expect would be given with them.

Moses is said to have been forty years old when he imprudently acted under an impulse in first attempting to vindicate his people; but here dates are very uncertain, as they are in regard to many things which are recorded in the Bible. At any rate, it is an incidental matter, and is not of much importance. As though the peasant Hebrew mother was so firmly linked with Moses in the brilliant court of Pharaoh that between her and him ran the umbilical cord of her heart, in the midst of scenes of grandeur he was the center of her admiration and affection, and his own heart was with his countrymen. Unwisely he slew an Egyptian that was smiting a Hebrew; and the next day, when he sought to perform another good act by separating two quarreling Hebrews, one of them turned upon him, and said, "Intendest thou to slay me as thou killedst the Egyptian?"

When Moses found that the thing was known, he feared and fled eastward to the land of Midian in the Sinaitic Peninsula, and there, having married a daughter of Jethro, the priest of Midian, he dwelt with him and kept his flocks. This man, who, for the age in which he lived, was encyclopedic in knowledge, became, for many long years—forty, the record says—a humble shepherd. What his thoughts and feelings were during that time you can imagine as well as I.

We now reach a scene in which this retirement comes to an end.

"Moses kept the flock of Jethro his father-in-law, the priest of Midian: and he led the flock to the backside of the desert, and came to the mountain of God, even to Horeb. And the angel of the Lord appeared unto him in a flame of fire out of the midst of a bush: and he looked, and, behold, the bush burned with fire, and the bush was not consumed."

It was doubtless an acacia bush, or tree, as that was almost the only tree in that region. It seemed luminous to his eye. It was burning, but the flame was innocuous. It was a light, a fire that did not consume.

"And Moses said, I will now turn aside, and see this great sight, why the bush is not burnt. And when the Lord saw that he turned aside to see, God called unto him out of the midst of the bush, and said, Moses, Moses. And he said, Here am I. And he said, Draw not nigh hither: put off thy shoes from off thy feet, for the place whereon thou standest is holy ground."

Wherever a man's soul is brought into the presence of God Almighty the ground is sacred, whether it be in a church or on a ledge, on a crag or in a cathedral. It is holy ground where a man consciously meets his God.

"Moreover he said, I am the God of thy father, the God of Abraham, the God of Isaac, and the God of Jacob."

In our day men do not need to be told who God is; he is the theme of inspiration from the cradle up: but in those early days men supposed the world to be populated with all sorts of gods, every great phenomenon being regarded by men as divine, or as the result of the action of some deity. There had come out of Padan-aram one man who held to the unity of God; who believed that the heavens above and the earth beneath were under the dominion of one thinking, willing, controlling God. To the Israelites that one God was unrepresented. There were to them no gods in the shape of naiads or spirits. There was only one God; and he was the God of Abraham, Isaac, and Jacob. These three patriarchs and the twelve chiefs of Israel bore down to us from antiquity the precious truth of one God. How far the Israelites had forgotten him in their Egyptian corruption, we do not know; how far even Moses may have wandered in religious speculation in his Egyptian education, we are not told. But his years of retirement and meditation had evidently prepared him for a great conviction.

"The Lord said, I have surely seen the affliction of my people which are in Egypt, and have heard their cry by reason of their taskmasters; for I know their sorrows; and I am come down to deliver them out of the hand of the Egyptians, and to bring them up out of that land unto a good land and a large, unto a land flowing with milk and honey; unto the place of the Canaanites, and the Hittites, and the Amorites, and the Perizzites, and the Hivites, and the Jebusites. Now therefore, behold, the cry of the children of Israel is come unto me: and I have also seen the oppression wherewith the Egyptians oppress them. Come now, therefore, and I will send thee unto Pharaoh, that thou mayest bring forth my people the children of Israel out of Egypt."

Those years in the wilderness had not been ineffectual in Moses. How ripe he was! He ran at first without any call, and, actuated by a vague, youthful, romantic enthusiasm, he meant, by his own right hand, to destroy the oppressors of his country. Yet now, chastened, enlarged in knowledge, when called to this very same task by the God of his fathers he shrank back in modesty, and said to God,—

"Who am I, that I should go unto Pharaoh, and that I should bring forth the children of Israel out of Egypt? And he said, Certainly I will be with thee; and this shall be a token unto thee, that I have sent thee: When thou hast brought forth the people out of Egypt, ye shall serve God upon this mountain.

"And Moses said unto God, Behold, when I come unto the children of Israel, and shall say unto them, The God of your fathers hath sent me unto you; and they shall say to me, What is his name? what shall I say unto them?"

Then comes one of the most sublime of enunciations.

"And God said unto Moses, I AM THAT I AM."

A God, he is, that cannot be represented by picture, by statue, nor by any language—a God so vast, so wonderful, so beyond the measure of human thought or conception, that he is undescribed and indescribable.

"And he said, Thus shalt thou say unto the children of Israel, I AM [the Living, the Existing] hath sent me unto you. And God said moreove. unto Moses, Thus shalt thou say unto the children of Israel, Jehovah, God of your fathers, the God of Abraham, the God of Isaac, and the God of Jacob, hath sent me unto you: this is my name forever, and this is my memorial unto all generations."

A little further on, God explains that he appeared unto Abraham and Isaac and Jacob as El Shaddai—*God Almighty*, but by his name Jehovah—*I Am* (or perhaps more strictly, *I Will Be*) was he not made known unto them. From this time forth in the Old Testament Scriptures the name appears; but, owing to the reverential fear of the Jews to pronounce it, it has been represented by the words *the Lord*. The name itself, however, is so full of meaning that it is a pity not to have retained it.*

"Go, and gather the elders of Israel together, and say unto them, Jehovah, God of your fathers, the God of Abraham, of Isaac, and of Jacob, appeared unto me, saying, I have surely visited you, and seen that which was done to you in Egypt: and I have said, I will bring you up out of the affliction of Egypt unto the land of the Canaanites, and the Hittites, and the Amorites, and the Perizzites, and the Hivites, and the Jebusites, unto a land flowing with milk and honey. And they shall hearken to thy voice: and thou shalt come, thou and the elders of Israel, unto the king of Egypt, and ye shall say unto him, Jehovah, the God of the Hebrews, hath met with us: and now let us go, we beseech thee, three days' journey into the wilderness, that we may sacrifice to Jehovah, our God. And I am sure that the king of Egypt will not let you go, no, not by a mighty hand. And I will stretch out my hand, and smite Egypt with all my wonders which I will do in the midst thereof: and after that he will let you go. And I will give this people favor in the sight of the Egyptians: and it shall come to pass, that, when ye go, ye shall not go empty: but every woman shall borrow of her neighbor, and of her that sojourneth in her house, jewels of silver, and jewels of gold, and raiment: and ye shall put them upon your sons, and upon your daughters; and ye shall spoil the Egyptians.

"And Moses answered and said, But, behold, they will not believe me, nor hearken unto my voice: for they will say, Jehovah hath not appeared unto thee."

---

* In the spirit of this, the name has been used in certain quoted Scriptural passages, where the personality of the God of the Hebrews in distinction from the "other gods," of Egypt and surrounding nations, seems to be the point of emphasis. The American members of the Old Testament Revision Company, in the Revised Version issued in 1885, express their preference to "Substitute the Divine name 'Jehovah' *wherever* it occurs in the Hebrew text for 'the LORD' and 'GOD.'"—*Editor*.

Then God gives him the first sign: casting his rod upon the ground it became a serpent, and at the command of God he seized it, when it again became a rod.

"And Jehovah said furthermore unto him, Put now thine hand into thy bosom. And he put his hand into his bosom: and when he took it out, behold, his hand was leprous as snow. And he said, Put thine hand into thy bosom again. And he put his hand into his bosom again; and plucked it out of his bosom, and, behold, it was turned again as his other flesh.

"And it shall come to pass, if they will not believe thee, neither hearken to the voice of the first sign, that they will believe the voice of the latter sign. And it shall come to pass, if they will not believe also these two signs, neither hearken unto thy voice, that thou shalt take of the water of the river, and pour it upon the dry land: and the water which thou takest out of the river shall become blood upon the dry land."

The Lord assured Moses that in these signs the most of his people would have faith that he came authenticated by the divine authority.

"And Moses said, O my Lord, I am not eloquent, neither heretofore, nor since thou hast spoken unto thy servant: but I am slow of speech, and of a slow tongue.

"And the Lord said unto him, Who hath made man's mouth? or who maketh the dumb, or deaf, or the seeing, or the blind? Is it not I, Jehovah? Now therefore go, and I will be with thy mouth, and teach thee what thou shalt say."

Reluctant Moses could not answer a word; but still he did not want to go.

"And he said, O my Lord, send, I pray thee, by the hand of him whom thou wilt send. And the anger of Jehovah was kindled against Moses, and he said, Is not Aaron the Levite thy brother? I know that he can speak well. And also, behold, he cometh forth to meet thee: and when he seeth thee, he will be glad in his heart. And thou shalt speak unto him, and put words in his mouth: and I will be with thy mouth, and with his mouth, and will teach you what ye shall do. And he shall be thy spokesman unto the people: and he shall be, even he shall be to thee instead of a mouth, and thou shalt be to him instead of God. And thou shalt take this rod in thine hand, wherewith thou shalt do signs."

We are to understand that from this time when Moses did anything publicly he did it through the ministration of Aaron.

Now we come to the journey of Moses with his wife and

two sons back to Egypt. There is a scene of which we can give no explanation.

"And it came to pass by the way in the inn, that the Lord met him and sought to kill him."

The possible explanation is that Moses was taken sick, but that his wife supposed him to be smitten by the Lord.

"And the Lord said to Aaron, Go into the wilderness to meet Moses. And he went, and met him in the mount of God, and kissed him. And Moses told Aaron all the words of the Lord who had sent him, and all the signs which he had commanded him. And Moses and Aaron went and gathered together all the elders of the children of Israel: and Aaron spake all the words which the Lord had spoken unto Moses, and did the signs in the sight of the people. And the people believed: and when they heard that the Lord had visited the children of Israel, and that he had looked upon their affliction, then they bowed their heads and worshiped."

A short life of faith and of reverence!

"And afterward Moses and Aaron went in, and told Pharaoh, Thus saith Jehovah, the God of Israel, Let my people go, that they may hold a feast unto me in the wilderness.

"And Pharaoh said, Who is Jehovah, that I should obey his voice to let Israel go? I know not Jehovah, neither will I let Israel go.

"And they said, The God of the Hebrews hath met with us: let us go, we pray thee, three days' journey into the desert, and sacrifice unto Jehovah our God; lest he fall upon us with pestilence, or with the sword.

"And the king of Egypt said unto them, Wherefore do ye, Moses and Aaron, let the people from their works [hinder them from their work]? Get you unto your burdens. And Pharaoh said, Behold, the people of the land now are many, and ye make them rest from their burdens. And Pharaoh commanded the same day the taskmasters of the people, and their officers, saying, Ye shall no more give the people straw to make brick, as heretofore: let them go and gather straw for themselves. And the tale of the bricks, which they did make heretofore, ye shall lay upon them; ye shall not diminish aught thereof: for they be idle; therefore they cry, saying, Let us go and sacrifice to our God. Let there more work be laid upon the men, that they may labor therein; and let them not regard vain words.

"So the people were scattered abroad throughout all the land of Egypt to gather stubble instead of straw. And the taskmasters hasted them, saying, Fulfill your works, your daily tasks, as when there was straw. And the officers of the children of Israel, which Pharaoh's taskmasters had set over them, were beaten, and demanded, Wherefore have ye not fulfilled your task in making brick both yesterday and to-day as heretofore?

"Then the officers of the children of Israel came and cried unto Pharaoh, saying, Wherefore dealest thou thus with thy servants? There is no straw given unto thy servants, and they say to us, Make brick: and, behold, thy servants are beaten; but the fault is in thine own people. But he said, Ye are idle, ye are idle: therefore ye say, Let us go and do sacrifice to Jehovah. Go therefore now, and work; for there shall no straw be given you, yet shall ye deliver the tale of bricks."

This was more than even slave human nature could bear; and when Moses and Aaron went back to meet them they said unto them,—

"Jehovah look upon you, and judge; because ye have made our savor to be abhorred in the eyes of Pharaoh, and in the eyes of his servants, to put a sword in their hand to slay us."

Again they turned on their emancipators that would have been.

"And Moses returned unto the Lord, and said, Lord, wherefore hast thou so evil entreated this people? why is it that thou hast sent me? For since I came to Pharaoh to speak in thy name, he hath done evil to this people: neither hast thou delivered thy people at all. Then the Lord said unto Moses, Now shalt thou see what I will do to Pharaoh: for with a strong hand shall he let them go, and with a strong hand shall he drive them out of his land."

After a rehearsal of the various points of history, to emphasize the memory of the fathers and of God's administration, there follows an account, doubtless taken from interjected fragments in the narrative, of the heads of the house of Israel.

"And the Lord spake unto Moses and unto Aaron, saying, When Pharaoh shall speak unto you, Show a miracle for you: then thou shalt say unto Aaron, Take thy rod, and cast it before Pharaoh, and it shall become a serpent. And Moses and Aaron went in unto Pharaoh, and they did so as the Lord had commanded: and Aaron cast down his rod before Pharaoh, and before his servants, and it became a serpent. Then Pharaoh also called the wise men and the sorcerers: now the magicians of Egypt, they also did in like manner with their enchantments. For they cast down every man his rod, and they became serpents: but Aaron's rod swallowed up their rods. And he hardened Pharaoh's heart, that he hearkened not unto them; as the Lord had said. And the Lord said unto Moses, Pharaoh's heart is hardened, he refuseth to let the people go. Get thee unto Pharaoh in the morning."

Now, by whichever theory men take of this history, we enter upon a scene which is of like interest—namely, what may be called the struggle between dynasty and democracy. It is a contest between the spirit of freedom and the spirit of oppression, between justice and liberty and proud monarchic power despotically established. The histories are of efforts to make slaves free, and of the bombarding, the beating down, of the dynastic oppressor. These histories follow in regular order; and it is to the points involved in them that all these miracles are addressed.

"And the Lord spake unto Moses, Say unto Aaron, Take thy rod, and stretch out thine hand upon the waters of Egypt, upon their streams, upon their rivers, and upon their ponds, and upon all their pools of water, that they may become blood; and that there may be blood throughout all the land of Egypt, both in vessels of wood, and in vessels of stone.

"And Moses and Aaron did so, as the Lord commanded; and he lifted up the rod, and smote the waters that were in the river, in the sight of Pharaoh, and in the sight of his servants; and all the waters that were in the river were turned to blood. And the fish that was in the river died; and the river stank, and the Egyptians could not drink of the water of the river; and there was blood throughout all the land of Egypt. And the magicians of Egypt did so with their enchantments: and Pharaoh's heart was hardened, neither did he hearken unto them; as the Lord had said. And Pharaoh turned and went into his house, neither did he set his heart to this also. And all the Egyptians digged around about the river for water to drink; for they could not drink of the water of the river."

Then Moses and Aaron go to Pharaoh again and threaten another plague upon him.

"And the Lord spake unto Moses, Go unto Pharaoh, and say unto him, Thus saith the Lord, Let my people go, that they may serve me. And if thou refuse to let them go, behold, I will smite all thy borders with frogs: and the river shall bring forth frogs abundantly, which shall go up and come into thine house, and into thy bedchamber, and upon thy bed, and into the house of thy servants, and upon thy people, and into thine ovens, and into thy kneadingtroughs: and the frogs shall come up both on thee, and upon thy people, and upon all thy servants. And the Lord spake unto Moses, Say unto Aaron, Stretch forth thine hand with thy rod over the streams, over the rivers, and over the ponds, and cause frogs to come up upon the land of Egypt."

A few frogs might be evaded or avoided, though with disgust; but to have the whole land carpeted with them, to step on them, to go wading among them as in the mud, and crushing them under one's feet, would be disagreeable, to say the least. There was not, perhaps, anything terrific in it but there was enough that was repulsive.

"Then Pharaoh called for Moses and Aaron, and said, Intreat Jehovah, that he may take away the frogs from me, and from my people; and I will let the people go, that they may do sacrifice unto Jehovah. And Moses said unto Pharaoh, Glory over me: when shall I intreat for thee, and for thy servants, and for thy people, to destroy the frogs from thee and thy houses, that they may remain in the river only? And he said, To-morrow. And he said, Be it according to thy word: that thou mayest know that there is none like unto Jehovah our God. And the frogs shall depart from thee, and from thy houses, and from thy servants, and from thy people; they shall remain in the river only.

"And Moses and Aaron went out from Pharaoh: and Moses cried unto the Lord because of the frogs which he had brought against Pharaoh. And the Lord did according to the word of Moses; and the frogs died out of the houses, out of the villages, and out of the fields. And they gathered them together upon heaps: and the land stank."

When the evil was removed Pharaoh returned to his obstinacy.

"And the Lord said unto Moses, Say unto Aaron, Stretch out thy rod, and smite the dust of the land, that it may become lice throughout all the land of Egypt."

This was bringing the matter home!

"And they did so; for Aaron stretched out his hand with his rod, and smote the dust of the earth, and it became lice in man, and in beast; all the dust of the land became lice throughout all the land of Egypt. And the magicians did so with their enchantments to bring forth lice, but they could not: so there were lice upon man, and upon beast. Then the magicians said unto Pharaoh, This is the finger of God: and Pharaoh's heart was hardened, and he hearkened not unto them; as the Lord had said.

"And the Lord said unto Moses, Rise up early in the morning, and stand before Pharaoh; lo, he cometh forth to the water; and say unto him, Thus saith Jehovah, Let my people go, that they may serve me. Else, if thou wilt not let my people go, behold, I will send swarms of flies upon thee, and upon thy servants, and upon thy people, and into thy houses: and the houses of the Egyptians shall be full of swarms of flies, and also the ground whereon they are. And I will sever in that day the land of Goshen, in which my people dwell, that no swarms of flies shall be there; to the end thou mayest know that I am Jehovah in the midst of the earth. And I will put a division between my people and thy people: to-morrow shall this sign be.

"And the Lord did so; and there came a grievous swarm of flies into the house of Pharaoh, and into his servants' houses, and into all the land of Egypt: the land was corrupted by reason of the swarm of flies. And Pharaoh called for Moses and for Aaron, and said, Go ye, sacrifice to your God in the land [that is, here, in Egypt]. And Moses said, It is not meet so to do; for we shall sacrifice the abomination of the Egyptians to the Lord our God: lo, shall we sacrifice the abomination of the Egyptians before their eyes, and will they not stone us? We will go three days' journey into the wilderness, and sacrifice to Jehovah our God; as he shall command us. And Pharaoh said, I will let you go, that ye may sacrifice to Jehovah, your God, in the wilderness; only ye shall not go very far away: intreat for me.

"And Moses said, Behold, I go out from thee, and I will intreat Jehovah that the swarms of flies may depart from Pharaoh, from his servants, and from his people, to-morrow: but let not Pharaoh deal deceitfully any more in not letting the people go to sacrifice to Jehovah.

"And Moses went out from Pharaoh, and intreated the Lord. And the Lord did according to the word of Moses; and he removed the swarms of flies from Pharaoh, from his servants, and from his people: there remained not one. And Pharaoh hardened his heart at this time also, neither would he let the people go."

Then still more strenuous measures were resorted to.

"All the cattle of Egypt died; but of the cattle of the children of Israel died not one. And Pharaoh sent, and, behold, there was not one of the cattle of the Israelites dead. And the heart of Pharaoh was hardened, and he did not let the people go.

"And the Lord said unto Moses and unto Aaron, Take to you handfuls of ashes of the furnace, and let Moses sprinkle it toward the heaven in the sight of Pharaoh. And it shall become small dust in all the land of Egypt, and shall be a boil breaking forth with blains upon man, and upon beast, throughout all the land of Egypt. And they took ashes of the furnace, and stood before Pharaoh; and Moses sprinkled it up toward heaven; and it became a boil breaking forth with blains upon man, and upon beast. And the magicians could not stand before Moses because of the boils; for the boil was upon the magicians, and upon all the Egyptians. And the Lord hardened the heart of Pharaoh, and he hearkened not unto them; as the Lord had spoken unto Moses.

"So there was hail, and fire mingled with the hail, very grievous, such as there was none like it in all the land of Egypt since it became a nation. And the hail smote throughout all the land of Egypt all that was in the field, both man and beast; and the hail smote every herb of the field, and brake every tree of the field. Only in the land of Goshen, where the children of Israel were, was there no hail."

Pharaoh now sent for Moses and Aaron, and confessed that he had sinned, and promised that if the thunderings and hail should be stopped he would let the people of Israel go. So they were stopped; but the king's heart was again hardened, and he refused to let them go. And Moses went once more to Pharaoh, and said,—

"Thus saith Jehovah God of the Hebrews, How long wilt thou refuse to humble thyself before me? Let my people go, that they may serve me. Else, if thou refuse to let my people go, behold, to-morrow will I bring the locusts into thy coast:"

and he described the plague that should be, and went out from Pharaoh.

"And Pharaoh's servants said unto him, How long shall this man be a snare unto us? let the men go, that they may serve Jehovah their God: knowest thou not yet that Egypt is destroyed? And Moses and Aaron were brought again unto Pharaoh: and he said unto them, Go, serve Jehovah your God: but who are they that shall go? And Moses said, We will go with our young and with our old, with our sons and with our daughters, with our flocks and with our herds will we go; for we must hold a feast unto Jehovah. And he said unto them, Let Jehovah be so with you, as I will let you go, and your little ones: look to it; for evil is before you. Not so: go now ye that are men, and serve the Lord; for that ye did desire. And they were driven out from Pharaoh's presence.

"And the Lord said unto Moses, Stretch out thine hand over the land of Egypt for the locusts, that they may come up upon the land of Egypt, and eat every herb of the land, even all that the hail hath left. And Moses stretched forth his rod over the land of Egypt, and the Lord brought an east wind upon the land all that day, and all that night; and when it was morning, the east wind brought the locusts. And the locusts went up over all the land of Egypt, and rested in all the coasts of Egypt: very grievous were they; before them there were no such locusts as they, neither after them shall be such. For they covered the face of the whole earth, so that the land was darkened; and they did eat every herb of the land, and all the fruit of the trees which the hail had left: and there remained not any green thing in the trees, or in the herbs of the field, through all the land of Egypt.

"Then Pharaoh called for Moses and Aaron in haste; and he said, I have sinned against Jehovah your God, and against you. Now therefore forgive, I pray thee, my sin only this once, and intreat Jehovah your God, that he may take away from me this death only. And he went out from Pharaoh, and intreated the Lord. And the Lord turned a mighty strong west wind, which took away the locusts, and cast them into the Red Sea; there remained not one locust in all the coasts of Egypt.

"But the Lord hardened Pharaoh's heart, so that he would not let the children of Israel go. And the Lord said unto Moses, Stretch out thine hand toward heaven, that there may be darkness over the land of Egypt, even darkness which may be felt. And Moses stretched forth his hand toward heaven; and there was a thick darkness in all the land of Egypt three days: they saw not one another, neither rose any from his place for three days: but all the children of Israel had light in their dwellings. And Pharaoh called unto Moses, and said, Go ye, serve Jehovah; only let your flocks and your herds be stayed; let your little ones also go with you. And Moses said, Thou must give us also sacrifices and burnt offerings, that we may sacrifice unto the Lord our God. Our cattle also shall go with us; there shall not an hoof be left behind; for thereof must we take to serve Jehovah our God; and we know not with what we must serve Jehovah, until we come thither. But the Lord hardened Pharaoh's heart, and he would not let them go. And Pharaoh said unto him, Get thee from me, take heed to thyself, see my face no more; for in that day thou seest my face thou shalt die.

"And Moses said, Thou hast spoken well, I will see thy face again no more."

Then a great plague was declared. The firstborn of every household in Egypt was to be stricken with death at the midnight hour, and it was this, as the most memorable event of their experience, that was to be handed down through all generations as a token of the power of God over his people. It was for this sake that the Feast of the Passover was then instituted, of which an account is given. The children of Israel were commanded to take lambs, preparing them in a certain way for eating, and they were to take hyssop branches, and with the blood of the lambs they were to smite the lintels of the doors and posts, that the destroying angel might pass by,—blood, among all ancient nations, being the symbol of life. Thus all the Israelites were protected.

And then, at midnight, the scourge came, and there was not a house in all the city, nor in all the suburbs, nor in all the villages, nor along the line of the great river, far and wide, that there was not lamentation, and the cry, " Death, Death is here!" Thereupon,—

"Pharaoh rose up in the night, he, and all his servants, and all the Egyptians; and there was a great cry in Egypt; for there was not a house where there was not one dead."

The whole people moved, that time, and were urgent upon the Israelites to send them out of the land in haste. So the Hebrews made their march. And what a march, without organization, it must have been! At any rate, they went forth, pursuing an eastward course. Instead of making directly for Canaan, the promised land, where it would have been necessary for them to meet a warlike people in fortified cities, they turned somewhat from the east toward the south, and came to the head of the Red Sea. There they found themselves surrounded on either side by mountains, with an arm of the sea before them. Pharaoh, having recovered sufficiently from the shock of the last plague which had been sent upon the Egyptians, had sent forth his army, and was pursuing them; and the Israelites cried out, charging Moses with having brought them out of Egypt that they might be destroyed in the wilderness.

But the Word of the Lord came unto Moses, saying, "Speak unto the children of Israel that they *go forward.*" According to the divine command Moses stretched his hand over the sea, and God, by a strong east wind, laid bare the sands, so that the fugitive throng passed on across, and landed upon the other side. Pharaoh's host followed after them. The force that had rolled back the waves was by the divine command suspended, and the waters returned and whelmed the Egyptians, and they were destroyed.

Here we leave the narrative, and, looking upon the far shore, in that motley crowd we behold two figures—Miriam and Moses—sister and brother.

"Then sang Moses and the children of Israel this song unto the Lord, and spake, saying,—

"I will sing unto the Lord, for he hath triumphed gloriously: The horse and his rider hath he thrown into the sea."

This sublime tragedy thus ends, not with the lurid light of the plagues that fell upon the obstinate monarch of Egypt; nor does it end, to our imagination, with the irregular movement of that great mob of Israelitish people : we have in our thought that people, brought out by a powerful hand and a stretched-out arm into a land of freedom, and behold them lingering upon the shore of the Red Sea, across which they have been so miraculously led, singing songs of triumph and joy and praise to Jehovah.

So, the mighty drama is accomplished. The name of one God, and only one, has been celebrated by mighty acts and wonderful judgments. The obstinacy of despotism has been beaten down. Emancipation has been declared, and is on the way toward realization.

If you regard this as history, it is memorable history. If you consider it as history couched in the form of magnificent drama, there is no other like it. There is no other drama that attempts to deal with the mighty theme of the breaking loose of a great people from an iron hand. There is no other drama whose actors are so sublime—whose heroes or prophets act, from day to day, under the inspiration of God himself. The heavens and the earth; the forces of nature; all the elements which men have been accustomed to regard as powers,—all of these are brought into play in this wonderful picture; and out of their desolate and abandoned condition this great nation, by the hand of their fathers' God, were transplanted into the school of the desert and the wilderness.

Our next discourse in this series will be a brief rehearsal of their passage from the side of the Red Sea to the banks of the Jordan ; and after that I shall undertake, if life and strength permit, a still more difficult task—namely, that of presenting the constitution which Moses framed for the education and government of that people. Our own constitution is one of the posterity of that of the wilderness. The timber that has been wrought into the fabric of this great nation was grown in the desert of Arabia, and the architect of the structure under whose roof we ourselves dwell was Moses—the greatest name of antiquity. If you take into consideration the various departments in which he served, if you bear in mind his prophetic gifts, his leadership and generalship, his constructive power in legislation, his administrative talent, his literary and poetic endowments, his is the greatest name—except the Name which is above every name—that ever dwelt upon the earth.

XI.

THE WILDERNESS AND SINAI.

"And thou shalt remember all the way which the Lord thy God led thee these forty years in the wilderness, to humble thee, and to prove thee, to know what was in thine heart, whether thou wouldest keep his commandments, or no. And he humbled thee, and suffered thee to hunger, and fed thee with manna, which thou knewest not, neither did thy fathers know; that he might make thee know that man doth not live by bread only, but by every word that proceedeth out of the mouth of the Lord doth man live."

LAST Sabbath night we dropped the history of the Israelites in their hour of triumph, upon the eastern shore of the western branch of the Red Sea, or the Gulf of Suez. At last Egypt was behind them. Their bondage was over. A new life was opening to them. It was but a little more than one hundred miles to the land that God had sworn to give to their fathers—Abraham, Isaac, and Jacob, and the twelve tribes; and the way was not difficult. It was the way of the caravans, over which almost all the commerce between the plain of Heliopolis, or what was the easterly part of the land of Goshen, and the southern part of Palestine, was carried on. Instead of following this road, Moses went three days into the wilderness; then he turned southward; and it was forty years before the tribes took possession of the promised land.

The question arises, Why should this have been? Why was not the ordinary path taken? If it be replied that there were necessities of discipline, as I shall show in a moment, it may be asked, Since God was in the way of working miracles, why did he not work a comprehensive miracle at this time? Why did he not inspire the people with miraculous courage? Why did he not disregard the Hivites, the Jebusites, and all the other *ites*, and let the people go at once into the promised land?

There were two reasons that I think will be obvious upon their being unfolded. In regard, first, to this working of miracles, neither then nor since—that is, neither in the Old Testament dispensation nor in the New—were miracles wrought for the sake of working them, nor for the sake of avoiding natural difficulties. They did not undertake to substitute divine omnipotence for human will, education, and faith. They were auxiliary, occasional; and they were always wrought, not for the purpose of relieving men from special personal troubles, but for the purpose of inspiring men that were rude and unenlightened with the highest conception of God, the Invisible—for the purpose of bringing down to human comprehension the fact that God maintained providence, ruled in heaven, and controlled natural law. In so far as it was necessary to fill the imagination with this sense of God, so far miracles became a part of the education of the people; but to go on with them, and take away all motive for exertion or courage or learning by making everything miraculously easy would have been to have reared idiots and not men.

The reason, then, why the direct path was not taken to Palestine was, first, a military one. It is true that the Israelites had men of war among them; it is true that it was the policy of Pharaoh to make these men defenders of the frontier, and along the line that separated the cultivated portion of Goshen from the wilderness (it should be called a wilderness, and not a desert) beyond. Along the line where he might fear the incursions of wandering tribes or great peoples—there, by policy, he encouraged military development. So, when the Israelites went out they were not to go devoid of experience in warfare, or of brave men, as we shall have occasion to show. Nevertheless, if there were a million or a million and a half (I should rather take the lower figure than the higher; because we are not altogether acquainted with enumeration as it existed at that time, and the tendency is to exaggerate numbers) that was a large band to move. There is nothing else in history like it. The only thing that approaches it is the account by De Quincey of the uprooting of the great Tartar tribe from the midst of Russia, and its march across the continent back again to the borders of China, the land of its fathers; and that was a horrible experience. There is not in any literature a more wonderful delineation of such a scene than that given by De Quincey. But this journey of the people of Israel was more methodical. It was like taking a great nation out of a fat valley, where they were slaves and idolaters, and setting them down in a hard pasturage country, where they were to be pupils. It was the School of the Wilderness to which they were going They were to become scholars.

It is probable that they did not advance more than ten miles a day. The women and children and flocks certainly could not have been moved faster than that. If they had crossed the southern borders of Palestine they would easily have been attacked in the front and flank by those who had possession of the land, whose business was warfare, and who were armed and always ready; so that the greatest disasters would have come to them. They were therefore turned away from the northern route to the east and south.

For another reason they were put through this passage of the wilderness. They were not fit for settlement in Palestine: they were as little fit for it as they were for fighting their way directly to it.

You will take notice that in our text the reason given for their carriage through the wilderness is that they might be educated—for that is the real meaning of the statement.

"Thou shalt remember all the way which Jehovah thy God led thee these forty years [this was after it was all over] in the wilderness, to humble thee and to prove thee, to know what was in thine heart, whether thou wouldest keep his commandments, or no."

They were going into a state of discipline, of schooling, that they might develop the moral, social, and civil qualities necessary for a permanent nationality.

"And he humbled thee, and suffered thee to hunger, and fed thee with manna, which thou knewest not, neither did thy fathers know; that he might make thee know that man doth not live by bread only, but by every word that proceedeth out of the mouth of the Lord doth man live."

They were to understand that God was the only true end of the highest manhood; and that they might develop this higher manhood in the center of the wilderness. For such a purpose as that the wilderness certainly was good. If the people were to be nationalized, if they were not to be scattered into alliances on the right and on the left, it was desirable that they should have their training in the wilderness, where they would be little liable to attack. They were to be compacted; they were to be brought into obedience; they were to have institutions; they were to be educated in laws and customs; and above all they were to have a spiritual religion opened up before them, with its truths and inspirations.

This was an immense undertaking. It was one of the most gigantic conceptions that ever entered into the heart of man—that of bringing a great people out from the midst of the most powerful military nation on the globe, taking them into a wilderness, where there were no cities, no villages, no industrial developments of any kind, and there drilling them as soldiers, breaking them in as citizens, regulating their habits, and inspiring in. them an *esprit de corps*, a national spirit of patriotism, that should hold them together; and doing these things chiefly by unfolding in them the idea of a pure theocracy, of only one God, holding in his hands the heaven above, the earth beneath, and all laws and influences.

To them the word *law*, as applied in the modern sense of the methods in which God's forces act, would mean nothing. It was long before the development of that theory in the human race What we call *natural laws* were not known for thousands of years after that time. Instead of the modern scientific knowledge of the method of God in the administration of his power through great natural agencies, it was indispensable that a ruder government should be resorted to ; and that ruder government was an impression upon their imagination that all the great elements of nature were, at one time or another, under the control—before their eyes, they being witnesses—of the God of Moses,—the invisible God, whom it was impossible to represent by picture or carved statue. A great nation, besotted, servile, could not have been taken and made to serve an invisible God, in Egypt, and along the valley of the Nile, where they had been used to seeing gods in animals and images and symbols on every side, and would have been subjected to the attack and solicitation of neighboring nations with their idolatrous tendencies.

There is one thought that may perhaps be of service here. That was a time in the history of the Israelites when their minds were not unfolded to the simplest ideas above material fact ; but now there has developed a divine economy by which even rude and coarse natures in almost all nations are brought into a fuller understanding of the divine nature. The truth comes in here which I mentioned in my second lecture—namely, that inspiration, or revelation, is limited by the receiving power of those to whom it is made, and that it is impossible to disclose any more of unseen truth than is within the capacity of the men to whom it is given to comprehend. All the world may be full of sunshine ; but if the roof be slate, and the windows be covered, and the doors be closed, there can be no sunshine in the house. There is darkness there. There can be in any structure no more of the light of the continental, atmospheric sun than can pass through the aperture by which it is admitted. And in dealing with the primitive races the divine interference was adapted not only to the wants of men, but to their ability to appropriate what they received. For those early ages would naturally be instituted an economy that to us would be full of strange lights and shadows. More advanced methods, that would be entirely understandable to you, would not have been understood by men who lived in the time of Moses. You can well see that what in the olden time was considered

14

manly wisdom is like nursery talk of later generations. The attempt to put into the minds of children ideas which they have had no experience to enable them to grasp, would be futile. How often the mother is obliged to say to the child, when it desires information on subjects that are above its comprehension, "Wait, my darling, till you are older, and then you will understand these things."

The problem of the instruction of the Israelites in the wilderness, then, was the problem of the nursery. It was like undertaking to put knowledge into the mind of an unknowing child. And if sometimes there seems to be a strange use of natural causes, and at times an abandonment of them, much must be attributed to our ignorance in the divine adaptation of means to ends; to the fact that in the early period of the human race there were obtusenesses of which we can form scarcely any conception, and which required striking methods to arouse the sluggish mentality below.

Another thing: when you think of the children of Israel as being in a "wilderness," you must not imagine that it was a desert, or such a wilderness as that west of Egypt, where sand hills roll as waves of the ocean. Far from it. Modern travelers say that there are but one or two places in the Sinaitic Peninsula where sand prevails, and that for the most part there is a rock formation there. The peninsula, or portion of the country inclosed between the outstretched arms of the Red Sea, is not, in shape, unlike a horse-shoe, bent out a little; and the central part of it is rocky upland. The lower section is mountainous. Between the mountains run sinuous valleys, not altogether barren, and yet not fertile like our western valleys, but, with their water courses, affording a very fair sustenance for herds, for flocks of sheep, and for goats. Here and there was an oasis on which grass and shrubs and herbs grew; and the Israelites went forth with large flocks and herds; and as they traveled from place to place, pasturing their animals as they went, much of their subsistence consisted of milk.

It is probable that in the ancient day there was far better herbage in that region than there is now. We know that in Palestine, for instance, in the time of the Old Testament Scripture, it was clothed with forests, while to-day there is not in all of Palestine a good-sized tree. For purposes of war, or other uses, the growth has been almost entirely cut away. Although there may be new growths coming afterward, especially on the part east of the Jordan, other portions have been denuded to such an extent that Abraham and Isaac and Jacob would not enter them. If they came to them and looked at them, they would pass them by. The same causes have laid bare the Sinaitic wilderness. There were formerly more trees, shrubs, undergrowth, and grasses there than there are to-day.

Looking, then, upon the mission of Moses, and his purpose to inform and train this horde of degraded slaves into a great nation, and looking upon this rocky and pastoral wilderness as a schoolhouse, let us follow them on their way to school.

First, we shall notice the three murmurings with which this part of their history opens.

"So Moses brought Israel from the Red Sea, and they went out into the wilderness of Shur; and they went three days in the wilderness, and found no water. And when they came to Marah, they could not drink of the waters of Marah, for they were bitter."

Probably they were alkaline.

"And the people murmured against Moses [of course against *Moses*—on the leader of any people come all the complaints], saying, What shall we drink? And he cried unto the Lord; and the Lord showed him a tree, which when he had cast into the waters the waters were made sweet: there he made for them a statute and an ordinance, and there he proved them, and said, If thou wilt diligently hearken to the voice of Jehovah thy God, and wilt do that which is right in his sight, and wilt give ear to his commandments, and keep all his statutes, I will put none of these diseases upon thee, which I have brought upon the Egyptians: for I am Jehovah that healeth thee."

Does anyone say that to work a miracle and sweeten a bitter spring is scarcely worthy of God, who is the governor of the processes of the natural world? But was it not worthy of Moses, the schoolmaster of a nation, was it not wise in him, when he desired to impress upon them the reality of the divine presence and power in every natural agency, to take an occasion like this to bring to bear upon the imagination and conviction of this great people the fact that God had sweetened these waters right before their eyes, and incline them to believe, and to say, "There is a God, an invisible Ruler, in the heaven"?

"And they came to Elim, where were twelve wells of water, and threescore and ten palm trees [this gathering of palm trees remains, and has increased to the number of some two thousand, we are told]. And they encamped there by the waters. And they took their journey from Elim, and all the congregation of the children of Israel came unto the wilderness of Sin, which is between Elim and Sinai, on the fifteenth day of the second month after their departing out of the land of Egypt.

"And the whole congregation of the children of Israel murmured against Moses and Aaron in the wilderness: and the children of Israel said unto them, Would to God we had died by the hand of Jehovah in the land of Egypt, when we sat by the flesh pots, and when we did eat bread to the full; for ye have brought us forth into this wilderness, to kill this whole assembly with hunger."

There you get the level of this people. The moment they were thirsty life was nothing, heroism was nothing, and religion was nothing, to them. The moment they were hungry there was nothing else in all the world, to their minds, but food. They lived for the belly.

"Then said the Lord unto Moses, Behold, I will rain bread from heaven for you; and the people shall go out and gather a certain rate every day, that I may prove them, whether they will walk in my law, or no. And it shall come to pass, that on the sixth day they shall prepare that which they bring in; and it shall be twice as much as they gather daily. And Moses and Aaron said unto all the children of Israel, At even, then ye shall know that Jehovah hath brought you out from the land of Egypt: and in the morning, then ye shall see the glory of Jehovah; for that he heareth your murmurings against Jehovah: and what are we, that ye murmur against us?"

It was as if they had said, "It is not our power or skill, but God, that is leading you."

"And Moses said, This shall be, when Jehovah shall give you in the evening flesh to eat, and in the morning bread to the full; for that Jehovah heareth your murmurings which ye murmur against him: and what are we? Your murmurings are not against us, but against Jehovah. And Moses spake unto Aaron, Say unto all the congregation of the children of Israel, Come near before the Lord: for he hath heard your murmurings. And it came to pass as Aaron spake unto the whole congregation of the children of Israel, that they looked toward the wilderness, and, behold, the glory of Jehovah appeared in the cloud [some light, some image, some illumination]. And Jehovah spake unto Moses, saying, I have heard the murmurings of the children of Israel: speak unto them, saying, At even ye shall eat flesh, and in the morning ye shall be filled with bread; and ye shall know that I am the Lord your God."

It was right to feed them, that they might know the reality of God, and of his presence with them.

"And it came to pass, that at even the quails came up, and covered the camp."

It is not necessary to suppose that in each case there was a turning aside from or overcoming of some known natural law, and introducing some natural law with which men were not before acquainted. Anything that is not understood, and that excites wonder, is regarded as a miracle; but that is not always true. This statement in regard to the quails is said to accord with a historical fact recurring to this day. We are told that they sometimes came in flocks that almost darkened the sun at certain periods; and very likely the account here given may have related to one of those instances. Whether it did or not, whether or not Moses' long years of familiarity in all this region gave him knowledge of such exceptional resources, whether the circumstance occurred first at that time or not, its coming at that time marked it to them as a divine interference.

Then came, the next morning, the miracle of the manna.

"And in the morning the dew lay round about the host. And when the dew that lay was gone up, behold, upon the face of the wilderness there lay a small round thing, as small as the hoar frost on the ground. And when the children of Israel saw it, they said one to another, It is manna: for they wist not what it was. And Moses said unto them, This is the bread which the Lord hath given you to eat."

I have been reading, this week, a long line of discussions on the part of men who want to show that what was called "manna" was an exudation from the acacia tree. They want to get around the miracle. I do not propose to get around it in any way, so long as there is no other solution than that of the statement here. You have got either to jump this statement or take it. There is no getting around it or modifying it.

You will take notice that there fell enough manna to feed about fifteen hundred thousand people. There must have been a good many acacia bushes to give out enough gum for the consumption of that number of people. They were to gather of this manna every morning on six days— an omer for every mouth. An omer is about three quarts; so there were three quarts for each man, woman, and child. They gathered it every day, a quart for a meal. That was for bread only. They were, of course, to have the nourishment which sprang from the flocks—the usual nourishment of wandering people. This continued during their whole stay in the regions of Sinai, Moab, and Kadesh, to Palestine; but when they crossed the Jordan, and came to Gilgal, and found old corn, they began to eat that. Then, and only then, the manna was withheld from them.

This is the statement; and if you can make any natural explanation of it you are more ingenious than I am, or than I can conceive anybody to be. It is in accordance with the faith of the people at the time, and of the people that came after them. It has entered into Christian literature everywhere, and Christian faith throughout the world. It is supposed that this manna fell down from heaven every morning. The falling down of manna every morning from heaven is very properly expressed, and likened to the down-coming of the divine influence upon our souls. The inspiration and the comfort of the Holy Ghost vouchsafed to men is represented, in the minds of men, by the descent of the manna to the people in the wilderness.

On the Sabbath there was to be no gathering. The acacia bushes would not bear on the Sabbath! On the day before they bore twice as much as on other week days, and the children of Israel were commanded to gather two omers; and although on every other day this exudation, this manna, would keep only during twenty-four hours, that which they gathered on Friday kept all that day and through the Sabbath. The amount of it, the continuance of it, and the peculiarities of its condition in their hands, all seem to lead to one single conclusion—either that the statement is absolute fiction or that it is a fact. If it is a fact it is a miracle,—and a most stupendous miracle. It stands over against the greatest miracle of Christ; for you will recall that while raising the dead was in some respects to us among the most wonderful acts wrought by Christ, yet a greater act performed by him was the feeding of the five thousand by the multiplying of the loaf. When this latter miracle was wrought it produced such an effect on the imagination of the people that they declared that God had come, that here was a king, and that he should be crowned; and they sought to take him by violence and compel him to lead them to glory and to victory. This sending of the manna was more impressive than the light that went by night and the cloud that went by day before the people of God.

The next and third murmuring was for the same reason—the want of something to drink.

"And all the congregation of the children of Israel journeyed from the wilderness of Sin, after their journeys, according to the commandment of the Lord, and pitched in Rephidim [the precise locality we cannot now determine], and there was no water for the people to drink. Wherefore the people did chide with Moses, and said, Give us water that we may drink. And Moses said unto them, Why chide ye with me? wherefore do ye tempt Jehovah? And the people thirsted there for water; and the people murmured against Moses, and said, Wherefore is this that thou hast brought us up out of Egypt, to kill us and our children and our cattle with thirst? And Moses cried unto Jehovah, saying, What shall I do unto this people? they be almost ready to stone me."

There never has been a king or president since that time who has not felt the same way. When anything goes wrong the people want to stone the leader or head of the party or nation.

"And Jehovah said unto Moses, Go on before the people, and take with thee of the elders of Israel; and thy rod, wherewith thou smotest the river, take in thine hand, and go. Behold, I will stand before thee there upon the rock in Horeb; and thou shalt smite the rock, and there shall come water out of it, that the people may drink. And Moses did so in the sight of the elders of Israel. And he called the name of the place Massah [Tempting, or Proving], and Meribah [Chiding, or Strife], because of the chiding of the children of Israel, and because they tempted the Lord, saying, Is Jehovah among us, or not?"

That event has wrought itself into the history of the world. The familiar and beautiful hymn—

> " Rock of ages, cleft for me,
> Let me hide myself in thee,"

had its origin in this scene.

Again, then, the people were supplied with water by the miraculous interposition of God through his servant Moses.

At this point the Israelites had their first conflict. Tidings came to them that a great people had broken into their pastoral grounds. Amalek had sent out couriers, gathered together a great army, and fallen upon the Israelites. By this time, doubtless, considerable order had been introduced into the camp of the children of Israel, and when Amalek attacked them they were not altogether unprepared for self-defense. Not much is told about the fighting; but the same thought runs through this part of the history as through other portions—namely, that of the attempt to fasten the minds of these idolaters upon the sustaining power and protection of their invisible God. Moses ascended a near hill, and stood as if imploring Jehovah, and as long as his hands were lifted up in an attitude of prayer, so long they made headway against the attacking tribe; but as his hands grew weary and fell, the conflict wavered. It is probable that the people saw it, and that whenever his hands were lowered they lost courage, while when they were lifted up they were inspired with heroism. We know how a fighting body, by a wave either of panic or enthusiasm, can be driven forward or backward at a critical moment. So Aaron, and Hur (who is represented to have been the husband of Miriam's sister), held up Moses' hands in prayer. This striking figure appears in literature the world over to express spiritual help given by men to one another.

The Amalekites were utterly defeated by the Israelites

under Joshua, who here first appears as a military leader. Just why Moses promulgated a decree of extermination against these first attackers of the Israelites, in the name of Jehovah, does not appear: perhaps because of some peculiar cruelty in their attack. But he did; and after the entrance into the promised land only a handful of the Amalekites remained. The decree uttered against them had been fulfilled.

Now we come to the most significant experience in all the wanderings of the Israelites. It occurred around about Sinai, in the peninsula, in the third month after the exodus from Egypt. There has been much discussion in respect to this mountain. There is a cluster of mountains, much like our White Mountains in New Hampshire, with which you are familiar. There are eight or ten peaks in the White Mountain cluster. The highest, Mount Washington, is well known. The question as to whether a particular event took place on one or another peak of a cluster of mountains may not be very important; and yet it may be exceedingly interesting. It is now pretty well accepted that Mount Sinai was located on the westward flank of this pile of rugged slopes.

We are to bear in mind that those mountains are not simply craggy hills. Their height varies from five to nine thousand miles—*feet*, I mean! I am not a worker of miracles, and therefore I correct myself, and reduce the quantity. Mount Washington is six thousand, three hundred feet high. The highest point in the Sinaitic group is between nine and ten thousand feet high. Besides being rugged, they are gloomy and grand. The whole neighborhood is impressive. The peculiar character of the air about them is such that a person reading in a low tone can be distinctly heard at a distance of sixty feet. The Bedouin Arabs say they can hear across the whole sea of Achbor on the east. This is probably an exaggeration, but it has some foundation in fact.

There is sufficient valley ground to accommodate the number of people that must have encamped there. If modern investigation had shown that there was not room enough for all those people, it would have gone very much against the narrative ; but there is the ground, and there is the mountain standing over against it. These mountains had been visited by the Egyptians. Some of their carving on the rocks there remains to this day.

The Israelites, then, after leaving Rephidim, came into the wilderness of Sinai, and were brought into this great camp-ground, in front of the mount, for the purpose of receiving the Word of God under conditions the most terrible and the most impressive.

The preparation for this deserves a moment's attention. There is given in the nineteenth chapter a reason for it.

"And Moses went up unto God, and the Lord called unto him out of the mountain, saying, Thus shalt thou say to the house of Jacob, and tell the children of Israel : Ye have seen what I did unto the Egyptians, and how I bare you on eagles' wings, and brought you unto myself. Now, therefore, if ye will obey my voice indeed, and keep my covenant, then ye shall be a peculiar treasure unto me above all people : for all the earth is mine : and ye shall be unto me a kingdom of priests, and an holy nation. These are the words which thou shalt speak unto the children of Israel."

Here the drama of emancipation is enunciated as a prelude, and the purpose of what is to follow, which is a moral one of transcendent importance, is made known. Moses commanded all the people to prepare themselves, to wash their clothes, and to practice abstinence from everything that would give sensuousness to their life ; for on the third day Jehovah should be manifested to them upon the mount. Bounds were set about the sacred ground, and no man was to touch the mount on pain of death, nor to approach it.

"And it came to pass on the third day in the morning, that there were thunders and lightnings, and a thick cloud upon the mount, and the voice of the trumpet exceeding loud ; so that all the people that was in the camp trembled. And Moses brought forth the people out of the camp to meet with God ; and they stood at the nether part of the mount. And Mount Sinai was altogether on a smoke, because Jehovah descended upon it in fire : and the smoke thereof ascended as the smoke of a furnace, and the whole mount [some ancient authorities make this *people*] quaked greatly.

And when the voice of the trumpet sounded long, and waxed louder and louder, Moses spake, and Jehovah answered him by a voice."

Compare the majesty and magnificence of this with all those scenes of the appearance of the gods that are mentioned in the Greek and Egyptian mythologies, and that were conceived of by the Romans. It stands without a parallel or an approach in any ancient descriptions of the appearance of God, and is worthy of the glory that has been ascribed to him.

"And the Lord came down upon Mount Sinai, on the top of the mount: and the Lord called Moses up to the top of the mount; and Moses went up. And the Lord said unto Moses, Go down, charge the people, lest they break through unto the Lord to gaze, and many of them perish. And let the priests also, which come near to the Lord, sanctify themselves, lest the Lord break forth upon them. And Moses said unto the Lord, The people cannot come up to Mount Sinai: for thou chargedst us, saying, Set bounds about the mount, and sanctify it."

They were to inspire the whole multitude with the profoundest awe and reverence, as in the very presence of their God.

"And the Lord said unto Moses, Thou shalt come up, thou, and Aaron with thee: but let not the priests and people come up."

"And God spake all these words, saying, I am Jehovah thy God, which have brought thee out of the land of Egypt, out of the house of bondage.

"Thou shalt have no other gods before me.

"Thou shalt not make unto thee any graven image, or any likeness of anything that is in heaven above, or that is in the earth beneath, or that is in the water under the earth: thou shalt not bow down thyself to them, nor serve them: for I Jehovah thy God am a jealous God, visiting the iniquity of the fathers upon the children unto the third and fourth generation of them that hate me; and showing mercy unto thousands of them that love me, and keep my commandments.

"Thou shalt not take the name of Jehovah thy God in vain; for Jehovah will not hold him guiltless that taketh his name in vain.

"Remember the Sabbath day, to keep it holy. Six days shalt thou labor, and do all thy work: but the seventh day is the Sabbath of Jehovah thy God: in it thou shalt not do any work, thou, nor thy son, nor thy daughter, thy manservant, nor thy maidservant, nor thy cattle, nor thy stranger that is within thy gates: for in six days Jehovah made heaven and earth, the sea, and all that in them is, and rested the seventh day: wherefore Jehovah blessed the Sabbath day, and hallowed it.

"Honor thy father and thy mother: that thy days may be long upon the land which Jehovah thy God giveth thee.

"Thou shalt not kill.
"Thou shalt not commit adultery.
"Thou shalt not steal.
"Thou shalt not bear false witness against thy neighbor.
"Thou shalt not covet thy neighbor's house, thou shalt not covet thy neighbor's wife, nor his manservant, nor his maidservant, nor his ox, nor his ass, nor anything that is thy neighbor's."

Moses abode in the mount, it is said, for forty days, receiving from God the whole form of service, and the whole so-called Levitical economy, to which, to a very large extent, the remainder of this book and the whole of the book of Leviticus are devoted. While he was in the mountain an extraordinary scene took place. I shall return to the Ten Commandments after I have finished the story.

It seems that during the long absence of Moses the people forgot their terror and their trembling, and, being released from the master-eye and the master-mind, began to fall back into the habits they had brought up with them from Egypt. They demanded of Aaron that he should make them a graven image of a god such as they had probably worshiped in Egypt, and he did so, making a golden calf, or bull—the Egyptian emblem of creative power—which they worshiped with great turbulence and noise.

"And Moses turned, and went down from the mount, and the two tables of the testimony were in his hand: the tables were written on both their sides; on the one side and on the other were they written. And the tables were the work of God, and the writing was the writing of God, graven upon the tables. And when Joshua heard the noise of the people as they shouted, he said unto Moses, There is a noise of war in the camp. And he said, It is not the voice of them that shout for mastery, neither is it the voice of them that cry for being overcome: but the noise of them that sing do I hear. And it came to pass, as soon as he came nigh unto the camp, that he saw the calf, and the dancing: and Moses' anger waxed hot."

No wonder!

"And he cast the tables out of his hands, and brake them beneath the mount."

It is not likely that he meant to break them, but they broke. Probably they were slabs of granite, thin but heavy; and in the impetuosity of his nature, during an outburst of that same fiery indignation which led him to slay the

Egyptian, under the influence of his rash temper, largely subdued, like coals raked up, dangerous, ready to flame forth, he cast the tables out of his hands, and broke them.

"And he took the calf which they had made, and burnt it in the fire, and ground it to powder, and strawed it upon the water, and made the children of Israel drink of it. And Moses said unto Aaron, What did this people unto thee, that thou hast brought so great a sin upon them? And Aaron said, Let not the anger of my lord wax hot: thou knowest the people, that they are set on mischief. For they said unto me, Make us gods, which shall go before us: for as for this Moses, the man that brought us up out of the land of Egypt, we wot not what is become of him. And I said unto them, Whosoever hath any gold, let them break it off. So they gave it me: then I cast it into the fire, and there came out this calf."

Fool! What a coward, what a liar, what a wretch, shirking all the blame from himself, and making up this miserable story! If a man will lie, he ought to lie somewhere along the border of the probable truth!

Then followed a scene of judgment most terrible:—

"Moses stood in the gate of the camp, and said, Who is on the Lord's side? let him come unto me. And all the sons of Levi gathered themselves together unto him. And he said unto them, Thus saith Jehovah, God of Israel, Put every man his sword by his side, and go in and out from gate to gate throughout the camp, and slay every man his brother, and every man his companion, and every man his neighbor. And the children of Levi did according to the word of Moses: and there fell of the people that day about three thousand men."

It was a time for surgery. This was a condition of things in which the whole scene of emancipation was likely to fall to the ground, and the grand experiment of education was in danger of ignominiously coming to naught; there must be some punishment which should strike the people with such terror and remorse as to bring to an end their defection. After having been, by Almighty God, rescued from the terrible plagues of Egypt; after having been, by the divine hand, borne across the sea, and through the wilderness, as on eagles' wings; after having been again and again supplied with food and water; after having been brought through scenes of terror to Mount Sinai, where most majestic and dramatic effects were produced upon them—after all these things, within the space of forty days, being left without a leader, they came down to what among more cultivated people, in later days, was called the worship of Venus. They were debauched. They were engaged in that which was worse than a drunken frolic. They were guilty of a heinous sin toward God. And when Moses visited them with such punishment as it is recorded that he did, it indicated a determination to produce upon them a wholesome and lasting moral impression.

I come back, now, for a moment, to a rendering of the Decalogue—the Ten Words—the Ten Commandments. These Commandments may be called the constitution of the Jewish people. Though there is chapter after chapter of directions concerning worship and civil economy,—for the Mosaic system included the total knowledge of civility,—the Ten Commandments were the marrow and center of that system; and they indicated that which was peculiar to the early period in which they were given, not by what they contained, so much as by what they omitted.

The Ten Commandments must underlie civilization to the end of the world—for there is in them something more fundamental than that which rests upon physical elements. The union of morality with spiritual religion was first made known here. It was here that man's duty toward God was first coupled with his duty toward men—for religion is the worship of God, and morality is the discharge of our duties toward our fellows; and here, first, in the history of literature, we find them joined together and forming one system. Their separation was the curse of all the other religious systems in the world. All other religions had in them worship, but not morality; here we find them united.

In the first place, standing above every other declaration is that of the unity of God; and the natural inference to be drawn from it is the denunciation of all forms of idolatry. The foremost conception was that of establishing a power in the minds of the people by unfolding to them the nature of God, and bringing them to believe that he governed the heavens and the earth, and that they were his peculiar people.

So, here, declaration is made of God; and it is remarkable that at so early a period the monotheistic idea, or the idea of the eternal unity of God, was developed in so clear and distinct a form. It was taught that there was one God, and only one; and that has been the salvation of religion through the ages.

What is still more striking, is, in the second Commandment, that God was to be forever to them an idea—a creature of the imagination. He was not to be represented to them by any outline of chalk or charcoal, nor by any picture or statue. He was not to be limned or carved. Nothing in the heavens—no brilliant star and no radiant sun—was to represent him. No phenomenal representation was to be made of him. Nothing on the earth or in the water was to portray him. No sensuous and physical thing should delineate him. The Infinite is boundless, and cannot be described by means of art or any outward object. In the forefront stands the Invisible and Indescribable, so vast that nothing in this world can represent it. The conception is a majestic one. And that is the purport of the first two Commandments; it will endure throughout the ages.

"Thou shalt not take the name of Jehovah thy God in vain; for Jehovah will not hold him guiltless that taketh his name in vain."

Irreverence for sacred things; playing the animal with supreme things; the degradation of things higher than ordinary life, which should lead men up from the depths of lower experience,—that is accursed. To go through a gallery of art, and slime the noblest pictures with mud, and deface or destroy the most magnificent marbles,—no man would permit that. The whole world would cry out against the desecration of beauty under such circumstances. Yet men think themselves justified in drawing down the sanctities of heaven,—those thoughts and feelings which have in them inspiration and elevation,—and defiling them, or using them for purposes of self-aggrandizement and low ambition; while here stands this command, which covers the whole ground of vulgarizing things that are high, and that are necessary to lift men up from low associations. "Thou shalt not take the name of the Lord thy God in vain" does not mean simply that men shall not curse, or even swear by that holy name to falsehood ; it includes the whole latitude and longitude of the realm of thought and feeling in which there is the desecration of whatever is sacred.

"Remember the Sabbath day, to keep it holy. Six days shalt thou labor, and do all thy work: but the seventh day is the Sabbath of Jehovah thy God: in it thou shalt not do any work, thou, nor thy son, nor thy daughter, thy manservant, nor thy maidservant, nor thy cattle, nor thy stranger that is within thy gates."

This commandment is an enunciation of the great law of humanity. It enjoins rest. Men are called upon to rest one day out of every seven. It is not a proscription of enjoyment or of social delight. It was not so carried out in the Jewish nation as to exclude these things ; on the contrary, it markedly included them. It merely says "Stop," to the plough. It says to the toiling yoke and to all tools, "Be still." It says to labor of every kind, "Cease." Its object is to give a pause : for sanctuary privileges, for instruction and reflection, for enjoyment,—in a word, for recreation. It is one of the most blessed provisions that ever came to the world. It stands, to-day, not on the ground of Levitical observance, but on the ground of universal humanity. The command is, "Rest," because the laboring race need rest ; and woe be to those industries and vocations that keep men toiling seven days every week in a ceaseless round, and give them no rest! Every man has a right to his seventh day of rest, everywhere, for purposes of joy, for purposes of society, and for purposes of moral culture ; and this will stand to the end of time.

Next to the worship of God is reverence for parents ; this is the foundation of the family.

"Honor thy father and thy mother : that thy days may be long upon the land which Jehovah thy God giveth thee."

There is no people who verify that more than the Jews. They are remarkable for sweetness and beauty of domestic life, and for health and length of days. To this hour, through all their medieval persecutions, in spite of all the horrible cruelty to which they have been subjected, they have been marked as a people of wonderful endurance and elasticity. Their life began in the household. The command, "Honor thy father and thy mother," has not been so implicitly obeyed in any other nation as among the Israelites; and in no other nation has been so signally realized the implied promise, "that thy days may be long in the land." As a nation, in spite of multiform adversity they have had notable prosperity, and you may depend upon it that in a country where the household is pure, and the father and mother are reverenced, there are laid foundations which revolution itself cannot destroy, and which no outward adversity can overthrow. The sanctuary of the household is in importance above every other thing.

Then comes the conflict in the relations of men.

"Thou shalt not kill."

That is a declaration of the sacredness of human life.

"Thou shalt not commit adultery."

Here the purity of the household is made the subject of a distinct command.

"Thou shalt not steal."

The sanctity of property is thus enunciated. The heathen doubtless in all ages have needed this injunction; and it is an injunction aimed at a socialistic abomination which prevails to-day. The results of a man's productive power are not to be taken from him without a suitable equivalent. Thou shalt not unjustly take from another that which he earns. The sacredness of property is the very foundation of civil society.

"Thou shalt not bear false witness against thy neighbor"— unless he is a politician, or a governor, or a candidate, or a president! But here it is put without exception. *Thou shalt not bear false witness against thy neighbor;* and you are not excused from obeying this command even if you are the editor of a religious paper. Nor are you excused from it because a man belongs to a different sect from that to which you belong, or because he is in a rival business, or because he stands over against you in the conflicts of life. You shall not bear false witness against your neighbor either by your tongue or by your ear. It is as bad for a man to quietly hear another man slandered as to slander him.

And, brethren, it is not enough for you to maintain in your speech and in your whole conduct the sanctity of the reputation of those around about you. There is a phase of honor far more sacred than that. There is in every man a silent judgment-seat, a chamber in his own thoughts, where he thinks evil or thinks well of his neighbors; where he looks upon them charitably or uncharitably; and you are violating one of the sanctities of God's Law when you dare to think unjustly of your fellow men. They are not present to hear your charge or to defend themselves against it; and if you condemn them, you condemn them unseen and unheard. In the silence of your thoughts you inflict the grossest injustice upon them. Every man who has the spirit of Christ, and professes to exemplify that spirit, is bound not only to abstain from outward misrepresentation and adverse criticism of men, as commanded by Moses, but to see to it that in his own thoughts men have justice done them.

"Thou shalt not covet thy neighbor's house, thou shalt not covet thy neighbor's wife, nor his manservant, nor his maidservant, nor his ox, nor his ass, nor anything that is thy neighbor's."

Envy, jealousy, and hunger for another's prosperity— these are a violation of the central canon of benevolence, and are forbidden.

Here, then, are the foundations of religion: in reverence toward God, in the sanctity of the household, in the sacredness of property, in a just conduct of mutual relations and intercourse of one with another. They are the foundation of worship within the bounds of civil society. What was lacking in these declarations of the early period were the elements of meekness, of self-denial, of love, and of self-sacrifice. These had not then been developed. They are fruits of the later economy set forth in the Sermon on the Mount. In the Ten Commandments we have the foundation, and in the Sermon on the Mount we have the superstructure. The Ten Commandments will always be needed because there will always be men in the wilderness; there will always be a detritus; there will always be a vast amount of barbarism and heathenism. In every generation the Ten Commandments will be as much wanted as ever they were. But they are not enough. They stand as the Law in respect to the lower forms of life. The higher forms—the graces, the effluences, the blossom, the fruit, the beauty of transcendent spirituality—these Christ came to develop, and they must be superadded to the Ten Commandments in order to make a complete whole, and thus will the Law be "fulfilled."

I shall close with only one reading, and that from the Twelfth Chapter of Hebrews, that I may put it in apposition and opposition to the scenes to which I have already called your attention. In speaking of the coming of men into the Christian disposition, the writer says:—

"Ye are not come unto the mount that might be touched, and that burned with fire, nor unto blackness, and darkness, and tempest, and the sound of a trumpet, and the voice of words; which voice they that heard intreated that the word should not be spoken to them any more: (For they could not endure that which was commanded, and if so much as a beast touch the mountain, it shall be stoned, or thrust through with a dart: and so terrible was the sight, that Moses said, I exceedingly fear and quake:) but ye are come unto Mount Sion, and unto the city of the living God, the heavenly Jerusalem, and to an innumerable company of angels, to the general assembly and church of the firstborn, which are written in heaven, and to God the judge of all, and to the spirits of just men made perfect, and to Jesus the mediator of the new covenant, and to the blood of sprinkling, that speaketh better things than that of Abel."

The world has had a long and weary march from Mount Sinai to Mount Zion. Woe be to him that insists upon making that march over again! For us, Mount Sinai stands afar off. We hear the thunder still, but we have learned in a better school. Inheriting the knowledge of ages, we have risen to a sublimer conception of God than any that can be made by quaking, by the voice of the trumpet or the sound of thunder. We have beheld Love instituted as the supreme and central power in this world. Not yet fixed, for the world and the church still vibrate, with incessant pendulum, between Sinai and Zion, between force and persuasion, between fear and affection, between the Law and the Gospel, between all that is severe and terrible and all that is lenient and comforting. But methinks that, more and more as the ages go on, men are brought into the spirit of the New Dispensation ; more and more the thunder ceases to be heard by mankind ; more and more we are lifted above its noise. To him who knows no love there must be fear ; but perfect love casts out fear : and he who stands in the sphere of hope and expectation is beyond the reach of the thunder and its quaking, and is not far from Mount Zion.

May God give to us all the spirit of the New Dispensation. While we are gratefully looking back to see the steps that have been taken to bring the human family up from their low estate at large, we may rejoice that along the slopes of Mount Sinai the human race is gradually advancing and rising toward Mount Zion that is above.

XII.

THE SABBATH.

"And he said unto them, the Sabbath was made for man, and not man for the Sabbath."—Mark ii. 27.

THIS is an additional clause to the passage which I read in the opening service, more fully recorded in Mark. "Therefore the son of man is Lord also of the Sabbath" occurs in both passages. I shall return, in due time, to the thought that is contained in this passage. In the discourses on the preceding Sunday nights I have taken a very general survey of the structure and contents of the book of Genesis and the book of Exodus. It has not been possible to expound all the points of interest. There are so many, in the light of modern experience and scholarship, that I should make but very slow progress if I attempted to unveil all of them. But if the external history of any people is more romantic and more acceptable, the institutions and interior economy of no other people is more important.

We have now come to that point in the books of the Old Testament where the Mosaic economy, as it has been called, is opened up. I confess that when I read of it in Exodus, in Leviticus, and in Deuteronomy, it seems to me as though it must strike an ordinary reader as a very strange jumble; because, as compared with our systems of law, which throughout the ages have been developed into logical sequences, and in which all the great interests of society are separated and treated one by one with minute

---

Sunday evening, January 12, 1879. LESSON: Luke vi. 1-12.

order and procedure, the Mosaic system is a jumble. The most contrary things lie together in the same bed. If in one verse it speaks of land, in the next verse it speaks of the household, and in the next it speaks of the relations of personal property. One thing treads upon another without any logical method. So it comes to pass that this economy would seem to be a collection of proverbs. They lie in juxtaposition, they touch, but they do not cohere. And it is my purpose, so far as it can be done without wearying you, to portray some of the great Mosaic institutions that have never been more profoundly or wisely or beneficially treated than they were in the economy of the wilderness. If you sympathize with me, you will be both grateful and surprised to see at how early a time some of the most useful elements of modern society had their origin, their development, and their establishment.

We are to bear in mind, then, in entering upon this general view, what was before the mind of this great lawgiver and leader — this man of antiquity who stands before the past as the vast statues of Egypt stood before their temples, so huge as to hide the very temples themselves. There never has been a name on earth of one who, in antiquity or in modern times, being a purely secular man, excelled him. We are to bear in mind that his was the first attempt of any considerable importance to organize human society around about an ideal, invisible God. It has been called "a theocracy"; and by that was meant, it has been more generally supposed, merely the rule of a priesthood. But it was a *bona fide* attempt on the part of Moses to organize a commonwealth that should have no visible head; that should be apparent to man only through the element of faith—the imagination sanctified to sacred uses. The source of all authority, the origin of all law, the process of all providence, was, in the mind of every one of the citizens, to be in the great commonwealth above. So that, while nature and primitive organization would be drawing men to the earth, because they were of the earth, there would be in the whole framework of their government elements that should draw them toward the invisible and superior.

It was designed to produce, by such a process as this, a people that should be, without exception, in the field, in the city, and in the way, filled with overflowing happiness. Happiness was the end that was being sought—happiness through righteousness, which everywhere is declared to bring forth peace and prosperity. Nor can I conceive of a more sublime motto than that which is given in the seventh of Deuteronomy, and the sixth verse. This is the last letter of Moses in the Book of Deuteronomy. He said, in his dying testimony:—

"Thou art an holy people unto Jehovah thy God: Jehovah thy God hath chosen thee to be a special people unto himself, above all people that are upon the face of the earth."

Here was the national motto: no lion emblazoned on a blood-red shield; no ravenous eagle; but, *Thou art a peculiar people whom God hath set apart for himself to make them a happy people.* Such was the legend that Moses gave in the furtherance of the great end of his life and mission.

Through their immediate and personal adhesion to God, then, he instituted various economies. The first one which we enter upon in the order of time is the Sabbath—the setting apart and consecration for rest of a seventh portion of every man's time. It is to this matter, whose importance far transcends our ordinary apprehension of it, that I wish to call your attention to-night.

There is mention of the observance of the seventh day —and it is the first mention of it—after the escape of the Israelites from Egypt, and while they were wandering in the desert, before they came to Mount Sinai, and when the manna fell from heaven. You will recollect that the command was to gather on the sixth day for both the sixth and the seventh; for, said Moses, To-morrow is a solemn rest, a holy Sabbath unto the Lord. And there was the correspondence of the miracle that if manna was gathered on any day except the sixth, and kept more than one day, it was corrupted, but that if gathered on the sixth day it was not corrupted when it was kept over a day. This marks the fact that before they received the law at Mount Sinai there had been introduced a recognition and an observance of the seventh day as Sabbath—rest-day—in the camp.

How far back this went no one can tell. All efforts to show that the Sabbath day was observed from the beginning have been, it seems to me, worse than failures. They have involved such a use of Scripture as would justify any amount of wrenching, special pleading, and perversion. There is no evidence in the whole history of the patriarchs that they ever observed that day. There is nothing to show that the seventh day, or any part of the time, was observed in Egypt. It may have been, but there is no evidence of it. They may, in those early times, have worn scarlet hoods, but there is no evidence of it. They may have had shoe-buckles, but there is no evidence of that. And there is no evidence that in any nation then, or at any anterior period in the Israelitish nation, the seventh day was observed. However that may be, it comes to our notice as being authoritatively established for regular observance only when the camp sat down before Mount Sinai, and it was commanded in the Decalogue.

Why the seventh day should have been chosen has been a matter of a good deal of debate. All nations have not accepted this. Some peoples have counted their week as five days, some as six days, and some as ten days, and though the greatest number of nations have had a week composed of seven days, and the inquiry is a natural one, How should they have fallen upon this seven-day week? the reason given is that in six days the Lord created the heaven and the earth, and rested on the seventh day. That may be a reason in regard to God, but it is not a reason in regard to nations. The presumption is that it is a legend transmuted into an allegation.

The more probable reason is this: In the early day the shepherd life predominated. You have never had any experience of such a life. We know very well that when men follow the sea they become observant of clouds, of wind, of phenomena that are strange to us. We know that Indians living in the woods sharply see in nature and cunningly use many things that are blind to us. We could not follow trails. We could not even find our way by means of the blazes of the frontiersmen of the forest. We, dwelling in cities and old communities, never had practice of this sort.

Now, people living on the plains, watching their flocks day and night, become companionable with the stars ; they learn to observe the heavens familiarly ; and there are influences—I do not mean magical or mystic influences, but a kind of education—derived from a contemplation of the stellar universe, by pastoral people, of which we know very little. The changing moon, whose changes average completion once in about twenty-eight days, being the nearest of the observed heavenly bodies, naturally attracted the attention of a pastoral people, and took priority in their mind ; and by dividing that period into quarters, roughly corresponding to the moon's changes, they got seven days. If this lunar theory is not correct, at any rate it is ingenious ; and it is supposed by many to have been the origin of the division of time into periods of seven days.

Around this reason was afterwards developed, I suppose, other reasons, of which I shall speak in a moment ; and among them was the legend or transmitted tradition of the days of the creation.

Let us now look at the position which the Sabbath takes in the Law, as it was given by Moses, or through Moses, to the people. There is a marked difference between the statement of Moses in Deuteronomy and that made by him in Exodus. I shall read both of them.

"Remember the Sabbath day, to keep it holy [that is, separate and apart from all others]. Six days shalt thou labor, and do all thy work : but the seventh day is the Sabbath of Jehovah thy God [Jehovah's rest] : in it thou shalt not do any work, thou, nor thy son, nor thy daughter, thy manservant, nor thy maidservant, nor thy cattle, nor thy stranger that is within thy gates : for in six days Jehovah made heaven and earth, the sea, and all that in them is, and rested the seventh day: wherefore Jehovah blessed the Sabbath day, and hallowed it."

So it stands in Exodus. In Deuteronomy it reads:—

"Keep the Sabbath day to sanctify it, as Jehovah thy God hath commanded thee. Six days shalt thou labor, and do all thy work: but the seventh day is the Sabbath of Jehovah thy God: in it thou shalt not do any work, thou, nor thy son, nor thy daughter, nor thy manservant, nor thy maidservant, nor thine ox, nor thine ass, nor any of thy cattle, nor thy stranger that is within thy gates; that thy manservant and thy maidservant may rest as well as thou."

These last words are not contained in Exodus; nor do they express the reason given in Exodus for keeping that day, that it was a celebration of creative rest. The added reason is stated as follows:—

"Remember that *thou* wast a servant in the land of Egypt, and that Jehovah thy God brought thee out thence through a mighty hand and by a stretched out arm: therefore Jehovah thy God commanded thee to keep the Sabbath day."

It was a day set forth in Deuteronomy to commemorate emancipation from Egyptian toil and bondage. It has a counterpart in the fact that the Israelites were emancipated from toil and bondage in Egypt when God brought them out from that land, and that the Sabbath day, among other things, was to celebrate this event. When you take both passages, and see that Moses left out the creative reason, and introduced another, it leads us to lend a more ready ear to the statement of those who say that, time after time, in the early periods, books were amended, not by making new books, but by taking an old one and adding to it. This was not unbefitting the simplicity of infantile authorship. Sometimes one reason was given and sometimes the other.

But the fundamental reason does not lie in these historical associations, however well adapted to catch and hold the attention of the Hebrews; it lies in the nature of the thing itself—what it is, why it is, and what the effect of it is, in the nature of things.

You will observe, in the first place, that in both accounts there is this one central idea, that one-seventh part of a man's time is redeemed from toil. Rest, *rest*, is the primary idea; and that falls in entirely with the whole constitution of man in every age and nation. We know very well that continuity within certain limited bounds is on the way to success, and we know that beyond those bounds it is on the way to disaster. We know that one single article of food, being continued for a long time, at last nauseates and disgusts. We know that things iterated, iterated, and iterated, often become hateful and injurious. One cannot be a wheel in a machine and revolve with perpetual revolution, and be a man. Variety, change, is indispensable to manhood. So there is appointed a great intermission during every single twenty-four hours. One-third of every man's life is a sabbath. In every day eight hours are a sabbath—a rest—unto man, unto nature, and, since God has arranged it, unto God. On this principle civilization develops more, apparently, than on any other; and it is on this principle that the commandment of the observance of one day in seven is founded. Whether or not one day in eight, one day in nine, or one day in ten would have done about as well as one day in seven, I do not know; but I think experience has shown to the satisfaction of man that one day in seven practically meets the exigencies of human life. It does not embarrass industry. About as often as that the human system needs a change—a change which comes from throwing off the habits of routine everyday industries, and giving the man head-room, breath-room, heart-room, and hand-room.

But then, take notice that while we have one day appointed for rest, there is not, so far as the Ten Commandments are concerned, a single word said about worship on that day. As we have been brought up, what we think of the Sabbath or Rest-day, is, that we must not talk loud; that we must not run about the house and make a noise; that we must be combed and dressed; that we must go to church; that we must unite in the religious services, whether they are light or heavy; that we must not, going back home, feel free to enjoy ourselves according to our nature; that we must walk with propriety; that we must be quiet; that we must not go visiting or riding; that we must not discharge ordinary duties; that we must keep the day as straight and as perpendicular as possible.

That idea of the Sabbath day remains without much decoration, without any considerable amount of relief, without a great deal of comfort, overruling instincts of a very wholesome nature. Such is about the notion derived from Puritan practice, strained through New England. Well, that was not the Sabbath day of Mount Sinai. Such a Sabbath was not known to the Jews. It is a modern invention. It is a perfect transformation.

"In it [the Sabbath day] thou shalt not do any work."

There is a command to rest, but there is no command to worship. Such was not the primitive injunction.

And yet, while this rest from work, as distinguished from the modern methods of Sunday keeping, was made prominent, it carried with it a great deal more than the mere idea of cessation from toil: it insisted on cessation from toil on the part of the poor and needy. It was the foundation on which was to be built protection of the rights sacred to individuality. The individual might read for himself.

"The seventh day is the Sabbath of Jehovah thy God: in it thou shalt not do any work [Look at the particularity of it], thou [head of the family], nor thy son, nor thy daughter [and as these might be exempt by favor, and the work might be shoved over to others], nor thy manservant, nor thy maidservant."

Then, as if that did not include enough, it goes on to secure humanity for the inferior creation:—

"Nor thy cattle."

And after emancipation, during one-seventh part of the time, had been provided for the man, and his whole household, including the servants, and his possessions,—the horse, the dog, the ox, the ass, everything that was his,—next came the Chinaman, I was going to say; but "thy stranger that is within thy gates" are the words in the Scripture record. All nations in antiquity were taught to hate strangers, who were often put to the sword in former days; but here comes this humane injunction: You shall treat the stranger as you treat your own self, your household, and your property. That made it more emphatic; and the reason given is, *that thy manservant and thy maidservant may rest as well as thou.* No aristocracy here! No privileged class! The kitchen and the parlor stand on the same rights. The man that goes afoot and the man that rides in his carriage stand before God with no distinction in this respect. If the democracy of Mount Sinai should sweep through life, what confusions and overturnings it would produce!

"The Lord loveth the stranger, in giving him food and raiment." Then this pathetic appeal is added: "Love *ye* therefore the stranger; for *ye were strangers in the land of Egypt.*"

Then there is the injunction to *remember those in bondage—to have compassion on those in bonds.*

So that, aside from the idea of the sanctity and antiquity of this portion of time—one day of rest in seven derived from the creative act—there came to them this national and patriotic reason: *You shall give a day of absolute rest to everything that lives and breathes within your land.* There was the Mosaic humanity.

Such was the spirit, not only of Moses, but of the Israelitish people—that is, those who represented the best estate of Hebrew thought and feeling. For, in all the backslidings and delinquencies of these people there were rising up priests and prophets and reformers who undertook to bring them back to obedience to their national laws; and you will find that in all the condemnations uttered by the prophets, greater or minor, it is the manhood on which their minds rest. Turn, for instance, to Amos, one of the minor prophets, the eighth chapter and the fourth verse, and read:—

"Hear this, O ye that swallow up the needy, even to make the poor of the land to fail, Saying, When will the new moon be gone, that we may sell corn? and the Sabbath, that we may set forth wheat, making the ephah small, and the shekel great [that is, making the measure small and the price large. You see the spirit of commerce was very ancient], and falsifying the balances by deceit? That we may buy the poor for silver, and the needy for a pair of shoes; yea, and sell the refuse of the wheat? Jehovah hath sworn by the excellency of Jacob, Surely I will never forget any of their works. Shall not the land tremble for this?"

Tremble for what? A technical violation of the Sabbath? No: for a violation of the Sabbath so as to oppress the poor and needy.

If you turn to the denunciations in Isaiah and Jeremiah, the marrow of them is this : not that men have gone aside from the observation of the Sabbath, but that they have gone aside from it in such a way as to overwhelm the poor and the needy. There never was a book in this world so anti-monarchical as the Old Testament; and there never was a book in which natural religion and natural humanity ran so deep and were so universal as in this same Old Testament, which is so despised, and which men say we have so outgrown that we do not need it any longer. It is true that the Old Testament is like an old pasture-field, and needs to be plowed—not, however, for the sake of throwing it away, but that we may use it more to our advantage, and make more out of it than is being made by neglect, by misrepresentation, or by Pharisaical stringency on minor matters.

It is, then, all the way down through the Old Testament, a plea for the Sabbath on account of the poor and needy. And when we come to the New Testament what do we find? We find Christ rising in the same spirit, and facing the perversions that had knitted up the Sabbath, and made it, as it were, a net, holding people in bondage and restriction, giving liberty only to those who were not poor and necessitous. He struck through this bondage and this restriction, and declared that the poor and needy were to be released. He said they were not made for the Sabbath, as if to keep that day were more important than to take care of the people.

Out upon your nefarious pretensions! he indignantly declared. Is not a man more valuable than a sheep?

There is no one of you that would not pull a sheep out of a ditch on the Sabbath; and yet you would prevent my healing a man that is blind, or that has a withered hand, on that holy day! My Father worketh hitherto on the Sabbath. Doth the sun stand still on the Sabbath; doth not the grass grow; doth not the genial spring bring forth the blade on the Sabbath day? My Father thinks, and wills, and plans, and blazes forth forever more, on Sabbaths and on week days. "My Father worketh hitherto, and I work;" but it is a work of humanity. It is a work that gives rest, recuperation, more life, more power: not a work of exhaustive care. It is not an everlasting grind at distasteful industry. It is a regeneration of man. It is a lifting up of new life in a man, and giving him opportunity to use that life rationally.

It was for such a Sabbath as this that Christ pleaded, and against the absurd and puerile restrictions of the narrow constructionists of the old Pharisaic period.

I shall not stop to amuse you with an account, at the present time (it may be in order to do it by and by), of what curious provisions were made for keeping the Sabbath day, as to when it came in and when it went out; as to what was work and what was not work; as to whether or not a man might have Gentile servants that were not forbidden to light fires and cook food. According to the Hebrew economy all work must end on the day before the Sabbath, and no excuse whatever was valid for putting even domestic labor upon the servants. This was carried to such an extent that we can scarcely read about it without a smile.

This division of time, then, though known to other nations, and possibly to the Patriarchs, was enforced and made into a positive institution only under the Hebrew Commonwealth. One-seventh part of the time was defended against avarice, against involuntary toil, against the mastery of man over man. When the seventh day came, the father and the son were both alike to God. The father could not say to the son, "Go," or "Do." The son was released, and the father and the son stood equal. On that Sabbath day a man could not be driven afield, or starved if he did not do a given amount of labor. The poorest man was even with the richest. There was no man that could force his fellow man to go forth and labor on that day. Every man stood in his full manhood. It was a day of emancipation. It perpetually set forth the liberation of the children of Israel from the bondage by which they were ground down in Egypt. So every seventh day God said to the great mass of poor, overworked and underfed people, "I release you to-day, and this is your vacation."

As a matter of history, also, it is true that the observance of the Sabbath was not in any sense restrictive or burdensome. While it set man free from servile toil, it did not have an equivalent of bondage in the form of worship. There are many ways in which a man can be oppressed. Not alone the hoe and the plow, but the Confession of Faith and the Catechism, may make men toil and sweat. A man may have rest from bone and muscle weariness, but may have ten times as much fatigue of brain. The day set as a pearl among all the others, and the most blessed of the seven, is the Sabbath : and it should be perpetually observed as a day of Rest.

There are some aspects of the Lord's day in my memory as a day of poetry. On that day it seemed to my young eyes as though the sacredness of God had descended from heaven and clothed the earth. Distances were never so long. Sounds were never so melodious. Never was there mystic brooding of heaven upon earth such as came down to my imagination on summer Sunday mornings that broke with light and beauty upon the Connecticut hills; and if then I could have been taken by the hand, and led into the garden of the Lord, and taught to hold communion with the invisible, there would not have been one dark spot on my recollection of the supreme beauty of that day of emancipation from labor of soul and body.

But alas for the catechism! Alas for the dinners of which I was defrauded because I could not learn it!

Alas for the hours when I was shut up in a room by myself and made to study it! Alas for the wearisomeness of going to church! Alas for the aching of my little legs that could not reach the floor, and swung from the high board seats! Alas for the rigor of that well-intended Puritan Sunday on which, though I rested in body, I was weary and worn out in mind! Though the sun came over the eastern horizon bringing scintillations of beauty and pleasure and even of heavenly imaginings to my youthful mind, when it went down over the western horizon there was nothing that said "Good riddance to you!" with the eagerness that I did; for the Sabbath was not a liberty to me : it was to me an imprisonment—a restriction of my freedom.

Now, this did not belong to the original Sabbath day. That day was not meant to be an oppression. It is a misuse of it that makes it a burden in any sense.

The obligation of the Sabbath is not derived from the sanctions of Mount Sinai nor from Moses. That day is obligatory upon us on account of our human nature. This goes deeper than either of the other reasons stated. That which experience, prolonged and various, determines to be best for each and for all, is the voice of God. That which, after suitable trial, is found to be most effectual in developing and advancing mankind, has a sanction that could not have been given by Mount Sinai. Nature, when at last we understand it, is the voice of God, and is as solemn as any recorded word; and the Sabbath day comes to us as divine because it comes with an experience that justifies its institution, that renders apparent its wisdom and humanity, and that makes it even more desirable now than it was in antiquity.

Hence, futile are all disputes about the transfer of the Jewish Sabbath to the Christian dispensation. Above all, futile are those Pharisaic difficulties which spring up as to what day we shall observe—whether we must go on observing the old Jewish Saturday, or whether there is any authority for observing our Sunday. As if men had kept track of the seventh day of creation, when God wound up his work, and rested! As if the Jews, or anybody, were sure of being on that very track! As if, in the vast confusions of time, there were any credible or authoritative record that could enable one to determine with certainty whether or not he was on the same road which was followed in this respect by men of primitive days! The question never was, whether the Sabbath should be the seventh day of the week: the question always was, whether it should be a seventh part of the week. It is one-seventh part that brings emancipation to every man, woman, and child—that releases from burden the whole community. That is the Sabbath—not the particular day on which it falls. If there is any sufficient reason for putting it on Monday, Monday is good enough; or on Tuesday, Tuesday is good enough; or on any other day, that day is good enough; but it is important that it should be observed on the same day by the whole nation, and by every nation, so that there shall be consentaneousness of observation, and so, fair-play and co-operation. It is not wise for one man to observe one day and another another; that would fill the community with infinite confusions and disputes: but while there should be one day of rest in each week, it is of no importance whether it falls on Saturday, on Sunday, or on any other day. There is no direct command on the subject. The only obligation resting upon us to observe Sunday is that which comes up through our nature. We are to do it because it is best for us, for our children, for our manservants, for our maidservants, for our beasts of burden, and for the stranger that is within our gates. Such is our duty in regard to the Sabbath day, and that is deep enough, broad enough, authoritative enough, for every wise man.

We need this day as much as it was needed by the people of the olden time. Indeed, we need it more than they did. While civilization has not changed the necessity for rest during one-seventh part of the time, it has made the need more imperative, because of the excessive toil of this age of the world; because of added cerebration. Not only do the bones and muscles need rest, but the whole head and nervous system need it. Reason, moral sentiment, domestic affection, and the ten thousand cares of complicated modern life, call out for rest more imperiously than ever they did in the wilderness, or in the primitive conditions of a simpler form of society. To-day the industry of the globe is such that the vast, uncountable majority of men are employed in drudgery. Taking the world through —and more and more as you come up into semi-civilization and civilization—men are working like machines, without any interest except that of getting their bread and raiment. Their wages, their means of livelihood, is all that they see coming from their incessant toil. Beyond that they have no share in that wealth which they are instrumental in producing. They weave with rapidly-flying shuttle, sending forth a gold-and-silver thread ; and the garments that come out of the loom are not for their wearing but for the wearing of others.

Never was there a period of the world in which the great mass of workingmen had so much right as now to demand absolute rest during one-seventh part of the time —so much right to come out of the dreary mine ; out of the dirty stithy ; out of the whirling factory ; out of the field, with its burdensome tasks ; out of the many subordinations that belong to the lower offices of complicated society.

This is eminently a day in which the bottom should come up to the top, and breathe. As you have seen, on some lake, at evening twilight, when man and beast and bird no longer vex, myriad little fishes dotting and dimpling the whole surface, as they freely rise out of the water to breathe the air, so on one day of the week every living creature has a right to come to the surface, as it were, and take in the sweet fresh air of God's day of rest.

Then, a question which belongs to the subject of the normal occupation of man, is that measureless fatigue which the competitions of business bring upon the intermediary classes. There is absolute remorselessness in the industry of these great cities. It may be likened to the revolution of a vast treadmill wheel, which goes round and round, so that when a person is once upon it he must keep stepping. The organized industries of society are so various, so extensive, so tremendous, that the master mechanic, the merchant, the lawyer, the teacher, everybody that lives by his brains, finds himself perpetually fagged, jaded, worn, till the very flesh cries out, and till the care-furrows upon the face show what is the stress to which he is subjected. And there is nothing that men given to toil need more than rest. If there be any difference between us and those that lived in antiquity, it is that we need a Sabbath more than they did.

But let us bear in mind that rest does not altogether mean non-laboriousness, though to some extent it means that. I do not hold the old Puritan views of Sunday. I try to follow the spirit of Christ.

When it was proposed that the city railroad cars should not run on Sunday, I was asked to sign a petition to that effect. I would not do it. I was glad that there was some way in which the crowded population of the city could get out once in seven days into the country. When it was proposed to open the public libraries and reading-rooms, and let men and women have an opportunity to read there on Sunday, it was resisted, and I defended it. I advocate it still. I believe in a church Sabbath such as has been transmitted to us by our fathers ; but I couple something else with it. I do not think Christian people do well by their servants, who live so affluently on the Sabbath day that those servants have no chance for rest ; or, if they do not have it on that day they ought to have it on another. I do not believe the ferryboats, or city railroads, or steamboats, or hotels, have any right, by paying extreme wages, or in any other way, to defraud the men who serve them of their Sabbath. I do not mean by this that boats and cars and hotels should not be run, but that if it is worth while to run them on that day, it is but right that there should be release of mind and body provided with rotation of duties, so that all should have a Sabbath every week.

It is said, "You want to send men to the country: what about the drivers and conductors? Don't they want a Sabbath?" Certainly they do; and I plead for them. There should be such arrangements that every conductor, every driver, every waiter, every cook, and everybody under him, should have a portion, at least, of every Sunday for rest, or if not of Sunday then of some other day. I plead for those that are on the great wheel of society, which is perpetually turning round and round, and that have no Sabbath. Though they may not miss it, we ought to miss it for them. It is for us to think for the unthinking, and to be wise for the unwise.

It is often said, "It is better for the laboring man that he should go out into the country than that he should stay at home and go to church." Well, if it is a question as to whether a man shall remain in his corner grocery or squalid garret or go to the country on Sunday, let him go to the country, in God's name! If it is a question as to whether he shall spend Sunday on the street corners or whether he shall go into the open fields on that day in summer, there can be no doubt as to which is best. It is far more wholesome for him to go into the open fields, especially if he carries with him the spirit of the Old and New Testaments.

But is that the best way in which the laboring man can spend the Sabbath? Is there not a better way for him to rest even than that? What we want for rest on Sunday is change, variety, to give vitality to that part of ourselves which is not much developed during the other six days of the week; and no men need so much cerebral stimulus as men who give six days out of every seven to muscular or mechanical work. To make a man think with the highest faculties, to give him inspiration, poetry, moral emotion—that is a renovation such as cannot come by merely snoring on a bed, or walking in a garden or field; and I hold that every man, in proportion as he labors during the week, needs the spiritualization and uplifting which come from gathering for public worship, with its songs and teachings.

If, therefore, having this rest of change for one class of faculties, men also take social joy in another class, I have not one word to say against that. I believe in it. I do not believe that men are to be tied up. Although the Jews were put to death if they worked on the Sabbath, they had festivities all day long. It was a day of rejoicing, of singing, of merriment. In the time of Christ it was a day of feasting, and he himself went on Sabbath days to feasts at rich men's houses. He would have been turned out of the Presbytery, out of the Council, in other words, out of the church, if he had done that in New England. There are things that Paul and his Master did in their time which they could not have done if they had lived in our time.

So, the true Christian Sabbath is one in which a man rests from labor, and which reinvigorates his social affections. And what a blessed day it is that brings a man into better acquaintance with his wife and children, and into fuller fellowship with his neighbors! How much of rust would be rubbed off if there were universal sanctifying intercourse, so that men should everywhere meet as Christian neighbors and households!

We want more relaxation in our Sundays. And I must utter another protest. I must raise my voice against the want of a proper distribution of the duties of a wise observance of the Sabbath. There are persons in every church in this community who are overburdened with labor. There are those who rise early for private devotion, and then care for the children, and then attend the preaching services in the forenoon, and then go to the Sunday-school in the afternoon, and then take part in a prayer-meeting, and then go to the night service, and then return home overwearied and stupid. That is what they call "keeping Sunday." Nobody has any business to keep Sunday in that way,—making it the hardest day of the whole week. No man should be overtasked. Everyone should have something to do, so as to make the day easier for all. But some willing workers take upon themselves so much that they are spiritual slaves on the Lord's day. To them, instead of being a day of illumination it is a day of severe drudgery.

Of course, I do not have any rest on Sunday. There is no Sunday for me when you have it. To me it is the hardest day of the whole week. Were it not that I take my rest in installments out of the other days I should be sabbathless. So it must be, from the very organization of society, with those who preach the Gospel. But for the great mass of those who are engaged in heavy, exhausting labor on other days during the week, Sunday is the day of rest.

Therefore, from every consideration, it behooves us to be thankful for the primitive institution of the Sabbath ; for that Mosaic economy whose fruits have come down to us ; for that experience which has taught us to base the observance of the Sabbath, not on a historic command, not on a word pronounced, but on an experience four thousand years deep, and as wide as the human family, whatever the obscuration, the perplexity, and the limitation may be with which we have received it. Circumcision has gone, sacrifices have gone, Mosaic laws and governments have gone ; but the Sabbath moves on. Like the pillar of fire that went by night before the Israelites in the desert, it is luminous. It leads forward the civilization of the present. Commencing in remote antiquity, it has come down to us dropping honey upon the ages as it came ; it has been an unspeakable blessing to the races of mankind ; it has brought to us an experience mightier than the voices of Mount Sinai ; and it is for us to make it more melodious and sweeter, and to send it as a grand chant of liberty down through the ages that are yet to come, until at last the earthly Sabbath shall mingle with the heavenly Sabbath, and the heaven and earth shall be one, to rejoice together forever more.

XIII.

MOSAIC INSTITUTES:

HUMANITY.

I PROPOSE to enter, to-night, upon an exposition of the laws of Moses. I shall not discuss the question of their historical development; for, whether the Pentateuch represents a work accomplished and recorded in the lifetime of Moses, or whether upon the basis of such a record it received additional elements at the hands of scribes from age to age, so that we owe it, as many scholars think, in its present form, to the age following Solomon, while a matter of some historical interest, it is not a matter of sufficient interest to my purpose for me to discuss it. Whatever may have been the origin of the Pentateuch, there it stands; and it contains a complete system of customs, rules, regulations, and laws, besides an account of some institutions.

When you examine the laws that are embodied in this system you will perceive at once that the popular notion that all of them were whispered into the ears of Moses by the lips of Jehovah when he was upon the Mount, and that Moses was a writing machine who took down what was dictated to him, is not sustained by the facts. It will be found that many of these laws were handed down from the patriarchs, having been held by them in common with the race from which they sprang, and that they represented a given state of attainment in antiquity. It will be found that many of the customs sprang up in the primi-

---

Sunday evening, February 2, 1879. LESSON: Mark xii. 1-34.

tive period, when large numbers of Israelites resided in Egypt, in the land of Goshen. It will be found that there are reminiscences, hints, suggestions, remolded or borrowed from the Egyptians. We are to bear in mind that Moses himself was educated in all the wisdom of Egypt; and it is scarcely possible that he should not carry with him some of the elements that were incorporated into the system which he was to establish in the promised land. It will be seen, also, that many of the precepts were gathered from the experiences of the desert.

So the laws and institutions of Moses represent a wide field. As a matter of fact we are not at liberty to say that they were all told him at once, and that he wrote them down as they were given to him of God. They were developed under a divine providence that worked through hundreds of years.

This does not detract at all from the divinity of their inspiration; it merely gives us another view of the method by which divine laws were made known to men. As they stand in the Pentateuch one is at first almost discouraged in attempting to comprehend them. There is no order in their arrangement. They may be said, in one sense, to be jumbled up. All sorts of laws on all sorts of subjects are strung together in juxtaposition, but without any logical relation or scientific classification. And they are repeated. You find them stated in Exodus; you find them made known again in Leviticus; you find them restated in Numbers; and you find them more at large set forth in Deuteronomy. So there is at once a sense of repetitiousness, and almost of incongruity. It was not given to that early time philosophically to classify, to develop, as the Romans did first, largely, laws pertaining to certain subjects, to gather them together, and to give them a logical unfolding and natural sequence; such classification or development did not belong to the literature or genius of Semitic antiquity. We are to take the Mosaic institutes as we find them. I think that if you follow me in examining and attempting to classify them, you will agree with me, before we are done, that they are abundantly rich ; and I shall be surprised if you are not surprised at the extent of this richness. You will find in the Old Testament Scriptures much ore that you have not yet dug, and will acknowledge that the Old Testament is not used up yet. There are here laws that cover the whole range of society life ; laws pertaining to the individual, to the household, to national and civil life ; laws relating to home and foreign policy ; laws having to do with property and commerce ; laws that regulated public worship and determined religion with all its requirements ; in short, laws that affected the whole moral, social, and civil estate of man.

There is a vague popular idea that the laws of Moses concern themselves chiefly with forms and ceremonies and sacrifices ; but I think you will be surprised to find how much of wise injunction and restriction was contained in them which is yet needed in the world, concerning everyday business and home life.

Especially I shall ask your attention, to-night, to the consideration that was given by the great lawgiver of antiquity to the matter of humanity. The foundation principle, we are informed by our Master, of the whole economy, was, " Thou shalt love the Lord thy God with all thy heart, and with all thy soul, and with all thy mind. This is the first and great commandment. And the second is like unto it : Thou shalt love thy neighbor as thyself." "On these two commandments hang all the Law and the Prophets," said Christ. I shall put the more important last, and discuss the second first.

Thou shalt love thy neighbor as thyself. It becomes a matter of very great interest,—and it ought to be something more than curiosity,—how the Mosaic enactments came to contain this injunction quoted by our Master, which he said contained the whole intent and meaning of the Old Testament Scriptures. When you examine it, is it true to fact? The more strict duties imposed as acts of worship I shall not discuss, but I shall consider the duties of man to man, and shall not by any means exhaust them to-night.

In the first place, you are to bear in mind that the Israelites were to be an agricultural and not a commercial people. They sprang from a pastoral nation. Much in their habits began in Egypt, where they were semi-pastoral—pastoral and agricultural. They resumed again in the wilderness their pastoral life. It was the design of their leader and lawgiver that when they entered the promised land agriculture should be the basis of their industry,—that the State should live by agriculture, not commerce. One reason was that intense love of nature which was a large element in the Hebrew make-up—the keeping of men in communion with the great natural world. Another reason was the fact that commerce was so undeveloped at that time that it made manifest to the mind of Moses only its dangers. Still another reason was the fact that an agricultural people are not a roving people. They can be held. They can be made obedient to fixed laws. They do not fritter away home influence by foreign travel. They are not apt to import new customs. And if it was the intent of the lawgiver to develop a high moral state in the Israelitish people, it was desirable that they should stay at home where they could be indoctrinated in wholesome laws. That which is alleged to have been cruel in the Old Testament economy, such, for instance, as the cutting off of nations, I think will receive, if not a perfect solution, yet much amelioration, when we consider that the object of the lawgiver was to keep this nation separate from every other till they had been thoroughly educated in the new idea of a pure and holy God, ruling pure and holy men.

In short, as the mother keeps the children at home, sequesters them, lest they be injured by a neighborhood which is injurious to the welfare of children, and does not send them out until they have attained character and manhood, and then lets them go forth, so the divine economy in antiquity was to take this select people—the peculiar people of God—and bury them, as it were, in obscurity, and develop them until they should attain such moral stature that it should be safe for them to go out; and then came the words, "Go ye now into all the world." To maintain this separateness, and repel the temptations that came from heathen nations, often required a degree of severity, not to say cruelty, which shocks men in modern times— although I think modern times to be far more refinedly cruel than antiquity was.

When the Hebrews took possession by violence of the promised land it was distributed first among the tribes, and then, within the tribes, it was apportioned so that every family had its share. But no man held his land in fee-simple; neither was it held in fee-simple by the priests or by the government: for God was their King; and the theory announced and followed was that all the territory belonged to God. The consequence was that when it was distributed to the holders they were tenants, and not owners. And they paid rent (what is called "tithes") for the support of priestly tribes, and of the State. Therefore, according to the Mosaic plan, the Jews never owned the soil in fee-simple in the early day.

You will find this distinctly stated in Leviticus, the twenty-fifth chapter: "The land shall not be sold forever [in perpetuity]: for the land is mine; for ye are strangers and sojourners with me." The land could be exchanged between man and man, but it could not be sold forever. All purchases of land were subject to redemption whenever the seller chose to redeem it, or, if he could not do it, whenever his next of kin chose to redeem it.

Wherever there was a sale of land, it was under these limitations and conditions. And once in fifty years all land came back anyhow. There were seven days, and one was a day of rest. Then there were seven years, with a sabbatic year of rest. Then there were seven times seven years, making forty-nine, and the fiftieth was the jubilee, or great year of rest.

Now, in the partition of land it was leased, subject to redemption at whatever time the man leasing chose to redeem it; or, if he could not do it, at whatever time some rich kin could redeem it; and it was always subject to inevitable return to the original household or family on the fiftieth year. So it was not in the power of any one tribe gradually to accumulate or appropriate land of another tribe; nor was it in the power of one strong man gradually to gather territory into his hands, and leave the great majority of his fellows destitute of soil. To those who have given thought to the land question, especially in the old and crowded territories of England, there is much food for reflection in this land theory and law contained in the Mosaic institutes, especially as to its bearing on man's treatment of man.

Another peculiarity in regard to the land and its cultivation was this: that the land could only be cultivated six years out of seven. It was not permitted to cultivate the land at all the seventh year. It was to have a rest. And the promise was that if they would obey the commandments of God he would make the sixth year so fruitful that with the natural wild increase of the fields, forests, orchards, and gardens, the whole seventh year should be abundantly supplied with food. They were not to plow, nor reap, nor in anywise pursue the industries of agriculture. The whole land had to have its rest, an entire year of it, every seven years.

The Hebrews being placed on this land, the most striking feature that arrests our attention is the extraordinary humanity that was commanded and that was developed under the Mosaic economy. The sacredness of human life was the very first step. It was made sacred by every device.

"Whoso sheddeth man's blood, by man shall his blood be shed."

Murder was death to the murderer. No compromise was permitted at that time. There were no courts such as clear murderers in our day. There was no provision that sought to build up a reputation by snatching from punishment notorious murderers, as there are nowadays in every State of our Union. Whoever took the life of a man forfeited his own life; and it was expressly forbidden to make any compromise, even if the criminal offered untold money for his life. He was a murderer, and he must pay the penalty by death. It was made a crime to be so much as careless of life. If a man committed manslaughter, if, without intending it, by accident, he destroyed his neighbor, if by some chance stroke, not seeing the victim, he in any way destroyed human life, it was the right of the next of kin to the man killed to pursue and slay the slayer, if he could do so before he got into a city of refuge. The unintentional destruction of life was ranked with murder; but cities of refuge were made both east and west of the river Jordan, to which men who had accidentally destroyed the life of another man could flee. It was commanded that the roads be kept open so that men under such circumstances could travel easily, and reach one of these cities, and be safe. Thus when one man by some mischance killed a fellow man, he dropped his flail or spade, or whatever else he might have in his hand, and fled; for the avenger of the spilled blood, the next of kin, was straightway in pursuit of him, to kill him if he overtook him; but if he reached a city of refuge before he was overtaken, he could not be harmed. Yet, lest men who had committed murder should pretend that it was accidental when it was intentional, it was retained that every man who should flee to a city of refuge for preservation should be tried by the officers of the city, who would listen to his story, and to the pursuer's story, and who, if they judged him to be innocent would give him refuge, but who, if they judged him to be guilty, would deny him shelter within the city's bounds, thus leaving him to be deprived of his life, which he had forfeited. This sacredness of life under the law of Moses stands out in singular contrast to the indifference of life which prevailed among all the ancient nations, and even that which obtains in these later days. Not only was the murderer to be destroyed; not only was manslaughter to be in some sense punished, in order that men might take care; but even carelessness such that a man's life should be destroyed by an animal was made penal as to the owner. You will find this to be one of the earliest declarations. It is contained in the twenty-first chapter of Exodus, and is again mentioned in later enactments.

"If an ox gore a man or a woman, that they die: then the ox shall be surely stoned, and his flesh shall not be eaten; but the owner of the ox shall be quit. But if the ox were wont to push with his horn in time past, and it hath been testified to his owner, and he hath not kept him in, but that he hath killed a man or a woman; the ox shall be stoned, and his owner also shall be put to death."

It is as if it were said, human life is so sacred that you must not only not murder, but you must not even be careless, lest your carelessness may lead to the destruction of human life; and your responsibility for care against accident extends even to your animals. If some animal suddenly develops fury which he never exhibited before, that animal shall be accursed. You shall not eat him, and he shall not be eaten. He is impure. Human life was so sacred that the wild animal was condemned to destruction if he destroyed it. And on the other hand, if the owner of the animal knew that he was dangerous, and did not keep him in or slaughter him, and he destroyed a man or a woman, not only was the animal subject to destruction, but the owner was condemned to death.

Is there a rumseller in this town that does not know what it is to have his cups push with the horns? Is there a man that is selling liquid damnation, day and night, who does not know what is the peril that it carries with it? Do not we know that there are ten thousand devilish bulls that push with the horns as dangerously as any animal, and that intoxicating drink is one of them? And is the dealer in such drink to go scot-free? Might we not wisely go back for our laws to the desert, and take counsel of Moses and the old Israelites?

Still further the sacredness of human life was defended. If a man were found dead in any neighborhood, and no one knew how he came to lose his life, then there was to be an accounting. It was such a discipline as was very effectually used in our war, and such as is used in all great wars. Where soldiers are being picked off, where the guards of railroads are being lurked after and destroyed, the inhabitants of the township or county in which the occurrence takes place are held responsible for it. The neighborhood shall pay for men picked off in that way.

It is supposed that this provision is modern, but it is very ancient. You will find, for instance, in the twenty-first chapter of Deuteronomy, the following :—

"If one be found slain in the land which the Lord thy God giveth thee to possess it, lying in the field, and it be not known who hath slain him : then thy elders and thy judges shall come forth, and they shall measure unto the cities which are round about him that is slain : and it shall be, that the city which is next unto the slain man, even the elders of that city shall take an heifer, which hath not been wrought with, and which hath not drawn in the yoke ; and the elders of that city shall bring down the heifer unto a rough valley, which is neither eared nor sown, and shall strike off the heifer's neck there in the valley.

"And the priests the sons of Levi shall come near ; for them the Lord thy God hath chosen to minister unto him, and to bless in the name of the Lord ; and by their word shall every controversy and every stroke be tried : and all the elders of that city, that are next unto the slain man, shall wash their hands over the heifer that is beheaded in the valley : and they shall answer and say, Our hands have not shed this blood, neither have our eyes seen it. Be merciful, O Lord, unto [Forgive, O Lord,] thy people Israel, whom thou hast redeemed, and lay not innocent blood unto thy people of Israel's charge.

"And the blood shall be forgiven them."

There is but one case that I have found in which human life may be peremptorily taken, and no account be given, and that is where a man is a thief and a robber, and is discovered breaking into a house to steal. The owner or occupant of that house may destroy him at once, and be clear. I wish that Mosaic economy were more prevalent in our time. It is the impunity that robbers have, it is the cowardly manhood with which men betray their trust in failing to defend their own possessions, and allowing a thief to take anything he pleases, and go, rather than hurt him—it is this that gives such encouragement to burglars, whereas, if nine men out of every ten who enter a house for the purpose of robbing it were slaughtered, robbers would be very soon diminished and the community would be a great deal better off.

But while the whole question of the sanctity of human life is disclosed by this brief examination of the laws of Moses, I would not have you suppose that it begins or ends here. This is but a single specimen, though it lies at the root of society.

I wish, next, to call your attention to the profound concern which the State, as organized by Moses, was called upon to take for the poor and the unfortunate. In the first place, it was ordained, in the twenty-third chapter of Deuteronomy, and the twenty-fourth and twenty-fifth verses, that any man suffering from hunger, and walking through his neighbor's field or orchard or garden, had a right to eat whatever he wanted—whether melons, apples, or what not. He must not pocket them, or walk off with them in a bag, but no man that was hungry was to be denied the privilege of satisfying his hunger.

"When thou comest into thy neighbor's vineyard, then thou mayest eat grapes thy fill at thine own pleasure ; but thou shalt not put any in thy vessel. When thou comest into the standing corn of thy neighbor, then thou mayest pluck the ears with thine hand; but thou shalt not move a sickle unto thy neighbor's standing corn."

The poor were not to starve, property was not so sacred as human life, and whoever had food in the field owned it only up to the point where a fellow being was perishing with hunger : then it belonged to the man that needed it—so much of it as he needed.

More than that, the poor man had a right to glean. That right is set forth so strongly in the next chapter—the twenty-fourth—that I will read an extract from it.

"When thou cuttest down thine harvest in thy field, and hast forgot a sheaf in the field, thou shalt not go again to fetch it."

If it slid off the cart behind you and you did not know it, and it was hid by a tree or stone, or if you forgot it, let it stay there.

"It shall be for the stranger, for the fatherless, and for the widow: that the Lord thy God may bless thee in all the work of thine hands. When thou beatest thine olive tree, thou shalt not go over the boughs again [the second time, that is]: it shall be for the stranger, for the fatherless, and for the widow. When thou gatherest the grapes of thy vineyard, thou shalt not glean it afterward: it shall be for the stranger, for the fatherless, and for the widow. And thou shalt remember that thou wast a bondman in the land of Egypt: therefore I command thee to do this thing."

What humanity there was in it!

You have read the inimitable story of Ruth and Boaz. There is portrayed in an exquisite idyllic picture this great beneficence, by which every man was obliged, as it were, to make the poor partners of his prosperity.

Great consideration, also, was shown toward the poor in the matter of their wages.

"Thou shalt not oppress a hired servant that is poor and needy, whether he be of thy brethren, or of thy strangers that are in thy land within thy gates."

He was not speaking of the Chinese at that time: he was speaking of strangers that belonged around about the head of the Kedron.

"At his day [that is, the day on which he earns it] thou shalt give him his hire, neither shall the sun go down upon it; for he is poor, and setteth his heart upon it: lest he cry against thee unto the Lord, and it be sin unto thee."

In the matter of paying wages as soon as they are earned, would it not be worth while to have the law of Moses instituted in some of our families where we do not pay up the servants for weeks and months? Would it not be well to have some of Moses' laws enforced in some of the business houses in New York, and in the great manufacturing centers where caps, shirts, and clothes are made, where the wages are cut down to the lowest point, and where the employees find it hard to get what is promised them?

There is in New York an institution that has the blessing of God on it. It is an association of gentlemen and ladies to enforce the payment of their wages to the poor, and hundreds and thousands of dollars have been collected through the beneficence of this association without a penny's expense to those for whom it was collected. It is not modern, however. The origin of it was in the Mosaic institutes. Men were commanded to pay the poor their wages, and to pay them the day they earned them, not only because they were poor, but because in dealing with the poor men were forbidden all usury; and that does not mean excessive interest, but any interest,—usance,—payment for the use of the loan.

"Thou shalt not lend upon usury to thy brother."

This was not a commercial nation, and interest then did not bear the same relation to money that it does now. The Hebrews were an agricultural people, and they had no occasion for borrowing capital, as we have, for purposes of development. Men worked day by day, and yet, on account of inequality of soil, or because of difference of skill, or for other reasons, some men were in penury and want while others had an abundance; and men were forbidden to lend to their brethren and charge them anything for the accommodation.

"Thou shalt not lend upon usury to thy brother; usury of money, usury of victuals, usury of anything that is lent upon usury: unto a stranger thou mayest lend upon usury; but unto thy brother thou shalt not lend upon usury: that the Lord thy God may bless thee in all that thou settest thine hand to in the land whither thou goest to possess it."

And if they got in debt one to another, there was a limit even to the obligation of a debt that was incurred; for it is implied that debts not paid, or unliquidated, by reason of inability, in process of time became outlawed; and every seventh year settled all debts. In other words, there was a periodical bankrupt act by which everything unsettled when the seventh year came round settled itself. No man could be tied up all his life on account of what he owed; and no one could make poor men literally his slaves, under the pressure of constantly accumulating debt. They rose up every seventh year free from the debts under which they had been struggling. What wisdom! What humanity!

But it might be that men, under such circumstances as these, would shut up their hearts against their neighbors, since they could not take usury, and since debts incurred and not paid were quashed on the seventh year; but provision was made against that.

"At the end of every seven years thou shalt make a release. And this is the manner of the release : Every creditor that lendeth aught unto his neighbor shall release it; he shall not exact it of his neighbor, or of his brother ; because it is called the Lord's release. Of a foreigner thou mayest exact it again : but that which is thine with thy brother thine hand shall release ; save when there shall be no poor among you ; for the Lord shall greatly bless thee in the land which the Lord thy God giveth thee for an inheritance to possess it : only if thou carefully hearken unto the voice of the Lord thy God, to observe to do all these commandments which I command thee this day. For the Lord thy God blesseth thee, as he promised thee : and thou shalt lend unto many nations, but thou shalt not borrow ; and thou shalt reign over many nations, but they shall not reign over thee.

" If there be among you a poor man of one of thy brethren within any of thy gates in thy land which the Lord thy God giveth thee, thou shalt not harden thine heart, nor shut thine hand from thy poor brother : but thou shalt open thine hand wide unto him, and shalt surely lend him sufficient for his need, in that which he wanteth. Beware that there be not a thought in thy wicked heart, saying, The seventh year, the year of release, is at hand ; and thine eye be evil against thy poor brother, and thou givest him naught ; and he cry unto the Lord against thee, and it be sin unto thee. Thou shalt surely give him, and thine heart shall not be grieved when thou givest unto him : because that for this thing the Lord thy God shall bless thee in all thy works, and in all that thou puttest thine hand unto.

" For the poor shall never cease out of the land : therefore I command thee, saying, Thou shalt open thine hand wide unto thy brother, to thy poor, and to thy needy, in thy land."

Further than this, where men lent on the promise of repayment, and the borrower was unable to keep his promise, humanity was also enjoined, showing that the heart of the lawgiver, as inspired by the wisdom and goodness of God, was in intimate sympathy with the helpless and the needy. Turn to the twenty-fourth chapter of Deuteronomy and you will find him speaking after this manner :—

"No man shall take the nether or the upper millstone to pledge."

It is not likely that it was our ordinary kind of mill. In antiquity mills were as portable as old-fashioned hand coffee-mills, with a revolving stone turned by hand. Again :—

"When thou dost lend thy brother anything, thou shalt not go into his house to fetch his pledge. Thou shalt stand abroad, and the man to whom thou dost lend shall bring out the pledge abroad unto thee. And if the man be poor, thou shalt not sleep with his pledge."

In other words, you are not to issue an execution, and, taking the officer, or yourself acting as an officer, go in and pick out the best things you can find, and remove them. The man himself is to be allowed to select what he can easiest spare. If he select a garment (and one who is poor has nothing better than that, often) you have no right to keep it. As to setting a man's furniture out on the sidewalk, as to taking his bed from under him, as to kicking him into the street,—it is an outrage that never entered into the head of Moses, even to forbid it.

More than this, you will observe that while there was a distinction made between the Israelites and foreigners there was no discrimination that was oppressive. There was to be a greater degree of love and a larger exercise of humanity toward the Hebrews; but there was the most explicit provision made for kindness in the treatment of the foreigner. If you will turn to the book of Exodus you will be struck with the ground and reason given for it. In the twelfth chapter and the forty-ninth verse is this command:—

"One law shall be to him that is homeborn, and unto the stranger that sojourneth among you."

"When a stranger shall sojourn with thee, and will keep the passover to the Lord, let all his males be circumcised [enter into Abraham's covenant with God], and then let him come near and keep it; and he shall be as one that is born in the land: for no uncircumcised person shall eat thereof."

He may come in and take part with you if he please; but if he do not please you shall not press him. Toleration, a large consideration of the natural rights of men, is a very striking feature here.

Look at the repetitious care with which the rights of men, as distinguished from Jewish rights, are set forth and guarded in the nineteenth chapter of Leviticus, the thirty-third and thirty-fourth verses:—

"And if a stranger sojourn with thee in your land, ye shall not vex him. But the stranger that dwelleth with you shall be unto you as one born among you, and thou shalt love him as thyself; for ye were strangers in the land of Egypt: I am Jehovah your God."

Look at the repetition, also, in Deuteronomy, which is

even stronger yet, in some respects, in the tenth chapter, from the seventeenth verse to the nineteenth :—

"For Jehovah your God is God of gods, and Lord of lords, a great God, a mighty, and a terrible, which regardeth not persons, nor taketh reward: he doth execute the judgment of the fatherless and widow, and loveth the stranger, in giving him food and raiment. Love ye therefore the stranger: for ye were strangers in the land of Egypt."

Hear this, ye Christian people that have trod down the African as dirt in the street! Hear this, O Christian nation that is destroying, not the stranger in the land, but the original occupant, who held possession of it before ye came hither! Hear this, ye that refuse to let China stand by herself, that broke down her towers and demanded that she should come forth and become one of the nations of the earth, and that then, when she came forth reluctantly, and sent out her scholars, teachers, and laborers into our land, said, "The Chinaman must go"—that said, first, "He shall not stay at home;" and, second, "He shall not abide here; he shall be swept into the ocean!" Nearly four thousand years have gone, and the world in many regards has been ripened, but the heart of this people to-day is coarser and harder than it was when Moses led the Israelites in the desert. *There shall be one law for him that is homeborn and for him that comes among you*—one law for the German, one law for the Irishman, one law for the American, and, as God is just, one law for the Chinaman, throughout this land! Are we to sit supine and indifferent—we that have the whole thunder of the Old Testament rising up against us? Are we to say, "Politicians are doing it, and we shall lose the election if we interfere"? Is iniquity to be enforced as law, and are provisions for the protection of our fellow men to go by default, and are the very foundations on which this great nation stands to be undermined, and are those that are working these mischiefs to be tolerated without rebuke and indignation? The judgments of God will neither linger nor slumber. Accursed be the nation that despises the poor and maltreats the stranger! Accursed be the people that execute injustice upon the head of the helpless and those that are ready to perish ! I care nothing for politics, but I care everything for principle. I care nothing for party, this or that, compared with the honor of our people—compared with the glory of this great freeborn nation, that ought to be ashamed to set an example that would make the desert blush for inhumanity !

Pardon me—I must go back to Moses ; and it is a great way back ! I wish to call your attention to another feature in the development of the great humanity of the laws of Moses, namely, the nature of the punishments among the Jews as contrasted with the penalties inflicted by other nations. The national punishment was stoning. Death by that mode is probably as easy as death by almost any other mode. A sound blow on the head settles it. After receiving such a blow men are no longer conscious, and therefore do not suffer. Stoning was the national method of execution. The sword came next—especially in the cases of those that suffered by reason of sentence of war. Beside this, there were no cruel punishments of men among the Israelites. In other nations men were slowly roasted in ashes and embers ; their feet were cut off ; their hands were removed ; their eyes were put out ; they were sawn asunder ; they were impaled, a stake being driven through the whole length of their bodies ; and they were crucified ; all of these were foreign punishments : but the legislation of Moses was stainless in that regard. There was not a cruel punishment permitted by it. It allowed no torments. While it insisted upon exact justice, it was administered with the greatest humanity capable of producing the required effect.

But look at the bloody laws of England. Look at our own earlier legislation. We ought to be ashamed to compare it with the Mosaic humanities.

Not only were all these things true that I have mentioned to-night, but I call your attention briefly to the extraordinary stretch of humane principles toward slaves, animals, and nature itself. There is not a parallel in the legislation of any nation.

In the first place, it was forbidden to make slaves of Hebrews even in the sense in which it was permitted to make slaves of foreigners. You might hire or take a man for service for six years, and he would go free on the seventh year. That was the extent of the service that was allowed to be inflicted on a native born Hebrew. It was like hiring a man for a term of years. The Roman law of slavery never prevailed in Judea or Palestine—that accursed law that disfranchised a man and took away his manhood, and ranked him as an animal, and bought and sold him without regard to his feeling or interest. The feature of Roman slavery which under American slavery allowed the making of the condition of the slave as bad as it might be, was unknown to the Jews.

Under the Jewish system the slave had a right to redeem himself if he could. Nay, if he was maltreated, if a brutal master smote him so as to maim him, that set him free. If he lost an eye, that emancipated him. If the treatment he received in the household was such that he fled, that fact was considered to be evidence that he was oppressed ; and it was forbidden that he be caught and returned to his master. It was taken for granted that persons from foreign nations would find their condition as slaves so much better that they would not run away unless there was good reason for it ; and anything like our Fugitive Slave Law could not have been thought of in the time of Moses. It took about four thousand years of religion to develop that abomination.

Nay, more : around about the service of foreign-born men, such as it was, were thrown all the alleviations that belong to the native population. These men had the Sabbath to themselves as much as the Jews. The sabbatic year was theirs as much as it was their masters'. The great jubilee, also, was theirs as much as it was their masters'. They partook of all great festivals. They had a right to be circumcised and become Hebrews by adoption. If they did not want to be set free the master had to make provision for them.

"And it shall be, if he say unto thee, I will not go away from thee; because he loveth thee and thine house, because he is well with thee; then thou shalt take an awl, and thrust it through his ear unto the door, and he shall be thy servant forever."

I do not recollect the record of a case in which any American slave who was offered his freedom, and given permission to go, loved servitude better than emancipation; and what must have been the nature of Jewish slavery when this enactment was made? The time has gone by for us to be interested in this subject as we should have been twenty years ago.

As I have said, not only slaves but animals were not to be abused. It was forbidden to muzzle the ox that trod out the corn. As the poor had a right to glean, so, when the crop was being threshed, the ox had a right to eat what he needed, and he was not to be muzzled. And if mercy was to be shown toward an animal, how much more should mercy be shown toward a man, who is so much better than an ox!

Again, you will find this decree:—

"Thou shalt not seethe a kid in his mother's milk."

In other words, the parental relation was to be so sacred that a Jew should, by association, shrink from slaying a kid, a lamb, or a calf, and then cooking it in its mother's milk. It ought to shock one's sensibility, and it did theirs. What humanity to animals, that even their parental feelings were to be respected! They were defended from becoming victims to those horrible, over-boiling human lusts which existed in contemporaneous nations.

And even nature was treated with great tenderness. Allow me to read from Leviticus, the nineteenth chapter and the twenty-third verse, a remarkable enactment.

"When ye shall come into the land, and shall have planted all manner of trees for food, then ye shall count the fruit thereof as uncircumcised: three years shall it be as uncircumcised unto you: it shall not be eaten of. But in the fourth year all the fruit thereof shall be holy to praise Jehovah withal. And in the fifth year shall ye eat of the fruit thereof, that it may yield unto you the increase thereof: I am Jehovah your God."

If anyone planted a grape vine he was forbidden to gather

the tender fruit, the first little clusters, for four years of its bearing, and so weaken its growth ; but after that the vine was strong enough to bear harvests and to admit of their being gathered and consumed without injury.

And if a bird's nest chanced to be in the way, in any tree, or on the ground, they were commanded not to destroy it. To the bird, the sweet singer, the minister of joy, they were to be humane.

Be humane, then, to the bird ; be humane to the animal ; be humane to the slave ; and be humane to the foreigner. Take care of the poor, and take care of your neighbor. When Christ said, "Love thy neighbor as thyself," he gave out the key with which to unlock the Old Testament. But I have not told you the half of it yet ; and I shall resume the subject next Sabbath evening.

XIV.

MOSAIC INSTITUTES:
THE HOUSEHOLD.

"When thy son asketh thee in time to come, saying, What mean the testimonies, and the statutes, and the judgments, which the Lord our God hath commanded you? Then thou shalt say unto thy son, We were Pharaoh's bondmen in Egypt; and the Lord brought us out of Egypt with a mighty hand: and the Lord showed signs and wonders, great and sore, upon Egypt, upon Pharaoh, and upon all his household, before our eyes: and he brought us out from thence, that he might bring us in, to give us the land which he sware unto our fathers. And the Lord commanded us to do all these statutes, to fear the Lord our God, for our good always, that he might preserve us alive, as it is at this day. And it shall be our righteousness, if we observe to do all these commandments before the Lord our God, as he hath commanded us."—Deut. vi. 20-25.

It may seem as though it were a more profitable thing to discuss living nations and contemporaneous events than to go back thousands of years to an early people, in an Oriental land, of a different language, and of different habits, hunting up the memorials of antiquity; but, quite aside from any archeological curiosity, we have a very special interest in the study of the early history of the Hebrews; for scarcely less directly descended from that people are they that came from the loins of the Hebrews than we, who are descended from their spiritual loins. The Hebrew laws—the Hebrew Scriptures—have been especial companions of the reformers, martyrs, witnesses, confessors of the truth throughout Christendom. Those

---

Sunday evening, February 16, 1879. LESSON: Deut. vii 6-25.

Scriptures were largely issued in stormy times; and, ever since, men in stormy times, under pressure, have found them eminently congenial to themselves. Although the New Testament was not disregarded by our Puritan ancestors, it must be said that they lived largely in the spirit of the Old Testament, and were greatly fashioned by the Hebrew spirit, which gave to England, and to New England, a kind of intellectual lineage, heart lineage, and political lineage. We have the Greek metaphysics and philosophy, and we have the Hebrew moral sense; and though they strive mightily, and are not always reconcilable with each other, yet we are the children of both. Therefore we have a heritage in these old Scriptures. They are the birthplace of our thoughts. They are the roots from which we are now gathering fruit for many of our dearest institutions. We know not how large a part of that which dignifies life, and gives value to everything around about us, we owe to the spirit of Moses, to the institutions of Moses, and to the wonderful developments of the Hebrew people.

I proceed, to-night, to review certain elements that belong to the constitution of the Hebrew polity. In my last lecture of this series, delivered two weeks ago, I attempted to show the spirit of humanity which ran through the whole Mosaic economy, that it was of the largest type, how it bound men together by the cords of a loving hopefulness, working in every relation of society, and taking charge of the poor and ignorant. I undertook to explain that the laws of Moses were protective of the wants of the laboring classes, and of the weak and necessitous, dealing considerately not only with the poor in all their interests, but with the slaves; and were eminently humane toward the stranger; such being the spirit of administration throughout the best years of the Hebrew commonwealth. I undertook to demonstrate that even with their culprits and in administering justice there was no inhumanity; that while other nations were tormenting men for the sake of tormenting them, such cruelty was never known to the old Hebrews; that unnecessary pain in punishment was avoided by them; that their whole economy was humane. I attempted to show that their humanity went still further, and included the entire animal kingdom—bird and beast.

This whole line of thought might be diversified and intensified; but let us pass on, to-night, to the development of other elements, and of those that are perhaps more important.

I propose to speak of the condition of woman, and of the condition of the family or household, as they existed under the ordinances of Moses, and as to a large extent they have existed in practical life until this day. It should be borne in mind, however, that it would be very unfair to bring to bear upon this matter the advanced conditions and notions of modern society. It would not be reasonable for us to take the results of the experimentation of thousands of years on the globe, and go back to the twilight of antiquity, and especially to Oriental peoples, and measure their economies by that which is now ascertained to be best. This would be as unjust as it would be to take the latest astronomical discoveries and methods and make them the criterion for judging of the attainments of the earliest astronomers of the world. We are to remember that the Hebrews were an early nation, and we are not to be surprised at much that we find in their history. The theory of inspiration which we hold does not oblige us to suppose that everything which is recorded in the Old Testament sprang directly from the hand of God; but it does require us to suppose that there was a supervising providence by which the nascent human race was step by step developed through childhood and onward. Therefore you shall find in the inspired Word records of legislation in antiquity that would be utterly intolerable as applied to our day, while in the infancy of the race, if they were not permissible, they were at any rate to a degree excusable.

I need not say to you that outside of our later modern

nations the condition of any community may be ascertained beyond peradventure by the condition of woman in it. There never has been a nation, nor will there ever be a nation, having prolonged prosperity along with inferior women; and there never has been a nation, nor will there ever be a nation, without a wholesome, strong, and progressive prosperity along with honor to women. Therefore, in examining critically the condition of any nation, one of the primary questions is, "What has been the condition of its women? Were they slaves; were they creatures of amusement; were they mere servants of the kitchen: or, were they honored as the equals of men?" We must bear in mind that although the style of womanhood among the Jews was inferior as compared with womanhood now, yet it was, as compared with that of neighboring nations, eminently advanced. The Hebrews only, in antiquity, so far as I recollect, put any degree of honor upon women. But, in the condition of a nation's women you shall find the unmistakable traces of its barbarism or civilization.

The primitive law undoubtedly was that of power. Men worshiped power. It was the august power of nature that suggested to them deities. Among men those were the heroes who had power—the Samsons of antiquity. A Hercules was a hero in the olden time. Low, muscular strength was first in favor, but afterwards the ability to control and lead men; then wealth; and then pomp and glory, as elements of power, were objects of admiration.

From the beginning woman, as weaker than man, was disesteemed; she was not admired; and such was the course of human thought down to within a comparatively recent period. You will find, therefore, clear indications of this in the primitive condition of the Hebrew women.

With this explanation, I shall call your attention to the remarkable superiority of womanhood among the Hebrews as compared with every other contemporaneous people. In the first place, a woman in her father's house was simply a servant. The birth of a daughter in antiquity did not bring half so much joy as the birth of a son. As a child a woman was salable. The father could send his daughter to market at any time he pleased. At that early time property had not, to use a modern phraseology, differentiated. Whatever a man had or controlled was property. It was at a comparatively late day that men began to consider that property must mean *things*, and not persons. In ancient times property meant persons, if one had the control of persons; and in the Hebrew economy the daughter was the father's property just as much as a book or an invention that comes from my brain is my property; and he had absolute control not only of her liberty but of her life as well. She had no free choice as to matrimony. Her father gave her away, and of course always for a consideration. When the father was dead then the brother took his place; and in either case she had no volition of her own. She inherited nothing by law except where, from lack of male inheritors, the estate was likely to go out of the family. In that case she was a "Jack-at-a-pinch" heir. Such things mark the genius of an age. An espoused virgin if derelict in chastity was put to death; but her seducer was exonerated. He was a man, and she was nothing but a woman! The same thing has come down to us. The fault of the woman is unpardoned and unpardonable, but the fault of the man is condoned by society; and he walks among men and women with unblushing cheek, while she walks no more among men or women. Under Moses, however, if the woman were a wife, then both man and woman were put to death.

When married—and here the light begins to dawn—the Hebrew woman was never made the slave of bondage or toil. She was not put to severe tasks, as the squaw is, or as many Oriental woman were. Among the Hebrews the hardest industry was always imposed upon men. The woman was a housekeeper, and did the things that were to be done within the house, not being a field laborer. She was admitted to the society of men. She was not veiled. She did not need to be ashamed of her face. She ate with her husband—a thing which the Greek wife was not allowed to do in any well-regulated family. It would have been considered a breach of decorum for a Greek woman to sit at table with her husband if he chose to deny her the privilege,—for then, as now, men were more sensitive on some points of etiquette than concerning actual morality. But the Hebrew woman was not her husband's slave; she was his companion. She sat with him and communed with him. She took part with him in all public services. When he went up to Jerusalem to attend the great annual service she went with him. She could not offer sacrifice as he could, but to her was permitted the sacred song and the sacred dance. She took part generally in the religious observances of her people.

More than that, there is this remarkable peculiarity of the Hebrew nation, that from the earliest day they never stood in the way of extraordinary genius in man or in woman. They made no distinction of sex in that regard. If Miriam could sing and rejoice, Miriam was permitted to sing and rejoice : there was no public sentiment or prejudice that rendered her obnoxious. If Deborah had the gifts of a leader and judge, there was no objection raised to her exercising those gifts. Huldah, the prophetess, in times of uncertainty and apprehension, was sent for, because it was thought that better wisdom could be obtained from this venerable woman than from men. And from the beginning to the end of the Hebrew economy, if a woman was a poet, an orator, a prophet,—anything that would be considered honorable in a man,—she was at liberty to develop it. But it was only among the Hebrews, except in royal families, or in the families of the nobility, that women received such consideration.

Therefore, in reading the Scriptures both of the Old and the New Testaments, unless your attention has been called to the matter in detail, you will scarcely think of women in conditions other than those in which they exist among us. Samuel's mother, Elizabeth, Mary, and Martha, the women who accompanied Christ—to whom he looked a portion of the time for his support, and who afterwards consorted with the apostles, and were organic parts of the primitive church—women such as these were honored in the old Hebrew commonwealth.

But there was one vice which existed among the Hebrews. The origin of it is obscure. It was conspicuous, because it stood in such contrast with the many virtues of that nation. Polygamy was permitted among them. We learn in Genesis that monogamy was an ordinance of God; and yet when we come down in the history of the Hebrews we find that the great patriarchs were exceptions, and that in the time of Moses not only did polygamy exist, but ordinances were enacted which took it for granted that it was permitted by Moses. To those who hold to the doctrine of verbal and absolute inspiration here is a predicament; for if you insist that Moses enacted every single one of his ordinances because God commanded him to do it, you are obliged to take the ground that God ordained polygamy, since Moses recognizes it. He never once directly or indirectly forbids it.

We are not to suppose that there was no secular reason for this. At that time, when property in men was not distinguished from property in matter, men owned their wives and made them servants; and there was thus a property temptation for a man to own his cook, his chambermaid, all those who served him. The prevailing economy was such as to lead a man to wish to control and multiply his industrial forces.

This vice was permitted, I suppose, for another reason. The peculiar attraction of idolatry in the Pagan nations was not the polytheistic idea, but the element of sanctified lust. There was no one idolatrous service known to antiquity in which physical lusts and appetites did not play an important part; and it was this fact that drew the Israelites to the right and to the left continually. A multiplication of wives was an evil, and one that loudly called for restriction; yet it may be supposed that the great lawgiver tolerated it under certain limitations, with the idea that there was in it that which would keep the people from worse defections. Universal experience has determined that polygamy is a wrong, not to woman alone, but to her children; nor to them alone, but to the husband; nor to him alone, but to the whole household estate; nor to it alone, but to the entire nation. There never was a people since the world began that could maintain existence without a fatal weakness, where polygamy was in the household. Never was there a nation that was able to sustain itself against adversity without being monogamous — and there never will be one. Yet, for the Hebrews it was far better than to be running after the pagan gods and their obscene rites, as they were so often seduced into doing.

Strangely, in the midst of this great civilized nation of ours, that boasts of its Christianity, there has broken out this system, organized and enforced; and the power of Christianity has not thus far been able to cope with it; nor is there any prospect that it will be able to cope with it. Happily, Utah does not vote on national questions, and therefore it may be that politicians will legislate so as to insure a final extinguishment of this terrible mischief in our midst. If Utah were a State the evil would not be overthrown, because votes are the gods of our representatives at Washington; but she is not, and her polygamy will die under the pressure of surrounding education, thrift, and industrial and commercial activity.

The life of the children among the Hebrews, according to the spirit and letter of the Mosaic economy, was very precious. The murder of children, whether it was antenatal, or whether it was by their exposure after birth, was punishable by death. The destruction of children's lives in all nations around about was very widespread, such was the barbarous condition of things in those times. But nothing of that kind was allowed for a moment under the economy of Moses. If a woman destroyed her coming child, she was, under the Mosaic law, a murderer with deeper guilt than if she slew a child that was actually born. It would be well if the humanity toward childhood of that economy could be made imperative in modern times. Talk of the slaughter of the innocents by Herod! In these cities innocents are slaughtered by hundreds and thousands;—and it is not accounted an unvirtuous thing.

When you look at the economy of the family among the Hebrews, at every step the light grows brighter, and the picture is more beautiful. Around about the household were statutes the most rigorous. Infidelity to the marriage relation on the part of a man was punishable with death. Divorces were facile, but not on the part of women. No woman could bring a petition of divorce from her husband, but a man could get a divorce from his wife. Yet this did not take place largely in the earlier times. It developed to a greater extent in the later and more luxurious days. At the time of Christ, although polygamy had gone very much out of existence, it existed among the rich, and a man could obtain a divorce pretty much at his own option. And he found reason enough. If his wife was a little old, if she was troublesome on account of sickness, or if for any other reason she did not please him, he could put her away, and if she was innocent of any impropriety he could give her an honorable dismissal.

Now, when Christ forbade divorce, the whole spirit and temper of his command on that subject was to right the condition of woman, to make her marital relations permanent, and not dependent on the mere whim and caprice of her husband.

The condition of the family is a matter with which the statutes of Moses are never done with dealing. You are to bear in mind that in antiquity there were no such schools as we have; that there was no provision for universal education; that there were no books for the young; that knowledge had not been developed except in very limited spheres. And yet there was the greatest pains taken to educate the children. Let me read you one or two passages; as, for instance, in Deuteronomy, the sixth chapter and the sixth verse, where the education of children is insisted upon:—

"And these words, which I command thee this day, shall be in thine heart: and thou shalt teach them diligently unto thy children, and shalt talk of them when thou sittest in thine house, and when thou walkest by the way, and when thou liest down, and when thou risest up. And thou shalt bind them for a sign upon thine hand, and they shall be as frontlets between thine eyes. And thou shalt write them upon the posts of thy house, and on thy gates. And it shall be, when Jehovah thy God shall have brought thee into the land which he sware unto thy fathers, to Abraham, to Isaac, and to Jacob, to give thee great and goodly cities, which thou buildedst not, and houses full of all good things, which thou filledst not, and wells digged, which thou diggedst not, vineyards and olive trees, which thou plantedst not ; when thou shalt have eaten and be full ; then beware lest thou forget Jehovah, which brought thee forth out of the land of Egypt, from the house of bondage."

This was the height of teaching. Every house was a schoolhouse. Father and mother were school-teachers. And they were to teach, not once in a while, on the Sabbath, or at the great festivals, but incessantly. The teaching was to be the household conversation. It was to be the talk in the field, as the parents and the children walked together. It was to be their familiar discourse wherever they were in the ways of living. The parents were to be constantly storing the minds of their children with knowledge.

Knowledge of what? First, of the whole national history—of all matters that belonged to the State, and then of the statutes and ordinances of God that belonged to property, and neighborhood, and service, with this grand text which evermore shone as the very fountain of all duty, *Thou shalt love the Lord thy God, and honor Him, and thou shalt love thy neighbor as thyself.*

The whole scope of political economy or civility, as far as known among them, was taught to their children by the Hebrews. The whole science of life, so far as it was known among them—this, the Mosaic law said, they were to teach rising up and sitting down, perpetually. And they did it.

Labor was enjoined and made honorable. One of the proverbs of the old Jews was, "Whoever brings up a child without a trade brings him up to steal." However high a family was in social position, it was the habit of the Jews to teach every boy a trade, as he might see the day when it would be necessary for him to labor with his hands. It was wisdom in them to bring up their children to industry, and see that they had training such that if worse came to worst they would have a calling by which they could earn their bread. It was sought to give every man the capacity to take care of himself, so that there should be no poor people in the land. So successfully was this policy carried out that it has been said that the word *beggar* does not exist in the Hebrew tongue. Hear that, Ireland! Hear that, Italy! And all this sprang, not from climate or condition, but from the application of the Mosaic economy to the education of the people.

Moreover, the children were not brought up to follow simply what seemed good in their own sight: they were brought up to courtesy, to obedience, to reverence, to industry, and to morality. And the parent held no slender rod in such a matter as that. In the twenty-first chapter of Exodus, the fifteenth and seventeenth verses, you will find the following:—

"He that smiteth his father, or his mother, shall surely be put to death."
"He that curseth his father, or his mother, shall surely be put to death."

Veneration for parents is made obligatory. "Honor thy father and thy mother, that thy days may be long in the land which the Lord thy God giveth thee," was sounded in the ears of children from the earliest moment; and the violation of that command brought death.

Still more imperatively is it laid down in the twenty-first chapter of Deuteronomy, from the eighteenth verse onward:—

"If a man have a stubborn and rebellious son, which will not obey the voice of his father, or the voice of his mother, and that, when they have chastened him, will not hearken unto them: then shall his father and his mother lay hold on him, and bring him out unto the elders of his city, and unto the gate of his place; and they shall say unto the elders of his city, This our son is stubborn and rebellious, he will not obey our voice; he is a glutton and a drunkard. And all the men of his city shall stone him with stones, that he die: so shalt thou put evil away from among you; and all Israel shall hear, and fear."

Need I tell you that the Jews, being brought up in the household on that pattern, very soon became a thoroughbred people? The family was their special glory. Upon it was concentrated all their institutions and economy. It was the fountain of fountains. It was the institution that bred institutions. It was that toward which the natural affections, the educated understanding, and the statutory arrangements of the Mosaic economy, chiefly tended.

If you ask me, How is it that this people are set upon, dispersed, abused, persecuted, and made recipients of more injustice than ever fell upon the heads of any other people, and that yet they cling together, and maintain their nationality, and endure, and overcome, and exert such a power among the nations of the earth? I reply that it is because of the Mosaic economy in which they have been educated, and which has continued the family relations which it instituted. By that economy they have been brought from barbarism to civilization; and their strength to-day—in addition to what they have gained in common with other civilized nations—is what it always has been in Mosaism. That people which consists of groups of households, in which the children are developed into the highest forms of manhood, is indestructible; it will never be caught in a storm so severe that it will founder; and such a people are the Jews.

Contrast, for one moment, the condition of woman—the wife and the mother—in the Hebrew commonwealth with the condition of woman in contemporaneous neighboring nations, as, for instance, the Greek. In Greece not only was woman a slave, a working creature, but she was debarred from the privilege of public service. She was not permitted to sit at table with her lord and master; she was not allowed even to go to the door to see what was taking place in the street, unless she was densely veiled; moreover, she must be veiled or she could not sit in an assembly; she had no part or lot in the administration of public affairs; and she was denied the enjoyment of knowledge. I do not mean that her education was neglected, and that she must grow up ignorant; but there was a state of public sentiment in Greece such that if a woman showed evidence of refinement and education it was taken for granted that she had lost her purity. The whole Greek mind and conscience had come to associate ignorance with virtue and intelligence with vice, so that one was the sign of the other. There were among the women of Greece a class who were educated. They were taught in history, in philosophy, in music, in art, and in statesmanship. They were educated as far as the then knowledge of the world was capable of being carried. There were no men in Greece that were more highly endowed with knowledge than many Greek women. But who were they? Women who devoted themselves to the pleasure of wealthy and cultivated men, and who wished to make themselves attractive. If a woman meant to be a professional harlot, no pains was spared in educating her; but if a woman meant to be a mother, respected and honored, she must not be educated, because an educated woman and a harlot had come to be identical in the Greek mind. That is the reason why the Apostle Paul says to the Corinthians, "Let your women keep silence in the churches." It was feared that if they spoke in the churches it would be said, "They are impure persons, and the churches encourage licentiousness." Such was the condition of things in Greece at that time.

It has been remarked in regard to the Greeks that, in spite of their wonderful genius and acquirements in all intellectual and esthetic directions, they had not enough conscience to frame a constitution that would endure, or to maintain an administration of public affairs, and that they were so corrupt that Sodom and Gomorrah could have gone to school to them and learned of them in the lore of corruption.

But the Hebrew nation were of a very different type. In spite of their passionate nature and their lapses under the allurements of surrounding vicious nations, under the Mosaic economy they were trained to a general character of purity and moral uprightness. They established and maintained the family; they honored womanhood; and they educated their children in obedience and love.

So, then, let me say in closing, that we are indebted to the Hebrews for the very roots of our best institutions, and among others for the family, out of which comes all the sweetness of life. We are indebted to the Hebrew polity, more than to anything else in antiquity, for the position of woman in our day.

And let me say another thing: no genuine religious idea is without value. While the Roman adoration of the Virgin Mary is distasteful to our Protestant minds, we are indebted for the chivalry and heroism with which we look upon womanhood largely to that idea of transcendent purity and beauty handed down through the growing ages. I have, in almost every room in my house, from the hands of one artist or another, an engraving of the Madonna and child. To the devout eye of the Catholic it means the *Mother of God;* to me it means *mother.* To them the babe means *the Son of God;* to me it means *childhood.* I look upon the mother and child, and bless God that that idea, begotten in old Hebrew times, at last ripened and came down through the medieval ages to our day, and shines out from so many canvases for the elevation of our ideal of home, for the gratification of our purest imagination and our esthetic taste, and brightens by its influence ten thousand times ten thousand households. All this we owe to Mosaic institutions.

Let us not, therefore, say that the Old Testament has served its purpose; that we have got through with it; that the New Testament is sufficient for us. There is treasure in the Old Testament, for us, if we know where to look for it.

XV.

MOSAIC INSTITUTES:

SOCIAL OBSERVANCE.

"Ye shall therefore keep all my statutes, and all my judgments, and do them: that the land, whither I bring you to dwell therein, spew you not out. And ye shall not walk in the manners of the nation which I cast out before you: for they committed all these things, and therefore I abhorred them. But I have said unto you, Ye shall inherit their land, and I will give it unto you to possess it, a land that floweth with milk and honey: I am the Lord your God, which have separated you from other peoples. Ye shall therefore put difference between clean beasts and unclean, and between unclean fowls and clean: and ye shall not make your souls abominable by beast, or by fowl, or by any manner of living thing that creepeth on the ground, which I have separated from you as unclean. And ye shall be holy unto me: for I the Lord am holy, and have severed you from other peoples, that ye should be mine."—Lev. xx. 22–26.

THERE have been but two great original nations that have had universal power upon the manhood of mankind— the Hebrew and the Greek.

To the end of the world the Greeks will be masters of the intellectual elements and stimulators of universal thought in its relations to abstract philosophy and to the elements of beauty. Further than this they did not go. They were empty and void and bankrupt of all true religion and all morality. They were a people immoral, indecent, rotten to the very core and backbone, and in time they were dissolved in their own bestialities; but intellectually they were the schoolmasters of the ages.

The Hebrew people, though not deficient in understand-

Sunday evening, February 23, 1879. LESSON: Psa. cxxxix.

ing and in wisdom, had their power on the moral element of man, and they have disclosed a longing for the higher life,—an earnest conscience burdened and grieved at sinfulness, and a yearning for an apprehension of true righteousness, that has not been equaled, and that has made them masters of the soul. From the days of the fathers to the end of time the Hebrew spirit will be, as it were, the priest and the religious teacher of the universal conscience and the universal heart. The Roman people were legislators and administrators; other nations have been great organizers: but the world has never felt the power either of their philosophical reason or of their conscience as it has felt the power of the Greeks and the Hebrews.

Every man admits that, not excluding the understanding, the moral element in man is transcendently the greatest; and the Hebrew people were pre-eminently, I will not say the authors of morality, but the expounders of it, as it stands in their nature and their history. As they were, so to speak, the priests, it is a matter of vital importance to know something of their origin and of the institutions to which they were trained. What if they were crude, what if they were secular, what if they were not up to the standard of the present age in civilization; they yet should have a profound interest to every man who spiritually comes from Abraham. We are to bear in mind that the New Testament is an outburst of blossoms and new leaves from solid wood of the Old Testament; and we ought never to forget that He whom we worship above all others was a Jew, trained in all the lore of the Old Testament. There is not a line which we trace on which his eye has not lingered. Not only the Prophecies with their thunders, and the Psalms with their sweet influences, and the Histories with their instructions, but the institutions, as well, of the old Hebrews, were the subject-matter of Christ's education in his childhood and in his manhood; and are all these things to be disengaged and set afloat and lost to us? It is squandering treasure to set aside the Old Testament.

And yet, apart from its antiquity, it has been a matter of

severest criticism, and justly, if you are to accept the old theory of inspiration, as if everything that was recorded was mandatory, and proceeded from the direct will of God. The Old Testament cannot, if it be put on that ground, justify the enormous slaughters or hideous cruelties which, in any age, cannot be justified according to the moral sense in which we are educated by the New Testament.

But, aside from that, we are to regard the books of the Old Testament as recording the best account of those ancient times, given by the best men, under such influence as they were capable of receiving from the divine afflatus, and as representing, therefore, an honest endeavor to show the highest truth as well as it could be shown at that time, when the human soul, the channel of its transmission, was not redeemed from external and incidental liabilities to error—as, indeed, it is not altogether, even yet! While on this particular ground we can defy scoffing criticism and misjudgment, we are also able even more effectually to resist those minor strictures which are directed toward a great deal of the Mosaic economy. The statutes have been subjected, in detail, to criticism and ridicule, as being puerile and meaningless, tending to produce a separation of nations from neighboring nations, to lead to dissensions between brethren, and to create a narrow superstition, instead of a generous religion founded upon the nature of things.

Now, in order to judge of any institution wisely it is always necessary, first, to consider whether the end sought by that institution is a worthy end, and, second, to examine whether the means used for accomplishing this are well adapted to secure it. As to what was the great drift of the Mosaic institutions we are not left in doubt. It was designed to build up "a peculiar people, zealous of good works," above all the other peoples that lived upon the earth. It was to develop a nation that, in its whole religious, civil, and industrial economy should represent the utmost purity, equity, activity, and prosperity. The end was certainly noble. Were the laws and institutions worthy by which that end was sought? In judging both of the objects aimed at and of the means by which it is attempted to achieve those objects, we must take into view, not what would seem wise to us, in our circumstances, at this late period of time: we must go back to the age in which the events under consideration occurred, to the particular races concerned, and to the circumstances of the individuals who enacted those events.

In this case, here was a rising people. They were to become a settled nation. The pastoral life to which they had been accustomed was to be changed to an agricultural life. With the establishing of a hereditarily pastoral people as an agricultural people there would of necessity be some things that seem essentially unwise. It could not be but that in the process of changing a wandering tribe to a settled people there would be more or less imperfections. Commerce springs up in a later period. Agriculture can go only a certain way alone. It must be followed by manufacturing. And manufacturing must always be accompanied by commerce. This belongs to a later period of development. A primitive people, savages, must become pastoral; and a pastoral people, always semi-civilized, must become agricultural; and the agricultural people must become manufacturing and commercial. But in the beginning it would not have done to have commerce incorporated into the Hebrew economy. If they had gone to Tyre and Sidon they would have been swept away by the corruptions that on every side were to be found among those commercial people of the Orient, who were corrupt and corrupting. Therefore the Hebrews must be held separate while in training.

A people of low moral consciousness were to be educated to morality. A sensuous race, subject to superstition and idolatry, were to be brought to a spiritual worship of the one God. And people facile to all temptations of the flesh were to be kept away from the miasm of licentiousness.

When, therefore, you consider the customs of which I shall speak to-night very briefly and cursorily, you are to bear in mind that they were substantially such as we yet practice toward our children in the family and in our schools. We hold our children not subject to a direct and promiscuous intercourse with the world while yet they are children. We do not let them know even things that it is proper that they should know later. We treat them as children, and do not suffer them to go out into society until they are equipped with habits and principles. This approves itself as wise to the enlightened judgment. And it was important that the Israelites in Palestine should be held apart from all damaging intercourse with neighboring nations until such time as they could bear the world's intercourse.

Idolatry, as it prevailed at that early period, was not half so bad in its theology as in its license. The most damnable element in the systems of the nations of antiquity was their licentiousness, their lust. License of every form was wrought into a ritual. In their temples were prostitutes. The temple of Venus at Corinth maintained a thousand prostitutes as ministers of worship. By express law in Babylon all women were subject to gross indignities. From the East were introduced into Rome ideas which led to outrageous sensualism.

So when you note the nations that surrounded the Israelites, you find that these people required a worship founded not only on intelligence, but on out-reaching virtue and purity. When, therefore, we find in the law of Moses, as we do, an enactment that no father should make a harlot of his daughter, we open our eyes with astonishment until we come to reflect that it was a principle of the religion of all the nations around about the Israelites to carry their daughters as an offering to their gods ; that a prostitution of them was an act of dedication to actual worship ; and that this ordinance of Moses was an ordinance of purity for the cleansing of the atmosphere in which the people lived,

If we turn to Leviticus, which is supposed to be wholly a book of ritualism, but which is full of other elements of profound interest, we shall find, in the nineteenth chapter, the twenty-sixth verse and onward, certain Mosaic duties which have been ridiculed as being unworthy of the divine inspiration—as being perhaps permissible to superstitious and degraded priests, but inconsistent with anything like authentic divine commandment. The idea that God ever promulgated such duties is laughed at as utterly improbable.

"Ye shall not eat anything with the blood: neither shall ye use enchantment, nor observe times. Ye shall not round the corners of your heads, neither shalt thou mar the corners of thy beard. Ye shall not make any cuttings in your flesh for the dead, nor print any marks upon you: I am Jehovah. Do not prostitute thy daughter, to cause her to be a harlot; lest the land fall to whoredom, and the land become full of wickedness. Ye shall keep my sabbaths, and reverence my sanctuary: I am Jehovah. Regard not them that have familiar spirits, neither seek after wizards, to be defiled by them: I am Jehovah your God. Thou shalt rise up before the hoary head, and honor the face of the old man, and fear thy God: I am Jehovah."

Let us look a little at this. It does seem, when a man is told that the Mosaic institutes contain God's inspired laws, and when he finds in them the precept for the barber shop, "Ye shall not round the corners of your heads, neither shalt thou mar the corners of thy beard," as though these were matters fit for ridicule. It would seem as though a divine ordinance requiring a man to trim his beard or cut his hair in a particular way was rather small, to say the least. But there is great and remarkable meaning in this ordinance. Look at the tonsure of the Roman priesthood. If they make it signify the crown of thorns which the Master wore, is it of no account? When you understand the thought with which their heads are shaven as they are it is of a great deal of account. It is not a barber's matter, it is a matter as deep as the soul, under such circumstances.

Is our flag, that floats over ship or fort, of no account? When it rises, every morning, before our eyes, at yonder fortification, with the rising sun, and goes down with the sun at night, is it merely a matter of bunting—red, white, and blue? Does it mean nothing but just cloth? It means everything that there is in the national heart and life. It is the banner that stands universally for all that pertains to us as a civilized nation.

Now, in heathen nations the cutting of the hair and beard was indicative of the religious worship of the wearer. Cutting the hair in a given way was supposed to imply adhesion to the gods of the foul idolaters, and cutting it in a certain other way was supposed to indicate fidelity to the God of the Hebrews. When, therefore, Moses said to the people of Israel, "Ye shall not round the corners of your heads, nor mar the corners of thy beard," it was a good deal. It was a separation between them and the customs of the idolatrous nations around about them.

Was there no difference, in our civil war, between blue and butternut? To-day a man can wear butternut or any other color he pleases, and no man shall call him to account for it; but during that strife it meant all the difference between friends and enemies—between men for the Union and men for the Confederacy. It indicated a separation between them as wide as the whole economy of society. The cropped round-head of the Puritan and flowing locks of the Cavalier will occur as a similar badge of distinction. And thus, even in so small a matter as a lock of hair, there may be conditions in which shall be represented separations between those who were devoted to the pure Jehovah and those who were wedded to idolatry.

Consider also some other elements.

"Ye shall not eat anything with the blood: neither shall ye use enchantment, nor observe times."

It was not that they were not to observe days and nights and months and years; that was universal and right; but it was a dissuasion against the observance of what are called "signs,"—auguries such as are observed by many common people even to-day under the influence of superstition; and how wise was that economy which led Moses to forbid the Israelites, in the first place, to go to wizards, soothsayers, practicers of second-sight, or those that had mediumistic powers — persons that professed to know by intuition what was happening or what was going to happen to men! From the beginning of the race down to the present day people have been deluded by pretenders like these; and it is more or less the case in our time that necromancy, witchcraft, the mediumistic art, has been practiced with immoral effects. Therefore, in the economy of Moses, which was to redeem the people of Israel, and bring them upon the plane of reason, this was a very wise enactment, though men have made light of it as meddling with an inconsequent, insignificant thing.

"Ye shall not make any cuttings in your flesh for the dead, nor print any marks upon you: I am Jehovah."

We know what the custom was—especially among zealots, or enthusiasts. We know how they would disfigure themselves. We know how they used to cut their bodies with stones. We know how it was oftentimes carried to permanent dismemberment. And the enactment of Moses, which required men to regard their bodies as sacred, and not to be wantonly disfigured in the mummery of pagan rites, was very humane, though it has been subject to ridicule.

"Thou shalt rise up before the hoary head, and honor the face of the old man, and fear thy God."

The child that is not taught to reverence his parents in the family will not reverence the magistrate out of the family; and the child that has no reverence for the magistrate will never reverence God. The way to reverence God is to practice reverence among the people with whom we dwell. The way to worship God whom we have not seen is to show consideration toward those in the midst of whom we move. When you take even these minute commands, and see what the objects of them were, and what the prevailing circumstances were, they rise from insignificance and triviality, and become important factors of education. All these and many other things carry in them the fundamental idea which Moses sought to inculcate among the people of Israel—namely, the idea of separation from the heathen peoples about them. Again and again and again he endeavored to impress them with the thought that they were a peculiar people—a people separated from the world. They were to be reminded of it by their clothes, by their industry, by everything that went on in the house and in the field, as well as in the worship of the sanctuary.

Look, for instance, in Deuteronomy, the twenty-second chapter, at the commands that are given there:—

"The woman shall not wear that which pertaineth unto a man, neither shall a man put on a woman's garment: for all that do so are abomination unto Jehovah thy God."

We all know that it is becoming a custom of every nation that men and women shall dress differently, not only for convenience, but because it promotes morality. There was a special reason for this in Moses' time, because in many of the neighboring nations the idolatrous worship required change and interchange of dress. This was the case in the later worship of Bacchus, and some of the most eminent historical characters figured in it. But there was something else; the idea of national separation was all the time carried foward in that matter, also.

"Thou shalt not sow thy vineyard with divers seeds: lest the fruit of thy seed which thou hast sown, and the fruit of thy vineyard, be defiled. Thou shalt not plow with an ox and an ass together. Thou shalt not wear a garment of divers sorts, as of woolen and linen together."

Those look like sumptuary laws, insignificant, this requiring of separateness, things of a kind being kept by themselves, and things different not being allowed to be promiscuously mixed; barley, for instance, being kept with barley, and wheat with wheat, contrary to the practice of modern times, when a farmer mixes various kinds of grass and other seeds in the sowing. Among the Jews there was the idea that seeds must be kept separate one from another, as they, being a peculiar people, must be separated from all other peoples. They were not allowed to twist together woolen and linen; not because it was cheaper, not because there was any intrinsic unfitness in their being united, but because everything must be held to its original simplicity, as it were, to signify and constantly enforce the separation of the people Israel.

So in their husbandry, in the manufactures of the loom, in the very dresses they wore, in all the economy of life, there were these silent indications, these little witnesses, saying to the Israelites, "Ye are a peculiar people, separated from every other. Ye are not Ammonites, or Amorites, or Jebusites, or Hivites; ye are not of Egypt, or Canaan, or Assyria, or Babylon; ye are a people consecrated and brought up of God to be a peculiar people, that in you should be developed a righteousness that by and by shall break forth as a sun, and shine to the uttermost parts of the earth."

Now, when you consider what a crude people the Hebrews were, and how they would be tempted to take on their neighbors' manners and customs, and mix with other nations, you will perceive that there was much substantial importance attaching to these signs and symbols, though to us they seem very insignificant if we read about them without recollecting that that childish, unformed people were being developed in moral sense, and that they were being so trained that they should be made sensitive to right and wrong. One of the functions of the Mosaic economy was to unfold the conscience. In this day, by force of long culture in Christian households, children are to a large extent born with innate tendencies toward right and away from wrong; and certainly with these tendencies it is easier to lead them in true courses than would otherwise be the case. We had a good start at birth; we came from a thoroughbred stock: but the question is, "How shall men who began low down, and whose appetites are animal, be led to be heedful and aspiring? How shall they be taught to discriminate between right and wrong? How shall they be helped to fortify themselves against the evil influences by which they are surrounded? That is the profound problem which Moses endeavored to solve; and the peculiar training to which he subjected the Jews had a constant tendency to broaden their knowledge of right and wrong, of purity and impurity.

Turn to the eleventh chapter of Leviticus. I shall not read all the chapters bearing on this subject, but I will take from the eleventh enough to give an insight into the economy of Moses.

"Speak unto the children of Israel, saying, These are the beasts which ye shall eat among all the beasts that are on the earth. Whatsoever parteth the hoof, and is cloven-footed, and cheweth the cud, among the beasts, that shall ye eat. Nevertheless, these shall ye not eat of them that chew the cud, or of them that divide the hoof: as the camel, because he cheweth the cud, but divideth not the hoof; he is unclean unto you. And the coney, because he cheweth the cud, but divideth not the hoof; he is unclean unto you. And the hare, because he cheweth the cud, but divideth not the hoof; he is unclean unto you. And the swine, though he divide the hoof, and be cloven-footed, yet he cheweth not the cud; he is unclean to you. Of their flesh shall ye not eat, and their carcass shall ye not touch; they are unclean to you.

"These shall ye eat of all that are in the waters: whatsoever hath fins and scales in the waters, in the seas, and in the rivers, them shall ye eat. And all that have not fins and scales in the seas, and in the rivers, of all that move in the waters, and of any living thing which is in the waters, they shall be an abomination unto you: they shall be even an abomination unto you; ye shall not eat of their flesh, but ye shall have their carcasses in abomination. Whatsoever hath no fins nor scales in the waters, that shall be an abomination unto you.

"And these are they which ye shall have in abomination among the fowls; they shall not be eaten, they are an abomination: the eagle, and the ossifrage, and the ospray, and the vulture, and the kite after his kind; every raven after his kind; and the owl, and the night-hawk, and the cuckoo, and the hawk after his kind, and the little owl, and the cormorant, and the great owl, and the swan, and the pelican, and the gier eagle, and the stork, the heron after her kind, and the lapwing, and the bat. All fowls that creep, going upon all four, shall be an abomination unto you.

"Yet these may ye eat of every flying creeping thing that goeth upon all four, which have legs above their feet, to leap withal upon the earth; even these of them ye may eat; the locust after his kind, and the bald locust after his kind, and the beetle after his kind, and the grasshopper after his kind. But all other flying creeping things, which have four feet, shall be an abomination unto you. And for these ye shall be unclean: whosoever toucheth the carcass of them shall be unclean until the even. And whosoever beareth aught of the carcass of them shall wash his clothes, and be unclean until the even."

In the first place, it is a matter striking in the economy

of Moses that the health of the people was looked after. We have no medical treatise that is more minutely careful in regard to the securing of ventilation and the removal of miasma than were the provisions of the Mosaic commonwealth. And as to articles clean and unclean, although we may eat some that were proscribed by Moses, in the main the beasts and birds that he prohibited have not been eaten by civilized men, and have not been regarded as wholesome food. Men do not generally care to eat the horse and the zebra. Everywhere men eat the elk and the ox. The eating of swine's flesh was forbidden by Moses. We are to bear in mind that in the climate in which the Israelites dwelt oily meat could not be eaten with the same impunity that it can in colder regions; so too with fish not having scales, like the bull-pout and the eel, they are oily and indigestible, and, like the forbidden birds of prey, they feed upon carrion. Thus there was a reason for their not eating certain kinds of food, beyond the question of ceremonial cleanness or uncleanness.

And the matter of uncleanness was sometimes carried to a remarkable degree. If a dead insect fell into a dish for the table, that dish must not be eaten, just as with us if a cockroach gets into a plate of food, the whole has to go. In our modern restaurants they would take out the cockroach and give you the food. I prefer to board with Moses. According to the Mosaic prescription, if a man bore a pitcher of water, and a dead insect fell into it, he must break the pitcher as well as throw away the water. This was no hardship, considering the sort of pitchers they had in the early days. It might seem otherwise in our modern times of exquisite ceramic ware. In those days a broken pitcher was no loss, because one could be made in ten minutes.

There were cases in which the law against handling unclean things was enforced to a singular extent. If a man was made unclean by touching a dead body, anyone that he touched was unclean; and anyone that *he* touched was also unclean; and so on. There were four degrees of uncleanness by successive contacts. Such was the length to which the Mosaic system carried this matter; but it was all in the direction of compelling carefulness and punishing carelessness, as children are trained at school.

I will not go further in this direction to-night. I do not desire to weary you with extended commentaries on the economy of Moses; and this evening's discourse has been intended only to illustrate the general principle underlying its many regulations—the necessity of separating Israel from surrounding nations, and of impressing their untutored natures with precept upon precept of wisdom enforced by line upon line of minute observance.

I will close to-night by calling your attention to a dramatic scene in the history of this people to which I alluded in an earlier discourse. When you consider what an uncultivated and naturally imaginative and superstitious people they were, you will recognize how striking that drama must have been. I need not go back to the grandeur and unsurpassable sublimity of that spectacle wherein the great congregation of Israel, in an oasis of the desert, came to a narrow plain at the foot of Mount Sinai, and saw the flame and heard the Voice when Moses received the law at the hands of Majesty. That the impression produced by this exhibition must have been very powerful is shown by the fact that from time immemorial writers have striven to adequately picture it.

There was another scene which, though of a different character, was as full of sublime grandeur as that. Moses ordained that when all the statutes which he had developed had been practiced by the children of Israel in their wanderings until they came to the border of the promised land, so soon as they had gone over the Jordan, the law should be ratified by the acclamation of the people, and under circumstances which should indelibly impress its sanctity upon their minds. Crossing the Jordan before Jericho, and passing over the plains of Mamre, they came to two mountains—that at the north, Ebal, and that at the south, Gerizim, with a valley between them. It was here that the ceremonies took place which are described in the twenty-seventh chapter of Deuteronomy:—

"And Moses with the elders of Israel commanded the people, saying, Keep all the commandments which I command you this day. And it shall be on the day when ye shall pass over Jordan unto the land which Jehovah thy God giveth thee, that thou shalt set thee up great stones, and plaster them with plaster [that being the way in which they wrought]: and thou shalt write upon them all the words of this law [the Ten Commandments], when thou art passed over, that thou mayest go in unto the land which Jehovah thy God giveth thee, a land that floweth with milk and honey; as Jehovah God of thy fathers hath promised thee. Therefore it shall be when ye be gone over Jordan, that ye shall set up these stones, which I command you this day, in Mount Ebal, and thou shalt plaster them with plaster. And there shalt thou build an altar unto Jehovah thy God, an altar of stones: thou shalt not lift up any iron tool upon them. Thou shalt build the altar of Jehovah thy God of whole stones: and thou shalt offer burnt offerings thereon unto Jehovah thy God: and thou shalt offer peace offerings, and shalt eat there, and rejoice before Jehovah thy God. And thou shalt write upon the stones all the words of this law very plainly.

"And Moses and the priests the Levites spake unto all Israel, saying, Take heed, and hearken, O Israel; this day thou art become the people of Jehovah thy God. Thou shalt therefore obey the voice of Jehovah thy God, and do his commandments and his statutes, which I command thee this day. And Moses charged the people the same day, saying, These shall stand upon Mount Gerizim to bless the people, when ye are come over Jordan; Simeon, and Levi, and Judah, and Issachar, and Joseph, and Benjamin, [the favorite ones; the beautiful natures]: and these shall stand upon Mount Ebal to curse; Reuben, Gad, and Asher, and Zebulun, Dan, and Naphtali."

When all things were prepared, at a signal from the priests, the blessings and the curses that attended the fulfillment or the violation of the law of God were uttered, and were echoed from one mountain to the other.

"And the Levites shall speak, and say unto all the men of Israel with a loud voice, Cursed be the man that maketh any graven or molten image, an abomination unto Jehovah, the work of the hands of the craftsman, and putteth it in a secret place."

And so soon as the echo of that had died away, the whole congregation of people on Ebal and Gerizim, and all that were between, with a sound like that of many waters, cried out, *Amen!* And from Mount Gerizim on the other side came the corresponding blessing to those that worshiped the one true God. Then the whole people gave out the response, *Amen!* Then Mount Ebal thundered back another curse. Then Gerizim sent forth another blessing. So these gigantic mountains answered each other with curses and blessings like echoes in the storms of the Alps, resounding from peak to peak. And finally the vast assembly dispersed.

Thus was ratified, in a manner than which there could have been none more impressive upon the imagination and the senses, the law promulgated by Moses, the people invoking upon themselves the curses of disobedience and the blessings of obedience. It was the carrying out of that economy which was meant to bring the children of Israel up from barbarism and idolatry to civilization and the worship of Jehovah. It was a ceremony so striking and so sublime that it could never die out of the memory, and could never cease to elevate the imagination of those who were participants in it.

I bear witness that, though it be professionally my business to study the Word of God, the more I read and ponder the contents of the Old Testament the more are my admiration and reverence for that book increased ; and those who have not found this to be so should give more attention to that book as a means of better understanding the New Testament.

In the West, a venerable preacher who drew very much of his instruction from the Old Testament was called to order in a council of ministers for placing too much stress upon the Old Testament writings. They told him he should preach more from the New Testament and less from the Old. "Brethren," said he, "I am a soldier, and I find that the way to make a good shot is to draw the foresight through the hindsight. By my experience I am convinced that if in preaching a minister would make a good shot, he can do it best by drawing the foresight of the New Testament through the hindsight of the Old. In that way he can be more sure that he is giving his people the real Word of God." And my own belief is that, though the Old Testament is to be read with discrimination, and in the light of the knowledge that has accumulated about it during the ages that have passed since it was written, you will find within the lids of that book honey in the honey-comb. There are rude places in it; but as travelers through deserts and over mountains here and there find sweet little valleys, so in reading the Old Testament you will find exquisite histories, beautiful scenes, and profound wisdom, such as are not contained in any other literature on the globe.

XVI.

THE FEAST OF TABERNACLES.

"Go ye up unto this feast: I go not up yet unto this feast; for my time is not yet full come. When he had said these words unto them, he abode still in Galilee. But when his brethren were gone up, then went he also up unto the feast, not openly, but as it were in secret."—Jno. vii. 8–10.

THIS was the Feast of Tabernacles, as we are informed in the second verse of this chapter. The continued existence and flourishing of the great feasts of the Jews are indicated by this passage from the life of our Saviour, not only, but by others showing his interest in them, and his observance of them. We shall have occasion, this evening, in going on with our account of the Mosaic economy, to pay attention to the development and offices of these great annual festivals of the Jews; but, before this, a word upon the sacrifices that formed the worship and ministration of the priesthood and the Levitical order.

On few subjects has there been so much discussion to so little purpose as on the origin and meaning of the sacrifices—the *Divine Offerings*, as they are perhaps more fitly called in the Old Testament. Sacrifices or offerings have belonged to every nation and tribe on the globe. It may suffice to remark, in a general way, that they represented the efforts of men to conciliate their gods. They existed long before the time of Moses. They were known to the patriarchs. They were known and practiced in the land from which the patriarchs came out. They were common to all the nations around about.

The development of the sacrificial system varied in

Sunday evening, March 1, 1879. LESSON: Psa. xcvii.

different lands—in Egypt, in Chaldea, in Persia, and in Syria; their diversities were almost as great as those of the languages and customs themselves; but there was this common root in them—namely, conciliation; access to the reigning invisible powers; offerings of placation; testimonials of devotion, of reverence or honor. From that simple beginning they were differentiated; and in the Mosaic system it was sought by sacrifices to attach to almost every one of the interests of life associations of its relation to the ruling power of the nation—Jehovah. There was scarcely a thing in the person, in the family, in the grain that sprang from the ground, in the fruit that grew in the vineyard, in anything that belonged to them in the nature of prosperity or of wealth, that in one way or another was not, by being offered solemnly and religiously, made to bear a relation in their thought to the overruling God. In the Tabernacle, and afterwards more signally in the Temple, the sacrifices or offerings were so organized that their observance should honor and reverence God.

Whether or not the modern argument derived from the great sacrifice of Christ and the atoning power of his suffering and death are legitimately deduced from the Jewish ideas I will not undertake to say. I will say simply this: that modern thought has not made allowance enough for the real thought of antiquity, and that into the sacrifices that are celebrated in the Old Testament, and that had their fulfillment and completion in the Lord Jesus Christ, we have injected a modern element of thought that did not exist among the orthodox Jews of the old dispensation.

Their sacrifices were official—that is, while it was the common business of members of the family to make offerings to God, the more solemn offerings were made through the ministration of the priests.

You will recollect that there was one tribe set apart for the services of the sanctuary. The Levites and the priests did not represent in the ancient economy what the priesthood does in our day. Priests in modern economy are an instructed class, for administration in religious and moral thought and service. While they were yet in the wilderness the Levites and the priests were really the standing army of the Jews; and throughout the greater part of their national existence the office of the priest was far more nearly allied to that of the butcher than to that of the orator, or expositor, or preacher. Moreover, the greatest generals of the nation were drawn from the priestly order. The Levites were the defending power. They were the military centers. Whenever the armies were arrayed for offense or defense they were headed by their Levitical officers. When the sacrifices were offered up in the Temple, although there were prayers, and chants, and various other solemnities by others, yet the blood-offerings were made by the Levites. There were offerings of grain, and fruits, and frankincense, and what not, which they did not direct; but when bullocks, and goats, and lambs, and turtle doves were to be sacrificed, these were offered up through the Levites, or the priesthood.

If you will read the account of the dedication of the Temple of Solomon, you will see what a business it was. It is scarcely possible for our modern imagination not to be shocked at the scenes of blood which must needs have taken place every year, two or three times, in connection with the sacrificial rites of the Jews.

We cannot conceive of a service of that kind in which, in succession, bullocks and lambs were knocked down, and the priests stood by to take the blood that flowed from the necks of these animals. Literally, a whole river of blood ran, in these sacrifices, through days and days. The huge abattoirs in some of our towns are inadequate to represent what took place in those early times. The slaughter of hundreds of thousands of animals in the great sacrificial service of the Temple is so barren to every conception we have, that we can scarcely go back to-day in our thought and gain any realization of the scenes that were enacted then.

With us, blood means *death;* we have hardly a single conception, that is not artificial, which gives us any pleasant association in regard to these things. But to the Jews they had pleasant associations. "The blood is the *life,*" said Moses. Blood, as the universal symbol of life, was connected with their deepest thoughts and most sacred feelings. Here is a gulf between them and us.

Now, although the priests ministered somewhat in instruction, although some of them read the Psalms, or the Law, yet the great body of them were men of robust strength, stalwart, lusty, who could wield the battle-axe, or the butcher's axe, as the case might be; and they stood almost as far apart as it is possible to conceive of their standing from the priesthood as it is organized in modern times and as it exists in our Roman Catholic and Episcopal churches. In the Presbyterian, the Congregational, the Baptist, and other churches there is no priesthood. These churches have a ministry, not a priesthood, and they are exempt from many of the vexations and perplexities which belong to a priesthood. It would seem as though it would be a very dangerous thing to have introduced into a commonwealth a whole tribe of privileged men that stood between the people and God, and that therefore substantially owned the national conscience; but experience shows that perhaps in this case less harm flowed from it than ever before or since. It is notorious that the priesthood, the world around, has had a supremacy over the imaginations, the fears, and the consciences of men, and that, too, through the instrumentality of elements taken up and augmented by worldly ambition and organization. But this inheres in the nature of things. It is the tendency of human nature to look up, to aspire; and any man that officially represents, or any class of men that represent, higher conceptions of life and duty than the average will draw to them the thoughts and the reverence of the masses of mankind. It cannot be helped; and oftentimes persons will receive homage when individually they may be unworthy of it; for, with all the gravitation that there is in man's passions toward evil, there is also a struggle, feeble or strong as the case may be, of the divine principle in human nature, toward light and purity and elevation, and thus toward what stands for those loftier aims.

In general, according to the civilization and knowledge of the globe, the priesthood represent the best elements of human nature, and strive to draw people up to those elements; but when they are organized as a class, with peculiar privileges, when they gather wealth to themselves, and when political power comes into their hands as well, then they become a very dangerous class. It is dangerous in a great community to have any class which is immovable, and in which there is no circulation from the bottom to the top.

Now, the Levites had no possessions. They had places appointed for them, but it does not appear that they took possession of many of them. They were made to be dependent upon the voluntary contributions of the people. Tithes were the support on which they lived, and it was a very moderate support. And they never, in history, grew to be a rich or a dangerous class. One striking fact is that these priests, especially if they were high priests, even if they were most degenerate, were dear to the people—to the common people—and were regarded as in some sense of them, among them, and belonging to them. The Levitical economy was not one that separated the priests from the people in such a way that they lost sympathy with them. On the other hand, there was a feeling of mutual companionship.

I pass, now, to the discussion of some other elements of this great enginery of the commonwealth of Israel which have not received, it seems to me, that consideration which really belongs to them. There were three great festivals appointed by Moses, which, although they were intermitted, and although they lapsed at times, were in existence down to the time of our Lord, and after the city of Jerusalem was broken up by the Romans and the Jewish people were scattered. The first of these was the Feast of the Passover, the second was the Pentecost, and the third was the Feast of the Tabernacles.

The Feast of the Passover was designed to commemorate and to bear with it the whole breadth of the moral instruction which belonged to the sublime providence of God by which, when the firstborn of Egypt were destroyed, the destroying angel passed over the places where his chosen ones lived and saved them. It became an ordinance in Israel that every year, upon an appointed day, there should be a memorable and solemn convocation of the people, and that this should be the general ground and reason of it. The sacrifices, the songs and chants, the various emblematical services, were arranged around about that historic center.

Then, counting fifty days or seven weeks from the Passover, came the Feast of the Pentecost (*the Fiftieth*). That was more in the nature of a Thanksgiving, and celebration of the in-gathering, for it represented the nation in the act of bringing the first fruits of all the products of the field, and offering them up at the hands of the priests as a testimony of thanks to God.

Later on, in October, when they had gathered their grapes, their olives, their figs, and their latest fruits of the field, came the Feast of Tabernacles. This last, however, had a prior or larger historical element than the Pentecost, in that it celebrated the residence of the people in the wilderness, when they had no fields to sow, no pasturage, no oil, no wine, no vineyards.

If the Passover was the most solemn and profoundly religious, the Feast of Tabernacles was by all odds the most convivial and joyous of these three feasts. The Feast of the Passover occupied seven days, the Feast of the Pentecost one day, and the Feast of Tabernacles eight days.

By and by there was a fourth festival added, which was in full operation in the time of the apostles—namely, the Feast of Purim, established by Mordecai on account of the escape of the Jews from the persecutions of Haman in

Persia. This feast did not belong to the trio appointed by the Mosaic laws. There were other great festivals and fasts. I pass these all by, and confine my attention to the three great feasts established by the institutes of Moses.

It was in accordance with the ordinance of Moses that at these three periods every male whose age and condition would permit, should go up to the Tabernacle (or to Jerusalem after the Temple had been established), leaving their possessions and so much of their families as were to remain behind, but taking their families, even including their little children, if they pleased. Three times a year the whole nation rose up, as it were, to its feet, formed vast caravans, and proceeded to the appointed place. Multitudes came from the north and the upper line of Galilee down by the western shore of that sea. They came from the northwest, crossing the plain of Esdraelon, meeting just below the Sea of Galilee, crossed over Jordan, and went down on a better caravan road on the eastern side, as far as Jericho, a little above the point where the Jordan empties into the Dead Sea, and thence, recrossing the river, passed on to Jerusalem. And in approaching Jerusalem when near to Bethany they came to a most resplendent view.

Those that lived in the mountainous country came from the west. And from various directions came those that were in the southern and western parts. These had but two or three days' journey; but those in the extreme north made the distance in four, five, and six days, according to whether there were women and children among them, or whether they were all robust men.

From the moment of their starting until their return, the whole nation was one vast singing-school. They were perpetually chanting songs to Jehovah. On departing from their homes they left behind them houses, farms, cattle, horses, even their little children,—for usually it was not till the age of twelve that children were taken up to the feasts; and thousands, tens of thousands especially at evening, as they settled down in their picnic camps, would be heard to join in these songs ; and among the voices of the multitude might be distinguished those of children and trembling old men. How well their tender thoughts and feelings were expressed by such a Psalm as this :—

"I will lift up mine eyes unto the hills, from whence cometh my help. My help cometh from the Lord, which made heaven and earth. He will not suffer thy foot to be moved: he that keepeth thee will not slumber. Behold, he that keepeth Israel shall neither slumber nor sleep. The Lord is thy keeper: the Lord is thy shade upon thy right hand. The sun shall not smite thee by day, nor the moon by night. The Lord shall preserve thee from all evil: he shall preserve thy soul. The Lord shall preserve thy going out and thy coming in from this time forth, and even for evermore."

How beautiful, that those who took this journey trusted to the Lord all that they left behind which was dear to them! For, as you will bear in mind, it was the promise of God that if they would keep his commandments and observe his ordinances when they went to these feasts he would withhold their enemies so that they should not attack their homes in their absence—a promise which was kept. I shall resume, a little later, some account of the use of the Psalms on this journey.

Look, for a moment, at what the effect must have been of these great annual migrations by which, from end to end of Palestine, the whole people were taken out of their regular habits. It does men good to take them out of their habits—to drive them out of the store and make them forget it; to draw them away from their offices, and cause them to think of something else besides their toil. It would do a world of good, if, two or three times a year, every housekeeper could make a pilgrimage, and forget tubs, kneading troughs, the cares of home—if now and then she could, as it were, be sent out to grass. And consider what an effect it must have had upon that whole nation to have the family care very much surceased—to have everybody, on every side, fall into line in neighborly ways, and walk one, two, three, four, five days, to Jerusalem, spend there a week, and then go back, three or four weeks being utterly broken up from the associations of the household. What chance could there have been for care to plow furrows on the brows of such folks? It is a good thing once in a while to intermit cultivation, let the soil rest, and allow the rain to beat upon it, and the light and air to come into it ; and it is a good thing to break up the monotony of life, and let in relaxation where there is constant, solid employment.

So it was, in a very simple and natural manner, with the Israelites ; these pilgrimages gave them elasticity, and even relieved labor from its toilsomeness : for you must bear in mind that slaves under such circumstances had the privileges of their masters. They were not to be debarred from the enjoyment of these festivities. The stranger himself was also permitted to partake of them.

Consider what is the condition of the oppression-bound countries of Europe. How ignorant they are ! How unelastic they are ! How mechanical they are ! How narrow their ideas are ! If you contrast them with the versatile, active, energetic, all-sided Yankees of this country, that travel incessantly, that are alert, day and night, all over the land, you will see what might be effected by a provision of this kind among a people like the children of Israel.

Then, it was the beginning of a peripatetic education. It was not the Greeks alone that instructed men while they were walking. The Israelites, in conversation by the way, taught the people, both old and young. Much of the intercourse of neighbors with neighbors on the road was in the nature of academic instruction. Have you never heard men that lived in the country, after returning from large towns where they had been on market days, tell what they had seen, what they had done, and what others had done? I remember hearing an old farmer of Massachusetts in whose family I was interested, on his coming back from Boston, give an account of having heard Dr. Lyman Beecher preach a sermon. He described the congregation, and told what the text was, how the sermon was divided, and how the subject was treated ; and I never shall forget how the children sat around and listened to all these things. And consider how much two or three million people, going together to Jerusalem, and attending the Feast of Tabernacles, and returning, would have to talk about. Consider how eager they would be, in mixing their companies as they did, to tell one another what had happened in their town, in their province, or in their neighborhood. With a week of journeying on their hands, they would have time to unfold all the news there was; and it could not be but that they would enjoy opportunities for education, and derive larger conceptions of what was going on around about them. It was a substitute, in some sense, for modern newspapers—for everybody found out what nobody had any business to know. Everybody heard every rumor that had been circulated in any neighborhood about anybody. They had nothing to do but to talk over such things, and they generally talked. The cases were discussed of the man who had gone up and of the man who had gone down; of the persons who had died, and of the persons who had got married; of those who had failed, of those who had cheated, and of those who had performed honorable deeds. These and many other subjects relating to men and things, as well as the weightier matters of the Law, would naturally be made topics of conversation on the road and during the time that was spent in Jerusalem, by the vast multitudes that gathered there on these occasions. After being there seven days they would go back pretty full of news again, and undoubtedly they kept one another well "posted."

This may seem to have been not altogether desirable; but it is very desirable to keep people stirring, and to keep them interested and excited about something. There is nothing so bad for human nature as stupid, sodden indifference, although there are different degrees of merit in excitement; but the prime condition of the benefit of men is that they shall be excited; and surely the Israelites were kept wide-awake.

Besides, you are to bear in mind that these great migrations were a means of keeping family ties bright. If, on the one hand, they promoted the worship of the invisible God, on the other hand they enhanced in the minds of the Jewish people the sanctity of the family. As I have said before, I consider the power of the family among the Israelites as being the saving element in their earthly nationality. That which has carried them through the flood of persecution to which they have been subjected has been their conception of the family. This conception has come down to us; and we are indebted in this respect more largely to the Israelites than to any other nation, or than to all other nations on the globe.

Now, in this periodical migration of the people, on their return they were undoubtedly met by neighbors and relatives who remained behind, and it is presumed that they came together and indulged in social amenities such as we enjoy on Christmas and Thanksgiving days. We can readily understand that they had ample opportunities to learn about each other when we bear in mind that they were able three times a year to make these pilgrimages. It was a wonderful element in keeping bright the fire of the family altar of love.

Then consider, again, how, under such circumstances, the feeling of patriotism would be kindled. They worshiped, not only, but they worshiped under forms that brought to memory the great events of their history. Those feasts were not like the roaring Fourth of July celebrations of our Independence, where we substitute noise for brains—nothing of that kind. In their magnificent psalms they chanted on the road the events of their history. But the structure of the psalms must be borne in mind. They are in a form that is adapted to pronunciation and response by answering choirs. I have heard persons complain of antiphonal singing, with choirs standing over against each other in church and answering one another, as new fangled; but such singing is older than hymns. It seems to belong to the childhood of all nations. They have that kind of singing on plantations in the South.

One man sings, and then comes the chorus of all the rest. And the Israelites, on the way to Jerusalem as well as during the festive days, were accustomed to chant their songs in that manner.

Let us consider, for instance, the one hundred and thirty-fifth and the one hundred and thirty-sixth Psalms:—

"Praise Jehovah. Praise ye the name of Jehovah; praise him, O ye servants of Jehovah. Ye that stand in the house of Jehovah, in the courts of the house of our God, praise Jehovah; for Jehovah is good."

The response would come, like thunder,—

"Sing praises unto his name; for it is pleasant. For Jehovah hath chosen Jacob unto himself, and Israel for his peculiar treasure. For I know that Jehovah is great, and that our Jehovah is above all gods. Whatsoever Jehovah pleased, that did he in heaven, and in earth, in the seas, and all deep places. He causeth the vapors to ascend from the ends of the earth; he maketh lightnings for the rain; he bringeth the wind out of his treasuries: who smote the firstborn of Egypt, both of man and beast: who sent tokens and wonders into the midst of thee, O Egypt, upon Pharaoh, and upon all his servants: who smote great nations, and slew mighty kings."

There is something grand in this, when you consider that vast multitude coming, in various bands, from every direction, meeting, and with endless reverberating song chanting, day and evening, the great events of their national history.

"Who smote great nations, and slew mighty kings; Sihon king of the Amorites, and Og king of Bashan, and all the kingdoms of Canaan: and gave their land for an heritage, an heritage unto Israel his people. Thy name, O Jehovah, endureth forever; and thy memorial, O Jehovah, throughout all generations. For Jehovah will judge his people, and he will repent himself concerning his servants. The idols of the heathen are silver and gold, the work of men's hands.

"They have mouths, but they speak not; eyes have they, but they see not; they have ears, but they hear not; neither is there any breath in their mouths. They that make them are like unto them: so is every one that trusteth in them.

"Bless Jehovah, O house of Israel: bless Jehovah, O house of Aaron: bless Jehovah, O house of Levi: ye that fear Jehovah, bless Jehovah. Blessed be Jehovah out of Zion, which dwelleth at Jerusalem. Praise ye Jehovah."

Not one of these Psalms, but scores and scores of them, were perfectly familiar, residing in the memory of those great crowds, and were chanted by them all the way up to Jerusalem and back again. Thus the little children learned the songs, learned the history of the nation, learned the names of the Israelitish heroes, and coupled these patriotic themes with the ministration of divine providence, so that their religion had in it the most profound moral sensibilities.

Then this mingling of the people in their upward march and in their return broke up the tendency to tribal narrowness and sectionalism, in a manner that we scarcely should have anticipated. They were mixed together. They formed pleasing acquaintances on the road—for they dwelt separately. The law of property was such that the inheritance of each tribe was kept with that tribe; and the marriage laws were such that the property reverted to the tribe, no matter to whom the possessor was married; but this tribal exclusiveness was met and modified by the threefold mixture, every year, of the people who swarmed along the great highways and camped about Jerusalem.

When they once had arrived at Jerusalem they were to abide there from one to two weeks. Josephus, speaking of one occasion, says there were three millions of people that had come up to Jerusalem at the time of the Roman invasion and the besieging of the city. The number seems so great that many have doubted it; yet, when you come to make an estimate, the number must be counted by millions; and you may as well say three millions as two millions; for, if two millions could have been taken care of, three millions could have been. If such large multitudes were looked after during the passage through the Wilderness, they could also be cared for during their attendance at the Feast of Tabernacles; especially as each family group largely took care of itself.

Their manner of camping was very simple. All the hills around Jerusalem were clothed with people dwelling in booths, tents, or tabernacles. There they abode and observed various ceremonies of the Temple. The Temple itself occupied about a ten-acre space. Some of the ceremonies were resplendent. The conditions imposed and the offices enjoined by the ritual, while they were in some respects superstitious and burdensome, in many other respects were spectacular, impressive, and very powerful on the imagination.

It was in connection with the Festival of which we read in the Gospels—considered the greatest day of joy known to the Jewish people—that the old rabbis used to say, "He who has not been present at a Feast of the Tabernacles knows not what it is to be joyful." The people were carried to such a degree of exhilaration, and it was so socially contagious and infectious, that these three millions were as good as mad for joy around about that old city.

You are to bear in mind that the day was one of holy convocation. A portion of each day was set apart for solemn religious services, and the rest of the day was devoted to social conviviality. These things were ordered. Hospitality was a religious law. The people were commanded to provide for the stranger, for the orphan, for the widow, and for the Levite. Their housekeeping was very simple. Their hospitality was a kind of friendly interchange. They occupied themselves a whole week in such social economy; and this was interlaced, mixed up, with most solemn observances, led on by the priesthood. Can you conceive of anything that would appeal more strongly to the imagination of the Jews than these Feasts of the Tabernacles, and the customs and ceremonies which accompanied them? There never was an educating system which compared with that of Moses in its various particulars.

There is another element that I want you to bear in mind. I do not know where you will find anywhere else a real provision for dancing in the ordinances of religion for the purpose of producing piety. To be sure there were single instances of the sort; dancing was a religious service in Greece and Rome: but among the classic nations and other pagans it was a part of the most licentious rites. Where else can you find that to dance was to bring to mind a holy God? That is not generally the association connected with dancing in our time; but among the Hebrews dancing was made a part of the religious ceremonial in such a sense that it was allied to religious feeling; and, moreover, religious feeling and the whole economy of religion were to produce amusement, gratification, happiness, over and above that which came from mere religious instruction, from general social intercourse, or from home life. The economy of the Hebrew commonwealth was organized to produce happiness, as if it were a moral quality, and as if the production of it were worthy of the priesthood.

The Puritans went into the Old Testament and borrowed from it profound conceptions of moral purity, of righteousness, and of the rigor of an executed law; but the Puritans left behind them the sweet blossom of joy. The rounded-out fruit of this element they did not incorporate into their system—and for reasons that were very plain. Music, dancing, pictures, architecture, had been taken possession of by superstition; and where there has been gross superstition iconoclasm must follow. So the Puritans broke down all these fair and pleasant things. And we came from them. We came from the loins of New England, very largely, where men of granite were made—and they *were* men of granite, men of power, men of stability, foundation-men on whom could be built a commonwealth; but men that had no moss, no vines, no beauty except the inherent beauty of moral grandeur. Their churches were all plain. There was no provision in them for amusement. The only amusement they had was that of going to church; and that was not so amusing as one might suppose who did not know how the places of worship were built.

I have a vivid recollection of what going to church was in my boyhood on Litchfield hill—especially in winter. It was a bleak place. The winds held jubilee. Tribes of winds repaired to that hill, not three times a year, but at all times of the year. And the church was in some respects a cheerless place. There was little or no provision for comfort or for decoration. Beauty was a thing scarcely thought of. It was not sought to promote joy. The plan of procedure was quite unlike that of the Hebrew commonwealth, which looked upon joy not simply as an accompaniment to religion, but as part and parcel of it. The Jews sanctified joy, and made it serve the Lord.

Wesley said that we had given our best songs and music to the devil, and that he thought it right to make reprisals and get them back again. To a large extent the church has lost its hold upon the imaginative and social elements of life, provision for which has been universally made in the constitution of men; largely, religion has lost its hold upon them: but Moses, that wise old man of the desert, wrought them into his system; and not only at these festivals, but elsewhere, the people were instructed to observe them. The people were made happy, they were kept happy, and happiness was inculcated as a duty.

I think no one can understand the Psalms if he does not know how they were used on these and other great occasions. I have read one or two of them to you; but consider for a moment what the effect would be in an ancient Jewish congregation if the minister should get up and read, "I was glad when they said unto me, Let us go unto the house of the Lord. Our feet shall stand within thy gates, O Jerusalem." Even we do not need to hear that Psalm read a great many times in order to be deeply impressed by it; but to any Hebrew gathering it was resplendent with associations. From the farthest north, the region of perpetual snows, groups, families, neighborhoods, had gathered themselves in preparation for the journey to Jerusalem; at every path and road they had joined other bands; thus the multitude steadily grew. There was the boy who had never before been to Jerusalem, but whose imagination had been fired by accounts of its magnificence; there was the maiden that walked, peradventure, by the side of him who was to be her husband; there was the sturdy old father of eighty, who was proud to be able to say that he could do as much as any of his boys; there was the mother who also kept her place in the company. And so they proceeded on their journey; they went on, day and night, conversing and singing; they passed by the Jordan and Jericho. At last they caught a glimpse of the Temple; and soon the city in all its glory stood before them in the broad valley beneath. The morning sun was rising when they came to that scene, and the tears ran down their cheeks, while they chanted this Psalm:—

"I was glad when they said unto me, Let us go unto the house of Jehovah. Our feet shall stand within thy gates, O Jerusalem. Jerusalem is builded as a city that is compact together: whither the tribes go up, the tribes of Jehovah, unto the testimony of Israel, to give thanks unto the name of Jehovah. For there are set thrones of judgment, the thrones of the house of David. Pray for the peace of Jerusalem: they shall prosper that love thee. Peace be within thy walls, and prosperity within thy palaces. For my brethren and companions' sakes, I will now say, Peace be within thee. Because of the house of Jehovah our God I will seek thy good."

What a greeting was this! And when it came from thousands—from millions—of people, how impressive it must have been! And afterwards, when the joy had somewhat subsided, and the great multitude had had their various entertainments, and they stood singing some of these songs about the sections of the Temple in which the priests and Levites were gathered,—for it rose section upon section, court upon court,—standing near the great altar, imagine the priests giving out a verse of one of these Psalms; and then, at a signal, the immense crowd, stretching as far as the eye could reach, down on one side and up on the other, giving back the response, all the horns and instruments sending forth a blast like the roll of thunder; followed by the giving out by the priests and Levites another part of the parallelism, and at a second signal the vast multitude again responding in a voice like the sound of many waters. Is it strange that, under such circumstances, the people went home loving Jerusalem? Is it strange that they were glad to go unto the house of the Lord? Is it strange that, from time to time, they reassembled with enthusiasm at these feasts? Is it strange that, under such discipline, their patriotism was stimulated? Is it strange that they learned to reverence God as they saw him manifested in the firmament, in the clouds, in the storm, in the earthquake, and the volcano? Is it strange that beyond compare this people have been the most remarkable people on earth in the perpetuity of their characteristics and in the permanence of their institutions? There is no element among us that is more transcendent than the power which was developed in the economy of the old Mosaic commonwealth.

XVII.

IN THE LAND OF MOAB.

"Now when John had heard in the prison the works of Christ, he sent two of his disciples."—Matt. xi. 2.

THE prison in which John the Baptist lay was in the castle of Machærus on the east side of the Dead Sea. A castle built upon a high crag overlooked the land of Moab on the left hand; the Dead Sea in front, and the great plain of Moab around about the Jordan, over against Jericho, and extending north as far as Lebanon. It was this crag, or a neighboring one, from which Moses had taken his survey of the promised land. It was from this point that Balaam, called to curse Israel in behalf of Balak, had been seized with a spirit of prophecy, and blessed those for whom his monarch sought cursing. Perhaps there is not—certainly there is not east of the Jordan—any place that has more Biblical associations connected with it than this land of Moab; and my remarks to-night will hover around about the scenes that transpired there.

We have been for several Sabbath evenings occupying ourselves with the interior economy of the Israelites—their constitution, their laws, their great national observances—for the sake of coming into some knowledge of the spirit and genius of this remarkable people and sympathy therewith. Historically tracing their career, we left them on the plains in front of Mount Sinai. After devious wanderings, thirty-eight years having expired, and all that were twenty-one years of age when they left Egypt having been num-

---

Sunday evening, March 16, 1879. LESSON: John xi. 2-15.

bered with the dead, at last they had come to the point at which we resume our narrative—to the southern border of Palestine, but eastward, on account of the warlike people that dwelt just below Palestine. They took a detour, not following the table-land close by the Dead Sea, but going far east of it, avoiding Moab.

Here the strength of blood is a notable fact. The Israelites were descendants of Abraham, whose relationship and intimacy with Lot you will remember; and the people of Ammon and Moab were the direct descendants of Lot after the destruction of the cities of the plain. Hundreds of years had passed away, and generation after generation had slept; and yet, when Moses came to bring the descendants of Abraham into the promised land, he held the territory of Moab and the territory of Ammon sacred, on account of the relationship of Abraham and Lot, and asked permission to pass through these territories. And when the people were afraid of his great multitude, he turned aside from their boundaries; and, flushed with recent victories, he passed by them without harming their fields, without plucking clusters from their vineyards, and without even drinking out of their wells that lay all throughout the king's highway.

The Israelites, at the time of this narrative, had camped down near the Jordan, on what were called "the plains of Moab." The Moabites had occupied the territory clear up on the east of the Dead Sea, but had been driven back by their enemies, and now they only held the land up to the river Arnon, about halfway between the northern and southern ends of that sea; the Israelites camping north and east of them. Thus, partly surrounding the Moabites, the Hebrews were in a position such that they might cut them off on the north; and the king, Balak, felt considerable uneasiness,—and had reason to be uneasy, for he did not know at what moment this great victorious people would roll like an avalanche over him and dispossess him of what was left to him of the Moabitish country. As the land was very rich for agricultural purposes, and as he, therefore, was all the more reluctant to give it up, he determined to take spiritual as well as carnal weapons and destroy this on-coming host. So he sent far across the desert and summoned the most eminent prophet of his nation and of his time, Balaam by name; and there is not, in the whole compass of Old Testament Scripture, anything more sublime than the utterances which issued from the mouth of this prophet—a man reared, undoubtedly, under heathen auspices, but standing as evidence that while heathenism was imperfect in its conceptions of God, abhorrent in mingling worship with lusts and appetites, miserably corrupt in morals and in the higher forms of ethics, there nevertheless existed in its men and in its worship certain great truths both of God and of moral government; and nowhere more than in the Old Testament is there a tribute paid to the natural religion which prevailed in nations outside of the Israelites. We have been brought up to suppose that there was no true knowledge of God except in Israel; but history does not conform to any such notion as that. There was a great deal of knowledge of God in other nations, although it was adulterated and mixed with much that went far to destroy its moral effect. In the original the greater part of this history is in the form of poetry. In our authorized version the poetry does not appear. The poetry of the old Hebrews was not, like ours, in rhyme. It was peculiar to their literature, but it was arithmetical and rhythmic to a degree.

"The children of Israel set forward, and pitched in the plains of Moab on this side Jordan by Jericho [that is, over against Jericho].* And Balak the son of Zippor saw all that Israel had done to the Amorites. And Moab was sore afraid of the people, because they were many: and Moab was distressed because of the children of Israel."

How great that distress was will be more apparent if you turn to a remarkable passage in Micah, where is recorded a conversation between Balaam and King Balak which is recorded nowhere else, and which is generally regarded by

---

* The Revised Version (1885) has it, "pitched . . beyond the Jordan at Jericho."—Numbers, xxii. 1.—*Editor*.

wise and learned students of the Bible as being a historical record of a conversation that positively took place :—

"I brought thee up out of the land of Egypt, and redeemed thee out of the house of servants; and I sent before thee Moses, Aaron, and Miriam. O my people, remember now what Balak king of Moab consulted, and what Balaam the son of Beor answered him from Shittim unto Gilgal; that ye may know the righteousness of the Lord."

Then follows the conversation. Says the king :—

"Wherewith shall I come before the Lord, and bow myself before the high God? shall I come before him with burnt offerings, with calves of a year old? Will the Lord be pleased with thousands of rams, or with ten thousands of rivers of oil? shall I give my firstborn for my transgression, the fruit of my body for the sin of my soul?"

This is not poetry. In times of desperate emergency and need, when the danger was utter, human sacrifices were made, and the heir apparent was the favorite sacrifice. King Balak was driven to that extremity in the presence of this armed host, and he asked Balaam what sacrifices he should make—whether they should be sacrifices of his flocks and herds, or whether he should give his son—the fruit of his body for the sin of his soul.

And the reply is ever memorable :—

"He hath showed thee, O man, what is good; and what doth the Lord require of thee, but to do justly and to love mercy, and to walk humbly with thy God?"

But, to return to the narrative.

"And Moab said unto the elders of Midian, Now shall this company lick up all that are round about us, as the ox licketh up the grass of the field. And Balak the son of Zippor was king of the Moabites at that time. He sent messengers therefore unto Balaam the son of Beor to Pethor, which is by the river of the land of the children of his people, to call him, saying, Behold there is a people come out from Egypt: behold, they cover the face of the earth, and they abide over against me: come now therefore, I pray thee, curse me this people; for they are too mighty for me: peradventure I shall prevail, that we may smite them, and that I may drive them out of the land: for I wot that he whom thou blessest is blessed, and he whom thou cursest is cursed."

This not only indicates a prophet of very great reputation, but also the superstitious idea that a remarkable man, called on the eve of some campaign, had a power which was equivalent to sorcery—the power, as it were, of breathing mildew, so that his curse would make a difference with the fate of the adversary.

"And the elders of Moab and the elders of Midian departed with the rewards of divination in their hand; and they came unto Balaam, and spake unto him the words of Balak."

Now you will bear in mind that in this narrative (and I shall return to it), as in all that very early day, dreams were supposed to be divine revelations. They are yet, by the superstitious and the ignorant; but then they were thought to be the voice and teaching of God in such a sense that where things had been seen by men in a vision they were to be regarded as prophecies or histories. The events that took place in dreams at night were looked upon in the morning as veritable facts. Such being the case, those events were recorded, and they passed down into history. There is many and many a time when in the Old Testament record God is represented as telling a man to do abominable things—as, in a dream of the night, coming to him and addressing to him such and such commands. Sleeping and waking revelations were regarded as alike historical and actual; and many of them have come down to us in these old records as if the events described happened in the sight of all men.

Balaam returns no answer to these emissaries of Balak, but says:—

"Lodge here this night, and I will bring you word again, as the Lord shall speak unto me: and the princes of Moab abode with Balaam. And God came unto Balaam, and said, What men are these with thee? And Balaam said unto God, Balak, the son of Zippor, king of Moab, hath sent unto me, saying, Behold, there is a people come out of Egypt, which covereth the face of the earth: come now, curse me them; peradventure I shall be able to overcome them, and drive them out. And God said unto Balaam, Thou shalt not go with them; thou shalt not curse the people: for they are blessed."

I do not undertake to say that there was no divine influence exerted on the mind of the prophet: I only express my conviction that these were visions of the night. Nevertheless, as I have often told you, the instances of men gifted with the prophetic temperament, both in the Bible and out of it, are too frequent for us to doubt the existence of natures which are at times exceedingly sensitive to outer influences—certainly physical, and I believe also spiritual.

"And Balaam rose up in the morning, and said unto the princes of Balak, Get you into your land: for the Lord refuseth to give me leave to go with you. And the princes of Moab rose up, and they went unto Balak, and said, Balaam refuseth to come with us. And Balak sent yet again princes, more, and more honorable than they."

He thought the prophet had an eye to a good bargain, and that he had not sent enough presents, and dignitaries, and promises of exaltation. So he sent a much better salary.

"And they came to Balaam, and said to him, Thus saith Balak the son of Zippor, Let nothing, I pray thee, hinder thee from coming unto me: for I will promote thee unto very great honor, and I will do whatsoever thou sayest unto me: come therefore, I pray thee, curse me this people. And Balaam answered and said unto the servants of Balak, If Balak would give me his house full of silver and gold, I cannot go beyond the word of the Lord my God, to do less or more. Now therefore, I pray you, tarry ye also here this night, that I may know what the Lord will say unto me more.

"And God came unto Balaam at night, and said unto him, If the men come to call thee, rise up, and go with them; but yet the word which I shall say unto thee, that shalt thou do.

"And Balaam rose up in the morning, and saddled his ass, and went with the princes of Moab."

Now comes a paragraph which I am going to read just as it stands, and on which I shall then make a few remarks.

"And God's anger was kindled because he went: and the angel of the Lord stood in the way for an adversary against him. Now he was riding upon his ass, and his two servants were with him. And the ass saw the angel of the Lord standing in the way, and his sword drawn in his hand: and the ass turned aside out of the way, and went into the field: and Balaam smote the ass, to turn her into the way. But the angel of the Lord stood in a path of the vineyards, a wall being on this side, and a wall on that side. And when the ass saw the angel of the Lord, she thrust herself unto the wall, and crushed Balaam's foot against the wall: and he smote her again. And the angel of the Lord went further, and stood in a narrow place, where was no way to turn either to the right hand or to the left. And when the ass saw the angel of the Lord, she fell down under Balaam: and Balaam's anger was kindled [when a horse stumbles men always thrash him], and he smote the ass with a staff. And the Lord opened the mouth of the ass, and she said unto Balaam, What have I done unto thee, that thou hast smitten me these three times? And Balaam said unto the ass, Because thou hast mocked me: I would there were a sword in mine hand, for now would I kill thee. And the ass said unto Balaam, Am not I thine ass, upon which thou hast ridden ever since I was thine unto this day? was I ever wont to do so unto thee?"

This is a very interesting conversation.

"And he said, Nay. Then the Lord opened the eyes of Balaam, and he saw the angel of the Lord standing in the way, and his sword drawn in his hand: and he bowed down his head, and fell flat on his face. And the angel of the Lord said unto him, Wherefore hast thou smitten thine ass these three times? Behold, I went out to withstand thee, because thy way is perverse before me: and the ass saw me, and turned from me these three times: unless she had turned from me, surely now also I had slain thee, and saved her alive. And Balaam said unto the angel of the Lord, I have sinned; for I knew not that thou stoodest in the way against me: now therefore, if it displease thee, I will get me back again. And the angel of the Lord said unto Balaam, Go with the men: but only the word that I shall speak unto thee, that thou shalt speak. So Balaam went with the princes of Balak."

This is just exactly what we might expect of an imagative and yet superstitious-minded man like Balaam. It is about what one might suppose would arise in the visions of the night and seem to him to be notable fact. Even in times of superstition it must have startled a man to hear, of all things on earth, an ass talking, and talking good sense, and getting the better of an argument between himself and his master. But you are all aware that in dreams there is no such thing as incongruity. In dreams the most astonishing combinations occur without the slightest surprise. One would not be at all surprised, in dreaming at night, if he should hear a grasshopper sing like a canary bird. Nothing that happens in dreams is considered strange or mysterious. Fear and shame frequently come in dreams, but almost never a sense of right or wrong. So we can understand how Balaam, having this dream in the night, thought it to be real, and recited it in the morning as veritable truth.

One way in which commentators have sought to avoid difficulty has been by accepting this as historical; it is held up as a piece of history. We know that the history of the Moabites is being somewhat exhumed. You will recollect that some years ago we had intelligence that what was called "the Moabitish stone" had been discovered, that there were elaborate inscriptions upon it, and that on being deciphered it tallied exactly with many points of history as related in the Old Testament. But it is thought by many who have made a study of the history of Moab that this whole passage was transferred from the Moabitish records into the writings of the Old Testament.

Another evidence of what I have said to the effect that the Old Testament is not a history written continuously by the same men, but is a compilation, is the fact that even in the writings of Moses there are fables introduced; that impressions in the public mind were caught up by him and answered in his writings; that many accounts of things which were said to have transpired even after his time found their way into the text of his books.

This account, therefore, is not at all strange if it be simply the superstitious account of the Moabites in the form of the experience of their great prophet.

"When Balak heard that Balaam was come, he went out to meet him unto a city of Moab, which is in the border of Arnon, which is in the utmost coast. And Balak said unto Balaam, Did I not earnestly send unto thee to call thee? wherefore camest thou not unto me? am I not able indeed to promote thee to honor? And Balaam said unto Balak, Lo, I am come unto thee: have I now any power at all to say anything? the word that God putteth in my mouth, that shall I speak."

We are not to suppose that these persons were deceivers, impostors. There is such a thing even in our time and in our colder clime as men rising quite out of their normal or ordinary condition into a species of excitement, a state of exaltation; you might say that the personality of such individuals is different in their lower or usual condition from what it is in their higher or abnormal condition; and these old heathen prophets of the highly-strung, nervous Asiatic races undoubtedly rose into an exalted state such that their language and their conduct at such times were very different from ordinary.

"And Balaam went with Balak, and they came unto Kirjath-huzoth. And Balak offered oxen and sheep, and sent to Balaam, and to the princes that were with him. And it came to pass on the morrow, that Balak took Balaam, and brought him up into the high places of Baal, that thence he might see the utmost part of the people."

That is, he ascended the highest crag. I can see him, in imagination, standing there, weird, venerable, perplexed, and looking up at the heaven, to the left far into the wilderness on the south, into the land of Judea on the west across the Dead Sea, and northward on the right hand over the whole encamped host of Israel, and seeing the towers of the cities of Palestine gleaming in the morning sun, and the rolling land clear on to the white-topped Mount Lebanon. Not a great while after, his great peer and rival, Moses, also stood, probably, not far from the same spot; and very near the spot on which, later, was the tower of Machærus, in which John lay a prisoner, and out of which he looked, no longer with physical eyes upon the geographical features of the country, but with spiritual vision over all the land, and, knowing that the kingdom of God was coming, sent his disciples to ask Jesus, "Art thou he that should come, or do we look for another?"

Here were these great men—John, whom Christ pronounced the most eminent of worthies; Moses, the most remarkable lawgiver of all the world; and Balaam, the oldest representative of twilight prophets that belonged to the heathen nations. They were strangely gathered on this one mountain, Nebo, or Pisgah, which has been consecrated in sacred song.

"And the Lord put a word in Balaam's mouth, and said, Return unto Balak, and thus thou shalt speak.

"And he returned unto him, and, lo, he stood by his burnt sacrifice, he, and all the princes of Moab. And he took up his parable, and said:*

"Balak the King of Moab hath brought me
   From Aram, out of the mountains of the east, saying:
   Come, curse me Jacob,

---

* Balaam's "Parables" are here divided into poetic lines, according to the Revised Version; the phraseology, however, remains that of the King James version, used by Mr. Beecher.—*Editor.*

And come, defy Israel.
How shall I curse, whom God hath not cursed?
Or how shall I defy, whom the Lord hath not defied?
For from the top of the rocks I see him,
And from the hills I behold him:
Lo, the people shall dwell alone,
And shall not be reckoned among the nations.
Who can count the dust of Jacob,
And the number of the fourth part of Israel?
Let me die the death of the righteous,
And let my last end be like his!

"And Balak said unto Balaam, What hast thou done unto me? I took thee to curse mine enemies, and, behold, thou hast blessed them altogether. And he answered and said, Must I not take heed to speak that which the Lord hath put in my mouth? And Balak said unto him, Come, I pray thee, with me unto another place, from whence thou mayest see them: thou shalt see but the utmost part of them, and shalt not see them all: and curse me them from thence. And he brought him into the field of Zophim, to the top of Pisgah, and built seven altars, and offered a bullock and a ram on every altar.

"And he said unto Balak, Stand here by thy burnt offering, while I meet the Lord yonder. And the Lord met Balaam, and put a word in his mouth, and said, Go again unto Balak, and say thus.

"And when he came to him, behold, he stood by his burnt offering, and the princes of Moab with him. And Balak said unto him, What hath the Lord spoken? And he took up his parable, and said,

" Rise up, Balak, and hear;
Hearken unto me, thou son of Zippor:
God is not a man, that he should lie;
Neither the son of man, that he should repent:
Hath he said, and shall he not do it?
Or hath he spoken, and shall he not make it good?
Behold, I have received commandment to bless:
And he hath blessed, and I cannot reverse it.
He hath not beheld iniquity in Jacob,
Neither hath he seen perverseness in Israel:
The Lord his God is with him,
And the shout of a king is among them.
God brought them out of Egypt;
He hath as it were the strength of an unicorn.*
Surely there is no enchantment against Jacob,
Neither is there any divination against Israel:
According to this time it shall be said of Jacob and of Israel,
What hath God wrought!
Behold, the people shall rise up as a great lion,

---
* Wild-ox.

And lift up himself as a young lion:
He shall not lie down until he eat of the prey,
And drink the blood of the slain.

"And Balak said unto Balaam, Neither curse them at all, nor bless them at all."

It was as much as to say, in a kingly way, "Hold your tongue!"

"But Balaam answered and said unto Balak, Told not I thee, saying, All that the Lord speaketh, that I must do? And Balak said unto Balaam, Come, I pray thee, I will bring thee unto another place."

It used to be thought that certain places were favorable —that some were enchanted—that some were under magical spells; and having tried twice, Balak thought that perhaps elsewhere the desired curse might be granted.

"Peradventure it will please God that thou mayest curse me them from thence."

But after sacrificing again Balaam felt that it was not the will of God to curse Israel.

"And when Balaam saw that it pleased the Lord to bless Israel, he went not, as at other times, to seek for enchantments, but he set his face toward the wilderness. And Balaam lifted up his eyes, and he saw Israel abiding in his tents according to their tribes; and the spirit of God came upon him. And he took up his parable, and said,

"Balaam, the son of Beor hath said,
And the man whose eyes are open hath said:
He hath said, which heard the words of God,
Which saw the vision of the Almighty,
Falling into a trance, but having his eyes open:
How goodly are thy tents, O Jacob,
And thy tabernacles, O Israel!
As the valleys are they spread forth,
As gardens by the river's side,
As the trees of lign-aloes which the Lord hath planted,
And as cedar trees beside the waters.
He shall pour the water out of his buckets,
And his seed shall be in many waters,
And his king shall be higher than Agag,
And his kingdom shall be exalted.
God brought him forth out of Egypt;
He hath as it were the strength of an unicorn:
He shall eat up the nations his enemies,
And shall break their bones,
And pierce them through with his arrows.

> He couched, he lay down as a lion,
> And as a great lion: who shall stir him up?
> Blessed is he that blesseth thee,
> And cursed is he that curseth thee.

"And Balak's anger was kindled against Balaam, and he smote his hands together."

He was very angry. He had sought out Balaam; he had intreated him, he had commanded him to come; in vain. At last, in answer to yet greater presents and honors, the prophet came; and he had sought enchantments and sacrifices for the formulation of the curse; but when he spoke, he spoke blessings. With change of place and change of enchantments, he again blessed the Israelites. And now, when—lifted above enchantments, and under the influence of the spirit of God—Balaam blessed them again, Balak was hot with anger, and slapped his hands together, as a man about to fight.

"And Balak said unto Balaam, I called thee to curse mine enemies, and, behold, thou hast altogether blessed them these three times. Therefore now flee thou to thy place: I thought to promote thee unto great honor; but, lo, the Lord hath kept thee back from honor."

Balaam was not scared a bit.

"And Balaam said unto Balak, Spake I not also to thy messengers which thou sentest unto me, saying, If Balak would give me his house full of silver and gold, I cannot go beyond the commandment of the Lord, to do either good or bad of mine own mind; but what the Lord saith, that will I speak? And now, behold, I go unto my people: come therefore, and I will advertise thee what this people shall do to thy people in the latter days. And he took up his parable, and said,

> "Balaam the son of Beor hath said,
> And the man whose eyes are open hath said:
> He hath said, which heard the words of God,
> And knew the knowledge of the Most High,
> Which saw the vision of the Almighty,
> Falling into a trance, but having his eyes open."

He was himself conscious of passing into a trance state.

> "I shall see him, but not now:
> I shall behold him, but not nigh:
> There shall come a Star out of Jacob,
> And a Scepter shall rise out of Israel,
> And shall smite the corners of Moab,

And destroy all the children of Sheth.
And Edom shall be a possession,
Seir also shall be a possession for his enemies;
And Israel shall do valiantly.
Out of Jacob shall come he that shall have dominion,
And shall destroy him that remaineth of the city.

"And when he looked on Amalek, he took up his parable, and said,
"Amalek was the first of the nations;
But his latter end shall be that he perish for ever.

"And he looked on the Kenites, and took up his parable, and said,
"Strong is thy dwelling place,
And thou puttest thy nest in a rock.
Nevertheless the Kenite shall be wasted,
Until Asshur shall carry thee away captive.

"And he took up his parable, and said,
"Alas, who shall live when God doeth this!
And ships shall come from the coast of Chittim,
And shall afflict Asshur, and shall afflict Eber,
And he also shall perish for ever.

"And Balaam rose up, and went and returned to his place: and Balak also went his way."

Now, this sublime strain of poetry, or prophecy, or whatever you may call it, throws a great light upon the actual condition of things outside of Israel—upon the character of some of the men that served as priests and prophets in the midst of heathen worship. They were evidently not altogether given over to superstition and priestcraft and self-seeking.

Yet, when Balaam returned to his own people he did not do it without degenerating and falling back into his ordinary nature again. He counseled, it would seem, that though Balak could not by the hand of violence prevail against the adversary he might by craft and cunning. It was in accordance with his counsel that the minions of Moab went forth to inveigle and seduce the Israelites, giving rise to some of the most terrible penalties that Moses ever inflicted. Afterwards, in the war between the Israelites and the Ammonites, Balaam was slain.

I suppose more sermons have been preached on the subject of Balaam than on almost any other; and yet there is a great deal of mystery connected with this story. It is so different from the ordinary lines of modern experience that we have no measures or rules by which we can adjudicate it. It stands to me as a cloudy, sublime drama.

Not long after this the word of the Lord came to Moses to lay aside his burdens. You will remember that according to the statements of the old records Moses was eighty years of age when he went out to deliver his brethren. He had never been with them until he was about forty years of age, and then he had to exile himself in Midian. He is spoken of as the meekest man, though not in the sense in which we understand the word *meek*. Indeed, we have no equivalent of the original word that is translated *meek*. It signifies that quality which ennobles a strong and wise man in the continual modesty of his own merit and excellence. You will bear in mind how disinterested he was. You will recollect that though he was the reputed son of the Egyptian king, though he was a member of the royal family, yet, when he saw his own people oppressed, he undertook their vindication, he lost his standing at court, and was driven out. How faithfully he served for many years his father-in-law Jethro, we know. And when he was called of God to serve Him, he was so determined in his humble opinion of himself that he pled and pled and pled to be excused, until the anger of the Lord was aroused against him. And when he at last yielded to the divine wish, he besought God to let Aaron be the real leader, and he the counselor. Yet at every step he was the man that gathered together out of Egypt and out of contemporaneous nations the best parts, and fitted and molded them for his own people. He was the center of authority. And although in military matters Joshua was the general, Moses was, after all, the legislator and judge and real leader, going on in the march through the wilderness bearing its multiplied cares and labors until at last he came to the border of the promised land.

And now the word of the Lord came to him, "Thou shalt not go over." He had been telling his people for forty years that they were to pass to a land of milk and honey which had been promised to their fathers. It was the thought of his life, it was the desire and the mission of his soul, having piloted the people so long and so far, to be permitted to introduce them into the promised land ; and finally, when he stood over against that land, the Lord said unto him, " Thou shalt not go over." He is the prototype, the representative, of those noble men in every age who have wrought all their life long to pave the way for the success of those that came after them—of the men that laid right foundations ; as Luther, who died without seeing the results of his labor ; of men who perished on the scaffold to give liberty of thought to their fellow men, dying without beholding the change ; of missionaries who planted the seeds of civilization and religion, but reaped none of the fruits of those seeds ; of inventors who made valuable discoveries, and died poor that others might take what they had accomplished and carry it out to success. The victory of one man is founded on the defeat of a predecessor, time and time again, in this life.

Now Moses had, if ever any man had, a right to walk with unabated strength and undimmed eye across the border and into the promised land. But God said to him, "Get thou up upon the top of Nebo." It was probably the same mountain top from which Balaam had overlooked it. There God showed his faithful servant a vision of the promised land, not in a dream, but by a visible representation to the eye that understands what it sees ; and there, — without companion or spectator, alone, — died Moses. He left the greatest name of antiquity—for personal purity, for grandeur of conception, for wisdom of judgment, and for good conduct of the affairs of state on the largest scale during the longest period—the man that laid the foundations on which modern commonwealths have been built. He stood alone ; and who dying, does not stand alone ? That is the one act in which there can be no companionship. Though a million are around about us, the moment comes, in passing away, when we are as solitary as if we dwelt in the great desert of Sahara, or in the very midst of the ocean itself; and if Moses had given up his breath to God surrounded by myriads of his people he would have been as much alone as when he stood upon the summit of Mount Nebo on the top of Pisgah, to deliver up his soul. He was buried in one of those ravines: but no man knows where.

As Moses drew near to the appointed bound of his life he gave three songs to literature, but one of which I shall recite in your hearing. He gave the song in which is recounted the history of God's dealings with the people of Israel, which is contained in the thirty-second chapter of Deuteronomy and which occupies a wide space. He gave, also, the prophetic song describing blessings and curses upon the tribes, after the manner of Abraham and of Jacob. He likewise gave forth the grand funeral song of the ages. Imagine the astonishment he must have felt when the tidings came that he must needs depart, and when, seized with a poetic fervor, he indited this Psalm:—

> "Lord, thou hast been our dwelling place
> In all generations.
> Before the mountains were brought forth,
> Or ever thou hadst formed the earth and the world,
> Even from everlasting to everlasting, thou art God.
> Thou turnest man to destruction;
> And sayest, Return, ye children of men."

He had seen a whole generation of his people perish in the wilderness.

> "For a thousand years in thy sight
> Are but as yesterday when it is past,
> And as a watch in the night.
> Thou carriest them away as with a flood; they are as a sleep:
> In the morning they are like grass which groweth up.
> In the morning it flourisheth, and groweth up;
> In the evening it is cut down, and withereth."

When children look forward, how long the years are! When they become old men and look back across the great line of years, how short those years are! How slow time pulsates, to the young! How like an arrow it flies, to the old! And where has there ever been a more sublime expression of it than this?

> "For we are consumed by thine anger,
> And by thy wrath are we troubled.
> Thou hast set our iniquities before thee,
> Our secret sins in the light of thy countenance.
> For all our days are passed away in thy wrath:
> We spend our years as a tale that is told.
> The days of our years are threescore years and ten;
> And if by reason of strength they be fourscore years,
> Yet is their strength labor and sorrow;
> For it is soon cut off, and we fly away.
> Who knoweth the power of thine anger?
> Even according to thy fear, so is thy wrath.
> So teach us to number our days,
> That we may apply our hearts unto wisdom.
> Return, O Lord, how long?
> And let it repent thee concerning thy servants.
> O satisfy us early with thy mercy;
> That we may rejoice and be glad all our days."

There is in the close of the history of this great personage, Moses, a singular parallel to the doctrine which he taught all his life long. Nowhere would he allow any visible image or symbol of the eternal God to be carved or erected. The God of his people must be the Invisible One who made the heaven and the earth. He had himself been their leader; and when the time came for him to depart, he would withdraw himself absolutely from the sight of men. They should not have even his bones or his sepulcher to materialize or to worship. So when he died he was hidden, and the people never knew where his grave was. Full of years and full of honor, his natural force was not diminished, nor was his eye dimmed; and he went out of sight. As the old prophet Elijah disappeared, so his great precursor, Moses, disappeared from among the people, and gave them no chance to build over him a statue or monument around which they could gather for superstitious worship; and he became an invisible power. Having taught the invisible God, he was caught up into His presence, and became himself to his people like his God, an invisible authority which should lift their minds upward and not downward.

XVIII.

CAMPAIGNS OF JOSHUA.

It is somewhat perilous for men to examine certain parts of the Old Testament. They who do it have to carry burdens. If we do it not, however, we need not think that it will not be done. There are more and more men reading the Old Testament in critical mood and expressing themselves unfavorably in respect to it, and the public mind is being filled with conflicting ideas regarding its contents. Therefore, it is a part of the duty of every man who ministers to an intelligent and reflecting congregation to grapple with facts. This I have been attempting; and I confess, to-night, that in the cursory rather than critical examination of the books of the Old Testament which I have been making with you through the past few months, I have encountered difficulties the most serious.

I may say, honestly, that I am not myself content with the result of my own examinations of the subjects to which I have called your attention. After every consideration that I can bring to bear upon them, there are parts of this history that leave on my mind a very sad and mournful impression. Honesty requires me to say so much. I would not willingly deceive you. Not for the world would I say I believe a thing when I do not believe it; nor would I urge you to believe what I do not myself believe. I try to be honest with you; and perhaps on that account you will be the more ready to listen to me, when I say that my difficulties lie further back, in the main, than those which are ordinarily alleged, and that the usual difficulties are to a certain extent susceptible of explanation which, if it

---

Sunday evening, March 23, 1879. Lesson: Psa. cxxxv.

does not cure, certainly alleviates. Alleviation is the most I can promise to-night.

We will consider this evening a portion of the military campaigns of Joshua. We closed, last Sunday night, the account of the leadership of that great and noble man, Moses. After he had received the warning of God that his time was come, he called, appointed, and consecrated or ordained Joshua (in Hebrew, *Yehoshua*, Jehovah helps) to take his place. Moses had instituted a great policy, but the carrying out of that policy required military administration. Joshua appears to have been by nature, and also by experience, a notable general, and his name must rank among the great military geniuses of history.

It was under his command, all the way through the wilderness, that the Israelitish armies were able to beat off the assaults made upon them by the Midianites, and by the other adversaries east of the Jordan, and to take possession of the whole country of Canaan afterwards.

Before entering into some account of the campaigns of Joshua, let me ask your attention to what may be called the military commission of Moses recorded in the twentieth chapter of Deuteronomy. You will perceive here perhaps the most extraordinary mixture of humanity and severity that is found in literature :—

"When thou goest out to battle against thine enemies, and seest horses and chariots, and a people more than thou, be not afraid of them: for Jehovah thy God is with thee, which brought thee up out of the land of Egypt. And it shall be, when ye are come nigh unto the battle, that the priests shall approach and speak unto the people [now look at the tenderness and the humanity that are here exhibited], and shall say unto them, Hear, O Israel, ye approach this day unto battle against your enemies: let not your hearts faint, fear not, and do not tremble, neither be ye terrified because of them; for Jehovah your God is he that goeth with you, to fight for you against your enemies, to save you. And the officers shall speak unto the people, saying, What man is there that hath built a new house, and hath not dedicated it? Let him go and return to his house, lest he die in the battle, and another man dedicate it."

That is as beautiful a piece of poetic humanity as is anywhere recorded. It is as if it were said, Where a young man has just laid the foundation of his house, do not destroy him; let him go out of the battle, and return to his home; there are enough to take his place.

"And what man is he that hath planted a vineyard, and hath not yet eaten of it? Let him also go and return unto his house, lest he die in the battle, and another man eat of it."

That, too, betokens tender-hearted kindness in brooding over and caring for young life.

"And what man is there that hath betrothed a wife, and hath not taken her? let him go and return unto his house, lest he die in the battle, and another man take her."

He that hath dwelt with the woman of his love through a score of years has a thousand memories and associations that are more precious than those of a young man; nevertheless, the universal feeling of the race is that when love first blossoms, and the young are about to establish a household, that is one of the most exquisite phases of experience in human life; and the lawgiver put his command over it and protected it, by saying, Do not let such a man go to battle and be slain.

"And the officers shall speak further unto the people, and they shall say, What man is there that is fearful and faint-hearted? let him go and return unto his house, lest his brethren's heart faint as well as his heart."

There was not only wisdom in guarding against the contagion of panic fear, but humanity toward the man who was without physical courage. There are a great many men who have no backbone; and they are men, too. They did not make themselves. They did not pick out the qualities that were to be put into the machinery of their minds. And if a man was by nature wanting in this respect, it shows the humanity of the old Mosaic code that it protected him. Such men are not protected in modern times very much.

"And it shall be, when the officers have made an end of speaking unto the people, that they shall make captains of the armies to lead the people."

And I must not fail to add one other command of this extraordinary charge, which occurs at the end of it.

"When thou shalt besiege a city a long time, in making war against it to take it, thou shalt not destroy the trees thereof by forcing an axe against them: for thou mayest eat of them, and thou shalt not cut them down (for the tree of the field is man's life) to employ them in the siege: only the trees which thou knowest that they be not trees for meat, thou shalt destroy and cut them down; and thou shalt build bulwarks against the city that maketh war with thee, until it be subdued."

When the Prussians surrounded Paris, their lines lay among grounds and gardens that had in them all sorts of flowers and plants and beautiful things that had been handed down from father to son in their magnificence, and these were all swept away by the besom of destruction; but Moses commanded that when a city was besieged for the purpose of taking it, no trees that bore fruit that men lived upon should be destroyed. He required that there should be tenderness shown to trees, even.

That quality of compassion reigns through the Mosaic economy. The internal history of the Israelites develops the most exquisite portrayals of gentleness, and sweetness, and patience, and disinterestedness, and humanity. Therefore, the contrast is the more striking when you find coupled with them gross barbarities.

"When thou comest nigh unto a city to fight against it [that is to say, alien cities], then proclaim peace unto it. And it shall be, if it make thee answer of peace, and open unto thee, then it shall be, that all the people that is found therein shall be tributaries unto thee, and they shall serve thee. And if it will make no peace with thee, but will make war against thee, then thou shalt besiege it: and when Jehovah thy God hath delivered it into thine hands, thou shalt smite every male thereof with the edge of the sword: but the women, and the little ones, and the cattle, and all that is in the city, even all the spoil thereof, shalt thou take unto thyself; and thou shalt eat the spoil of thine enemies, which Jehovah thy God hath given thee. Thus shalt thou do unto all the cities which are very far off from thee, which are not of the cities of these nations. But of the cities of these people, which Jehovah thy God doth give thee for an inheritance, thou shalt save alive nothing that breatheth: but thou shalt utterly destroy them; namely, the Hittites, and the Amorites, the Canaanites, and the Perizzites, the Hivites, and the Jebusites; as Jehovah thy God hath commanded thee."

Absolute, murderous annihilation to all cities, without exception, situated westward of the Jordan, was the stern command of Moses; and this was the commission of war which he gave to Joshua. But now hear the reason for it:—

"That they teach you not to do after all their abominations, which they have done unto their gods; so should ye sin against Jehovah your God."

In pursuance of this command Joshua entered upon the work faithfully and very successfully. An account of the campaign against the Midianites is narrated in the thirty-first chapter of Numbers.

"Jehovah spake unto Moses, saying, Avenge the children of Israel of the Midianites: afterward shalt thou be gathered unto thy people."

Every tribe gave a thousand men. The Midianites represented the Bedouin Arabs. They were a shepherd people yet. They were addicted to war yet. Like other tribes of the desert they were armed with spears. Portions of them inhabited the Sinaitic peninsula, and they stretched eastward to the south and east of Canaan as far as Moab; and you will remember that it was with the Midianites that Balak the Moabite conspired, first to attack, and then—warned from that by Balaam's blessing instead of cursing—to seduce, the Israelites. Dwelling quietly, at this particular time, they were not prepared for an attack; and with about thirteen thousand men Joshua dashed into their midst and slew the five kings of Midian; and in this battle Balaam was also slain.

"And the children of Israel took all the women of Midian captives, and their little ones, and took the spoil of all their cattle, and all their flocks, and all their goods. And they burnt all their cities wherein they dwelt, and all their goodly castles, with fire. And they took all the spoil, and all the prey, both of men and of beasts.

"And they brought the captives, and the prey, and the spoil, unto Moses, and Eleazar the priest, and unto the congregation of the children of Israel, unto the camp at the plains of Moab, which are by Jordan near Jericho. And Moses, and Eleazar the priest, and all the princes of the congregation, went forth to meet them without the camp. And Moses was wroth with the officers of the host, with the captains over thousands, and captains over hundreds, which came from the battle. And Moses said unto them, Have ye saved all the women alive? Behold, these caused the children of Israel, through the counsel of Balaam, to commit trespass against Jehovah in the matter of Peor, and there was a plague among the congregation of Jehovah. Now therefore kill every male among the little ones, and kill every woman that hath known man by lying with him. But all the women children, that have not known a man by lying with him, keep alive for yourselves. And do ye abide without the camp seven days: whosoever hath killed any person, and whosoever hath touched any slain, purify both yourselves and your captives on the third day, and on the seventh day."

After having touched a dead body they had to abide seven days outside to purify themselves; but after having slaughtered all the men, all the boys, and all the women with the exception of the children girls, they felt no compunction whatever!*

Having cleared their way by conflicts with the tribes on the east of the Jordan, — the Amorites; Sihon, king of Heshbon; and Og, king of Bashan,—they crossed the Jordan and encamped at Gilgal. At that point, it is said, the manna ceased to fall, and they ate of the grain of the country.

There is here a gem interposed such as you find not infrequently in the fragmentary records of the Old Testament, without any prelude to explain it. We have a remarkable episode in respect to Joshua.

"And it came to pass, when Joshua was by Jericho, that he lifted up his eyes and looked, and, behold, there stood a man over against him with his sword drawn in his hand: and Joshua went unto him, and said unto him, Art thou for us, or for our adversaries? And he said, Nay; but as captain of the host of Jehovah am I now come. And Joshua fell on his face to the earth, and did worship, and said unto him, What saith my lord unto his servant? And the captain of Jehovah's host said unto Joshua, Loose thy shoe from off thy foot: for the place whereon thou standest is holy. And Joshua did so."

That is the whole story. If you say, "That is an actual historical fact," it is rather a remarkable fact that an angel of the Lord should come to Joshua, and tell him to take his shoes off, and leave him without saying anything more; but if you give to it a higher meaning it is something sub-

---

* This rough surgery for a foul and deadly disease, however, was enforced by Moses with equal severity upon the Israelites themselves. When the Israelites at Peor yielded to the seductions of the daughters of Moab and united in their licentious worship of their gods, Moses commanded: "Take all the chiefs of the people and hang them up unto Jehovah before the sun, that the fierce anger of Jehovah may turn away from Israel." And moreover a punitive "plague" slew "twenty and four thousand" of the children of Israel. Numbers xxv. 1-9.—*Editor*.

lime. If Joshua slumbered, if his soul was working upon the great task that had been given him to accomplish,—the conquest of Palestine,—and if in his sleep there seemed to come to him the great captain of Jehovah's host, saying to him, "Thou art on a holy spot," and then disappearing, that would be sublime as a vision of the night. When he rose in the morning, without a doubt he said, " I have seen the messenger of Jehovah, and I know it is a sacred cause to which I am called."

It was by visions that men of old thought they received messages from God ; and doubtless some of their visions were divine messages : but dreams are very uncertain messengers, and while some of them might have carried the truth some of them might have carried errors.

Next (and I have omitted a great deal that belongs to this history, because it is not pertinent, particularly, to the line of difficulties which I am treating to-night) comes the fall of Jericho, described in the sixth chapter of the Book of Joshua. The people were to make a procession around the city for seven days, on the last day compassing the city seven times ; then the priests were to blow the trumpets, and the people were to shout ; and then the walls of the city would fall. The command was obeyed, and the city was taken possession of, and all that were in it were utterly destroyed with the edge of the sword,—man and woman, young and old, ox, and sheep, and ass,—with the following exceptions :—

"Joshua had said unto the two men that had spied out the country, Go into the harlot's house [the woman who had harbored two Israelitish scouts and helped them to escape, and to whom they had sworn to protect her when their armies should come], and bring out thence the woman, and all that she hath, as ye sware unto her. And the young men that were spies went in, and brought out Rahab, and her father, and her mother, and her brethren, and all that she had ; and they brought out all her kindred, and left them without the camp of Israel. And they burnt the city with fire, and all that was therein: only the silver, and the gold, and the vessels of brass and of iron, they put into the treasury of the house of the Lord."

Such was the destruction of Jericho.

In the eighth chapter of Joshua we have an account of

the siege and overthrow of Ai. It seems that in the destruction of Jericho a man named Achan had purloined and hidden gold. It was not exactly defalcation; it was the primitive form of that which we do in our time far more skillfully. It was converting to private use that which had been devoted to the general treasury. It was counted a great sin then—a sin sufficient to bring down upon the Israelites divine punishment; because it was direct disobedience of orders issued in the divine name. In this case it was found out, and retribution followed. For Joshua sent up only about three thousand men against Ai; and the inhabitants came out and drove them off, and slew a great many of them; and Joshua cast himself down before the Lord, and mourned, and said:—

"O Lord, what shall I say, when Israel turneth their backs before their enemies!"

That was a striking manifestation of patriotic feeling, in which he identified himself with the cause of God and his people, and took the shame of their cowardice upon himself.

"For the Canaanites and all the inhabitants of the land shall hear of it, and shall environ us round, and cut off our name from the earth: and what wilt thou do unto thy great name?"

He had thrown himself down on the very ground in his mortification; and it is rather remarkable, the way in which God is represented as having looked upon a man crawling on the earth as a worm.

"And the Lord said unto Joshua, Get thee up; wherefore liest thou thus upon thy face?"

A great many men seem to think that God likes them if they wallow; but God does not like to see a man behave himself unseemly any more than we do. Men recount their sins, and bemoan their unworthiness, and tell what worms they are; but God would say to those who carry their humility to a morbid extreme, " Get up! wherefore do you lie thus upon your faces?"

Then followed the discovery that Achan had taken and hidden for himself portions of "the devoted thing" commanded to be cast into the treasury of Jehovah from out of the spoil of Jericho; and the stoning and burning of Achan and, according to the custom of the time, of all his family and possessions. Thus, the nation having been purged of its disobedience, Joshua was once more inspired with courage and a better wisdom for the battle.

Regarding himself as in communication with the divine Spirit, and acting in accordance with a new plan, which he accepted as an order of God, Joshua laid an ambush for Ai. He sent some thirty thousand men secretly, at night, to lie over behind, on the north side of it. The next morning, with five thousand under his command, he approached the city as aforetime, and, as before, the people of Ai rushed out into battle. Then Joshua, making a feint of defeat, took his men off nimbly; and the men of Ai ran after them, when Joshua stretched toward the city the spear he had in his hand, and the ambush arose quickly out of their place, and ran into the city from behind, took possession of it, and set fire to it. And as the men of Ai, seeing the city in flames behind them, started homeward, the Israelitish host closed in on them, and between their two bodies ground the enemy to powder. The king of Ai was taken alive and brought to Joshua, and was hanged.

"And it came to pass, when Israel had made an end of slaying all the inhabitants of Ai in the field, in the wilderness wherein they chased them, and when they were all fallen on the edge of the sword, until they were consumed, that all the Israelites returned unto Ai, and smote it with the edge of the sword. And so it was, that all that fell that day, both of men and women, were twelve thousand, even all the men of Ai. For Joshua drew not his hand back, wherewith he stretched out the spear, until he had utterly destroyed all the inhabitants of Ai. Only the cattle and the spoil of that city Israel took for a prey unto themselves, according unto the word of the Lord which he commanded Joshua. And Joshua burnt Ai, and made it an heap forever, even a desolation unto this day. And the king of Ai he hanged on a tree until eventide: and as soon as the sun was down, Joshua commanded that they should take his carcass down from the tree, and cast it at the entering of the gate of the city, and raise thereon a great heap of stones, that remaineth unto this day."

There is the account of the destruction of Ai. Following this came the erection of an altar of thanksgiving to

Jehovah in Mount Ebal, and the reading of the blessings and cursings of the Law to the people assembled before that hill and Mount Gerizim, in the heart of the country where Jacob digged his famous well, and where Shechem, Samaria, and other later names made a locality second in notability only to Jerusalem. The fame of Jericho and Ai had gone abroad in the land, and the kings or chiefs of all the country round about and beyond Jordan "gathered themselves together, to fight with Joshua and with Israel."

Next comes a pretty piece of strategy. It seems that the captains of Gibeon—a city greater than Ai—had more policy than courage, or else they had more sagacity; for, being satisfied in their minds that the Israelites were going to overrun and take possession of the land, they summoned their chief men, they clad them in their old clothes, they put on their feet shoes that were clouted and worn, they provided mouldy bread for their haversacks, and, unshaved and in every way disfigured, they went as a deputation to Joshua, and said, "We, of a far-off nation, have heard that God is with this people, and that they are going to be triumphant, and we desire to make peace and enter into a covenant with them."

Joshua, well pleased with their message, and seeing on looking into their pouches what sort of bread they were munching, and being satisfied, on beholding their worn-out shoes and clothes, that they had come a great distance, entered into a covenant with them that he would defend them, and never in any way assault them. Though it came out after two or three days who they were, it is to the honor of Joshua that he kept his word. Still, though he did not destroy them, he made the Gibeonites to be hewers of wood and drawers of water.

As soon as it was known to the Amorites throughout Palestine and the region to the southeast of the Dead Sea that the Gibeonites had made peace with Joshua, and betrayed their country's cause, the five great kings of that land determined that they would sweep away Gibeon at once; and they called together their men of war in great numbers, and drew near to the city, surrounding it. The Gibeonites sent to Joshua, imploring him to come to their succor; and he went all night from Gilgal, came suddenly upon the five kings, defeated them, and chased them to the south, to the west, to the east, and to the northwest. A great many people escaped into their fenced cities; and the five kings took refuge in the cave of Makkedah, somewhat to the southwest of Jericho, Gilgal, and Ai.

"And it came to pass, when Joshua and the children of Israel had made an end of slaying them with a very great slaughter, till they were consumed, that the rest which remained of them entered into fenced cities. And all the people returned to the camp to Joshua at Makkedah in peace: none moved his tongue against any of the children of Israel. Then said Joshua, Open the mouth of the cave, and bring out those five kings unto me out of the cave. And they did so, and brought forth those five kings unto him out of the cave, the king of Jerusalem, the king of Hebron, the king of Jarmuth, the king of Lachish, and the king of Eglon.

"And it came to pass, when they brought out those kings unto Joshua, that Joshua called for all the men of Israel, and said unto the captains of the men of war which went with him, Come near, put your feet upon the necks of these kings. And they came near, and put their feet upon the necks of them. And Joshua said unto them, Fear not, nor be dismayed, be strong and of good courage: for thus shall Jehovah do to all your enemies against whom ye fight. And afterward Joshua smote them, and slew them, and hanged them on five trees: and they were hanging upon the trees until the evening. And it came to pass at the time of the going down of the sun, that Joshua commanded, and they took them down off the trees, and cast them into the cave wherein they had been hid, and laid great stones in the cave's mouth, which remain until this very day."

After this comes the narration of the confederacy in the North. By this time Joshua had, with his battles, pretty nearly subdued Judah, the land which afterwards became Judea. It was a work which, although it is narrated in a few chapters, went through several years. It was about seven years before Joshua brought to an end his campaigns, and took possession of the whole land.

After these campaigns in central Palestine, five more "kings" in the extreme north gathered themselves near the waters of Merom—a small lake north of Gennesaret. It is a little to the south of the source of the Jordan, lying, therefore, at the very foot of Mount Lebanon. Here Joshua entered into battle with the five kings of the North, and utterly defeated them, and drove them helter-skelter, slaughtered the host, took their cities and destroyed the inhabitants of them, and in many cases swept away the oxen, the horses, all living things. From the beginning to the end, through six years, an annihilating campaign was carried on by Joshua, and it is alleged that at every step he was acting under the instruction of God.

The first difficulty that occurs to me in regard to this whole matter is the right of the Israelites to take Palestine, anyhow. It is said that God had a right to parcel out the inhabitants of the land as he pleased; and if there was any evidence of a divine plan by which men were elected according to their merit this would be an entirely adequate answer. The power of God to act justly toward nations or individuals no man denies. I aver that the right of God always moves within the lines of justice and of truth. The right of God to do as he has a mind to is to be admitted when the mind of God is represented as doing right, but under no other circumstances. God has no right to be selfish,—less than any other being in the universe. God has no right to be cruel,—less than any other being in the universe. God has no right to lie,—less than any other being in the universe. He is the Head, the Exemplar; and by as much as he is superior to all other beings he is included in those laws which he lays upon men. If he lays upon them the laws of justice, and kindness, and truth, and humanity, he himself is bound by those laws; and to allege injustice, cruelty, falsity, and inhumanity as coming from the inspiration of God seems to me, to speak moderately, a very great inconsistency.

That there were wise reasons for dispersing the inhabitants of Palestine I do not deny; I rather lean to the impression that there were such reasons: but not on the general ground that God has a right to do with his own people what he pleases. I do not believe God thought only of the Israelites. There were millions upon millions of men on the earth; and do you suppose God did not care for all of them? Is it your belief that when he looked forth upon the world the only people he saw were the Israelites? That is the quintessence of national vanity for the Jews; and for us, of superstition. We are not to suppose that a thing was right merely because it favored the Israelites; and yet, that was their national feeling, carried to an unjustifiable although perhaps natural extent. That it was within the divine purpose so to separate one people from all others that it should become a schoolmaster of generations is an idea not unworthy of our conception as a part of God's plan; and that, in order to the carrying out of that purpose, it was necessary that they should be penned up, as it were, where they would not be unduly exposed to those temptations to which all mankind in that age of the world were liable, I can conceive to be rational: but to say that, to the end that there might be in Palestine a school of which the Israelites should be the teachers, the other nations must be driven out, and that if they would not go out they must be exterminated, is to appeal neither to reason nor to common sense.

I am not satisfied with the theory that God has the same "right" to exterminate nations by the hands of other nations that he has to destroy men by earthquakes and pestilences. Destruction by these latter causes falls out under God's great natural laws. It is not to be supposed that he would make men executioners of destruction. It would not seem to be a very wise method of preparing them for the coming of Christ, for greater humanity, and for wiser civility. And yet there are those who justify the above reasoning on the ground that there must be means for the accomplishment of ends. They say, for instance, "If men are to go to school there must be a schoolhouse; and if that schoolhouse is infested by people who interfere with its legitimate use, and they refuse to depart, they must be removed." But that does not justify revenge. Moses charged the people to wipe out the remembrance of Amalek. They were to do it by way of retaliation. It has no justification. It was just as bad in Moses as in anybody else, to avenge an old grudge. There is no worthy end to be gained by it. The best that can be said is that it was of the spirit of the time.

It may be that Joshua was justified in taking the cities of Palestine, it may be that he was justified in the extermination of those cities; but he was not justified in heaping contempt upon the five kings whom he had taken, by having his captains tread on their necks. It was according to the human spirit of that day; but it was not according to the spirit of God, as revealed by Jesus Christ. I lift up this conduct before the tribunal of the New Testament, and ask whether, in the light of the spirit and temper of Christ, it can be justified. If you say that by criticising such things in the Old Testament we shall destroy the force of the Bible on the common people, my reply is that if you do not do something to remove the stigma of such things from the name of God you will destroy the true idea of God himself among thinking people. The attempt to save the Bible by destroying God is a poor bargain.

That there were instructions given, duties prescribed, by God, I do not doubt; but that men, in fulfilling those duties, in obeying those instructions, brought in many human elements I cannot doubt. I will not undertake to contravene the laws of justice and humanity by making any apologetic argument. I will call things by their right names. Cruelty is cruelty; justice is justice; love is love; truth is truth; humanity is humanity. If these nations were to be removed "by the hand of God," why were they not swept off by a plague or calamity? Why must three million men be made executioners, and go into the promised land wet with blood from their fingers to their shoulders?

And yet, we are to bear in mind that the reason of these things was not bloodthirstiness. Turn, if you please, to the seventh chapter of Deuteronomy, and see what was the impulse from which they sprang—for, although I do not think it removes all the difficulties, it certainly in a measure explains and alleviates them. It was not simply cruelty that inspired them.

"When Jehovah thy God shall bring thee into the land whither thou goest to possess it, and hath cast out many nations before thee, the Hittites, and the Girgashites, and the Amorites, and the Canaanites, and the Perizzites, and the Hivites, and the Jebusites, seven nations greater and mightier than thou; and when Jehovah thy God shall deliver them before thee; thou shalt smite them, and utterly destroy them; thou shalt make no covenant with them, nor show mercy unto them: neither shalt thou make marriages with them; thy daughter thou shalt not give unto his son, nor his daughter shalt thou take unto thy son. For they will turn away thy son from following me, that they may serve other gods: so will the anger of Jehovah be kindled against you, and destroy thee suddenly. But thus shall ye deal with them; ye shall destroy their altars, and break down their images, and cut down their groves, and burn their graven images with fire. For thou art an holy people unto Jehovah thy God."

That does not mean that they were perfect, but that they were set apart—that is the meaning of "holy"—to attain a morality better than that which had been attained by any other people.

"Jehovah thy God hath chosen thee to be a special people unto himself, above all people that are on the face of the earth."

That was the message.

So, then, the people were not to turn aside from God; and time and time again the reason why the pagan people were to be cut off, was that they would corrupt the Israelites, and turn and lead them away from righteousness; or, that they had already begun to do so.

Now, you are to bear in mind that the "jealousy" of Jehovah against other gods was not an ecclesiastical or theological jealousy. The reason why idolatry was so accursed, was not that it was a wrong theory of God or moral government: the reason was that the god of these idolatrous nations was a god fashioned out of their animal propensities. They worshiped a god of their lusts. The whole service of their gods employed the gratifying of the basest passions that can degrade the human body. Licentiousness was a part of their service. We have a record of how, when the Israelites came into the presence of the Midianites, the women of Moab and the women of the Midianites, at the suggestion of Balaam, coaxed the people of Israel into the commission of gross immoralities. It was this corrupting worship, this basilar lust, that made the idolatry of neighboring nations so dangerous to the children of Israel. There is nothing so contagious, nothing that men can so little resist, nothing that when it comes into laxity of public sentiment is so destructive to the virtue and stability of a commonwealth, as these sexual abominations; and the Israelites were brought into the presence of nations that were saturated with such elements, and whose whole religion was a deification of Venus. If the Israelites were to settle down among nations like those, the experiment of making them a moral people could not be made with any hope of success; and that the Israelites might become a powerful nation with households in which purity reigned (and, as I have shown, the families of the children of Israel have been singular for their purity) was one reason for the cutting off, the destruction, of those peoples.

If, then, we want an apology for this career of annihilation, the best thing we can say is, that a course may be right and necessary in the very earliest periods of human existence which becomes afterwards, in an advanced state of humanity, abominable and utterly unjustifiable. Back, through thousands of years, in the rude ages of mankind, a certain policy may have been allowable which in a later age is positively criminal. And we do not know enough, in detail, genealogically or specifically, of the nations of primitive antiquity, to sit in such rigorous judgment over the conduct of Joshua and the armies of Israel as we should if we were considering events that took place within the last two thousand years. One thing I know, that this policy of early times recorded in the Old Testament, if judged by the tribunal of the New Testament, cannot stand for a moment. It is foreign to the spirit of Christ. You cannot conceive of Christ looking upon such slaughter as is represented as having taken place in olden times, and approving it. Nor can you reconcile the revelation of a God, made known in the shedding of his own blood through his Son that the world might be redeemed from sin, with this account of a God that employed millions of men to shed the blood of hundreds of thousands. The light of the New Testament thrown upon such transactions condemns them.

If you say that in those ancient periods there was no opportunity to disclose the fruits of the Spirit that came out in the time of Christ, that may be an alleviation; but it will not justify the destruction of men, women, and children by hundreds of thousands. If you say that in the remote ages there might have been reasons for this which we do not know anything about, I assent to that.

Am I asked, then, "Do you hold that the Old Testament is a good book? Do you hold that it is a profitable book?" I answer: Do you hold that this world is a good and profitable world while there are thousands of bad things in it? Certainly it is. The chief tendencies are toward right; the great natural laws work for right: but entanglements arise from the interference of the human will, from the slow and imperfect growth of the moral sense, and from other causes. It is a mixed world; the moral development of men is required to enable them to know what is good and what is evil, what is right and what is wrong; and while this development is being wrought out there will of necessity be incongruities and inconsistences. You cannot make veterans of men that have not been in a fight. You must give them a chance to learn before you expect them to know. The Old Testament is a history of the education of men, and we are not to suppose that all they did was right because they thought God commanded it. We are to go through that history and take that which is good in the sight of God, and reject that which is not good.

We are to bear in mind that though the Bible is bound up as one book, it is made up of many distinct books, recording events that took place sometimes a hundred years apart, and sometimes a thousand years apart, and that a flaw in the validity of one would not make any difference with the validity of the rest. Men seem to think that the Old Testament is like a man who, if you take his bowels out, is gone; but you can take from the Bible this, that, or the other book without invalidating the remaining books. The contents of the Old Testament must stand or fall as divinely inspired, according as they agree or disagree with the moral judgments formed in the school of Jesus Christ. While you will see in the Old Testament the rudeness of primary beginnings, the infirmities of a race during the period of its childhood, the faults that belong to undeveloped human nature, on the other side you will see that the people of God in those far-off ages were aspiring after something higher; that they were endeavoring to follow nobler and nobler conceptions; that they were seeking to cleanse themselves from the impurities of heathendom; that they were striving after a better national life. The tendency, the spirit, of the Old Testament is upward, and it is not dragged down by these occasional aberrations or exaggerations of human passion. The Old Testament is full of material for instruction, and I think that in the hands of intelligent men it will be even more operative in the future than it has been in the past.

Meanwhile, let us rejoice that we are living in a time in which the light of the New Testament is to be our guide. Let us be thankful that our walks are cast in palmier, more cheering, and more comforting days than those in which the patriarchs stumbled. We do not see men as trees walking, as even the early lawgiver did. We are walking in the clearer light of the Son of God. We have not, indeed, lived up to the revelation that is made of Jesus Christ. We do not yet understand the fullness of the meaning of his words. We understand the Old Testament, the wisdom of it, its utmost stretch; but the interior spiritual revelations made by Jesus Christ, and through his apostles, we have not fathomed. The world has not yet come up to a position in which it understands them. The book of John is an unfathomable ocean yet, to mankind. The race is not ready to take possession of it.

It is for us, then, neither to deride the Old Testament nor to destroy it. We are reverently to read the history of the old patriarchs, and, putting a cloak over our shoulders, to go backward and cover its nakedness. Those that have no regard for it, and that make it a matter of ribald, witty, insensate attack, I cannot sympathize with. On the other hand, I would not be led away by the extreme school who claim that everything recorded in that history is right. I would take the great middle ground of discrimination, and, with the knowledge derived from later times, go back and see how the childhood of the human race staggered, what men did when they thought they were following the commands of God, and how long it was before they began to act with superior reason and a nobler conscience.

But let us beware. One utterance of the Saviour has in it great meat,—and great warning.

"Thou, Capernaum, which art exalted unto heaven, shall be brought down to hell."

There may be some excuse for men that lived in their passions and appetites, in an early time, to do the things they did; but for us there can be no excuse if we follow their example. The clearer our light, the greater our duty. For us to fall into the pit in which they of old stumbled —for us to be cruel, inhuman, unmerciful, and salacious— is thrice a crime, as compared with the criminality of those who in the primitive ages walked by doubtful light and with uncertain guidance.

XIX.

A TIME OF DEGRADATION.

BEFORE we go on, following the story of the Israelites, let us see exactly where we are. Let us get a bird's-eye view of this history. The first six books of the Old Testament are closely connected. The call of Abraham was the starting-point. He dwelt beyond the Euphrates, on the east. His own father was an idolater. He was commissioned to go forth as an emigrant. What the call was we do not know in full. Abraham appears as a very notable person; and on the whole, down to the time of Moses, he was beyond all odds the noblest man that appeared in the drama that was enacting in his time. He was a simple shepherd chief; he gave no literature, he organized no institutions, he apparently exerted no other influence than that which he put forth as the head of a great family, tending toward equity and largeness of mind in human life, and a belief in a supreme and invisible God.

Next came Isaac—doubtless a very sweet and lovable man, but colorless and powerless—a mere connecting link between Abraham and Jacob.

Jacob was a politician the first part of his life, and the latter part of his life he was a statesman. The politician is one that works by expedients, and the statesman is one that works according to great principles. In the early part of his life Jacob wrought by expedients that would not bear the test of modern morality, although then they were not considered as disreputable as they are (theoretically) in our day.

Sunday evening, March 30, 1879.   LESSON: Psa. lxxx.

Then came the heads of the twelve tribes—the sons of Jacob; and the less said about them the better.

Then there was a period of four hundred years during which, so far as any account we have is concerned, there was no divine guidance. It is as if the Lord God had absolutely forgotten the whole set. They sank out of view. At the end of that period Moses appeared, and his appearance was followed by a romantic history of him and his people. He organized them into a commonwealth, and conducted them through the great wilderness, where they abode as a nomadic nation for a period of about forty years, through the whole of which time he may be said to have been incubating the laws and institutes, the manners and customs, of this great multitude, now increased to millions. So long as he lived things went from worse to better, steadily.

Then came the time in which Moses laid down his rule, and appointed Joshua to be his successor. Under Joshua it was that the whole tract of country bordering on the Jordan was taken possession of.

West and east of the Sea of Galilee is a country very much like the lava beds in which our Modoc Indians hid themselves—a basaltic neighborhood of most extraordinary character, in which were almost inexpugnable cities. Their strong defensive positions and the warlike character of their occupants called forth the skill of Joshua's leadership and the courage of the Israelites—a courage which was undoubtedly religious. The enthusiasm (some would call it the fanaticism of religious faith and zeal) with which they plucked from the hands of that warlike people this territory is a marvel that is not sufficiently appreciated in modern times. It was a wonderful conquest—more so than that further south, east of the Jordan, of which we have a fuller account. Under the leadership of Joshua the Israelites passed over the Jordan, and entered upon a series of sieges and campaigns, running through a period of from six to seven years, during which time the main part of the land was taken possession of. Many of the cities were not subdued, and the fastnesses in the mountains were still held by the occupants; but substantially the great country was conquered from the river Jordan to the Sea on the west, and from the desert on the south to the sides of Mount Lebanon on the north. At this period it was that Joshua, being now one hundred and ten years old, laid down both his responsibility and his life.

It is very remarkable to see how, from time to time, the nascent and crude form of the democratic spirit was developed in this nation. I know not that it was in any other. Certainly it was not in any contemporaneous nation. In great emergencies Moses called together the chiefs of the tribes and heads of families, and all the priests and officers, and the people, and proclaimed the law and the policy, and rolled the responsibility upon them all. In some cases it took place in a dramatic form. It did when, in fulfillment of the command of Moses, the tribes were gathered between Mount Gerizim and Mount Ebal, and the whole law was read to them, and they said Amen to the blessings that were to follow obedience, and Amen to the curses that were to follow disobedience. That was, in some sense, putting to vote to the whole assembled nation, as represented by its men, and pre-eminently by its chief men, the question of national fidelity to God and national fealty to law.

Now, it is not to be supposed, as the population at that time amounted to vast numbers of people, that there could be a single assembly in which one man could address them all. The proclamation was probably made after this fashion: Joshua, or whoever was the chief and responsible magistrate, gathered in groups the priests and officers, and told them what was to be said to the people, and they in turn declared to their tribes or sections the word that was spoken to them. From them it was distributed to the great crowd. And then, at some signal, the voice of the whole people—men, women, and children—was lifted up, and with thunder, and acclamation such as probably has never been known in any nation since, they all bore witness, and gave their solemn vows and covenants, committing themselves both to the Law and to the procedures that were to fall out under that law.

When Washington retired from the magistracy he gave his farewell address; and when Joshua laid down his authority he gave his farewell address. The whole is contained in the last chapters of the book of Joshua. It contains some intimations of the state of the people which are worthy of our consideration before we go further.

"And Joshua gathered all the tribes of Israel to Shechem, and called for the elders of Israel, and for their heads, and for their judges, and for their officers; and they presented themselves before God. And Joshua said unto all the people, Thus saith Jehovah God of Israel."

Then he went through an inventory of everything that had happened, after which he said:—

"Now therefore fear Jehovah, and serve him in sincerity and in truth: and put away the gods which your fathers served on the other side of the flood*[that is, the other side of the river Euphrates] and in Egypt; and serve ye Jehovah. And if it seem evil unto you to serve Jehovah, choose you this day whom ye will serve; whether the gods which your fathers served that were on the other side of the flood, or the gods of the Amorites, in whose land ye dwell: but as for me and my house, we will serve Jehovah.

"And the people answered and said, God forbid that we should forsake Jehovah, to serve other gods: for Jehovah our God, he it is that brought us up and our fathers out of the land of Egypt, from the house of bondage, and which did those great signs in our sight, and preserved us in all the way wherein we went, and among all the people through whom we passed: and Jehovah drave out from before us all the people, even the Amorites which dwelt in the land: therefore will we also serve Jehovah; for he is our God."

Then rested the historical account; and Joshua said to the people:—

"Ye cannot serve Jehovah: for he is an holy God; he is a jealous God; he will not forgive your transgressions nor your sins. If ye forsake Jehovah, and serve strange gods, then he will turn and do you hurt, and consume you, after that he hath done you good. And the people said unto Joshua, Nay; but we will serve Jehovah. And Joshua said unto the people, Ye are witnesses against yourselves that ye have chosen you Jehovah, to serve him. And they said, We are witnesses. Now therefore put away, said he, the strange gods which are among you, and incline your heart unto Jehovah

---

* "Beyond the River," says the *Revised Version*.

God of Israel. And the people said unto Joshua, Jehovah our God will we serve, and his voice will we obey.

"So Joshua made a covenant with the people that day, and set them a statute and an ordinance in Shechem."

If that was not putting the thing to the vote, if it was not an election, I do not know what is one.

The earliest records, so far as I know, of organized popular voting on a large scale, were these appeals to the people, who had presented to them a great national question, who adjudicated it, and who by the most solemn act decreed it.

It seems that, after all their oppressions in Egypt, after their wanderings there, and after all their instructions, right under the eyes of Moses, these people had been smuggling their gods along with them. They were carrying their little contemptible godlings in their pockets, as it were; and when Joshua was brought to the leadership he discovered it. He found it more and more disclosed after Moses' death; and he made it a special point before he left his position and gave up his responsibility, to expose the people, and bring them to the public declaration that they would throw away their idols and worship the one invisible and only God. Having done this, he died, and was buried.

Joshua was an honest, moral, straightforward soldier. He was not a man of ideas, except as to military operation; he was not a man that took in to a very great extent the moral truth that existed in the teaching of Moses; nor had he a very full, comprehensive view of the institutions of the lawgiver. He was one who, having been a soldier, obeyed commands; and when Moses said "Go," he went; and when Moses said "Come," he came. Having obeyed, he was fit to command, and Moses retained him to take charge of the people, and to drive out the nations that inhabited Palestine. It was a bad business in the light in which we look at it in modern times. If there is any amelioration of the fact it is to be derived from the inchoate and undeveloped condition of mankind in that remote antiquity.

We may comfort ourselves with the consideration that this nation were dispossessing adversaries that had done the same thing to nations anterior to themselves, as those adversaries had done to still earlier tribes. There were no such laws of national rectitude at that time as we have now. It was then the habit of men, if they wanted anything, to take it if they could. It is very different in our day. If we want a thing, we go about getting it with infinite pretenses and all sorts of excuses. When we do not like the Chinamen, we find a thousand "moral" reasons why they should be kicked out. When a nation does not like the Jews, it finds "moral" reasons why they ought to be ejected. When Germany wants Alsace and Lorraine, she sees "moral" reasons why she should possess herself of them. But when the Israelites, under the direction of Joshua, wanted the territory occupied by other nations, they had a simpler and more direct way of getting it. There was no complaint; there was no inquiry; there were no scruples. Joshua obeyed what he understood to be the divine command. While he was not a man of broad thought nor of deep moral power, he was an obedient, an honest, a very thorough man; soldier-like and true to the religious, civil, and military instructions of Moses, his great leader. And he was influential; for it is recorded that after his death the influence of Moses and of Joshua that had been exerted upon this people continued during the lifetime of that generation.

For a while, then, things went on harmoniously, and with a certain degree of prosperity. Then a remarkable event took place. When Phinehas—that roaring priest who taught with the sword (it is doubtful which was the better fighter, Joshua or Phinehas)—was dead, and the elders that acted under their influence were also dead, there came a sudden sinking, prostration, of moral order and religion.

The record from the first shows no continuity of that Providence by which revelations or divine inspirations were given. Abraham was called from beyond the Euphrates, we know not how many thousands of years after our race began, who, according to this history, seems to have been the first man that was inspired. Then inspiration lulled; Isaac and Jacob seem to have been only once or twice inspired during their lives. It then ceased during the four hundred years in Egypt. It began again with Moses, and apparently continued till the termination of the régime finished by Joshua. Then it suddenly ceased once more, and had only the most fitful renewals down as late as the time of Samuel. Then it blazed out again, and continued until the period of David and Solomon, and the prophets that were contemporaneous with the Kings. Then it lulled again, and there was no organized, regular, consequent form of inspiration, down to the days of John the Baptist and Jesus Christ.

I shall not to-night go into an examination, which may perhaps befit a later occasion, of what were the different kinds of inspiration; but I have called your attention to the intermission or long pauses of it, which will give us some clew to the theory of the Bible on this subject.

When Joshua died there was, it seems, no magistrate raised up to take his place. There was no provision made for the leadership of the Israelites. There was no such organization of the priesthood as gave them power or influence. No means had been instituted for the regular education of the people. There was no plan entered into for assembling the people that they might choose a ruler. Things appear to have been left to take care of themselves. The remaining Canaanitish tribes — those that had not been cut off—soon began to intermarry with the Hebrews throughout the whole length and breadth of the land. It is declared that the Israelites gave their daughters to the Canaanites, the Hittites, the Amorites, the Perizzites, the Hivites, and the Jebusites, and that these tribes gave their daughters to the Israelites; so that in the early period of the residence of the children of Israel in the land of Palestine their blood was mixed with the Phenician blood, which was the civilized blood of antiquity (for the Phenicians were the merchants and travelers of their time, and the enlighteners of those around about them). And the worst of it was that these intermarriages led the Hebrews to the adoption of the worship of Baal and of Ashtaroth. I shall not go into an explanation of the interior nature of these gods : suffice it to say that for all modern purposes you may call Baal *Jupiter*, and Ashtaroth *Venus*. The worship of Baal and Ashtaroth was most corrupt. The true religion was thus for the time overlaid through the intermarriages of the Israelites with the other peoples of the land.

What then was the condition into which the children of Israel slumped? It was as if one were traveling on a macadamized highway, and it suddenly terminated in a mud road ; or, as if from some bluff he slid suddenly down into the fathomless mud of the valley below. The Israelites, that had been walking on a high plain, seemed, at the close of the generation which Joshua led, to plunge down into the depths of stupidity, superstition, ignorance, and corruption : and I shall read you two histories, simply as specimens.

"There was a man of Mount Ephraim [or the hill country of Ephraim], whose name was Micah."

Ephraim lay very nearly in the region which was afterwards called Samaria. It was probably between Jerusalem and the southern border of that region.

"He said unto his mother, The eleven hundred shekels of silver that were taken from thee, about which thou cursedst, and spakest of also in mine ears, behold, the silver is with me ; I took it."

That is to say : Mother, that silver about which you made such a scolding, I have—I took it.

"And his mother said, Blessed be thou of Jehovah, my son."

She did not care so much that the fellow was a thief ; but that he had the money, and that she was going to get it again, opened the flood-gates of gratitude, and she blessed him.

"And when he had restored the eleven hundred shekels of silver to his mother, his mother said [Now see the piety of it], I had wholly dedicated the silver unto Jehovah from my hand for my son, to make a graven image and a molten image : now therefore I will restore it unto thee. Yet he restored the money unto his mother; and his mother took two hundred shekels of silver, and gave them to the founder, who made thereof a graven image and a molten image: and they were in the house of Micah. And the man Micah had an house of gods [that is, he had a chapel, a little temple-like room], and made an ephod [priest's garment], and teraphim [household idols], and consecrated one of his sons, who became his priest. In those days there was no king in Israel, but every man did that which was right in his own eyes."

There is a very good beginning to show the condition in which the people lived.

"And there was a young man out of Beth-lehem-judah of the family of Judah, who was a Levite [He belonged to the regular order: he had been set apart in the historic manner. The man Micah was one of the dissenters, and he had taken his own way of consecrating his own priest in that little chapel of the silver gods]. And he sojourned there. And the man departed out of the city from Beth-lehem-judah to sojourn where he could find a place [He was out looking for a parish]: and he came to Mount Ephraim to the house of Micah, as he journeyed. And Micah said unto him, Whence comest thou? And he said unto him, I am a Levite of Beth-lehem-judah, and I go to sojourn where I may find a place. And Micah said unto him, Dwell with me, and be unto me a father and a priest, and I will give thee ten shekels of silver by the year, and a suit of apparel, and thy victuals."

A very good settlement!

"So the Levite went in. And the Levite was content to dwell with the man; and the young man was unto him as one of his sons. And Micah consecrated the Levite; and the young man became his priest, and was in the house of Micah.

"Then said Micah, Now know I that Jehovah will do me good, seeing I have a Levite to my priest."

So you see, having a fine church, a properly ordained minister, and great prosperity, as an indication of religion, is not modern: it began as far back as the time of the Judges. There is here, about morality, not a word; about reverence, not a word; about purity, truth, and justice, not a word: but they had set up certain silver gods, they had got hold of a regularly ordained Levite, he was settled on a proper salary, and they said, "Now we are all right with God." Conventional religion!

Well, this is not the whole story; but it is a good door by which to enter into it:—

"In those days there was no king in Israel: and in those days the tribe of the Danites sought them an inheritance to dwell in; for unto that day all their inheritance had not fallen unto them among the tribes of Israel. And the children of Dan sent of their family five men from their coasts, men of valor, from Zorah, and from Eshtaol, to spy out the land, and to search it; and they said unto them, Go, search the land: who when they came to Mount Ephraim, to the house of Micah, they lodged there.

"When they were by the house of Micah, they knew the voice of the young man the Levite: and they turned in thither, and said unto him, Who brought thee hither? and what makest thou in this place? and what hast thou here? And he said unto them, Thus and thus dealeth Micah with me, and hath hired me, and I am his priest. And they said unto him, Ask counsel, we pray thee, of God, that we may know whether our way which we go shall be prosperous."

They were out on a stealing-bout, as the account will show. Evil men like to have the varnish of religion over their acts. These were freebooters, about to commit one of the most atrocious of crimes, and they went to have the god inquired of, and the god that they went to have inquired of was the one that was made of silver.

"And the priest said unto them, Go in peace: before Jehovah is your way wherein ye go."

There never was a man that wanted a priest to prophesy things otherwise than just as he would like to have them.

"Then the five men departed, and came to Laish."

It was perhaps two or three days' journey to the north, past the western border of the Sea of Galilee, and up to the roots of Lebanon. Laish was a quiet city, as you will see, built by the Sidonians, or those that dwelt upon the border of the Mediterranean. Tyre and Sidon were cities that had but a very narrow strip of cultivatable land by the Mediterranean, and they were obliged, as they grew large and had a teeming population, to make provision to feed themselves by bringing corn from elsewhere. So they opened highways to the east, coming through the sides of the mountains, and built strong forts; and in a beautiful valley they placed an agricultural colony; and this colony was raising corn and sending it to the seaport to feed this commercial people. Such was Laish.

"They came to Laish, and saw the people that were therein, how they dwelt careless, after the manner of the Zidonians, quiet and secure; and there was no magistrate in the land, that might put them to shame in anything; and they were far from the Zidonians, and had no business with any man."

Nobody took any particular interest in them; they were not defended in any way; they were an agricultural people, and they were a great way from the mother that sent them out as a colony. They were a charming morsel. And these men were very much like a fox that, after wandering about in search of prey, should return and say, "Yes, I have found where the hens roost. There is no dog there. The man is a good sound sleeper. He don't know what is going on in the night. And the hens are fat. To-morrow we will go and take possession of that hen-roost."

"And they [the scouts] came unto their brethren to Zorah and Eshtaol: and their brethren said unto them, What say ye? And they said, Arise, that we may go up against them: for we have seen the land, and, behold, it is very good: and are ye still? be not slothful to go, and to enter to possess the land. When ye go, ye shall come unto a people secure, and to a large land: for God hath given it into your hands; a place where there is no want of anything that is in the earth."

They smacked their lips over that God-given providence.

"And there went from thence of the family of the Danites, out of Zorah and out of Eshtaol, six hundred men appointed with weapons of war. And they went up, and pitched in Kirjath-jearim, in Judah: wherefore they called that place Mahaneh-dan * unto this day: behold, it is behind Kirjath-jearim. And they passed thence unto Mount Ephraim, and came unto the house of Micah.

"Then answered the five men that went to spy out the country of Laish, and said unto their brethren, Do ye know that there is in these houses an ephod, and teraphim, and a graven image, and a molten image? now therefore consider what ye have to do."

Now for a little pious practice by the way. They must have the sanctions of religion.

"And they turned thitherward, and came to the house of the young man the Levite, even unto the house of Micah, and saluted him. And the six hundred men appointed with their weapons of war, which were of the children of Dan, stood by the entering of the gate.

"And the five men that went to spy out the land went up, and came in thither, and took the graven image, and the ephod, and the teraphim, and the molten image: and the priest stood in the entering of the gate with the

---

* "The camp of Dan." *Rev. Vers margin.*

six hundred men that were appointed with weapons of war. And these went into Micah's house, and fetched the carved image, the ephod, and the teraphim, and the molten image.

"Then said the priest unto them, What do ye? And they said unto him, Hold thy peace, lay thine hand upon thy mouth, and go with us, and be to us a father and a priest: is it better for thee to be a priest unto the house of one man, or that thou be a priest unto a tribe and a family in Israel?"

He had a larger call.

"And the priest's heart was glad, and he took the ephod, and the teraphim, and the graven image, and went in the midst of the people. So they turned and departed, and put the little ones and the cattle and the carriage before them."

Having stolen the man's religion, and his priest, and utterly cut him off from all divine communications by stealing his idols, they were very happy, and now were going to execute the word of the Lord on Laish.

"And when they were a good way from the house of Micah, the men that were in the houses near to Micah's house were gathered together, and overtook the children of Dan [for Micah did not like it]. And they cried unto the children of Dan.

"And they turned their faces, and said unto Micah, What aileth thee, that thou comest with such a company?"

It was impertinent in him.

"And he said, Ye have taken away my gods which I made, and the priest, and ye are gone away: and what have I more? and what is this that ye say unto me, What aileth thee?

"And the children of Dan said unto him, Let not thy voice be heard among us, lest angry fellows run upon thee, and thou lose thy life, with the lives of thy household."

Good advice!

"And the children of Dan went their way: and when Micah saw that they were too strong for him, he turned and went back unto his house.

"And they took the things which Micah had made, and the priest which he had, and came unto Laish, unto a people that were at quiet and secure: and they smote them with the edge of the sword, and burnt the city with fire. And there was no deliverer, because it was far from Zidon, and they had no business with any man; and it was in the valley that lieth by Beth-rehob.

"And they built a city, and dwelt therein. And they called the name of the city Dan, after the name of Dan their father, who was born unto Israel: howbeit the name of the city was Laish at the first. And the children of Dan [Pious souls!] set up the graven image: and Jonathan, the son of Gershom, the son of Manasseh, he and his sons were priests to the tribe of Dan until the day of the captivity of the land. And they set them up Micah's graven image, which he made, all the time that the house of God was in Shiloh."

Consider what is the condition of a people in which a transaction of this kind could take place without remark. Consider what a degradation they had fallen into. They had not lost all sense of religion, but it had degenerated into a most stupid superstition. Although they used the name of Jehovah, the name of God, yet they made him as a molten image to be worshiped ; and others stole it, and carried it off on a freebooters' expedition, to plunder the quiet agricultural people of the extreme north, and then put their idols into a temple there. And they all felt happy—all except Micah ; and Micah had to go home without any religion or any god. The probability is that his mother was dead, and had spent all the silver, so that he could not make another.

Well, there is even worse than this ; but I cannot enter upon it to-night. "Every man," it says, "did that which was right in his own eyes." You must bear in mind that there are no roads known to-day such as were then employed except the one from Beyrout to the east: there were not roads then, but paths. Wheel conveyances people knew nothing about in that mountainous country. There was very little intercourse between the inhabitants of the different sections at that time. The Israelites had no Jerusalem ; points outside of the city may have been taken, but the stronghold had not. No temple had been built, nor was there any central point either of religion or of government. There was no order anywhere thereabouts. The rulers, if such they might be called, winked at everything.

It is true, human nature now is about the same as it was then, with the exception of the varnish you put on it. In the olden time they did not varnish it. They did what they pleased without disguise. And the natural result followed.

We perceive, in going forward with this history, the moral corruption which takes place when men lose the restraint of a true God—a God of righteousness. When misconception of moral government and of the divine nature is such as to give a-loose to all their appetites and passions, the consequence is not simply personal wrong and personal degradation : it works out from the individual into the community. One thing is absolutely certain : that a people who are morally corrupt, and worship Baal and Ashtaroth, are utterly incompetent to form and maintain a government; and they go into anarchy. If a government is maintained over any people it must be an absolute despotism, or else it must be a government of self-control which lays upon every man the duty of virtue and self-denial. As long as the great lawgiver lived, and there was a considerable degree of faith in the one invisible God, Jehovah, who legislated for righteousness and upright dealing, so long the Israelitish people could not be shaken asunder in the desert by the assault of the Amalekites, of the Midianites, of the Moabites, nor of the Amorites ; they were compacted together, and strong enough to overrun any of the other tribes, and endure any hardships that could be brought upon them : but the moment they passed out from under that generic influence, and began to worship gods that, instead of binding them to virtuous living, opened to them the flood-gates of lust, they were dissolved, and sins of license and of licentiousness became characteristic of their whole condition.

And is there no warning in this episode of the history of the children of Israel to us? Is it possible to maintain a sound municipal government where the great majority are inclined to avarice, addicted to strong drink, given over to their passions, and utterly free from restraint? You cannot maintain a government except on the basis of purity, equity, and righteousness.

We see that so long as there were raised up for the Israelites great leaders, it was possible to hold the nation to its integrity, but that just as soon as these leaders died the nation found itself unable to maintain itself, and ran down into a fearful degradation. Where a great body of people are ignorant, and where they are comparatively non-moral, leadership is indispensable to the continuity of their existence and of their prosperity. And when, by education, both intellectual and moral, the rank and file of a whole community are lifted up, great men apparently disappear. Great men, as we call them, appear chiefly in the early stages of civilization. It is often said that we have no great men such as lived a hundred or two hundred years ago. The fact is, not that there is a paucity of great men, but that the whole community has been carried up so high that the difference between the best men and the average men is far less than it used to be. We have just as able men as there ever were, but the distance from the bottom to the top is not so great as formerly it was. The bottom has been going up. Therefore we have not leaders such as those that existed in earlier days. Leaders are not so much needed where there is an intelligent people,—except in times of great public disturbance, when they reappear. The voice of the people may become, and often is, the voice of God. But where the great body of the people are ignorant, or superstitious, or immoral, then there is no salvation for them unless there are great leaders; and when these arise they must necessarily be despotic, arbitrary, absolute.

So then, if a people want great men to lead them, they must consent to take them on the condition of their own inferiority; but there is no condition so fortunate for any nation as that in which the average education and the average morality of the whole community is graded so high that the people guide themselves, and public sentiment becomes the Moses and the Joshua. Take care of the public sentiment of any community, and you have all the leadership that is needful: destroy the public sentiment of any community and you must needs raise up some arbitrary leader, some absolute guide.

Happily, those far distant days of intermittent light have passed away. The rude and imperfect methods through which the divine will was communicated by men of old were like the stammering and lisping pronunciations of children. In these later days, not by dreams, not by prophets, but by his own son, God has made known his will unto us; and the knowledge of the truth revealed to us through the Lord Jesus Christ no longer needs to be in the hands of priests. It has entered into the common thought and the common feeling of nations, and there is a practical gospel—framing laws, carving out institutions, guiding administrations, and creating public policies. To-day the mind and will of God are disseminated, not through select classes, not so much by individual teachers, but by and through the common sense and the consciousness of the common people in Christian nations. And results show that the revelations of God through these influences are far more effective and enduring than the feeble lights that gleamed in antiquity.

XX.

GIDEON.

There were three periods through which the Israelites passed before they came to the point of revival under monarchy—the period of captivity in Egypt, the period of schooling in the great desert, and the period between the death of Joshua under the general régime of Moses and the time of Samuel. Upon this last period we have entered already, and our path through it we must pursue for the present.

The time between the death of Joshua and the ascendency of Samuel and Saul may be considered as a second Egypt—the Egypt of Palestine; for the people sunk into gross darkness. They degenerated very rapidly when the bonds of a more rigid authority were loosened, and they were left to themselves in a great degree; for now, no longer in a camp where, as a congregation, they could be overlooked and controlled by the eye and hand of Moses, they were scattered up and down through the whole land, and were under the dominion of general influences, and subject to the workings of that divine method of education which is operative upon all nations. I must dissent entirely from the view of those who undertake to find in the evolution of the Israelitish history a specification of divine influence that excludes natural causes, or that leaves upon the mind the impression that there was toward this people an administration that differs in kind from God's administration over every people. It has been assumed, on the whole, that natural causes have occupied a very unimportant place,—a place not only secondary, but basilar,—and

---

Sunday evening, April 13, 1879. Lesson: Psa. xx.

that substantially the Israelites were brooded and developed under a special divine influence that differed from that exerted on any other nation either before or since.

Now, I hold that there was a divine communication with the Israelites, because I believe there is a divine communication with universal humanity, and always has been. I therefore am prepared to assent to special messages, to special appearances, to visions, and to miracles or wonders: but these were occasional; in many periods they were rare; and the main instrumentalities by which the Israelitish people evolved from their low condition to a higher estate were great natural causes, as we call them. Christian people have been afraid of Nature, and in ignoring that element as a divine influence they have struck out of God's hand his own scepter. They have been so anxious to believe God does things by direct volition that they have left out of sight the fact that he organizes and puts in operation events and methods by which he influences men and nations throughout the whole globe. I believe that not only men—in their social conditions and mutual influences—but that the climate, that the air, that the winds, that the light, that mountains, that stones, that water, that birds and beasts, that all things, are God's ministers, his servants, and that it is through their ministration, by means of them, that he evolves the results which he accomplishes.

Let us follow out still further the history of the period on which we have entered. The Israelites, having lost their ordained leaders, became a mob, facile to temptation. During that period, in which Israel was broken and carried away captive, we shall see a strange mixture. We shall discern the steady operation of causes both in their degeneration and in their reconstruction. We shall observe, sparkling here and there, the mystic light of inspiration. It is dramatic to the last degree; and the record of it is most picturesque. We could not afford to lose out of the Old Testament that book of Judges, which carries us back to the early history of manhood, to the way in which men lived, and to the method by which God rescued them, or sought to do so.

We begin, this evening, the history of Gideon, and of his ministration over Israel.

The Midianites were descendants of Abraham through Keturah, and their chief habitation was in northern Arabia, that skirted the eastern part of the southern line of Palestine itself. The Israelites, as you remember, had already had some dealings with the Midianites. Joined with the Amalekites, they were overthrown by the hand of Joshua, under the regency of Moses. They seem to have been quiet for a time after they were decimated by war; but men breed fast in those Oriental deserts, and though it would be supposed that their courage would be broken and their force destroyed forever, they were soon found to exist in great numbers and with remarkable power. They broke over the Jordan, swarming the eastern parts of Palestine. The description of their operations is very emphatic.

You must imagine them as Bedouin Arabs, with their tents and their camels, pursuing their vocation as robbers, waiting until the people had sowed their fields with barley and wheat, until their crops had matured, and until their vines were loaded with ripe grapes, and then rushing in and taking possession of all their harvests, and levying tribute, in an orderly manner. Thus they carried on this illicit robbery; and to such extent did they ravage the land that the people, when threshing the grain, did not dare to do it by oxen or flail out of doors, but did it in the wine-press, that they might hide it from the Midianites that hovered around to seize any plunder that lay about loose. The Israelites of all the region were driven by these invaders into the caves and caverns as well as the mountains of the limestone region in which they dwelt. They were reduced very low, and they had to hide their food, and crawl like insects into the rifts of rocks or caverns, in order to escape the outrages to which the Midianites sought to subject them. It was more than human nature could bear. Not only had they come to this oppression, but, broken in spirit, they had given way to their passions, and gone back to the idolatrous and licentious worship of Baal. The worship of the true God had disappeared from among them.

But we are told somewhat earlier in the book of Judges, first in a sentence that is repeated again and again as if to intensify its meaning in connection with the woes that came upon the people :—

"And the children of Israel did that which was evil in the sight of Jehovah, and served the Baalim. . . . they forsook Jehovah, and served Baal and the Ashtaroth. And the anger of Jehovah was kindled against Israel, and he delivered them into the hands of spoilers."

Yet, from time to time, " it repented Jehovah because of their groaning by reason of them that oppressed and vexed them, and he raised them up judges "—champions— who saved them out of the hand of their enemies. We are about to look at one of these patriotic heroes.

"There came an angel of the Lord, and sat under an oak which was in Ophrah, that pertained unto Joash the Abi-ezrite: and his son Gideon threshed wheat by the wine-press, to hide it from the Midianites."

The locality is not distinctly known, but it is highly probable that it was in the upper border of Aram, near the valley of Jezreel—in that general neighborhood.

"And the angel of Jehovah appeared unto him [Gideon], and said unto him, Jehovah is with thee, thou mighty man of valor."

You take notice that when God calls men he always calls *men*. You cannot find a record of God's calling, for any great purpose, a poor, miserable, shiftless wretch. When he calls he knows what he wants, and he generally calls men that are men from their mother's womb. More than that, when a man is a *man*—and because of it—he hears God call when nobody else does.

Gideon was a man of the right sort. He was a patriot. His heart burned within him. He deplored the oppression of his people. He felt outraged by their idolatry and moral degradation. He grieved over their sufferings. He was a just man. And that was the message conveyed to him by the angel that appeared to him.

"And Gideon said unto him, O my lord, if Jehovah be with us, why then is all this befallen us? and where be all his miracles which our fathers told us of, saying, Did not Jehovah bring us up from Egypt? but now Jehovah hath forsaken us, and delivered us into the hands of the Midianites.

"And Jehovah looked upon him, and said, Go in this thy might, and thou shalt save Israel from the hand of the Midianites: have not I sent thee?"

It was the last thing that could have entered his mind, that he, a common working man, should be sent of God, and that he was to be brought to the position of a leader, a revolutionist, an emancipationist. He had not thought of such a thing before; so that with this new blaze of religion and patriotism firing his soul, he considered the matter modestly—as his greater predecessor Moses had done.

"And he said unto him, O my lord, wherewith shall I save Israel? behold, my family is poor in Manasseh, and I am the least [the youngest] in my father's house. And Jehovah said unto him, Surely I will be with thee, and thou shalt smite the Midianites as one man."

If any man feels that he is mightier than a host it is when he is conscious that God is with him. But Gideon was not flattered, and he was not credulous.

"And he said unto him, If now I have found grace in thy sight, then show me a sign that thou talkest with me."

It was an uncertain vision.

" Depart not hence, I pray thee, until I come unto thee, and bring forth my present [offering], and set it before thee.
"And he said, I will tarry until thou come again."

So Gideon went into the house, and prepared a kid, and some cakes, and brought them out, and put them on a stone, and the angel touched them with a rod, and there flamed fire, and Gideon was all a-quiver; for he, in common with all his people, was possessed with the idea that if any man looked upon divinity it would destroy him.

"And when Gideon perceived that he was an angel of Jehovah, Gideon said, Alas, O lord God! for because I have seen an angel of Jehovah face to face.

"And Jehovah said unto him, Peace be unto thee; fear not: thou shalt not die.

" Then Gideon built an altar there unto Jehovah, and called it Jehovah-shalom [Jehovah is peace]."

This is the opening history. Next it came to pass that God told Gideon to open the campaign, to throw down the challenge. How was that to be done? His father, Joash, had been probably led away into idolatry, and is supposed by many to have been a priest of Baal.

"Jehovah said unto him [either in a dream or in some other way by which he was impressed with it as with a vision], Take thy father's young bullock, even the second bullock of seven years old, and throw down the altar of Baal that thy father hath, and cut down the grove that is by it: and build an altar unto Jehovah thy God upon the top of this rock, in the ordered place, and take the second bullock, and offer a burnt sacrifice with the wood of the grove which thou shalt cut down."

The Hebrew word *ashera* that is translated *grove* has given rise to very much investigation. The general belief now is that it represented upright wooden images, or obelisks that stood for images, of divinities worshiped by licentious rites—Baal, Ashtaroth, and other such.

"Then Gideon took ten men of his servants, and did as Jehovah had said unto him: and so it was, because he feared his father's household, and the men of the city, that he could not do it by day, that he did it by night. And when the men of the city arose early in the morning, behold, the altar of Baal was cast down, and the grove was cut down that was by it, and the second bullock was offered upon the altar that was built. And they said one to another, Who hath done this thing?"

You may depend upon it, there was a buzzing.

"And when they inquired and asked, they said, Gideon the son of Joash hath done this thing. Then the men of the city said unto Joash, Bring out thy son, that he may die: because he hath cast down the altar of Baal, and because he hath cut down the grove that was by it."

It was an attack on their religion. No matter what men are doing—though they be wallowing in filth; though they be immoral, corrupt, superstitious, cruel and despotic to the last degree—touch their religion, and they will spring to its defense. Generally, the worse men are the more earnest they are to avenge what they call an insult to their religion. Here was their religion oppressing the people and treading out their very life; but when their altar was thrown down that was a reason for summoning the whole nation to defend that religion.

"Then all the Midianites and the Amalekites and the children of the east were gathered together, and went over, and pitched in the valley of Jezreel."

This was a little southwest of the Sea of Galilee. It was the way of caravans as they went toward Tyre and Sidon and the great East.

"But the spirit of Jehovah came upon Gideon,* and he blew a trumpet; and Abi-ezer was gathered after him. And he sent messengers throughout all Manasseh; who also was gathered after him: and he sent messengers unto Asher, and unto Zebulun, and unto Naphtali [all that region lying at the extreme north of Palestine]; and they came up to meet them."

This was like the gathering of clans. You that have read Scott's poetry will remember how the fiery cross was sent from tribe to tribe, from clan to clan. What magnificent descriptions the poet gives of the assembling of the Scottish hosts! That is the way the warlike tribes of old were called together. It took place under the command of Gideon. He blew the trumpet and brought the gathering tribes from the north, the east, and the west, for the national defense.

"And Gideon said unto God, If thou wilt save Israel by mine hand, as thou hast said, Behold, I will put a fleece of wool in the floor; and if the dew be on the fleece only, and it be dry upon all the earth beside, then shall I know that thou wilt save Israel by mine hand, as thou hast said. And it was so: for he rose up early on the morrow, and thrust the fleece together, and wringed the dew out of the fleece, a bowl full of water.

"And Gideon said unto God, Let not thine anger be hot against me, and I will speak but this once: let me prove, I pray thee, but this once with the fleece; let it now be dry only upon the fleece, and upon all the ground let there be dew. And God did so that night: for it was dry upon the fleece only, and there was dew on all the ground."

It was a very simple sign, and Gideon was a very simple man. Such a sign would not go a great way with you or me, because we are in a different age from that in which this occurrence took place; but it was sufficiently re-assuring to Gideon to give him certitude, faith,—in himself as an instrument of God, and in the cause which he was endeavoring to serve. Though you call it superstition,

---

* The margin of the Revised Version gives the vivid touch of direct translation: "clothed itself with Gideon."—*Editor.*

nevertheless it did the work appointed, and he was satisfied to go forward.

"Then Jerubbaal, who is Gideon, and all the people that were with him, rose up early, and pitched beside the well of Harod: so that the host of the Midianites were on the north side of them, by the hill of Moreh, in the valley."

It was high ground south of the plain of Jezreel, which looked down into that plain. They saw the hosts of the Midianites, with their allies, the Amalekites, described as being, for number, like grasshoppers—like those swarms of locusts with which we are too familiar in our own country, and which in the Orient have been observed from time immemorial: Gideon had gathered about thirty-two thousand men.

"And Jehovah said unto Gideon, The people that are with thee are too many for me to give the Midianites into their hands, lest Israel vaunt themselves against me, saying, Mine own hand hath saved me. Now therefore go to, proclaim in the ears of the people, saying, Whosoever is fearful and afraid, let him return and depart early from Mount Gilead. And there returned of the people twenty and two thousand."

Wonderful army! Twenty-two thousand cowards to about ten thousand men of pluck. That explains why there were too many of them, and why it was better that they should be sent home.

"And there remained ten thousand. And Jehovah said unto Gideon, The people are too many."

Undoubtedly, of that sort. So he commanded the number to be still further reduced, and the test of their fitness was very curious. Those that lapped water like a dog were dismissed; those that got down on their knees to drink were also set aside; but those that lapped, putting their hand to their mouth, of whom there were three hundred, he retained,—probably the trained fighters, who knew the surprises of battle too well to put their heads down beyond quick recovery, but raised the water to their mouths with their hands.

"And Jehovah said unto Gideon, By the three hundred men that lapped will I save you, and deliver the Midianites into thine hand: and let all the other people go every man unto his place."

"So the people took victuals in their hand, and their trumpets: and he sent all the rest of Israel every man unto his tent, and retained those three hundred men: and the host of Midian was beneath him in the valley.

"And it came to pass the same night, that Jehovah said unto him, Arise, get thee down unto the host; for I have delivered it into thine hand. But if thou fear to go down, go thou with Phurah thy servant down to the host: and thou shalt hear what they say; and afterward shall thine hands be strengthened to go down unto the host. [You will notice how much scouting and spying for information was done by all these Hebrew warriors.] Then went he down with Phurah his servant unto the outside of the armed men that were in the host [in the camp]. And the Midianites, and the Amalekites, and all the children of the east, lay along in the valley like grasshoppers for multitude; and their camels were without number, as the sand by the seaside for multitude.

"And when Gideon was come, behold, there was a man that told a dream unto his fellow, and said, Behold, I dreamed a dream, and, lo a cake of barley bread tumbled into the host of Midian, and came unto a tent, and smote it that it fell, and overturned it, that the tent lay along. And his fellow answered and said, This is nothing else save the sword of Gideon the son of Joash, a man of Israel: for into his hand hath God delivered Midian, and all the host."

When Gideon heard that he was well pleased. He understood it.

"And it was so, when Gideon heard the telling of the dream, and the interpretation thereof, that he worshiped, and returned into the host of Israel, and said, Arise; for Jehovah hath delivered into your hand the host of Midian."

Now comes the extraordinary arrangement of the battle. At about midnight he divided his three hundred men into companies of one hundred each, with not a sword, nor a bow, nor a sling, but a ram's-horn trumpet in the right hand, and a torch in the inside of a pitcher, as it is called, in the other. The pitchers were earthen vessels that protected the torches, as a lantern protects a lamp or a candle. They were so constructed that the light could not be blown out by the wind, and that it could be hidden. Such pitchers or lanterns are made yet in Oriental countries in which they carry torches or candles. About midnight, when the soldiers of Midian slept heavily, the band of Gideon came in from three different quarters, and suddenly broke their pitchers, and the three hundred torches flashed out upon the host. At the same time the three hundred trumpets sounded; and if you had ever heard one of those trumpets you would think it might wake up a dead man, and scare anybody; but three different bands, looking as if they were three different armies, pouring into the camp roused the whole host out of their sleep. "The sword of Jehovah and of Gideon!" shouted the three hundred; and the Midianites fled, panic-stricken, turning their swords upon one another in their fright and confusion.

You must bear in mind how easily any army may be surprised and thrown off their guard; and in the East, an army made up of mercurial and excitable people are peculiarly liable to panics of the most disastrous kinds. So this great host, supposing they were about to be consumed by these flashing red dragons, rushed headlong; and as, in the confusion, every one thought he was in the hands of the enemy, they smote each other, those that survived making their way as best they could toward the plains of Jezreel and the fords of the Jordan.

Then Gideon showed himself a general. He sent instant messengers throughout all the hill country of Ephraim, to the tribes that lived in the neighborhood of these fords, and asked them to come down against the Midianites, and hold the fords, while he with the tribes already gathered was pursuing the routed foe. The result was that only about fifteen thousand of that enormous host crossed the Jordan; for after the battle was fought, and the enemy were broken, every tribe from the north, and from the middle and lower parts of the land, rushed out to help destroy them. There is no trouble in obtaining recruits to an army after the foe is in flight.

"Come down [he said] against the Midianites, and take before them the waters unto Beth-barah and Jordan. Then all the men of Ephraim gathered themselves together, and took the waters unto Beth-barah and Jordan. And they took two princes of the Midianites, Oreb and Zeeb [that is to say, the Raven and the Wolf. Those were their names, as our Indian chiefs have names derived from animals]; and they slew Oreb upon the rock Oreb, and Zeeb they slew at the wine-press of Zeeb, and pursued Midian, and brought the heads of Oreb and Zeeb to Gideon on the other side Jordan.

"And the men of Ephraim said unto him [After it was well over, and all was sure and safe, their pride was a little hurt that another chieftain of another tribe had gained this victory], Why hast thou served us thus, that thou calledst us not, when thou wentest to fight with the Midianites? And they did chide with him sharply.

"And he said unto them [It is evident that he was a diplomat as well as a general], What have I done now in comparison of you? Is not the gleaning of the grapes of Ephraim better than the vintage of Abi-ezer? God hath delivered into your hands the princes of Midian, Oreb and Zeeb: and what was I able to do in comparison of you?

"Then their anger was abated toward him, when he had said that."

A sweet compliment will shut up an angry man's mouth.

"And Gideon came to Jordan, and passed over, he, and the three hundred men that were with him, faint, yet pursuing."

The Midianite remnant of some fifteen thousand had gone up one of the gorges and got upon the table-lands beyond into a secure place, had camped down, and were sleeping off their fatigue and fright; for they felt at last that they were secure; but Gideon pursued them up through this narrow defile, and came upon them unawares, and utterly routed and destroyed them. There fell, altogether, one hundred and twenty thousand Midianites.

On the way, however, Gideon asked relief and succor of those that he met in the road.

"And he said unto the men of Succoth, Give, I pray you, loaves of bread unto the people that follow me; for they be faint, and I am pursuing after Zebah and Zalmunna, kings of Midian. And the princes of Succoth said, Are the hands of Zebah and Zalmunna now in thine hand, that we should give bread unto thine army?"

They did not know but those kings might come back and destroy them, and they wanted to be sure that Gideon had captured them before they fed his men.

"Gideon said, Therefore when Jehovah hath delivered Zebah and Zalmunna into mine hand, then I will tear your flesh with the thorns of the wilderness and with briers."

So, too, with the men of Penuel, whose tower he said he would break down, because they refused him food during the pursuit. Returning from the battle, the victor caught a lad of Succoth and got him to describe the chief men of the place; then he took possession of it, and fulfilled his promise that he would tear their flesh with the thorns of the wilderness and with briers; and he did break down the tower of Penuel, and slew the men of the city.

Now comes an inimitable bit of sadness, and light in a dark place. The two Midianite kings, as they were called,—Zebah and Zalmunna,—were brought before Gideon.

"Then said he unto Zebah and Zalmunna, What manner of men were they whom ye slew at Tabor?"

We have no account of that to which reference is made except in this question.

"They answered, As thou art, so were they; each one resembled the children of a king. And he said, They were my brethren, even the sons of my mother: as the Lord liveth, if ye had saved them alive, I would not slay you.

"And he said unto Jether his firstborn, Up, and slay them. But the youth drew not his sword: for he feared, because he was yet a youth.

"Then Zebah and Zalmunna said, Rise thou, and fall upon us: for as the man is, so is his strength."

They wanted to be slain by a man. Their pride was touched by the idea that they were to be killed by a boy. There was an admirable element in their bold solicitation that they might be granted an honorable death, at the hands of a hero.

As a result of this great deliverance the natural enthusiasm of the people flamed out toward Gideon, and by a spontaneous acclamation he was called to be their king. And here shone out another noble trait.

"Then the men of Israel said unto Gideon, Rule thou over us, both thou, and thy son, and thy son's son also: for thou hast delivered us from the hand of Midian. And Gideon said unto them, I will not rule over you, neither shall my son rule over you: Jehovah shall rule over you."

That is all that is said here, and that is enough. A crown was offered him and his descendants, and he put it away both from himself and his family, and showed the secret of his influence and power—his belief in Jehovah, in an invisible God. But then he asked of them that they would give him all the ornaments that had been taken from their enemies.

"And Gideon said unto them, I would desire a request of you, that ye would give me every man the earrings of his prey. (For they had golden earrings, because they were Ishmaelites.) And they answered, We will willingly give them. And they spread a garment, and did cast therein every man the earrings of his prey. And the weight of the golden earrings that he requested was a thousand and seven hundred shekels of gold; beside ornaments, and collars, and purple raiment that was on the kings of Midian, and beside the chains that were about their camels' necks

"And Gideon made an ephod thereof, and put it in his city, even in Ophrah: and all Israel went thither a whoring after it: which thing became a snare unto Gideon, and to his house."

It is not to be supposed that Gideon sought to set up an idol: probably it was a clumsy attempt to construct a priestly garment with a breastplate, and an ephod (woven "of gold, blue, purple, scarlet, and fine twined linen" is the Levitical description) to which the breastplate was attached; and it is to be presumed that it was very gorgeous and very ample. It is not said that all the gold went into it. We cannot conceive that it could have consumed so much as was given to him.

"Thus was Midian subdued before the children of Israel, so that they lifted up their heads no more. The country was in quietness forty years in the days of Gideon."

So the Midianites, the Amalekites, with their tribes, pass out of the historical record.

"And Jerubbaal [Gideon] the son of Joash went and dwelt in his own house. And Gideon had threescore and ten sons of his body begotten: for he had many wives. And his concubine that was in Shechem, she also bare him a son, whose name he called Abimelech. And Gideon the son of Joash died in a good old age, and was buried in the sepulcher of Joash his father, in Ophrah of the Abi-ezrites."

You see what an irregular state of morals existed respecting the household; yet when you come upon the word "concubine" in the Old Testament Scriptures you must not attach to it the same odious meaning which is attached to it in our day. There were primary wives and secondary wives; and the secondary wives during the early history of the race were legal wives. They preserved their moral sense. Their position in the family was according to the custom and permission of the times. They were regular members of the household, although they occupied a subordinate station in it. It seems that one of the wives, or concubines (secondary wives) of Gideon was a Shechemite ; and it was of this foreign wife—foreign from the tribes of Israel—that Abimelech was born. After Gideon's death he came back to the people and conspired with them, and they, taking his part, made him king ; and one of his first acts of authority was to slay his brethren, the sons of Gideon, of whom there were some seventy. Then he went into various wars ; and there was rebellion against him ; and in quelling that rebellion he besieged a city, and made an attack upon it, and a woman threw part of a millstone off from the wall and hit him on the head. Then he called his armor-bearer, and said to him,—

"Draw thy sword, and slay me, that men say not of me, A woman slew him [Though thousands have died so, stabbed by the tongue, which is worse than any sword]. And his young man thrust him through, and he died [that he, too, might meet death at the hand of a man]."

After Abimelech came a succession of governors and rulers—Judges—whose acts are not given special record, and whose names are merely mentioned. And still the children of Israel did that which was evil in the sight of Jehovah ; over and again they fell into the hands of their enemies ; repeatedly arose champion-judges who recalled them from their evil lives and reorganized them for rescue and victory ; and again the story revolves,—

"But it came to pass, when the judge was dead, that they turned back, and dealt more corruptly than their fathers in following other gods to serve them."

Thus are we brought to the pathetic account of Jephthah and his daughter. After that follow the life and feats of Samson ; to be succeeded by the rise of the princely power of one Samuel. To these I shall begin to call your attention next Sabbath evening.

In looking back, now, upon the events of this dismal period of history, I do not know that they are any lower, judged by our moral sense, than much of the life that is going on around us to-day. Institutions that hide wickedness are as prevalent and as low now as ever they were known to be before the Flood, or since. There is a very respectable representation of Sodom and Gomorrah within twenty minutes' walk from the ferry in New York. There is beastliness, there are crimes, there are rotten vices, there are various forms of wickedness, festering in many and many a district close at hand, such as never were known in antiquity.

Take the tenement houses in New York. While they contain, perhaps, a population of five hundred thousand people, probably more than one hundred thousand of these are vice- and crime-breeders. The professors of medical institutions tell us that the diseases bred in these wretched lazar-houses are so various and so numerous that medical students are attracted to them as places where they can acquaint themselves with disorders that cannot be found in any other city in the land. And this multitude of crime-breeders fill our courts and jails and hospitals with human beings that probably stand lower in their moral conditions than any class in antiquity.

In the olden time people lived out of doors, and their lives were disclosed. They feared no man. Every one did that which was right in his own sight. Their acts were open, so that everybody could see them. The same kind of wickedness which they perpetrated is to a great extent indulged in to-day, only it is restrained by public sentiment and by police regulations. It is not at all to be wondered at that there was such wickedness in those ancient days. It certainly ought not to be wondered at by those who are familiar with the lives of multitudes of men in our modern cities. It was there, but it was not separated from the good. It was not repressed by law. Therefore it was like deadly poison filling the air with its destructive exhalations.

It was out of such material that the church came. Who would ever think, on opening the ground, and seeing the black dirt and manure, and casting the seed into it, that out of such filth there would come the fair stem and the pure, clean, white blossom, so fragrant and so beautiful!

And who, looking back into those pest holes of antiquity, so feculent with the depravity of the human passions, would suppose could come from them the glorious fruits of the gospel! Yet, in that matchless picture gallery, the eleventh of Hebrews, among the heroes held up to view are Rahab, the harlot, Barak, the general, Gideon, Jephthah, and Samson, and such as they, who were, after all, brought up in households of idolatry, and surrounded by all that was impure, but who believed in an invisible God. They had that saving quality which can come from nothing but the spiritual element. Show me a man who has no conscience, no heaven-born impulses, no sense of infinity, and I will show you a man who is unquestionably devoid of heroism. Show me a man who has these attributes, and I will show you a man who, though he may never be a hero, has in him that stuff from which, under favoring circumstances, heroes are made.

Let us bless God that the conditions in our well organized institution of the family, and that the influences which surround us in the street, are such as to inspire us to aim at higher and nobler lives ; and may we realize the responsibility which is laid upon us by our superior privileges to contribute to the elevation of others who are less fortunate in these respects than ourselves.

XXI.

JEPHTHAH.

In continuing these early tracings of the Scriptures, the more one reads them the more he feels the distance which there is between the Old Testament and the New. It is not a distance of time alone. The moral distance is even greater than the distance in chronology. The characters that rise up in the Old Testament are simply impossible to the New Testament history. We cannot conceive of anything that would be more astonishing than a character in the Gospels like that of the hilarious giant Samson, whose history will follow this, delineated from life, with his biography. The anachronism would be shocking. It would jar like discord in a symphony. Such a character does not belong to the New Testament age, nor to the New Testament style of thinking. Samson was a primitive man. So was Jephthah. All others who lived at the time when the history recorded in the book of Judges was enacted were primitive people. Even the prophet Samuel would be greatly out of place as one who figured in New Testament times. You could not connect him with any of the Apostles, and still less could you connect him with the Master. Conceive, for the moment, of that stern old priest bearing iron rule, and sitting at the feet of Jesus ; it would be like one of the gigantic Egyptian figures sitting before Apollo in the Grecian sculpture,—strong, harsh, rude, in contrast with perfection of beauty, inwardly and outwardly.

So then we find a great deal to learn, and very little to copy, in these ancient records. There is much that excites

---

Sunday evening, April 20, 1879. LESSON : Psa. cxli.

admiration and sympathy, but scarcely anything for imitation. The virtues of those of whom we read as having lived in the remote past were virtues that broke out in great power from untrained natural affections and gifts: but of that which we mean by grace, or of that which is the fruit of spiritual culture, begun early and continued through life, they had none. There was no provision for it—none in the Mosaic economy, and none in the institutions which we have spoken of thus far. For morality, yes; a great deal: and for that simple, single strain of religion which teaches man to look Godward, yes: but for the higher and finer grace of spirituality, no. That grew up apparently by and by of itself. That is to say, under that dispensation of Providence by which the best things are steadily evolved out of inferior things, gradually the world came to institutions higher and to culture deeper, and finally through Jesus Christ to a spirituality loftier than any that had been known on earth before.

There were three dramas enacted. I despair of being able, as I desired, to group them to-night, and present them in their threefold aspect. They are the three dramas that close the book of Judges.

They were geographically located at wide distances from each other. They are, first, the history of Jephthah, which took place on the eastern side of the Jordan; second, the history of the exit or partial exit of the tribe of Benjamin, which took place near the middle of Palestine; and, third, the history of Samson of the tribe of Dan, on the western border of that country, touching the very sea. That of Jephthah is in some respects more remarkable, having a deeper tragical element, with less rudeness, than either of the others.

Jephthah was an illegitimate child. When he grew to man's estate his father's other sons—his brothers—conceived against him a violent prejudice. Undoubtedly it arose from the strength of his character. Jephthah was a great man—or, as the record has it, a mighty man of valor—and they expelled him from the family.

"Thou shalt not inherit in our father's house; for thou art the son of a strange woman."

Family pride is a moral element which may be very cruel at times, but which yet is eminently conservative. It is a means of preserving honor; often it brings to bear upon men motives that hold them up when all other exterior things fail: and we cannot blame the brethren that they should not want the son of a strange woman to inherit with the legitimate children of the household.

"Then Jephthah fled from his brethren, and dwelt in the land of Tob."

Nobody knows where Tob was. Most likely it was in the extreme south of Moab, and on the borders of Arabia Petræa.

When Jephthah was thus expelled he became a chief—that is to say, a head-robber—and levied on the weak for all that was necessary to support himself and the followers who soon flocked to his leadership. We should have called him a freebooter. That calling was never very respectable, but it was much more nearly so in those days, when every man did that which was right in his own eyes, when no legitimate cause of action was deemed essential, and when nations had nothing to do but to eat each other up. Jephthah only did on a small scale that which nations were doing on a large scale. It did not seem so bad then as it does now, measured by our modern ideas; and we must not carry back our moral judgment to critically judge of the characters of men or their dealings then; for though cruelty is always cruelty, injustice is always injustice, and wickedness is always wickedness, yet the judgments which we pass upon relative wickedness, injustice, and cruelty vary in different ages, according to the degree of light and development which prevails; and at that time there was very little light and development, and a glorious opportunity for wrong-doing.

"And it came to pass in process of time, that the children of Ammon made war against Israel. And it was so, that when the children of Ammon made war against Israel, the elders of Gilead went to fetch Jephthah out of the land of Tob: and they said unto Jephthah, Come, and be our captain, that we may fight with the children of Ammon."

Then follows an exhibition of what you will find in Jephthah's character all the way through—brilliant common sense and sound reasoning. Though he was a man of violence, a rude man, you will be struck that at every step reason ran before his hands or his feet, and he acted along a line of thought.

"And Jephthah said unto the elders of Gilead, Did not ye hate me, and expel me out of my father's house? and why are ye come unto me now when ye are in distress?

"And the elders of Gilead said unto Jephthah, Therefore we turn again to thee now, that thou mayest go with us, and fight against the children of Ammon, and be our head over all the inhabitants of Gilead."

Now comes his forethought again. It was quite enough to be turned out once. He did not mean to run the chance of a second expulsion after he had delivered them, and so he comes to terms with them.

"And Jephthah said unto the elders of Gilead, If ye bring me home again to fight against the children of Ammon, and Jehovah deliver them before me, shall I be your head [I, a bastard, an exile, and an outcast]?"

He put it to them, whether they wanted to serve themselves by him at a pinch, or whether they meant that he should be their head as an established thing. He was determined that it should be understood that if he led their armies to victory he should have the glory and the authority.

"The elders of Gilead said unto Jephthah, Jehovah be witness between us, if we do not so according to thy words."

That was something worth while.

"Then Jephthah went with the elders of Gilead, and the people made him head and captain over them: and Jephthah uttered all his words before Jehovah in Mizpeh."

The Ammonites, it seems, had not actually commenced the invasion; they were gathering their forces: and the first step that Jephthah took was diplomatic. He sent out word to them, asking them why they were making war upon him and his people, and disturbing their peace.

"What hast thou to do with me, that thou art come against me to fight in my land?"

He had assumed, now, not simply the position but the tone of royalty.

"The king of the children of Ammon answered unto the messengers of Jephthah [and the answer seems at first to have been a perfectly satisfactory one], Because Israel took away my land, when they came up out of Egypt, from Arnon even unto Jabbok, and unto Jordan: now therefore restore those lands again peaceably."

If I were to read no further, everybody would say, "Well, they had the right of it; those were the lands of their fathers."

"And Jephthah sent messengers again unto the king of the children of Ammon: and said unto him, Thus saith Jephthah: Israel took not away the land of Moab, nor the land of the children of Ammon."

That is to say, Israel did not take it away ruthlessly or unjustly. Then he recites the history.

"When Israel came up from Egypt, and walked through the wilderness unto the Red Sea, and came to Kadesh; then Israel sent messengers unto the king of Edom, saying, Let me, I pray thee, pass through thy land: but the king of Edom would not hearken thereto. And in like manner they sent unto the king of Moab: but he would not consent: and Israel abode in Kadesh. Then they went along through the wilderness, and compassed the land of Edom, and the land of Moab, and came by the east side of the land of Moab, and pitched on the other side of Arnon, but came not within the border of Moab: for Arnon was the border of Moab. And Israel sent messengers unto Sihon king of the Amorites, the king of Heshbon; and Israel said unto him, Let us pass, we pray thee, through thy land into my place. But Sihon trusted not Israel to pass through his coast [his border]: but Sihon gathered all his people together, and pitched in Jahaz, and fought against Israel. And Jehovah the God of Israel delivered Sihon and all his people into the hand of Israel, and they smote them: so Israel possessed all the land of the Amorites, the inhabitants of that country. And they possessed all the coasts of the Amorites, from Arnon even unto Jabbok, and from the wilderness even unto Jordan.

"So now Jehovah the God of Israel hath dispossessed the Amorites from before his people Israel, and shouldest thou possess it?"

The argument is very conclusive: "You say you are going to get back your old country that we have wrested from you; but how came it to be in our possession? You would not permit us to go through it; and when we made a circuit clear around about Moab and the Amorites, and endeavored to pass by in the most peaceable manner, they sought our extermination, and we defended ourselves, and overthrew your fathers, and took your lands by a war which you yourselves brought on. It was not Israel, it was Jehovah the God of Israel, who took your land. Now, do you expect to get it back again?"

Then he makes an argument *ad hominem*. He throws the responsibility of their own god home upon them. "Whenever you go out under the direction of your god and gain a land by victory, do not you think yourselves entitled to it?"

"Wilt not thou possess that which Chemosh thy god giveth thee to possess? So whomsoever Jehovah our God shall drive out from before us, them will we possess."

He was ready to honor either of the titles. He recognized their divine Providence and that of the Israelites: but claimed precedence for his own God.

"And now art thou anything better than Balak the son of Zippor, king of Moab? did he ever strive against Israel, or did he ever fight against them? While Israel dwelt in Heshbon and her towns, and in Aroer and her towns, and in all the cities that be along by the coast of Arnon, three hundred years; why therefore did ye not recover them within that time?"

Possession is more than nine-tenths of the law, when possession is by the sword.

"Wherefore I have not sinned against thee, but thou doest me wrong to war against me: Jehovah the Judge, be judge this day between the children of Israel and the children of Ammon.

"Howbeit the king of the children of Ammon hearkened not unto the words of Jephthah which he sent him."

Thus far the diplomatic passage was carried before the war. Jephthah was on the defensive. He was not anxious to fight, but he justified the title of his people, and argued that if it was not just it ought to have been shown long before. The Israelites had dwelt there for three hundred years, they had gained a right to the lands by a protracted period of undisturbed possession, and the Ammonites had forfeited their title to them by non-use.

This discussion resulted in no agreement, and the war was to go on. So Jephthah gathered his hosts. They had a general; but they were superstitious,—for you find that an unintelligent religion is always superstition,—and there must be a vow and a covenant made with their God.

"And Jephthah vowed a vow unto Jehovah, and said, If thou shalt without fail deliver the children of Ammon into mine hands, then it shall be, that whatsoever* cometh forth of the doors of my house to meet me, when I return in peace from the children of Ammon, shall surely be Jehovah's, and I will offer it up for a burnt offering."

He had no business to make such a vow; and he had no business to keep it when it was made. No man has a right to break a pledge that he has unwittingly made, in respect to things that are moral, and are within the rightful control of his will. If, therefore, a man has made a vow, or covenant, or promise, without sufficient forethought of things that might come to pass, he must not draw back when he finds that it is to his damage; he must fulfill it, though it mulcts him, though it impoverishes him, so long as it is within the range of ordinary morality. But no man has a right to make a promise or covenant or vow that is extra-moral, outside of permission. Where a man makes a blind covenant, taking the chances of the future, it opens endless doors to possibility, and he has no right to keep that covenant when it may involve others in the grossest wrong, cruelty, or injustice. So, I repeat, Jephthah had no right to make the vow he did, it was morally improper; and he had no right to keep it, under the circumstances. If keeping it would have brought damage simply upon himself, it would have been his duty to keep it; but if one makes a vow that is wrong, he only makes it worse by keeping it. Jephthah, however, being superstitious, kept the covenant he made, though it was wrong.

"So Jephthah passed over unto the children of Ammon to fight against them; and Jehovah delivered them into his hands. And he smote them from Aroer, even till thou come to Minnith, even twenty cities, and unto the plain of the vineyards, with a very great slaughter. Thus the children of Ammon were subdued before the children of Israel."

Jephthah, flushed with victory, turned his steps home-

---

* Or "whosoever." *Rev. Vers. margin.*

ward. He was a redeemed exile. He should no longer endure the scorn of his brethren. He was now their head—the head of the house; more, he was the redeemer of his tribe and of his people, and their head also. And with what exultation, with what wild joy, did this heroic man approach his home! He had forgotten, doubtless, his vow; or, if he thought of it, he probably marveled what might be the first thing he should meet. It might be some of the flock of sheep, straying out upon the way in which he should come.

But no, it was his daughter!

"Jephthah came to Mizpeh unto his house, and, behold, his daughter came out to meet him with timbrels and with dances: and she was his only child; beside her he had neither son nor daughter."

Was there ever, since the world began, such a damsel, and such music, that greeted the eyes and ears of a father, as this sweet girl with her joyous dancing and her timbrels! Was there ever such a cruel dance as that with which she came out, bearing laurels in her hands to encircle the brow of her victorious father! With joy in her eyes, and love in her heart, and triumph on her brow, she went forth to meet him. The sight of her smote him as with a poisoned arrow. It fell upon him as darkness and midnight.

"And it came to pass, when he saw her, that he rent his clothes, and said, Alas, my daughter! thou hast brought me very low, and thou art one of them that trouble me: for I have opened my mouth unto Jehovah, and I cannot go back."

He was held fast by the terrible rashness of his vow. It was wrong; but he thought it was right. He sacrificed every instinct of a father, he trampled upon the strong feelings of a parent toward a child that he loved more than his own life, under the power of superstition. By this power were overruled in him all the great guiding principles of nature.

Now the daughter shines out beautiful as a star when the storm is lifted upon the horizon. There is not a lovelier phase, there is not a sweeter exhibition of woman's nature, in the whole compass of sacred history. There was no shock, no wild protest, no breaking down in grief. She sunk herself in the joy of her country and in the glory of her father.

"She said unto him, My father, if thou hast opened thy mouth unto Jehovah, do to me according to that which hath proceeded out of thy mouth."

Is there anything grander than that in human history? It was his only daughter, of tender years.

"Forasmuch as Jehovah hath taken vengeance for thee of thine enemies, even of the children of Ammon."

"My country has been saved, my father has been victorious, and what matters it what becomes of me? Let him fulfill his vow." Such was her thought.

"And she said unto her father, Let this thing be done for me: let me alone two months, that I may go up and down upon the mountains, and bewail my virginity, I and my fellows."

In a land where to be wed and become a mother of children was the highest earthly felicity, to be cut off in the morning of life, without conjugal love and household joy, was the greatest misfortune, and her only petition was this: "Since I must die thus, let me go and prepare myself by mourning and meditation in the mountain."

Dear child! She saw no little ones around her table, she experienced no love and no gratitude in a household in which she was the honored wife and mother; but to the end of the world thousands and tens of thousands will lift up their hearts in admiration and in praise of her. Her name has gathered to itself that which, if she had lived in the ordinary way of human life, she would never have inherited.

"And he said, Go."

If there was ever anything vexatious in connection with this account, it is the attempt of commentators, for the last two hundred years, to regulate the Old Testament by the ethics of the New, and to show that because the keeping of his vow by Jephthah would have been a cruel and wanton thing, it is not probable that he did it, making believe, that instead of sacrificing his daughter he dedicated her to eternal virginity in some retreat on the mountains.

You must bear in mind that among the peoples and in the time of Jephthah, and in the land where he lived, the sacrifice of men or their children was common. It was in accordance with the law. In close contiguity with that scene we have this record.

"When the king of Moab saw that the battle was too sore for him, he took with him seven hundred men that drew swords, to break through even unto the king of Edom: but they could not. Then he took his eldest son that should have reigned in his stead, and offered him for a burnt offering upon the wall. And there was great indignation against Israel: and they departed from him, and returned to their own land."

Here, within a very short period, was the instance of the sacrifice by the king of Moab of his eldest son, to propitiate the adverse god. We read in Micah that Balak offered to slay his eldest son if God would give him victory over the Israelites. Jephthah, who was living in that very region, and among this very people, made a covenant which amounted to a vow to sacrifice his only child. Indeed, the offering of Isaac by Abraham was a sort of shadow of that which prevailed throughout that land.

Unquestionably the daughter of Jephthah came back to her father's house, and gave up her sweet life, and was offered upon the altar as a lamb in sacrifice. A beautiful creature; a very sad death; but one of the sweetest of the scenes that lie along the mountains and rugged defiles of the Old Testament.

"And it came to pass, at the end of two months, that she returned unto her father, who did with her according to his vow which he had vowed: and she knew no man. And it was a custom in Israel, that the daughters of Israel went yearly to lament the daughter of Jephthah the Gileadite four days in a year."

There is only one more scene in the life of Jephthah, and that, too, is characteristic. You will recollect that, in the history of Gideon, after he had gained the victory by which he had rescued his country, as soon as he had taken the fords of the Jordan, and slain the common enemy, the Ephraimites arrogantly and enviously turned on him because they had not been in the battle, and said it was his fault. Precisely that identical thing takes place again.

"The men of Ephraim [the same tribe] gathered themselves together, and went northward, and said unto Jephthah, Wherefore passedst thou over to fight against the children of Ammon, and didst not call us to go with thee? we will burn thine house upon thee with fire."

Jephthah, instead of retorting, uses reason once more.

"I and my people were at great strife with the children of Ammon; and when I called you, ye delivered me not out of their hands. And when I saw that ye delivered me not, I put my life in my hands, and passed over against the children of Ammon, and Jehovah delivered them into my hand: wherefore then are ye come up unto me this day, to fight against me?"

The Ephraimites had gone beyond the Jordan into the land of Gilead, to seek him.

"Then Jephthah gathered together all the men of Gilead, and fought with Ephraim: and the men of Gilead smote Ephraim, because they said, Ye Gileadites are fugitives of Ephraim among the Ephraimites, and among the Manassites."

There was a feud between these two peoples. They were essentially of the same stock. The Ephraimites had possession on both sides of the Jordan. It was said of those on the east side—the Gileadites—that they were fugitives.

"And the Gileadites took the passages of Jordan before the Ephraimites: and it was so, that when those Ephraimites which were escaped said, Let me go over; that the men of Gilead said unto him, Art thou an Ephraimite? If he said, Nay; then said they unto him, Say now Shibboleth [meaning, probably, "a stream," and referring to the Jordan, which separated the two peoples]: and he said, Sibboleth: for he could not frame to pronounce it right."

It was like the failure of a German or a Frenchman to correctly pronounce some English word. Instead of giving the sound of *h* with that of *s*, the Gileadite made a simple hiss, and so betrayed his hostile nationality.

"Then they took him, and slew him."

They slew him because he could not say *Shibboleth*; and that kind of slaying has been going on ever since. When in the ordinances men cannot say *Shib*boleth, but say *Sib*boleth, they are slain with the sword of the church. Since there have been Christian denominations they have not given over making war one upon another on grounds as narrow as that between *shib* and *sib*. Every one mounts his conscience on some doctrinal distinction; and then the devil is riding on it,—for a fiery conscience is nearer like the devil than anything else that we know anything about.

"Jephthah judged Israel six years. Then died Jephthah the Gileadite, and was buried in one of the cities of Gilead."

The next account to which we come is that terrible one which is given in the nineteenth of Judges, and which is fit to be made known only because it gives such a portrayal of the whole way of life at that time. It is very hard for us to see how the Israelites were under a special providence, when we consider that they went through a period of three or four hundred years almost totally without any indications of leadership, except these sporadic local fighting-chiefs called judges, and that they left such an odious history as here follows.

"It came to pass in those days, when there was no king in Israel, that there was a certain Levite sojourning on the side of Mount Ephraim, who took to him a concubine [a kind of secondary wife] out of Beth-lehem-judah."

It seems that they had a quarrel, and she went home to her father. He could not live with her, nor could he live without her; and that is often the case.

"And her husband arose, and went after her, to speak friendly unto her, and to bring her again [Time and distance are oftentimes the best poultices for family difficulties], having his servant with him, and a couple of asses; and she brought him into her father's house [She seems to be placated now]; and when the father of the damsel saw him, he rejoiced to meet him."

Now comes a scene of great conviviality.

"And his father-in-law, the damsel's father, retained him; and he abode with him three days: so they did eat and drink, and lodged there."

That was all they had to do for amusement in those days.

"It came to pass on the fourth day, when they arose early in the morning, that he rose up to depart: and the damsel's father said unto his son-in-law, Comfort thine heart with a morsel of bread, and afterward go your way. And they sat down, and did eat and drink both of them together, for the damsel's father had said unto the man, Be content, I pray thee, and tarry all night, and let thine heart be merry. And when the man rose up to depart, his father-in-law urged him: therefore he lodged there again."

They had a bout—a three days' bout.

"He arose early in the morning on the fifth day to depart: and the damsel's father said, Comfort thine heart, I pray thee."

He was a good-natured, merry, hospitable old fellow. He was fond of good company, he liked this man,—who was probably a likable man.

"And they tarried until afternoon, and they did eat, both of them. And when the man rose up to depart, he, and his concubine, and his servant, his father-in-law, the damsel's father, said unto him, Behold, now the day draweth toward evening, I pray you tarry all night: behold, the day groweth to an end, lodge here, that thine heart may be merry: and to-morrow get you early on your way, that thou mayest go home. But the man would not tarry that night, but he rose up and departed, and came over against Jebus, which is Jerusalem; and there were with him two asses saddled, his concubine also was with him. And when they were by Jebus, the day was far spent; and the servant said unto his master, Come, I pray thee, and let us turn in into this city of the Jebusites, and lodge in it. And his master said unto him, We will not turn aside hither into the city of a stranger [You will recollect that Jebus, Jerusalem, was not subdued till after the time of David], that is not of the children of Israel; we will pass over to Gibeah."

That was one of their own country-place towns.

"And he said unto his servant, Come, and let us draw near to one of these places to lodge all night, in Gibeah, or in Ramah. And they passed on and went their way; and the sun went down upon them when they were by Gibeah, which belongeth to Benjamin. And they turned aside thither, to go in and to lodge in Gibeah: and when he went in, he sat him down in a street of the city [according to the way of the East]: for there was no man that took them into his house to lodging."

In that age and in that land inhospitality was a lack of humanity. In most places, even then, a stranger under such circumstances would have been invited to tarry; but it seems that in this city of unmitigated wickedness, Gibeah by name, the people were reduced to a condition as bad as that of the people of Sodom and Gomorrah.

"And, behold, there came an old man from his work out of the field at even, which was also of Mount Ephraim; and he sojourned in Gibeah: but the men of the place were Benjamites. And when he had lifted up his eyes, he saw a wayfaring man in the street of the city: and the old man said,

"Whither goest thou? and whence comest thou? And he said unto him, We are passing from Beth-lehem-judah toward the side of Mount Ephraim; from thence am I: and I went to Beth-lehem-judah, but I am now going to the house of Jehovah; and there is no man that receiveth me to house. Yet there is both straw and provender for our asses; and there is bread and wine also for me, and for thy handmaid, and for the young man which is with thy servants: there is no want of anything."

In other words, "I am not a pauper; I am not begging for anything; I have all that I want; I am not seeking for anything but shelter."

"And the old man said, Peace be with thee; howsoever let all thy wants lie upon me; only lodge not in the street. So he brought him into his house, and gave provender unto the asses: and they washed their feet, and did eat and drink."

Now came the terrible catastrophe. Men of the city, actuated by the most hideous depravity, besieged the house, and demanded the stranger. To protect him, the host laid hold on the man's concubine and took her out to them, and, when the woman was delivered to them, with ribaldry and unnatural cruelty they dragged her out and subjected her to the basest uses. The result is told in a few words that can hardly have a parallel for simplicity.

"Then came the woman in the dawning of the day, and fell down at the door of the man's house where her lord was, till it was light. And her lord rose up in the morning, and opened the doors of the house, and went out to go his way: and, behold, the woman his concubine was fallen down at the door of the house, and her hands were upon the threshold And he said unto her, Up, and let us be going. But none answered.

"Then the man took her up upon an ass, and the man rose up, and gat him unto his place. And when he was come into his house, he took a knife, and laid hold on his concubine, and divided her, together with her bones, into twelve pieces, and sent her into all the coasts of Israel.

"And it was so, that all that saw it said, There was no such deed done nor seen from the day that the children of Israel came up out of the land of Egypt unto this day: consider of it, take advice, and speak your minds."

What a messenger and what a message to send to all the tribes around about!

"Then all the children of Israel went out, and the congregation was gathered together as one man, from Dan even to Beer-sheba, with the land of Gilead, unto Jehovah in Mizpeh. And the chiefs of all the people, even of all the tribes of Israel, presented themselves in the assembly of the people of God, four hundred thousand footmen that drew sword. (Now the children of Benjamin heard that the children of Israel were gone up to Mizpeh.)

"Then said the children of Israel, Tell us, how was this wickedness? And the Levite, the husband of the woman that was slain, answered."

And he gives the story in brief, as it has already been narrated. Then he said:—

"Behold, ye are all children of Israel; give here your advice and counsel. And all the people arose as one man, saying, We will not any of us go to his tent, neither will we any of us turn into his house. But now this shall be the thing which we will do to Gibeah; we will go up by lot against it."

Lots were cast, and there were taken ten men out of a hundred, a hundred out of a thousand, and a thousand out of ten thousand, and they went up against Gibeah, and they assaulted it, and took it, and put to the sword all the men, women, and children in it—eleven tribes against this one; for when the tribe of Benjamin was told to deliver up the men that had done this wickedness, as a testimony of their horror, and to separate themselves from the guilt of this public crime, they refused. The tribal spirit ran high; they stood up for their own kin, and they went willingly to battle, bringing out their whole armed forces; for they were valiant men of war, and the eleven tribes had three successive days of obstinate fighting before subduing them. And it is said that, as a result, with the exception of about six hundred that shut themselves up in a cave, the Benjamites were all put to the sword, and the tribe was very nearly exterminated.

Then came a kind of popular revulsion. This was a time of strange contrasts. The people, aroused to fury against Benjamin by a sense of the wrong that had been committed, had emptied their cities and villages, and gone up, a great multitude, to avenge this crime, and they had all but cut off the tribe, having slain all the women, all the children, and all the men except about six hundred. Then they withdrew, and went back to the ark and the tabernacle, and were seized with a feeling of horror at the thought, "A tribe is blotted out in Israel!" That seemed to touch the very pride of the nation, that but eleven tribes remained. Six hundred men only lived of the thousands and tens of thousands of the inhabitants of Benjamin ; and there could be no households among them, for the people of Israel had sworn by a solemn oath unto the Lord that they would not allow one of their daughters to marry into that tribe. So there was mourning, and they said, "They have no wives, and although these six hundred remain there will be no posterity, and the tribe will be extinct."

But they fell upon a device which was peculiar to that age. They called for the record, and made an examination to see if all the people had come up upon the summons, and they found that none from Jabesh-gilead had come to the fight ; and therefore they walked over to Jabesh-gilead, and killed all the men and all the married women, and spared the young women, of whom there were four hundred, and called peaceably upon the six hundred children of Benjamin to come out from their hiding places, and all but two hundred of them had wives provided for them through this courting by the sword. Two hundred more were needed : but the Israelites had vowed that they would not allow any of their children to be married into that tribe ; and so they whispered to the Benjamites who had no wives that at Shiloh there were certain religious festivals and dances going on, and that if they would rush in and catch and run off with two hundred more virgins the parents should be argued with and placated, so that no harm should come of it. Thus, having taken four hundred maidens by the sword, and having stolen two hundred more, the Israelites fitted out the six hundred Benjamites with wives, and preserved the integrity of that tribe.

That is the second history. What a time ! What a state of society ! And these were "the people of God." They were a people that arrogated to themselves superiority. They were the people that had for hundreds and hundreds of years borne testimony that they were the peculiar people of God. And yet, in no age, and by no nation, were there ever performed more barbarous deeds than during three or four hundred years were performed in the history of this people.

Now, if we believe that God develops mankind by his divine providence, according to a method of evolution under natural law, we can bridge over this terrible gulf; but if we suppose that all this time these people were under the special guardianship and immediate direction of God, what are you going to do with these four hundred hideous years of darkness? And those parallel four hundred dreadful years in Egypt—what are you going to do with them? Along the line of the thought that there is a providence which works through natural law among the nations by a process of the unfolding of germinant moral sense, and tends toward civilization, morality, and spirituality, I can get relief; but along the other line I can get none.

In following these episodes, I have not always taken them in the order of their occurrence in the record, but rather have grouped them according to the chief elements they manifest. Our readings to-night have shown the power of superstition on rude natures and the readiness with which men find religious sanction for the devices and desires of their own hearts. The third of the three stories mentioned this evening as concluding our study of the time of the Judges is that of Samson, which we will consider next Sunday evening.

XXII.

SAMSON.

To-night, we deal with the last history that we shall consider in the book of Judges—the history of Samson.

I cannot afford to follow the example of spiritualizers who think it necessary or profitable to dress out the characters of antiquity with all the qualities which it would be possible for them to have if they lived in our time. It is true that now and then every age produces singular individuals that are well balanced, eminent in moral directions, intellectual and esthetic; but they are rare. For the most part, men who, having lived in the early ages, are reputed to have been great moral men, were rude and deficient to a degree that oftentimes would have made them not simply culpable but criminal if they had lived in our age. Yet, in their own age, either they were so useful in certain lines, or else they had singular qualities which were so eminent, that they are put in the calendar, I will not say of the saints, but of the heroes. Thus you will find in the eleventh chapter of Hebrews—a picture gallery of history—the names of Jephthah, of Samson, and of the harlot Rahab, as belonging to the list of persons eminent in the Israelitish history, who through faith in the invisible God of the Jews wrought wonders in times of personal and national tribulation.

Of the harlot Rahab we know nothing, except her kindness to the spies because from the history of the Hebrews she believed in their God, and helped them. Certainly her general character would not entitle her to have a name among the saints. Jephthah, a Bedouin Arab, was a free-

---

Sunday evening, April 27, 1879. Lesson: Psa. cxxxv.

booter, acting in accordance with the law of the strongest; but in one pre-eminent period of his life, inspired with patriotic valor in the name of his national God, he did great good to his people, rescuing them and then ruling them during the space of six years. Samson possessed traits which made him a conspicuous figure in the time in which he lived, and he was most useful to his own people: but he was no more a saint than Hercules was, or Goliath; and I cannot afford to invest him with a spiritual halo. In other words, I cannot consistently invest him with qualities that are utterly at variance with those that belonged to his nature.

There is much exaggeration in the usual treatment of all these characters, and even of so great a man of God as the prophet Samuel. It is amusing to read the pious things that are written of him. It is almost as good as a play. It is absolutely grotesque. It is absurd in the highest degree, to one who has a sense of humor.

I cannot deal so with Bible characters. I cannot undertake to make you believe that because a man figures in Old Testament history he was better than he would be if measured by canons of morality such as have been disclosed in this later time. We must judge greenness by ripeness; and it is the ethical clarity of the New Testament by which we must judge the sordid nature of men even in the very twilight dawn of human life. To be sure, we do not blame men for living low in those early ages as we should blame them if they were living thus now; but in describing them as heroes, and still more in speaking of them as prophets, we must measure their deficiencies by the ethics of the New Testament, and not attempt to spiritualize and slur over their faults, and undertake to show that when they did things criminal it was because God told them to. It will not answer to argue that it was right for this and that man in antiquity to steal, or murder, or commit acts of cruelty, because God commanded them to do these things. An influence that makes a man brutal may be inspiration, but it is not inspiration from above.

Now, while I delineate some of the peculiarities of the character of Samson you must bear with me if I analyze it, and give the facts as they are, and not as our Sunday-school classes have often been taught to think them to be.

There is a charming chapter, if you will make suitable allowance for the imperfections of the age to which it refers, the thirteenth of Judges, that opens with a simple history of the parents of Samson—Manoah and his wife. She had no name. In that age a woman had none of any consequence. Women may have had names, but it was generally unnecessary to record them. Therefore, " a certain woman " is often spoken of. As nowadays, in the theory of the law, a woman lapses and merges into her husband, and is known only as included in her husband, so in antiquity woman had little or no identity of her own. Manoah and his wife, therefore, figured together with one name between them.

It seems that this woman had a vision of angels, and it was repeated in dreams, concerning the birth of a child, which in those days, as in all times, was thought to be a blessing from the hand of God. The promise of children is divine, and to every noble nature the thought of bringing a child into life should be like a visit and vision of angels from God's very throne. It is the dearest, the divinest, the deepest, and the purest experience of human life.

The ministration of angels was not, however, in this case, so much to declare the coming birth as to declare that the child was to be a hero, and that it must be brought up with that thought in view. But is not every child a subject of angelic visitation ? Every mother's babe is perhaps capable of becoming a hero ; yet it is not every mother that brings her child up as if he were so.

So the father and mother were commanded to rear their child as a *Nazarite*, a word implying the primitive or undeveloped form of monk. It comes nearer to the monastic institution than anything else recorded in the Bible, of the history of this early period. It is true that monasticism, for the most part, gave men a local habitation, a seclusion from the family estate, not only, but from the civil occupations of life, shutting them up in a home provided expressly for them; but among the Hebrews, a Nazarite, although he separated himself from people in some respects, still commingled with them in other respects, and lived the ordinary life. As in the case of Samuel, Samson was brought up to separate himself from people by his habits of life. He was forbidden to taste the fruit of the vine. He was to be a teetotaler; and he grew up to great strength without a knowledge of stimulants as they were known in his nation and age.

More than that, he made himself peculiar by refusing to cut his hair. Undoubtedly he was a man of large stature, brawny, gigantic of bone and muscle, and with locks allowed to grow in full. The animal in him was mighty. His hair was unshorn and untrimmed. He was, however, in disposition not an ascetic; he was a jovial man. This was never with the hilarity of intoxicating drink; his joviality was the natural outflow of his own nature.

He is, indeed, almost the only man of the Old Testament the keynote of whose life seems to have been sportiveness or mirthfulness. Strange as it may seem, nearly every one of the delineations of Samson's character carries with it an element of almost irresistible jollity or humor. Although his various transactions were very rude and harsh, I think it will be found when we come to examine him from the standpoint of his own thought, that he had in him a kind of mirthful craft and cunning, and that he saw the great fun of things as well as the element of success that was in them.

Chapter thirteen closes with these words:—

"And the woman bare a son, and called his name Samson: and the child grew, and Jehovah blessed him. And the spirit of Jehovah began to move him at times in the camp of Dan between Zorah and Eshtaol."

Here, probably, is the history of twenty-five years compressed into two short verses. What are we to understand by these words? Looking at such a statement as this in the light of the facts of human life, of observation and experience, what may we conclude was the temperament he possessed?

There is a line that may be said to divide the whole human family of every nation. The few are above that line, and the vast multitude are below it. It is the line of power, inspiration, and exaltation. There is in the human constitution a capacity of sudden, powerful, concentrated thought or feeling. It may take on any one of several forms. A great many men are kindled slowly as green wood is. Other men are kindled fast, as dry wood is. Some, however, are capable of going off like gunpowder, suddenly, with intensity, at a word or at a thought, unbeknown to themselves and apparently uninvoked; there is that which pours the whole tide of their being out in one flame. This is the power of being what men call "inspired." The ancients considered it an act by which a god entered into a man and took possession of him, inspiring or breathing his own spirit into him. The best reason they could give for this sudden exaltation in a man was that he had a god in him that lifted him and carried him upward. He was godlike, according to their conception, so different was he from common men.

This condition depends upon the structure of the mind. It requires that a man should have a certain quality—fineness or susceptibility of nerve. More than that, it is not an effect without a cause; it is the result of a given combination of forces. And among these is the physical instrumentality of a sudden influx of blood upon the brain. But the current that comes to the brain should be stimulating. That is, the blood should be rich and full of power. And, moreover, the veins and arteries of the brain must act so that it can not only receive a sudden influx of power for instantaneous use, but can relieve itself with great freedom, or else there is danger of congestion and stupidity, caused by the throwing into it the whole force of circulation. The brain should be able to free itself easily, and with spontaneity, by a ready utilization — physical or mental or both—of any such excess of power that may be thrown upon it by the whole force that inheres in the man, whether that be greater or less.

Now, this susceptibility to inspiration is a matter of endowment at birth. No man by thinking can add one cubit to his stature; and no man by thinking can change his brain so that its structure shall not be what it was; nor can he change the construction of his organized body.

The old Roman writers used to say that a poet was born, not made. Education may enable a man to make rhymes, but not to write poetry. And thus, men that are capable of being inspired are so by nature. It is said of Jeremiah that he was called to be a prophet from his mother's womb. We should say in modern phrase that he had original adaptations to the prophetic function. And where a man has that inspirational force, that automatic action of mind, that sudden rushing energy which clothes him as in an instant with unusual power, it is born in him. It is never educated into a man. One having the elements of it may by education develop it, and make it more usable, or regulate it; but the fundamental conditions of it belong to the man's constitution.

This quality was not confined to the holy men of old, as they are called. In the time of the Israelites it broke out in every nation. Men that had this inspirational power were supposed to be channels through which the gods communicated. They were the men that governed the oracles. They were the Oriental leaders. If a man came into such a condition that he showed intense excitement he was thought to be possessed of a god. In some nations, even such persons as lunatics were considered sacred, and to harm them in any wise was like striking a god.

Where this sensibility of the whole cerebral system acted upon the physical frame, it made a man a warrior—not a warrior in the modern sense of being able to lay out and conduct large campaigns, but a warrior in battle, where inspiration enables one man to fire a thousand by his heroism, and lead them into the field as the lightning comes when once the cloud gives it out. Where it acted in the direction of the intellectual, it made men's reason powerful mainly in persuasion or demonstration. Where it acted in the direction of the imagination, it made them poets and orators. Where it acted with the moral sentiments as well as with the imagination, it made them prophets and preachers.

In Samson it was the lowest form. He was not a prophet, nor a preacher, nor a poet, nor a thinker. You might pluck his life bare from end to end and you could not find in it anything worth remembering of thought or feeling. He was utterly devoid of the higher forms of mental productiveness. And yet, Samson was a great man in his way. He was a genius of muscle. More than that, he was a genius of patriotism. There are four gradations in this direction. The first stage is where a man naturally loves himself; that is savagism. The second stage is where a man loves his tribe; tribal love is much higher than self-love. In the exercise of that love he begins to develop the generous sentiments of self-sacrifice. But a man is low down that has no enthusiasm except for himself and for his own tribe or family. The third stage is that of patriotism, where a man loves his nation; and that is a very great advance over the first and second stages, and carries with it signal benefits which they do not yield. But there is a stage which is higher than that, and which implies such a development of the moral and intellectual elements in a man that he comes into sympathy with the declaration of our Saviour that to him "the field is the world." This is the very highest point of development that is possible to the human race.

Samson stood, a great rude man, on the third plane. He loved himself, he loved his own household and friends, evidently, and he was so much a loving man that he loved his own people; but he did not love mankind.

As this man is described he is an instance of the great distinction which exists between Eastern and Western manners, and between the conceptions of the religious life as they exist in the East and in the West. He was a Jewish chief nearly resembling the founder of a monastic order. The founder of a monastic institution in medieval or modern times would be usually a man that denied himself of pleasure—who lived an ascetic life—utterly devoid of the ordinary passions and ambitions of men. Samson, who was an eminent example of the monastic order in antiquity, was very social, very genial, and very frolicsome, and anything but a model of propriety.

The first scene we have in which he figures is that of his courtship. You may wonder why this should be inserted in the Bible, when there were so many other things which men were dying for the lack of, that were left out; but so it is. Although it may be a stumbling-block in certain points of view, in other points of view it is of profound interest, as presenting a history of the manners of the times in which Samson lived.

"And Samson went down to Timnath, and saw a woman in Timnath of the daughters of the Philistines. And he came up, and told his father and his mother, and said, I have seen a woman in Timnath of the daughters of the Philistines: now therefore get her for me to wife."

In those days and lands, you know, wives were bought and sold like cattle. They are still, only it is done in a far more gracious manner than it used to be. The interior of the transaction is yet to a very great extent a mere matter of barter, but in the time of Samson it was exterior and obvious. Then, the father owned his children. Their life was in his hands. Their property was his, not alone in Israel but even so late as in Rome.

In this case Samson asks his father and mother to go and buy this girl for him. He liked her; but they didn't, —as is very often the fact.

"Then his father and his mother said unto him, Is there never a woman among the daughters of thy brethren, or among all my people, that thou goest to take a wife of the uncircumcised Philistines?"

They were right, as the sequel proved. To be sure, in the enthusiasm of young love, in the inexperienced glow of undisciplined affections, the young are apt to despise the counsel of father and mother, and to follow their own inclinations instead of considerations of fitness, adaptation, and propriety. If it were true that the enthusiasm of early love would bake bread, and make clothes, and till fields, and build houses, and promote family welfare in life, there would be more excuse for implicitly obeying its dictates. But it is not true. Still, I would not underrate it. I pity a man that never has had it. It may not be his fault. It is not the fault of a stick of wood that it cannot play a tune—but its misfortune. I cannot conceive that man to have the highest manhood who does not know how to be crazy, on proper occasions, with an enthusiasm which lifts him above calculation, above sordid motives. There is an inspiration of the inner, better, higher life under which such a thing is perfectly safe ; but in this lower life, environed with matter and material conditions, while there ought, surely, not to be less enthusiasm and disinterested love, there ought somewhere to be prudence. Generally speaking, the right place for the prudence is in father and mother ; and young people would do well to take heed to their counsels, as Samson did not. He got his pay for disregarding their advice, as we shall see.

"His father and his mother knew not that it was of Jehovah, that he sought an occasion against the Philistines : for at that time the Philistines had dominion over Israel. Then went Samson down, and his father and his mother, to Timnath, and came to the vineyards of Timnath."

They did not travel together ; for the scene with the lion took place when he was alone.

"And, behold, a young lion roared against him. And the spirit of Jehovah came mightily upon him, and he rent him as he would have rent a kid, and he had nothing in his hand : but he told not his father or his mother what he had done."

Samson evidently was no boaster. It has seemed strange to you and to me that a man should attack a lion and kill him with nothing in his hand ; but that is owing to the difference between you and me and Samson. If you suppose that which is recorded of him to be impossible, you are mistaken. It is recorded of not a few, and is not confined to sacred history. It will bring to mind the reply of David when he offered to go out against Goliath, and Saul told him he was a stripling too young to undertake so formidable a task. Said he :—

"Thy servant kept his father's sheep, and there came a lion, and a bear, and took a lamb out of the flock: and I went out after him, and smote him, and delivered it out of his mouth: and when he arose against me, I caught him by his beard, and smote him, and slew him. Thy servant slew both the lion and the bear."

There have been valiant men besides Baron Munchausen who have distinguished themselves by seizing wild beasts by the tongue or jaw and rending them asunder; and if others had done it there is no reason why we should not believe that Samson did it. Great things had been prophesied of him as a deliverer of his people; he had been trained in the idea; he felt his own strength; he *believed* in it as the gift of God,—and the inspiration that seized him was the flaming consciousness of victorious power.

"And he went down, and talked with the woman; and she pleased Samson well."

This seems to have been the second visit.

"After a time he returned to take her."

There is no further account given of the parental counsel; at any rate, they seem to have acquiesced. On his way,—

"He turned aside to see the carcass of the lion [the flesh had evidently decayed, leaving the ribs and other portions of the frame complete]; and, behold, there was a swarm of bees and honey in the carcass of the lion. And he took thereof in his hands, and went on eating, and came to his father and mother, and he gave them, and they did eat: but he told not them that he had taken the honey out of the carcass of the lion.

"And his father went down unto the woman: and Samson made there a feast."

It was his wedding feast. And now his sense of humor begins to appear.

"It came to pass, when they saw him, that they brought thirty companions to be with him. And Samson said unto them [the Philistines], I will now put forth a riddle unto you."

The propounding and guessing of riddles was one of the

common occupations of Oriental nations, clear down to the last days of the Israelites. They were not exactly conundrums, but questions that tested the ingenuity; and probably it was as good as many of the occupations that are pursued nowadays.

"If ye can certainly declare it me within the seven days of the feast, and find it out, then I will give you thirty sheets and thirty change of garments; but if ye cannot declare it me, then shall ye give me thirty sheets and thirty change of garments."

That is, he gave a riddle, and bet thirty sheets and thirty robes that they could not guess it, and they bet thirty sheets and thirty robes that they could. It was gambling, though it is described in decorous language; but a great deal of gambling goes on under pious phrases.

"And they said unto him, Put forth thy riddle, that we may hear it. And he said unto them, Out of the eater came forth meat, and out of the strong came forth sweetness."

I confess I should have been puzzled if that riddle had been put to me. I could not for the life of me have told what it meant. Apparently it might have related to any of a thousand things; but it was all the better for that.

"They could not in three days expound the riddle. And it came to pass on the seventh day, that they said unto Samson's wife, Entice thy husband, that he may declare unto us the riddle."

She was evidently a weak woman, who rather meant to do right, or who did not go to do wrong of her own accord. At any rate, this betrayal of her husband's interests would hardly seem to have been a proper proceeding at so early a period after one's wedding. She hesitated, probably; and, as she did so, they added:—

"Lest we burn thee and thy father's house with fire: have ye called us to take that we have? Is it not so?"

They wanted her to get Samson to tell her, and they wanted her then to tell them; and, when she hesitated, they charged her with having invited them to this feast for the purpose of robbing them, and threatened to take revenge by destroying her and her father's house if she did not comply with their request. She addressed to her husband the universal argument :—

"Samson's wife wept before him, and said:"—

What did she say? O, nothing new. There is nothing new under the sun. You will find that four thousand years ago human nature ran in the same channels that it does now. We are all going over and over again the old things.

"Samson's wife wept before him, and said, Thou dost but hate me, and lovest me not: thou hast put forth a riddle unto the children of my people, and hast not told it me. And he said unto her, Behold, I have not told it my father nor my mother, and shall I tell it thee? And she wept before him the seven days, while their feast lasted."

A very pleasant wedding festival they must have had; but continual dropping will wear away a stone.

"And it came to pass on the seventh day, that he told her, because she lay sore upon him."

A woman is just as weak as a child; a man could take her with two fingers and put her out of the door; and yet in a week a woman can weary a man into almost anything.

"And she told the riddle to the children of her people. And the men of the city said unto him on the seventh day before the sun went down, What is sweeter than honey? and what is stronger than a lion?

"And he said unto them, If ye had not ploughed with my heifer, ye had not found out my riddle."

Now, there was business!

"And the spirit of Jehovah came upon him [that is, in his indignation, tremendous power and courage rose up in him], and he went down to Ashkelon, and slew thirty men of them, and took their spoil, and gave change of garments unto them which expounded the riddle."

They won the bet, and they got the clothes; but who lost them? It was a very easy way of paying one's gambling debt.

"And his anger was kindled [That did not slake it. His indignation was like the sea, whose waves, even after the wind goes down, roll sometimes for days], and he went up to his father's house."

He abandoned the wife for the time being. He could not stand living with her; and, as it will appear, he could not stand living without her. Such is the history of thousands of men.

"But Samson's wife was given to his companion, whom he had used as his friend."

That was one of the band of thirty that had been invited to the house. Evidently Samson was partial to him, and he probably took Samson's place. There were no divorce proceedings; and it did not take long for the father who had given the damsel to one man, to give her, after he had gone off, to another. There was no law and no moral sentiment to prevent this.

"But it came to pass within a while after [you see how definite the statement is as to time], in the time of wheat harvest, that Samson visited his wife with a kid; and he said, I will go in to my wife into the chamber. But her father would not suffer him to go in. And her father said, I verily thought that thou hadst utterly hated her; therefore I gave her to thy companion: is not her younger sister fairer than she? Take her, I pray thee, instead of her."

When a man's heart is fixed upon a certain woman, she and she only will satisfy him. Others may be fairer and more suitable, but after all the secret intoxication is upon him and he will accept no substitute.

"And Samson said concerning them, Now shall I be more blameless than the Philistines, though I do them a displeasure.* And Samson went and caught three hundred foxes [Here, too, there is the utter absence of any record of time. There is no telling how long it took him to catch them], and took firebrands, and turned tail to tail, and put a firebrand in the midst between two tails. And when he had set the brands on fire, he let them go into the standing corn of the Philistines, and burnt up both the shocks, and also the standing corn, with the vineyards and olives."

This, too, has been a stumbling-block of wonder to a great many people. But, in the first place, we are to remember that in that hilly country animals, including foxes, were very numerous, that oftentimes they were found in flocks, and that they might have been gathered together and caught by driving them into corrals or prepared places. At any rate it was not a thing so impossible

---

* "This time shall I be quits with the Philistines, when I do them a mischief." *Rev. Vers. margin.*

but that one may believe it. Then as to tying firebrands between their tails after they were caught, that was not so difficult a matter. The reason why Samson tied the foxes together as he did was that if they had been allowed to go separately, they would have run away quickly and done little damage, but that being tied together they would attempt to run in different directions, and would be delayed so that the brands would have time to catch the dry straw, and insure the destruction of the whole crop.

Now you are to understand that this took place, not over a great extent of country, but only in the neighborhood of the thirty Philistines that got the sheets and robes; and if it still taxes your credulity, it is to be added that this is not a novel thing. It is recorded of Hannibal, you will recollect, that under certain circumstances he tied brands to the horns of two thousand oxen, and sent them out for devastation. The Romans, in festivals, were accustomed to tie brands to foxes and set them loose, as a kind of ceremony. We have accounts of tying brands to bullocks' tails, and watching their course to determine whether or not the gods were propitious. When you come to look into the customs which were prevalent as far down as the time when Rome was in her glory, the strangeness of this event to your mind will be somewhat alleviated.

"Then the Philistines said, Who hath done this? And they answered, Samson, the son-in-law of the Timnite, because he had taken his wife, and given her to his companion. And the Philistines came up, and burnt her and her father with fire."

That was a quick remedy. It was administered not simply in a spirit of wrath, but also with a desire to leave nothing to tempt Samson into that neighborhood thereafter.

"And Samson said unto them, Though ye have done this, yet will I be avenged of you, and after that I will cease."

In other words, "You have had your turn; now I will have mine : and the thing shall be ended."

"And he smote them hip and thigh with a great slaughter: and he went down and dwelt in the top of the rock Etam."

What unmannerly times! What a strange condition of human society!

"Then the Philistines went up, and pitched in Judah [for Israel at this time was under the dominion of the Philistines], and spread themselves in Lehi. And the men of Judah said, Why are ye come up against us?"

This evidently was a neighborhood matter. It was not known by the Israelites at large. They did not understand the reason of the invasion.

"They answered, To bind Samson are we come up, to do to him as he hath done to us.

"Then three thousand men of Judah went to the top of the rock Etam, and said to Samson, Knowest thou not that the Philistines are rulers over us? What is this that thou hast done unto us? And he said unto them, As they did unto me, so have I done unto them. And they said unto him, We are come down to bind thee, that we may deliver thee into the hand of the Philistines. And Samson said unto them, Swear unto me, that ye will not fall upon me yourselves. And they spake unto him, saying, No; but we will bind thee fast, and deliver thee into their hand: but surely we will not kill thee. And they bound him with two new cords, and brought him up from the rock."

I can imagine this great rollicking giant of a Samson sitting on the sides of the hills and grimly laughing while the foxes tugged at each other's tails with firebrands tied to them through the fields; there was something humorous in it to every man—except the one who owned the fields: and I can imagine how, when the three thousand Israelites came and told him that they had come to bind him and deliver him to his enemies, this hirsute, powerful man inwardly chuckled and put his hands up, and allowed them to tie him. Doubtless he really enjoyed being tied, knowing very well, as he did, what was in him.

"And when he came unto Lehi, the Philistines shouted against him: and the spirit of Jehovah came mightily upon him, and the cords that were upon his arms became as flax that was burnt with fire, and his bands loosed from off his hands.

"And he found a new jawbone of an ass, and put forth his hand, and took it, and slew a thousand men therewith. And Samson said, With the jawbone of an ass, heaps upon heaps, with the jaw of an ass have I slain a thousand men."

This, too, has been thought to be very wonderful; and it would be, for you or me. It was a *new* jawbone, with the juices of life not dried out of it ; and you will remember that, being the jawbone of an ass, it was very tough, and no mean weapon. As to the slaughter, it was not a difficult thing, under the circumstances, for him to kill so many men. He ran at them roaring and smiting ; and they were infected with panic, while he was actuated by enthusiastic courage. I quite believe the account.

Moreover, it was not the most active jawbone of an ass that ever was. Others have been as fatal in different ways and in different scenes !

"And he was sore athirst, and called on Jehovah, and said, Thou hast given this great deliverance into the hand of thy servant: and now shall I die for thirst, and fall into the hand of the uncircumcised? But God clave an hollow place that was in the jaw,* and there came water thereout ; and when he had drunk, his spirit came again, and he revived: wherefore he called the name thereof En-hakkore, which is in Lehi unto this day.

"And he judged Israel in the days of the Philistines twenty years."

Here you come to a more favorable aspect. Having delivered the people, the sense of power and of patriotism seems to have given him the best use of his judgment. They made their champion their ruler, and he judged and protected them for twenty years. His was a good nature. He was a kindly man. He was not a man of moderate passions ; he would have been marked in our day as a man grossly immoral : but he was a lover of his kin and of his country. He therefore had pre-eminent qualities for ruling in such a rude time as that in which he lived.

According to the account which is given of this man in later life, in the pursuit of illicit pleasures he found himself entrapped in the city of Gaza. As the people knew that he was there, they closed the gates, and determined, with the light of the morning, to secure him. "But he arose at midnight," it is recorded, "and took the doors of the gate of the city, and the two posts, and went away with them, bar and all, and put them upon his shoulders, and carried them up to the top of a hill that is before Hebron." How he must have enjoyed that—walking off

---

* "The hollow place that is in Lehi." *Rev. Vers. margin.*

with the very instruments of his captivity! If these gates were like the gates of some fortified cities of our time, they would weigh some forty thousand or fifty thousand pounds, and the tax on our credulity would be too heavy; but when we consider how the gates of cities or camps were built at that time, it is not difficult for us to believe this story. The gates spoken of here may have been such that it was quite within the power of so gigantic a man as Samson to carry them. There is nothing in the statement that need prevent our belief of it.

The next record of this man is not a very reputable one.

"And it came to pass afterwards, that he loved a woman in the valley of Sorek, whose name was Delilah."

Then comes the history of her enticing him. It is intensely natural, it is intensely human, and it is intensely miserable. He was now a public man, a magistrate, and he knew better. She, at the instigation of her people, the Philistines, persuaded him to declare wherein his strength lay. There are very few dramas written that, with so few simple touches, give so much interior history of the wiles of a cozening woman as does this of Delilah persuading Samson; of his making believe this, that, and the other thing; and of his finally, when wearied out by her importunities, telling her his secret. It is familiar. I need not detail all the ways in which he fooled her and her friends, nor the final way in which she induced him to fool himself.

"He told her all his heart, and said unto her, There hath not come a razor upon mine head; for I have been a Nazarite unto God from my mother's womb: if I be shaven, then my strength will go from me, and I shall become weak, and be like any other man.

"And when Delilah saw that he had told her all his heart, she sent and called for the lords of the Philistines, saying, Come up this once [She had called them twice before, but only to be laughed at by the jolly giant], for he hath shewed me all his heart. Then the lords of the Philistines came up unto her, and brought money in their hand."

Beautiful, cruel, worthless; rottener than the rot under the feet of the man that treads upon the fallen fruit of the orchard! Pretending to love him, giving herself to him in sacrilege of love, betraying him that really loved her, —and for money!

"And she made him sleep upon her knees; and she called for a man, and she caused him to shave off the seven locks of his head; and she began to afflict him, and his strength went from him. And she said, The Philistines be upon thee, Samson. And he awoke out of his sleep, and said, I will go out as at other times before, and shake myself. And he wist not that Jehovah was departed from him.

"But the Philistines took him, and put out his eyes, and brought him down to Gaza, and bound him with fetters of brass; and he did grind in the prison house."

Grinding was the most menial of offices in that land at that time; and this bereft, forlorn, coarse-grained man was reduced to the pitiful plight of public servitude of the most degrading character.

The account goes on to say that little by little Samson's hair grew again, and that with it came back his strength, his courage, his confidence, and his aptitude. Whether or not the long hair was the real secret of his enormous strength, it is clear that his *belief* in it was an essential element of his courage. And now he began to regain confidence. While yet in prison, he was brought out upon a great occasion to make sport for the Philistines,—probably in feats of strength. And he asked the lad who led him out to let him feel the columns which mainly supported the circular roof of the building in which the assembly was gathered, that he might rest, after his labors. When this request was granted, he uttered a cry to God, and then, exerting his immense strength, taking hold of the columns with his two hands, he bowed himself forward and wrenched the columns from their positions; and the roof, crowded with people, came down with a crash into the space below, and hundreds upon hundreds were destroyed, as well as Samson himself. He was sacrificed by his own act, together with thousands of his enemies—"men and women, and all the lords of the Philistines."

Now, looking upon this history at large, what is there in it that should have given it a place in the records of Scripture? This: that it is a fact; that it is a characteristic fact; that it is a revelation of the low state in which the best men of that time were living. And that is not all. It shows that there are periods in the history of nations in which a rude strength may be better than intellectual genius. Moses was a transcendently better man than Samson; he was one of the noblest men of all time; and yet, when he thought himself called on to exert his strength, he slew the Egyptian, and turned and ran. He was not fit for deeds that required great physical energy; but patience, wisdom, skill in organization, moral power—of these he had an ample endowment. In that later time, however, without a government, when every man did that which was right in his own sight, in a country without roads or institutions, there rose up this gigantic fellow, Samson, who brought fear to the hearts of the adversaries of his people; and he was adapted to the rudeness, the coarseness, the vulgarity of his time. It is often the case that a man who is not himself remarkable for goodness is in many respects better qualified for taking care of bad men than another man that is wholly good. I speak without disrespect, and with the utmost sincerity, and in some respects with sympathy, when I say that though Thaddeus Stevens was not a man whose character should be taken as a model for young men to build on, yet, as the founder of the common-school system of Pennsylvania, he has an enduring fame; and in national matters, at a time when men were treacherous, and when what we wanted was a man who dared to venture all for the land that he loved, to take a stalwart stand for freedom and against slavery, he loomed up a grand figure. Not for everything, but just for that, he made his mark; and his name will go down in history among the names of memorable men to whom the country is indebted.

While, then, Samson was fitted to his age, to his nation, and to the work that was to be accomplished, and according to the standard of that age was honorable and respectable, according to the standard of later times, and the conception of humanity which prevails to-day, he was one of the poorest specimens that could be selected from antiquity. But how many men to-day, no better than he in respect to the things in which he was bad, are not as good as he in respect to the things in which he was good! How many men are coarse, how many men are full of animal appetites, how many men are vindictive and cruel, how many men have no care for their families, still less for their country, and no thought except for their own physical enjoyment, and yet think themselves to be good because they are no worse than they are!

In looking back upon the history of the period that is described in the book of Judges I have merely to say, in conclusion, that this book is one of the most remarkable of the Old Testament. The simplicity of it, the picturesqueness of it, the wonderful variety of its contents, the honesty of it, make it a book that can be read with profit. There are some things in it that go as deep, and some that go as high, as the productions of any of the dramatists of the English language. But, quite aside from its literary merit, it is a book of inspiration and revelation. It reveals a state of society from which the world has emerged, and on our escape from which we ought to look with gratitude.

But we are not to suppose that the rude things recorded in it were the only things that were happening at the time to which it refers. During that very period of history were enacted scenes of beauty. Forth from it came strains of entrancing music. Upon the cheek of this rugged book of Judges lies the exquisite poem of Ruth. That charming idyl would seem almost like the song of children and the voice of mothers; it is pure, lovely, and in every way delightful. To that I shall call your attention next Sunday night.

XXIII.

NAOMI AND RUTH.

A DIAMOND in its rough and ordinary state is not lustrous nor beautiful; nor is it so until it has been ground, and artificial facets and angles are raised upon it: but when it has gone through the processes of being cut and polished it is one of the loveliest of gems. The pearl, however, suffers no hand to touch it. It is already perfect, and handling mars it.

There are many doctrinal passages in the Bible that are obscure, and that need much exposition to discover the precious truth within them. There are some—and we have come upon one of them to-night—that would be in danger of being dimmed and hurt if handled.

This book of Ruth has but four chapters; and yet, where can you find four other such chapters? It is not for everybody, nor for anybody at all times, to read this book. You cannot prepare to read it with your dictionary and your commentary. There are some strains of poetry which a man can read only when, in the mutations of feeling, he comes around to the very point of feeling from which those poems came. A man in the heyday of joy and hilarity cannot read the "In Memoriam" of Tennyson. A man cast into profound grief cannot enter into some of the most exquisite poems of joy and fantasy.

The book of Ruth should be read when the world has subsided from about us. You cannot read it nor understand it if you are cumbered with the habits of modern society, with our highly artificial conditions, with an utter

---

Sunday evening, May 4, 1879. LESSON: Psa. xxiii.

difference of standpoint as to manners and customs. It runs far back into antiquity. Its scenes were cast not only in a remote age and in an Oriental nation, but in a time of society that was very simple in occupations, being not pastoral, nor absolutely agricultural. Society had but little classification. Its life as well as its pursuits were very simple. No lordly dwellings were there for the rich, with hovels for the poor. Men lived very near to each other, both in locality and in condition. A little more land, a little more grain, a few more cattle, a few more robes, a little more gold or silver, differentiated the several classes; but men lived near together, and upon a level. In this state of society, if we come into sympathy with it, there is unfolded that exquisite idyl of antiquity in which there is not a malicious person; in which the Devil does not show so much as the top of his poll; in which all coarse passions are subordinated; in which the sweeter elements of life rise up and blossom. It is a garden of perfume from beginning to end, and it must be read in a spirit of reverence, and with a refined appreciation of natural virtues. That is what makes it so hard for me to do anything more than to read it—but I must do more.

"Now it came to pass in the days when the Judges ruled, that there was a famine in the land."

We have been wading through those times. We have had our hands full of the camp. We have marched with Moses and with Joshua. We have crossed the Jordan with them. We have gone into the seven years' war of dispossession and of possession. We emerged from that heroic age. We came into the slough of the times of the Judges, when every man did that which was right in his own eyes. We have oscillated with the people, plunging into captivity to paganism and the pagans, and then after many years coming forth under some natural leader that rose up and broke the chain, and led captivity captive. Our ears have been filled with the sounds of war—wars of wickedness and extermination; and the smell of blood has become stenchful to us. We are tired of freebooters, and Jephthahs, and Samsons. We have been in rough conflicts among a rude people in a cruel age.

Finally, the uproar ceases, and we find ourselves in a beautiful valley, as it were, walled in with mountains, fruitful, abounding in green pastures and still waters. The people lived a lovely life, in which there was not one single discord, and not one cacophonous sound.

Famines were common at that time, and are common in that land still, partly from want of skillful agriculture, and partly from climatic reasons.

We have somewhat the parallel of these famines, in Southern California. No husbandman can control the wind-currents and the moisture; and every five or seven years there comes a time when these currents and the moisture refuse to flow, and all summer long there is drought, drought, drought; and the pastures fail, and the sheep die by thousands, and the large adventurers are bankrupt,—except as they have learned the moistening of the soil by culture and by irrigation.

So it was in the hill country of Judah.

"There was a famine in the land. And a certain man of Beth-lehem-judah [there were two Bethlehems—Beth-lehem-judah and Bethlehem] went to sojourn in the country of Moab, he, and his wife, and his two sons. And the name of the man was Elimelech [*El*, in almost every case in which it is found in the Hebrew is equivalent to the word *god*: and *Elimelech* means *my god, my king*. A very great name; and a very good man he must have been that could carry such a name], and the name of his wife Naomi [which means *pleasant, lovely, beautiful*, not simply in the sense of comeliness, but in the sense of efflorescence of disposition. There is nothing in this world so beautiful as the shining forth of the soul of a woman], and the name of his two sons Mahlon and Chilion, Ephrathites of Beth-lehem-judah.

"And they came into the country of Moab, and continued there. And Elimelech Naomi's husband died; and she was left, and her two sons."

To the east of the Dead Sea is the territory of Moab. Although the western side of it is mountainous, consisting of a high plateau, the further east you go the more is it streaked with fertile pasture valleys. These were apparently watered by the streams that flowed down from the hills. Into this country Elimelech had gone to escape from the famine of his own land. Commentators have blamed him for going there. They have said that it was not for him to leave friends behind and come into a fat country himself. They have argued that he ought to have trusted God and stayed at home. As well might they have said that the Patriarchs ought never to have gone where they went. You might as well say that Jacob should not have sent his sons down to Egypt, but should have sat still and let the Lord deliver him, as to say that Elimelech should not have become an emigrant when he could find nothing to eat. If his neighbors and their families could not go, so much the worse for them.

But soon after his arrival in Moab he died. And what did the two sons do?

"They took them wives of the women of Moab; the name of the one was Orpah [*the hind*, or *roe*], and the name of the other Ruth [Many have supposed that meant, in the original, *the rose;* as you never can find out you may just as well call her Ruth] : and they dwelled there about ten years.

"And Mahlon and Chilion died also, both of them; and the woman was left of her two sons and her husband."

The Moabitish women seem to have been very engaging and very beautiful. That was their reputation. There are nations nowadays that have the same reputation. It is said that Circassia, and some of the neighboring hill countries, are famous for their beautiful daughters; and Moab seems to have had that peculiarity.

You will recollect that when Balaam was unable to make headway against Israel he counseled the Moabites to employ their women in devilish diplomacy in order to draw the children of Israel aside and corrupt them, that they did so, and that thus was brought terrific punishment from the hand of Moses. But four or five hundred years had passed, and Moab had built up again the diminished population, and the same peculiarities of physique seem to have gone on. Blood tells.

Mahlon and Chilion had married two of the daughters of Moab. They doubtless were beautiful. They certainly were good. This shows that although the Moabites were a vagrant nation all was not darkness in their midst. Their life was not wholly corrupt. The household among them had its pure atmosphere and its virtuous lives.

"Then she [Naomi, the pleasant and comely] arose with her daughters-in-law, that she might return from the country of Moab: for she had heard in the country of Moab how that the Lord had visited his people in giving them bread. Wherefore she went forth out of the place where she was, and her two daughters-in-law with her; and they went on the way to return unto the land of Judah."

But as they journeyed the magnanimous heart of Naomi pondered; she bethought her, and said, "Why, though I be a poor homeless widow, should I drag these my daughters-in-law out from among their kindred and away from their fathers' homes? Sweet, pleasant, they are to me; but why should I take them to share my poverty and my wretchedness?" So, with great generosity of heart she said to them,—

"Go, return each to her mother's house: the Lord deal kindly with you, as ye have dealt with the dead, and with me."

It was the voice of a wife whose husband was gone; it was the voice of a mother whose sons were dead; it was the voice of a widowed stranger.

"The Lord grant [she said to them] that ye may find rest, each of you in the house of her husband. Then she kissed them; and they lifted up their voice, and wept.

"And they said unto her, Surely we will return with thee unto thy people. And Naomi said, Turn again, my daughters; why will ye go with me? Are there yet any more sons in my womb, that they may be your husbands? Turn again, my daughters, go your way: for I am too old to have an husband. If I should say, I have hope, if I should have an husband also to-night, and should also bear sons; would ye tarry for them till they were grown? Would ye stay for them from having husbands? Nay, my daughters; for it grieveth me much for your sakes that the hand of the Lord is gone out against me.

"And they lifted up their voice, and wept again: and Orpah kissed her mother-in-law [that was the sign of farewell]; but Ruth clave unto her."

Orpah was sincere, she was true, she loved her mother-in-law, she clung to her: nevertheless, her heart was warm for her father's house, for the friends she had left behind, for the country of her nativity; and, being in a strait betwixt two, and acting under the influence of a natural generous affection, she went back and settled again in her father's household.

But Ruth had more personal attachment, and she remained with their mother-in-law.

"And she [Naomi] said, Behold, thy sister-in-law is gone back unto her people, and unto her gods: return thou after thy sister-in-law.

"And Ruth said, Entreat me not to leave thee, or to return from following after thee: for whither thou goest, I will go; and where thou lodgest, I will lodge: thy people shall be my people, and thy God my God. Where thou diest, will I die, and there will I be buried; the Lord do so to me, and more also, if aught but death part thee and me."

If ever heart had tongue, and spoke the words of love, simple, pure, and deep, that was the utterance of it; and it has passed into universal literature. It is diffused throughout poetry. It has almost become a proverb — this Moabitish maiden's beautiful and true love, that cared nothing for itself, but cared all for the one loved—it has sweetened the world; through four thousand years it has syllabled itself in almost every language, and is to-day as beautiful and true as it was when first uttered; and sorry am I for anybody that can read these words and keep dry eyes.

"When she saw that she was steadfastly minded to go with her, then she left speaking unto her."

I know that Naomi was glad, from the very bottom of her heart. She counseled her daughters-in-law to return, not because she felt that she could spare them,—she longed to keep them with her,—but because she thought it was best. Hers was ripe love, that showed itself in action. Ruth's was love midway, that showed itself not only in action but also in words.

"So they two went until they came to Beth-lehem."

And now we have the village life indeed. The word that comes in at the edge of the neighborhood runs from house to house, nobody knows how; but everybody has found out that Naomi has come back. The whole place is in excitement. When she went away she was the wife of a person of distinction; she belonged, that is to say, to the upper class. The upper class was not very far from the bottom, to be sure; but the upper class is the upper class everywhere.

> "And it came to pass, when they were come to Beth-lehem, that all the city was moved about them, and they said, Is this Naomi? And she said unto them, Call me not Naomi, call me Mara [Bitter]: for the Almighty hath dealt very bitterly with me."

With us names are mere bell-pulls and door-knockers—things hung on a man without any regard to their significance, to distinguish him from his neighbors; this is the case with all nations which are advanced in civilization; but in that primitive age, as also among our American Indians to-day, names were always significant, as they arose from external circumstances. You will recollect that passage of exceeding pathos where Rachel, in giving birth to Benjamin, as her soul was departing ("for she died," the narrative says), called his name Ben-oni, *Child of my Sorrow;* but the father in his pride and joy called him Benjamin, *Son of my Right hand.* So everywhere throughout the olden time you will find that names had meanings in them.

And this woman was called Naomi, the Pleasant, the Beautiful, the Comely; but she said, "Do not call me the Beautiful any more—call me the Bitter; for God hath dealt bitterly with me."

> "I went out full [with my husband and two sons], and the Lord hath brought me home again empty: why then call ye me Naomi, seeing the Lord hath testified against me, and the Almighty hath afflicted me? So Naomi returned, and Ruth the Moabitess, her daughter-in-law, with her, which returned out of the country of Moab: and they came to Beth-lehem in the beginning of barley harvest."

That is the first scene in this little drama. Now comes the next.

> "Naomi had a kinsman of her husband's, a mighty man of wealth, of the family of Elimelech; and his name was Boaz. And Ruth the Moabitess said unto Naomi, Let me now go to the field, and glean ears of corn after him in whose sight I shall find grace. And she said unto her, Go, my daughter."

Ruth betook herself to that which she thought would

support her mother. Her love was not simply sentiment—it was life and action; and she went forth, after the manner of that country, to earn her daily bread.

Now, support there was not very expensive, as we shall see by and by, where a rich man and his laborers would sit down contentedly to a meal of parched corn and rice. The luxury of such living did not require very severe toil; and yet this was the living of that day even among the rich. Now and then, however, there were great feasts, which contrasted strongly with the ordinary livelihood.

"And she went, and came, and gleaned in the field after the reapers: and her hap was to light on a part of the field belonging unto Boaz, who was of the kindred of Elimelech."

The *redeemer*, the *defender*—such is the original of that term *kinsman*. It sprang from the familiar habit of the Jewish people by which families were kept together, so that when a husband died the wife of the deceased was wedded to one of the brothers, or to some of his kindred. Hence he became her defender or redeemer. If the husband, dying, left landed property and a widow, it was not comely for her to marry out of the family connection, thus bringing another name or strain of blood into the possession of that property; for it was the policy of the Mosaic economy to keep the landed property together in certain families or tribes. There were what are called *levirate* (brother-in-law) marriages, whereby the widow of a son was united to the next son. They gave rise, you know, to the question which was put to our Saviour, in the New Testament, respecting the case in which a woman was married to seven successive brothers, and then died, and the question was asked, "Whose wife shall she be of the seven? for they all had her." Such a question as that would be impossible to our society, in our time; but among the Jews and in the East it fell in entirely with their manners and customs. It seemed both decorous and moral to them, though to us it would seem monstrous.

"Behold, Boaz came from Beth-lehem, and said unto the reapers, The Lord be with you. And they answered him, The Lord bless thee."

It was their ordinary mode of salutation. It was beautiful for the owner of a field to go forth and greet his reapers thus, and for them to greet him in the same spirit. What if a director of a railroad, nowadays, should come out in the morning, and say to his workmen, "The Lord be with you!" What would they think, or say? So it seems to us a wonderful period in which the householder and master addressed those who served him in these stately words, "The Lord be with you," and they said in reply, "The Lord bless thee." It was a good deal better than the best of our salutations. Take, for instance, our "Goodbye." That, you know, is "God be with you"—shrunk up to a skin.

"Then said Boaz unto his servant that was set over the reapers [for he had eyes in his head], Whose damsel is this?

"And the servant that was set over the reapers answered and said, It is the Moabitish damsel that came back with Naomi out of the country of Moab: and she said, I pray you, let me glean and gather after the reapers among the sheaves: so she came, and hath continued even from the morning until now, that she tarried a little in the house."

The custom of gleaning prevails in the East to-day that prevailed at that time. In Palestine you will find that men are cast in the same mold that they were when Ruth and Boaz lived. They talk in the same way. They reap in the same way. There has been no change there in the methods of agriculture for four thousand years.

"Then said Boaz unto Ruth, Hearest thou not, my daughter? Go not to glean in another field, neither go from hence, but abide here fast by my maidens: let thine eyes be on the field that they do reap, and go thou after them."

There is great benignity. "Do not go into any other field, where you may not be well treated: stay in my field." These rude reapers, gathered from every whither during harvest time, were not always select in their language, and they doubtless oftentimes had their equals in the stray women that bound up the sheaves. But Boaz seems to have had confidence in his own retainers, and said to Ruth, "Follow after my maidens." It was her protection that he had in mind.

"Have I not charged the young men that they shall not touch thee?"

In those far-off times, there was a man with a sensitive and delicate nature, and that was Boaz. He could not endure to see the rough hand of a coarse fellow slapping a woman's shoulders, or pinching her arms, or taking those rude liberties that are thought even by some young gentlemen in our day to be compatible with refinement. They had better turn back and go to school to Boaz. I am ashamed of many of the unlicked bears' cubs that pass themselves off for men of society at this advanced age of the world. Would that they were in the field reaping, and that Boaz was over them!

"And when thou art athirst, go unto the vessels, and drink of that which the young men have drawn.

"Then she fell on her face, and bowed herself to the ground, and said unto him, Why have I found grace in thine eyes, that thou shouldest take knowledge of me, seeing I am a stranger?"

She was as modest as she was sweet and beautiful.

"And Boaz answered and said unto her, It hath fully been shewed me, all that thou hast done unto thy mother-in-law since the death of thine husband: and how thou hast left thy father and thy mother, and the land of thy nativity, and art come unto a people which thou knewest not heretofore."

There is the history of love over and over and over again. The heart that loves lives for love's sake.

"The Lord recompense thy work, and a full reward be given thee of the Lord God of Israel, under whose wings thou art come to trust. Then she said, Let me find favor in thy sight, my lord; for that thou hast comforted me, and for that thou hast spoken friendly unto thine handmaid, though I be not like unto one of thine handmaidens."

She shrank from the comparison, and put herself lower than his handmaidens.

"And Boaz said unto her [she won him at every step by her tongue], At mealtime, come thou hither, and eat of the bread, and dip thy morsel in the vinegar. And she sat beside the reapers: and he reached her parched corn, and she did eat, and was sufficed, and left. And when she was risen up to glean, Boaz [he could not do enough; he began to feel very benevolent] commanded his young men, saying, Let her glean even among the sheaves, and reproach her not: and let fall also some of the handfuls of purpose for her, and leave them, that she may glean them, and rebuke her not. So she gleaned in the field until even, and beat out that she had gleaned: and it was about an ephah of barley."

What an ephah was we do not know, but it is computed to have been about fifty-five pounds of wheat. Whatever may have been the measure, it was evidently a very good day's gleaning in those simple times.

That is the second scene—the scene of the field. Next, Ruth returned to her mother-in-law. Now, Naomi had been a beautiful woman, doubtless, in her youth; and a handsome woman that is good becomes more handsome as she grows old. Where the disposition is bad no cosmetics can cover it; and no cosmetics are needed where there is goodness. I have no doubt that Naomi was still comely and beautiful though she called herself "Mara."

Nevertheless, good as she was, she was shrewd. A mother that has brought up children, and taken care of them for a long period, has a very good notion of management; and Naomi had a most sagacious idea of it.

"And she [Ruth] took it [the barley] up, and went into the city; and her mother-in-law saw what she had gleaned: and she brought forth, and gave to her that she had reserved after she was sufficed."

She had brought home some of the parched corn.

"And her mother-in-law said unto her, Where hast thou gleaned to-day; and where wroughtest thou? Blessed be he that did take knowledge of thee.

"And she shewed her mother-in-law with whom she had wrought, and said, The man's name with whom I wrought to-day is Boaz.

"And Naomi said unto her daughter-in-law, Blessed be he of the Lord, who hath not left off his kindness to the living and to the dead. And Naomi said unto her, The man is near of kin unto us, one of our next kinsmen."

There was light beginning to dawn on the darkness.

"And Ruth the Moabitess said, He said unto me also, Thou shalt keep fast by my young men, until they have ended all my harvest. And Naomi said unto Ruth her daughter-in-law, It is good, my daughter, that thou go out with his maidens, that they meet thee not in any other field.

"So she kept fast by the maidens of Boaz to glean unto the end of barley harvest and of wheat harvest; and dwelt with her mother-in-law."

Meantime, Naomi kept on thinking.

"Then Naomi her mother-in-law said unto her, My daughter, shall I not seek rest for thee, that it may be well with thee? And now is not Boaz of our kindred [our redeemer] with whose maidens thou wast? Behold, he winnoweth barley to-night in the threshing-floor."

When the barley was gathered from the sickle into sheaves, and threshed out, it was next carried to the winnowing floor; and then it was in the state in which men could steal it, if they wished—and there never was a time when somebody did not wish to steal. Therefore, it was the custom of the husbandman and householder to go down with his family and see to the winnowing, and sleep at night where his grain was. It was his year's livelihood, his treasure, and it must be looked after. Naomi knew the custom; and she said to her daughter-in-law—and there was nothing on earth purer, simpler, more righteous, according to the ideas and the customs of the country, than the directions given her:—

"Wash thyself, therefore, and anoint thee, and put thy raiment upon thee, and get thee down to the floor: but make not thyself known unto the man, until he shall have done eating and drinking. And it shall be, when he lieth down, that thou shalt mark the place where he shall lie, and thou shalt go in, and uncover his feet, and lay thee down; and he will tell thee what thou shalt do."

To the pure all things are pure. Custom determines what is right and wrong in social intercourse.

"And she said unto her, All that thou sayest unto me I will do. And she went down unto the floor, and did according to all that her mother-in-law bade her. And when Boaz had eaten and drunk, and his heart was merry, he went to lie down at the end of the heap of corn: and she came softly, and uncovered his feet, and laid her down.

"And it came to pass at midnight, that the man was afraid [startled], and turned himself: and, behold, a woman lay at his feet. And he said, Who art thou? And she answered, I am Ruth thine handmaid: spread therefore thy skirt over thine handmaid; for thou art a near kinsman.

"And he said, Blessed be thou of the Lord, my daughter: for thou hast shewed more kindness in the latter end than at the beginning, inasmuch as thou followedst not young men, whether poor or rich. And now, my daughter, fear not; I will do to thee all that thou requirest: for all the city of my people doth know that thou art a virtuous woman. And now it is true that I am thy near kinsman: howbeit there is a kinsman nearer than I. Tarry this night, and it shall be in the morning, that if he will perform unto thee the part of a kinsman, well; let him do the kinsman's part: but if he will not do the part of a kinsman to thee, then will I do the part of a kinsman to thee, as the Lord liveth: lie down until the morning.

"And she lay at his feet until the morning: and she rose up before one could know another. And he said, Let it not be known that a woman came into the floor [her reputation was dear to him]. Also he said, Bring the vail that thou hast upon thee, and hold it. And when she held it, he measured six measures of barley, and laid it on her: and she went into the city.

"And when she came to her mother-in-law, she said [for it was dark, so that she could not tell certainly who was coming], Who art thou, my daughter? And she told her all that the man had done to her. And she said, These six measures of barley gave he me; for he said to me, Go not empty unto thy mother-in-law. Then said she, Sit still, my daughter, until thou know how the matter will fall [She knew that the enchantment of love had begun. She had no fear but that Boaz would take the next proper step]: for the man will not be in rest, until he have finished the thing this day."

True! Wise old woman! She understood the case. This was the next scene in the drama. There was a courtship, in fact. It was not Boaz that in the first instance courted Ruth; she courted him. And similar instances have been occurring from that day until this—not in words, not in obvious ways, but in reality. A look is louder than speech. A gesture, a posture, winning sympathy, the very exhalation of virtue and of beauty, throw about a man an atmosphere of enchantment. Talk of a woman's being deprived of the privileges of approach! A true woman, with a great heart, emits an influence such that whoever comes within it is transfigured in all that he sees, and she walks a goddess before him.

Now comes the fourth scene, which reveals the manners and customs of the times. We have disclosed the method by which the transfer of property by levirate marriage took place.

"Then went Boaz up to the gate, and sat him down there."

They had no newspapers in those days. No notice was given. There was no probate court; nor was there any surrogate. Men settled their property transactions in a very simple way. Mahlon and Chilion had died. They had been heirs, in their lifetime, to certain landed property which belonged to their father Elimelech. The widows of

Mahlon and Chilion of course had a certain right to that real estate according to the Levitical law ; and there must be some plan by which they should be brought back by marriage into the family. They could not marry into any neighboring tribe without hazarding the family's ownership of the land that was possessed by their deceased husbands. There must be some kinsman to marry them. So Boaz went up and sat in the gate. He was his own officer, his own newspaper, his own court, and his own crier.

"And behold, the kinsman of whom Boaz spake came by [They are never in a hurry in the East : they could sit down and wait till those they wanted came along] ; unto whom he said, Ho, such a one ! turn aside, sit down here.

"And he turned aside, and sat down. And he took ten men of the elders of the city, and said, Sit ye down here. And they sat down [In that hot climate men are always willing to sit]. And he said unto the kinsman, Naomi, that is come again out of the country of Moab, selleth a parcel of land, which was our brother Elimelech's : and I thought to advertise thee, saying, Buy it before the inhabitants, and before the elders of my people. If thou wilt redeem it, redeem it : but if thou wilt not redeem it, then tell me, that I may know : for there is none to redeem it beside thee : and I am after thee.

"And he said, I will redeem it.

"Then said Boaz, What day thou buyest the field of the hand of Naomi, thou must buy it also of Ruth the Moabitess, the wife of the dead, to raise up the name of the dead upon his inheritance."

This kinsman evidently had not seen Ruth. She had not been reaping in his field, had not lain at his feet, had not eaten of his parched corn, and had not drunk of his wine.

"And the kinsman said, I cannot redeem it for myself, lest I mar mine own inheritance : redeem thou my right to thyself ; for I cannot redeem it. Now this was the manner in former time in Israel concerning redeeming and concerning changing, for to confirm all things ; a man plucked off his shoe, and gave it to his neighbor : and this was a testimony in Israel. Therefore the kinsman said unto Boaz, Buy it for thee. So he drew off his shoe.

"And Boaz said unto the elders, and unto all the people, Ye are witnesses this day, that I have bought all that was Elimelech's and all that was Chilion's and Mahlon's, of the hand of Naomi. Moreover Ruth the Moabitess, the wife of Mahlon, have I purchased to be my wife, to raise up the name of the dead upon his inheritance, that the name of the dead be not cut off from among his brethren, and from the gate of his place: ye are witnesses this day. And all the people that were in the gate, and the elders, said, We are witnesses. The Lord make the woman that is come into thine house like Rachel and like Leah, which two did build the house of Israel: and do thou worthily in Ephratah, and be famous in Beth-lehem: and let thy house be like the house of Pharez, whom Tamar bare unto Judah, of the seed which the Lord shall give thee of this young woman.

"So Boaz took Ruth, and she was his wife: and when he went in unto her, the Lord gave her conception, and she bare a son. And the women said unto Naomi, Blessed be the Lord, which hath not left thee this day without a kinsman, that his name may be famous in Israel. And he shall be unto thee a restorer of thy life, and a nourisher of thine old age: for thy daughter-in-law, which loveth thee, which is better to thee than seven sons, hath borne him.

"And Naomi took the child, and laid it in her bosom, and became nurse unto it. And the women her neighbors gave it a name, saying, There is a son born to Naomi; and they called his name Obed: he is the father of Jesse, the father of David."

And David stood in the ancestry of the Lord Jesus Christ; and he who is the Saviour of the whole world had thus mingled with his blood the blood of the Moabites,—though not alone through this strain, but through many others.

There are a great many things that may be said about that history. When this family went down into the land of Moab they were driven out of their own land by famine; and it was bad luck. When they got there Elimelech died;—bad luck again. After a little while the sons, being married, died;—bad luck still. Naomi, stripped of everything, denuded, a widow and a stranger, wandered back to her former home;—could anything be more dismal? And yet, these were the very steps by which she came into prosperity, not only into the re-establishment of herself in the household, but into the possession of the property of her ancestors. It teaches us the lesson that, when troubles come, if we bear them patiently we may be led out of them. It is God's way, to lead men out of trouble into brightness. If one has been struck by misfortune, let him not sink down under it, but remember that it may be one of the instrumentalities by which God is leading him to a greater prosperity.

I want to say a word here in respect to Naomi. She was a mother-in-law. Ever since men were born mothers-in-law have been at a discount. And yet, I should like to know how a man is going to have a wife if there are to be no mothers-in-law! And is it not time that there should be held up before men the true idea of this relation? I should like to know if there have not been more mothers-in-law blessed and harmonious than mothers-in-law discordant and evil. Do you know what a mother is? Do you know the days and months during which she carries the unborn babe, giving her very blood for its nourishment? Do you know the gate of outcry and anguish through which the child is born? Do you know how again the mother gives herself as the very food of the son or daughter over whom she rejoices? Do you know how many times the nights are turned into days in her watchfulness? Do you know how tired she often becomes from taking double labor upon herself for the child's sake? Do you know how impossible it is in sickness, though she may be more sick than the child, to weary her of care for it? Do you know how patient she is in her efforts to develop the boy or the girl? As she trains him or her, what fabrics of courage she weaves! what visions of hope she forms! what ambitions she conceives! what sacrifices she makes! How she rolls everything in life over upon her blessed son, proud of his growth in all that is good, exulting in his honor, and happy in his love! And when at last he comes to years of majority, and selects the partner of his life, the mother stands still to see him carried away by another, to see another take her place in his regard, to see herself dispossessed, for the time being, of the enthusiasm and the affection that once were hers; and it is not strange that there should be in the heart of even the best woman on earth a little rebellion under such circumstances.

Yet, mother, be patient! When children are married, and go away from home, they may be for a while absorbed in their new experiences; but as soon as cares and troubles overtake them you may be sure that they will come back, with more love and trust for you, and more need of you, than ever before. It is not to be wondered at, when a mother sees that for which she has given her life taken possession of by one that has not done a thing for it except in the coinage of God's mint of love, that she should protest for a season; and it is for the daughter-in-law to remember the feelings of the mother-in-law, and not everlastingly think that the mother-in-law should remember the feelings of the one that has come into the family. It is true that there are some proud and selfish mothers-in-law; and it is just as true that there are some proud and selfish daughters-in-law, as there are some proud and selfish children. And let me say that I think some of the most beautiful examples I have ever known in life have been those of the disinterested love of mothers to those that have come newly into the household—to sons' wives and daughters' husbands that have not been at first lovely, but have been made so by the all-embracing goodness of the mother-in-law.

One of the most delightful tributes paid to the mother-in-law that I ever heard was that of one of our foremost men,* who is highly respected, and who, on his wedding night said to the mother of his bride, "Mother, I never before knew how much Adam was to be pitied, who, in the nature of things, could not have had a mother-in-law."

Surely, Naomi was a lovely specimen of the mother-in-law; and her name ought to redeem from unmerited reproach this much-abused class of women.

Is it strange that the little fountain head of the streams that flowed, in this line of descent, to form the flood that at last came forth in the Lord Jesus Christ, should have been composed of such characters as Ruth and David? And might it not be expected—from the merely human side, even—that, with such an ancestry, he would make a

---

* Since he has recently passed away, honored, beloved, and regretted by the whole nation, it may not be improper to state that this was George William Curtis.—*Editor*.

grand prophet in Israel, and bring forth such perfect fruit as appeared in him?

After the roar of battle, when the army is removed from the field, and the hospital is abandoned; when the soldiers have gone home, and have been greeted, with music, with social exhilaration, with the ringing of bells, with lights in the windows; when there is joy in every home, and they have settled down into domestic peace, how strange is that peace in contrast with the rude alarms of war!

Out of the turbulent times, the dark days, of the Judges through which we have been finding our way, upon what have we come? This sweet idyl of Ruth, in which, from beginning to end, there is no discord; in which peace flows unbrokenly; and in which are manifested the purest feelings of patriotism and of love. The whole flow of the narrative is idyllic, pastoral, peaceful, beautiful. Its sentences sound in our ears, after we are done reading them, as the bell in the belfry still warbles through the air long after the tongue has ceased to strike. We leave it as a vision of beauty, a rare picture, an exquisite portrayal, made more beautiful because it comes from the thunder of war, and is interjected into the rude manners and gross morality of a far-removed age—beautiful as poetry, beautiful as a drama, and yet more admirable as a truth of history.

And now we may turn back and say, Good-bye, Samson, good-bye, Jephthah, good-bye, Benjamin, good-bye, Gideon, good-bye, Balak, good-bye, all you great swart, uncombed, harsh, mighty men, fitted for times of convulsion and revolution! Having said farewell to them, and passed through the lovelier scenes of Ruth, we have set our face forward toward the times of Samuel and Saul, and shall begin to behold the light of David's day and the Solomonic glory. I hope to be able at a future time to take up again the wonderful history from this point, and then I shall rejoice as the watcher rejoices who has waited through the night, and sees upon the horizon the first beams of twilight—the harbinger of day.

We have come to the close of this series of informal readings in the Jewish Scriptures of the Old Covenant. The term *Jew* has been a word of contempt. Among the Jews, as among us, there are disreputable classes. There never was a sea so pure that there was not mud at the bottom of it ; and there never was a race so pure that there was not a muddy class within it : but this Hebrew nation have brought to us many virtues, many sublime qualities that belong to manhood ; and as long as the Old Testament endures we ought to be grateful to it, and to the authors of it, for those sources and fountains of moral influence which have enhanced our prosperity. I declare to you that we have not got all the honey out of the lion yet ; we have not yet plucked all the flowers nor gathered all the grapes that grow on the vines of the Old Testament. When we walk up and down through its pages, no longer tied by a superstitious theory of verbal inspiration, and with freedom bring our reason to bear, and, as emancipated men, discriminate between truth and error, right and wrong, we shall have much to harvest out of this book. We shall learn much that will be of comfort to us in trial. We shall learn much of what the father is or ought to be to the family, and the citizen to the state. We shall learn many lessons of wisdom adapted to children, and to the young people when they set up for themselves. It is a book full of the most precious and sacred memories. It is a record of the experiences of four thousand years. It contains the best thoughts of the best men that the world has ever seen.

Stand, then, for the Word of God. Make it a light to your path and a lamp to your feet. Let it be your guide in the way of righteousness. Live by it, and die in its hope.

THE END.

"The Pulse-Beat of the Times."

THE CHRISTIAN UNION is a Family Paper for progressive people everywhere. It is a paper that can be depended on to tell comprehensively, candidly and compactly what is going on in the world—that provides the best reading for the whole family—that is wisely progressive—that looks on the bright side of life—that entertains by healthful fiction—that is religious without being pietistic, outspoken without being unfair, independent and not neutral in politics, sociology, and all other questions on which good men differ. It is emphatically a Paper of To-Day, dealing with questions as they arise, presenting and interpreting the news as it happens. The editors are LYMAN ABBOTT and HAMILTON W. MABIE. The price for a year's subscription is $3. What progressive men think of *The Christian Union* is illustrated by the extracts from recent letters which are appended:

Hon. HENRY L. DAWES, United States Senator, of Pittsfield, Massachusetts, writes: "I could not do without The Christian Union. It is high-toned, liberal and progressive in everything. In its discussion of public questions, as well as in its position as a religious newspaper, it is both progressive and conservative, able and quick to discern, avoiding all foolishness, and full of inspiration to those who are inquiring after the truth. It is a power for good wherever it goes."

Dr. C. H. PARKHURST, Pastor of the Madison Square Presbyterian Church, New York, writes: "The paper is bright and crisp and abreast of the times. Items of current interest, both at home and abroad, are treated by it in a masterly way. In its columns one feels the pulse-beat of the times. The spirit which animates it is broad and generous, uncompromising, but recognizing good wheresoever it is to be found."

The Christian Union,
CLINTON HALL,
Astor Place, New York.

Yale Lectures on Preaching.

By HENRY WARD BEECHER.

["Lyman Beecher Lectureship," Yale Theological Seminary.]

THREE VOLUMES IN ONE.

The First, Second and Third Series were at first published separately, aggregating $4.25 in price, and in that form sold nearly 20,000 volumes. The present edition groups the *three series in one volume*, at $2.00, thus bringing this most helpful and famous work within the reach of all.

FIRST SERIES: Personal Elements.

What is Preaching? Qualifications of the Preacher; The Personal Element in Oratory; The Study of Human Nature; The Psychological Working Elements; Rhetorical Drill and General Training; Rhetorical Illustrations; Health, as Related to Preaching; Sermon-Making; Love, the Central Element of the Christian Ministry.

SECOND SERIES: Social and Religious Machinery.

Choosing the Field; Prayer; The Prayer Meeting: its Methods and Benefits; The Prayer Meeting: its Helps and Hindrances; Relations of Music to Worship; Development of Social Elements; BibleClasses, Mission Schools, Lay Work; The Philosophy of Revivals; Revivals Subject to Law; The Conduct of Revivals; Bringing Men to Christ.

THIRD SERIES: Methods of Using Christian Doctrines.

The Preacher's Book; How to Use the Bible; The True Method of Presenting God; Conception of the Divinity; Practical Use of the Divine Ideal; The Manifestation of God through Christ; Views of the Divine Life in Human Conditions; Sins and Sinfulness; The Sense of Personal Sin; The Growth of Christian Life; Christian Manhood; Life and Immortality.

"Of intense interest to every minister."—*Watchman* (Baptist).

"Every Theological student, young minister. Bible-class teacher and laborer in mission-work, will be profited by the study of this thoughtful and interesting book."— *The Episcopalian* (Philadelphia).

"No homiletic advices can be more practical, as none can be more exhilarating."—*Christian Register* (Unitarian, Boston).

"No other man could have combined so much of the genuine gospel method of teaching and preaching into one volume."—*Methodist Recorder* (Pittsburgh).

"Characteristically sagacious, sensible, earnest, brilliant, witty and wise." *Chicago Advance* (Congregationalist).

"No preacher or Christian worker but will benefit himself and others by a knowledge of the principles and methods of one of the foremost preachers of the day."—*Sunday School Times* (Philadelphia).

"The secrets of successful pulpit work as explained by one of its masters."—*Baltimore Presbyterian.*

"Many of the sources of his extraordinary power are clearly set forth in these characteristic lectures." — *New York Observer.*

FORDS, HOWARD, & HULBERT, New York.

A Valuable Memorial.

A SUMMER IN ENGLAND
WITH
HENRY WARD BEECHER.

Giving Seventeen Sermons, four Popular Lectures ["The Reign of the Common People," "The Wastes and Burden of Society," "Conscience," and "Evolution and Religion." never before published] and eight Special Addresses, delivered by him in Great Britain during the season of 1886; with an Account of the Tour, expressions of British Public Opinion, and Personal Reminiscences. Edited by JAMES B. POND, Mr BEECHER'S business manager and traveling companion.

Crown 8vo, 702 pp   Artotype Portrait (1887) and 7 pp Autograph Fac-simile of MS. Notes. Garnet cloth, gilt top, $2.

"Valuable records [this, and the Speeches in England, 1863] of the great orator's two very memorable visits to the Mother Country—the first a national service, the last a personal gratification, such as fall to the experience of few men."—*The Nation* (N. Y.).

"The 'Summer' being the last of Mr. Beecher's life, and the work he did in his 'vacation' being almost as wonderful in amount and in influence as any of his earlier life."—*The Critic* (N. Y.).

"The 'Reign of the Common People,' one of the lectures most called for in England, is the best thing Beecher ever put to the consideration of a thinking man."—*Providence Journal*.

"They have almost the solemnity and value of 'last words.' It was the gathering of strength and eloquence before the days of silence."—*Phil Ledger*.

"The narrative is simple, straightforward, and full of interesting personal reminiscences. . . . The volume reflects great credit upon its editor."—*Boston Home Journal*.

"A fertility of intellectual production on the highest lines of forensic labor without parallel." *The Churchman*.

"The triumphal progress was a fitting climax to a remarkable career."—*Portland Transcript*.

HIS ONLY NOVEL.

NORWOOD: A Tale of Village Life in New England. By HENRY WARD BEECHER.

When ROBERT BONNER asked Mr BEECHER to write a story for the *New York Ledger*, the clergyman replied that he had no hesitation about doing it *if he thought he could*, and added:

"Scott did not write till he was over forty. Who knows but I may turn out a great novelist, and have it said when I am dead: After this distinguished novelist (who also sometimes preached) was fifty years old, he was found out by Robert Bonner to have a turn for fiction, etc., etc."

The effect of this story on the circulation of the *Ledger* justified Mr. Bonner's sagacity and enterprise; and when it was afterwards issued in book form, it very shortly sold over 60,000 copies. It has ever since remained a favorite with those who delight in the purity and beauty, the shrewd wit and homely wisdom, the quaint and sterling characters and the genuine rural loveliness of New England life.

"Embodies more of the high art of fiction than any half-dozen of the best novels of the best authors of the day. It will bear to be read and re-read as often as Dickens' 'Dombey' or 'David Copperfield.'"—*Albany Evening Journal*.

"Wholesome and delightful, to be taken up again and yet again with fresh pleasure."—*Chicago Standard*.

FORDS, HOWARD, & HULBERT, New York.

PLYMOUTH PULPIT SERMONS

BY

HENRY WARD BEECHER

Four Volumes, covering the period from Sept. 1873 to Sept. 1875.

About 600 pp. each, Garnet Cloth, $1.50 per vol.

"The late HENRY WARD BEECHER was, take him all in all, the most remarkable preacher and orator of this generation. His fertility of mind was inexhaustible. The publishers have rendered a public service in reprinting in a convenient form these sermons. . . . Printed on good paper and in good type, they are issued at a price which will put them within the reach of hundreds of young ministers and thousands of laymen, who retain their relish for original and vigorous thought presented with fervid eloquence."—*New York Evangelist.*

Vol. I.—Religion in Daily Life; Forelookings; Heroism; New Testament Theory of Evolution; The Atoning God; Prayer; Man's Two Natures; All-Sidedness in Christian Life; Fact and Fancy; Cuba; Moral Teaching of Suffering; How Goes the Battle? Nature of Christ; Working and Waiting; What is Christ to Me? Science of Right Living; Religious Constancy; Soul Power; Riches of God; St. Paul's Creed; The Departed Christ; Naturalness of Faith; Spiritual Manhood; The Debt of Strength; Special Providence; Keeping the Faith.

Vol. II.—Charles Sumner; Saved by Hope; The Primacy of Love; Foretokens of Resurrection; Summer in the Soul; Hindering Christianity; Soul-Relationship; Christian Joyfulness; Liberty in the Churches; The Temperance Question; God's Grace; Ideal Christianity; Problem of Life; Unjust Judgments; Immortality of Good Works; The Universal Heart of God; Delight of Self-Sacrifice; Truth Speaking; The Secret of the Cross; Resolving and Doing; Triumph of Goodness; Following Christ; Prayer and Providence; What is Religion? Christian Sympathy; Luminous Hours.

Vol. III.—Law and Liberty; Faint-Heartedness; As a Little Child; God's Will; Present use of Immortality; The Test of Church Worth; Peace in Christ; The Indwelling of Christ; The End and the Means; Saved by Grace; Soul-Rest; The World's Growth; Foundation Work; The Bible; The Work of Patience; Divine Love; Unworthy Pursuits; True Righteousness; Things of the Spirit; Christian Contentment; Moral Standards; Trials of Faith; Old Paths; Meekness, a Power; Extent of the Divine Law; Soul-Growth.

Vol. IV.—Christ Life; The Courtesy of Conscience; Love, the Key to Religion; Christianity Social; Morality and Religion; Law of Soul-Growth; Sources and Uses of Suffering; God's Dear Children; Grieving the Spirit; Working and Waiting; The Sure Foundation; Nurture of Noble Impulse; Sowing and Reaping; Soul Statistics; Secret of Christ's Power; The Communion of Saints; Christian Life a Struggle; The Prodigal Son; Universality of the Gospel; Economy in Small Things; Good Deeds Memorable; Divine Indwelling; Claims of the Spirit; The Kingdom Within; The New Birth; Perfection Through Love.

RECENT OPINIONS.

"They cover the period of Mr. Beecher's deepest trouble, 1873-1875, and the period in which his preaching had perhaps the ripest thought and the deepest spiritual life, . . . the ripest and best portion of his ministry."—*The Christian Union.*

"As one turns these wonderful pages, it is hard to think that the mind which speaks through them with such ever fresh power to interest. and often with such tremendous vitality and suasive strength, has ceased to act on earth."—*The Congregationalist*, Boston.

FORDS, HOWARD, & HULBERT, New York.

EVOLUTION AND RELIGION.

By HENRY WARD BEECHER.

PART I. Theoretical and Fundamental.—Eight Sermons discussing the bearings of the Evolutionary Philosophy on the executive doctrines of Evangelical Christianity. *Paper, 50 cents.*

Introductory: The Signs of the Times; Evolution in Human Consciousness of the Idea of God; The Two Revelations; The Inspiration of the Bible; The Sinfulness of Man; The New Birth; Divine Providence and Design; Evolution and the Church.

PART II. Practical and Vital.—Eighteen Sermons, with applications of the Evolutionary Philosophy to religious thought and life. *Paper, $1.*

Introductory: The Background of Mystery; The Manifold Christ; The Conversion of Force; The Drift of the Ages; The Hidden Man; The Rest of God; God's Loving Providence; New Testament Theory of Evolution; God's Goodness Man's Salvation; Poverty and the Gospel; God in the World; Jesus the True Ideal; The Growth of Creation; The Battle of Life; The Liberty of Christ; Concord, not Unison; The Liberty and Duty of the Pulpit; The Vitality of God's Truth.

Parts I and II, bound together in Cloth, 440 pages, $1.50.

"The spell of Mr. Beecher's genius has never been more powerfully exerted than in these sermons. His imagination was never more fervid and creative, nor his rhetoric finer. One is amazed at the sustained intellectual vigor that at so advanced an age is still so fresh and productive."—*Living Church*, Chicago.

"His intellectual vigor has never been questioned, and many will read with interest what he here puts forth as the matured convictions of a lifetime devoted to the study of the subjects herein treated."—*San Francisco Bulletin.*

"He casts upon the great fundamental doctrines of the Church, in succussion, the light of the Evolutionary theory; and those who felt assured before of their firm foundation, must yet confess that they take on new beauty and meaning under this light, while many will owe to this illumination no less than the renewal of a lost belief."—*Sacramento Record-Union.*

"The discourses [*Sermons in Part I*] are clear, sober, solid thought. Each link in the chain is complete and perfect in itself."—*Cornell Review.*

"Everyone [*Sermons in Part II*] is full and overflowing with stimulating thought, fresh views of great truths grown stale by monotony of iteration, inspiring impulses and strong mountings of devotion toward God, earnest benevolence and goodwill toward man, loyalty to Christ,—and in fact a gospel of good sense and hopeful Christianity, wrought out of a reverent study of God's ways of working in nature—physical, social, mental, moral, and spiritual."—*Providence Star.*

"It seems to me you keep all the most choice and precious things, only placing them on the right foundation; and how they can stand much longer on the old foundation I do not see. . . . Surely your book will bring light to many."—*From a Presbyterian Clergyman.*

FORDS, HOWARD, & HULBERT, New York.

Notable and Interesting Religious Books.

SIGNS OF PROMISE.

Sermons Preached in Plymouth Church, Brooklyn, 1887-1889.

BY LYMAN ABBOTT, D.D.

Eighteen Discourses. 12mo, cloth, gilt top. Price, $1.50.

"'Signs of Promise' is the fit title of the first volume of sermons preached in Plymouth Pulpit since its greatest occupant passed from earth. By all logical and intellectual inheritance, that pulpit is now worthily filled. . . . The Plymouth preacher of to-day shows us that God is, and not merely that he was. His words thrill with the currents of hope born of a survey of the past and making contact with the unseen future. . . . All of these sermons are strong, helpful and suggestive, and reveal the true prophet."—*The Critic,* New York.

"Clear and compact, and palpitate with the influences of the time. . . . One cannot read these sermons without being impressed with the ability with which the subjects are handled, and with many glowing passages which are eminently spiritual and uplifting."—*Christian Intelligencer,* New York.

"One of the favorite assertions of that supremely irritating created thing, the infidel who has not sufficient strength of mind to believe in aught but himself, is that Christianity is behind the times, is incapable of grappling with the problems of every-day life, and, indeed, blinds itself to their existence; and as this kind of infidel is common, and his cuckoo cry is all but continuous, it is a pleasure now and then to encounter a volume of sermons showing the keenest sensitiveness to current topics of interest. One need not agree with the author's theology; one may be a Buddhist or a Mohammedan and yet enjoy the manner in which such an one will attack and rout this species of infidel."—*Boston Herald.*

"Dr. Abbott is no copyist, but a man strong in his own peculiar powers and gifts."—*Christian Register.*

"Full of earnest and vigorous thought and are eminently stimulating. Even those who do not altogether agree with the author's theological positions will find much to be admired here and little to be condemned."—*Congregationalist.*

"A clew to Dr. Abbott's Beecher-like reception of all revelation, in Scripture nature or life, and to his ability to keep abreast with the stream of such revelation as it widens continually between the opposite but not opposing banks of theology and science."—*Brooklyn Eagle.*

SPIRIT AND LIFE.

Thoughts for To-Day.

BY AMORY H. BRADFORD, D.D.,

First Cong. Church, Montclair, N. J.

Twelve Discourses. 16mo, vellum cloth. Price, $1.00.

"It is evident to the laical mind that a certain tender, serious, humane spirit possesses men of this class, urging them to work for the good of man and the glory of God in nobler fashion, broader ways, than purely metaphysical schemes can ever hope to instigate."—*Boston Post.*

"We commend his volume heartily to those of our readers who desire to get an appreciative and wholly uncontroversial interpretation of the Bible which God is writing continuously in human hearts."—*The Christian Union,* N. Y.

"Rarely has there been published in this country a finer volume of sermons, of sermons more worthy of publication, or better fitted to be of actual helpfulness to Christian thought and the spiritual life."—*The Advance,* Chicago.

"The best modern preaching deals with spiritual wants and vital truths. Judged by this test, the sermons before us are worthy to be classed among the best sermons of the day."—*New Englander and Yale Review.*

FORDS, HOWARD, & HULBERT, New York.

www.ingramcontent.com/pod-product-compliance
Lightning Source LLC
Chambersburg PA
CBHW032130010526
44111CB00034B/571